The Sword Arm

The Sword Arm

Military Forces in the Twenty-First Century

Sanu Kainikara

Vij Books India Pvt Ltd

New Delhi (India)

Copyright © 2019, *Sanu Kainikara*

Dr Sanu Kainikara
416, The Ambassador Apartments
2 Grose Street
Deakin, ACT 2600, Australia
sanu.kainikara@gmail.com

First Published in 2019

ISBN : 978-93-88161-35-0 (Hardback)

ISBN : 978-93-88161-36-7 (ebook)

Designed and Setting by

Vij Books India Pvt Ltd
2/19, Ansari Road, Darya Ganj,
New Delhi - 110002, India
(www.vijbooks.com)
All rights reserved.

No part of this book may be reproduced, stored in a retrieval system, transmitted or utilized in any form or by any means, electronic, mechanical, photocopying, recording or otherwise, without the prior permission of the copyright owner. Application for such permission should be addressed to the author.

Dedicated

To the Warriors – Past and Present,
Whose service, bravery, loyalty and integrity,
Have never wavered

May the Sword Arm always be steadfast…

OTHER BOOKS BY SANU KAINIKARA

National Security, Strategy and Air Power

Papers on Air Power
Pathways to Victory
Red Air: Politics in Russian Air Power
Australian Security in the Asian Century
A Fresh Look at Air Power Doctrine
Friends in High Places (Editor)
Seven Perennial Challenges to Air Forces
The Art of Air Power: Sun Tzu Revisited
At the Critical Juncture
Essays on Air Power
The Bolt from the Blue
In the Bear's Shadow
Political Analysis
The Asian Crucible
Political Musings: Turmoil in the Middle-East
Political Musings: Asia in the Spotlight

The Indian History Series: From Indus to Independence
Volume I: Prehistory to the Fall of the Mauryas
Volume II: The Classical Age
Volume III: The Disintegration of Empires
Volume IV: The Onslaught of Islam
Volume V: The Delhi Sultanate

CONTENTS

Author's Preface   xi

Introduction   1

Section - I
National Security, Policy and Grand Strategy Shifting With the Sands of Time

Introduction		21
Chapter 1	The Rise of Nation States	27
Chapter 2	National Security	41
Chapter 3	Security, Policy and Strategy	61
Conclusion		

Section - II
The Evolving Geo-Political Environment International Strategic Trends

Introduction		83
Chapter 4	The Ever Changing World	87
Chapter 5	Global Strategic Environment	105
Chapter 6	Challenges to Geo-Political Stability	139
Chapter 7	Emergence of New Global Players	157
Conclusion		165

Section - III

The Future of Conflict
Contextualising War

Introduction		171
Chapter 8	Analysing War	175
Chapter 9	Factors affecting the Conduct of War	191
Chapter 10	Emerging Trends in the Conduct of War	201
Chapter 11	Irregular Warfare: The Asymmetric Core	209
Chapter 12	Challenges of a New Era	227
Conclusion		247

Section - IV

Military Forces: An Element of National Power
The Strategic Interface

Introduction		253
Chapter 13	The Power of Military Forces	259
Chapter 14	Future Conflict Trends: Impact on Military Forces	303
Conclusion		315

Section - V

The Sword Arm
Military Forces In The 21st Century

Introduction		321
Chapter 15	The Evolution and Mitigation of Threat	327
Chapter 16	The Dynamics of Resources	345
Chapter 17	Military Forces and Security Strategies	359
Chapter 18	Military Forces in the 21st Century	371

Chapter 19	The Military Force as an Instrument of Policy	399
Chapter 20	Strengthening Military Forces in a Democracy	413
Conclusion		429
Conclusion		435
Bibliography		453
Index		471

AUTHOR'S PREFACE

CRAFTING THE SWORD ARM

The continually changing norms within truly democratic nations and the impact of such changes, some made arbitrarily by the elected representatives of the nation, on the status of the military forces of the nation has been a topic of study for me for decades. Over the years I have noticed that the civilian leadership of most democratic nations display at least a slight discomfort when dealing with their military forces and its leadership. This wariness is visible in all democracies—from the most mature to the emerging pre-colonial ones—and is more manifest in nations where the military force is all-volunteer in composition. In analysing this phenomena I have come to the conclusion that the reasons for this awkwardness could be attributed to both the civilian and the military leadership in almost equal measure. It is also clear to me that this tension between the two will never go away completely, but will only ebb and flow, primarily under the influence of individual personalities.

If the civil-military relationship is always bound to suffer from some amount of anxiety, it is incumbent on both parties to study the fundamentals of the relationship and attempt to ameliorate it in the best possible manner, and to the amount possible. It is the earnestness, from both sides, with which this effort is undertaken that will mark the stability or otherwise of democratic nations. This fundamental fact is not readily visible to either a political or military analyst unless the person manages to cross over from one discipline to the other and back again; not an easy task. However, civil-military relations have to remain on an even keel and be able to withstand a great deal of turbulence—especially in times of relative peace—in order for the nation to be secure. National security is never challenged as much as when there is discernible dissonance between the civil and military leadership. A democratic nation creates, or accepts, a divide between the two at its own peril.

The other major factor that influences the status of military forces is the complex relationship that the military forces share with the broader 'civilian' society of the nation. The ethos of the nation as a whole towards the damage, destruction, and loss of life and treasure that the full employment of its military forces bring about; and the acceptance of the society of its commitment to provide tangible emotional and economic succour to the returning veterans of distant wars will directly influence the well-being of the warriors and indirectly determine the calibre and competency of national military forces. The profession of arms is not for the soft-hearted, but compassion towards the military forces has to be a demonstrated part of the national psyche if the force is to deliver what it is meant to—national security.

*   *   *   *   *

I started preliminary research for this book almost eight years ago, the pace being somewhat slow because of time constraints and other commitments. In fact for almost three years, while the concept of the book remained live, active thinking regarding the way forward and the research to further the writing remained dormant. In the end, about a year ago, the book overtook my vague and semi-existent plans for it and became an important element in my writing life. I somehow knew that the book had to be completed, although I am not able to clearly identify the impetus for the feeling or the actual events that led to the book assuming its own life, almost completely independent of my other commitments. In such circumstances an author is forced to go along with what the book dictates, becoming a follower rather than being the leader. In some cases, the esoteric and altruistic intentions with which the book was started gradually become the background rather than the core reason for writing it—the book assumes a superior position, demanding to be written. This has been the case with *The Sword Arm*. It was so exactingly insistent on wanting to be written that I was compelled to put aside other writing commitments to concentrate on it. I believe that this analysis must be brought to light as the ever-changing world is demanding much more than their traditional responsibilities from the military forces, while at the same time attempting to sideline them to the periphery of the national security equation. These two positions assumed by the national leadership of most democratic nations are non sequitur.

*   *   *   *   *

An author can, while writing the book, feel the flow, smell the freshness of the air that emanates from the pages, and know inherently whether the effort is grounded, or not, with each breath he or she takes. This is a feeling that can only come with complete involvement in writing the book, the toil, frustration at not getting the right expression and the hollow feeling that tells you that the turn of phrase is not one of beauty—adequateness is not sufficient to satisfy the inner urge, most of the time it is the exemplary that one seeks. The author knows where the sentences have come from, where the ideas have originated, where the flow of thought is bound to go, even if the thought-process takes a life of its own, for some books are like that—they have a life of their own. For me, this book has been one such occasion.

The author, especially of a book that is based on research of subjects of topical interest and one that attempts to push the envelope of contemporary thinking on the subject, is in turn both afraid and defiant. This is true at least when the writing begins. I have realised that at some stage in the process of writing, one crosses an invisible line and then one is not afraid anymore and one does not feel the need to be defiant either. The writing then becomes my opinions, hopefully well-expressed, and which I have the ability to explain logically, if needed. I am comfortable with the ideas that I have put across in this book; I have taken a great deal of time to think them through; I have debated them with some of my contemporaries; and even if any of my readers disagree with some of the premises that I have put forward, I believe that my opinions would also be respected.

*   *   *   *   *

The success of a book, I believe, lies in its ability to permit an intelligent reader to distil its contents to a concentrated and absolute essence. If the core of a large tome can be summed up in a page of few impeccable sentences, the author has reached near-perfection in explaining his thoughts through the medium of words. This is so since the reader and the author, more often than not, do not share a relationship other than that developed through the book. The one page, or few sentences, essence, is the most invaluable drops that must be savoured, since they form the intellectual output of the author. I will be most gratified if *The Sword Arm* reaches such a stage, wherein an intelligent reader is able to extract the essence of the book without having to take recourse to his or her own research. My fundamental objective of creating a book with clarity in expression and logic in explanation would have been achieved.

Sanu Kainikara

Canberra

January 2019

INTRODUCTION

WIELDING THE SWORD ARM IN DEMOCRACIES

From the very beginnings of history, when bands of humans wandered the earth in search of sustenance, a small group of armed men within the band were charged with ensuring the safety of the band. These bands developed into clans and then into organised societies and along with this development, the group that ensured the safety of the society gradually became military forces, which is today an indelible part of human society. The military forces, and its forbearers, are the only group whose contribution to the well-being of the broader society has not been seriously questioned in history. Their importance is still accepted with a minimum of debate. Since early to mid-20th century, the scope of involvement of national military forces in the safety and security of the nation-state has broadened considerably, especially since the understanding of national security itself is evolving.

The military forces of a nation, collectively the sword arm within the elements of national power in all democracies, are currently employed as the first responders to any and all challenges that threaten the status quo safety of the nation. They are also held as the visible indicator of the power, prestige and status of the nation. In the late-20th and early-21st centuries military forces have become one of the many elements of national power—playing its part in the national security calculus as both the supported and supporting component—although at the core it remains the steel around which other more malleable elements of power tend to be arranged to achieve national security objectives.

Even while there is accepted acknowledgement of the criticality of the military forces in securing the nation, the more stable democracies of the world consciously attempt to restrict the employment of these forces and, in some cases, also to dilute the capabilities resident in modern military forces. While restricting the possible employment of military forces may be a step forward in ensuring global stability, diluting their capabilities, and more importantly, curtailing their application at the operational level are harmful trends—both to the security of the nation and the well-being of the military forces. These attempts to place a confining cover over the military forces are couched in legislations and arbitrary rules that are imposed and which impinge on their operational effectiveness. These are retrograde steps in a world that is becoming increasingly volatile and multilateral, while also globalising at a pace and rate never seen before.

In the mid-20th century, the military forces of the newly de-colonised world brought about a different hue to the understanding of the capability and role of the military forces. The military forces of these nations had a less than optimum understanding and acceptance of the principles of democracy and of the role of military forces in ensuring national security. They perceived themselves not only as the arbitrators of national security but also as the saviours of the nation from a predatory political leadership. In misguided attempts to 'save' the nation, the military forces of a number of these countries took over the running of the state as military dictators. Military coup d'états occurred so many times in the last decades of the 20th century that they cannot be considered aberrations to the norm any more. These events have tarnished the image of military forces and also made the political leadership of the developing nations suspicious of its competence and capabilities. The distrust has manifested in a number of ways, most of it detrimental both to the nation and the military forces. The bottom line is that any action that is harmful to the efficacy of the military forces, directly or indirectly, also impinges on national security.

Although the misgivings in the relatively new democracies regarding the role and intentions of the military forces are not without cause, a majority of these forces remain forces-for-good. As long as the military forces function under the 'correct' line of command and strategic control, they will remain the cornerstone of all national security calculations. No other element of national power will be able to replace the capabilities that military forces bring to achieving national security objectives. The evolving broadening of the spectrum of military operations across the world is ample proof of the fundamental need within a democratic nation to create, sustain and employ a military force of sufficient calibre.

Military forces are at the forefront of securing the nation from multifaceted threats that have become complex and complicated. However, the world is traversing an age that seems to be in a continual state of war, waged more by amorphous organisations that do not represent nation-states, and pursue ideological rather than territorial or resource controlled objectives. Essentially, the prime objective is the control of the cognitive domain of the people. In these circumstances, the military force, while a crucial, and even critical, element in ensuring national security, will only be one part of the national response to threats and challenges.

The employment of military forces has so far been a tried and tested way to ensure national security. It is therefore not surprising that strategic thinkers through the ages—Sun Tzu, Kautilya, Machiavelli, Clausewitz—have struggled to find the answers to some basic questions that confound the application of lethal force in the pursuit of national security. How to win wars without having to fight battles? How to deal with a stronger power that is not aligned to one's own position? How to minimise the risk and casualties to one's own forces when lethal application of force becomes necessary? How to measure one's own potential and power vis-à-vis its effect on others? And many more.

International relations is the arena in which a nation establishes itself as a viable entity and claim its position in the comity of nations. This position is based on a liberal, realist dyad. Although some nations do not accept this assertion, no viable alternative has been suggested so far; and the application of force is not seen as a practical substitute to mould international relations, which is essential to develop a realistic world view. Therefore the pursuit of national security can be, at times, limited by foreign policy options available in a contextual manner. These options themselves could further be restricted by the limitations faced by the nation, becoming a self-perpetuating cycle by itself.

The last few decades of the 20th century saw the definitive widening of security perceptions with most nations connecting national security to the protection not only of its interests but also its core values. The connection between national security and national interests have become an indelible fact. Politico-economic and politico-military strategies, employed in a balanced tandem, create a conducive environment to protect national interests. In most cases, protection of national interests hinge on the creation of a territorial sphere of influence, through the threat or actual use of force if necessary. Such actions could also involve engaging neutral states that are in close proximity of the sphere of influence being established, through the strategies of influence and shape and coercion, if it becomes necessary.

Cooperative Security

In the past five decades or so the power distribution in the world has been such that it has not left any 'one nation' powerful enough to establish its writ on the rest of the world. While the US did have an opportunity to evolve as the one state to do so, the small window of opportunity was either not recognised or not taken advantage of, the leadership squandering the opportunity that comes to a nation but rarely in history. The end of the Cold War in the early 1990s was presumed to be the beginning of a unipolar world. However, it turned out to be the start of establishing a multipolar world that was more prone to chaos and confusion than during the Cold War. Again the increased geo-political complexity had not been anticipated.

In the prevailing multipolar security environment, even minor powers can manipulate and influence the flow of events to favour their nation. In turn, this situation has led to the development of security relationships, both regional and global, with partners and allies to maintain the status quo or re-establish stability through joint and concerted action. It has become imperative to embrace multilateral initiatives as the focus for ensuring global security and stability. In order to ensure the viability of such initiatives, and further multilateral security alliances, more stable nations and middle power nations have to become partners in such ventures. The fundamental aim is the avoidance of armed conflict of all kinds and if the application of lethal force becomes a necessity, then it has to be ensured that military forces of the necessary calibre, quality, competence, and efficiency are available to do so.

A multilateral approach to ensuring peace and stability requires each of the nations involved to possess sufficient national capacity to assess, plan and assist inter-agency peace keeping, stabilisation and reconstruction efforts. In this practice the bigger nations should assist the smaller powers and boost their capabilities. The entire enterprise needs pre-planning, sufficiency in training and assured inter-operability. Multilateral engagement encompasses military to military contact, confidence-building measures and joint exercises as part of a coalition or as allies.

Partners and Allies

All sovereign nations are continually on the lookout for assured national security and therefore understand the need to have partners and allies to create a viable security shield. Partners are like-minded nations who could, when necessary, form coalitions to address emerging common threats. Such a group of nations may not have a formalised alliance between them and may not also have commonality of equipment, concepts of operations or even fighting ethos in their military forces. Partner nations will have to exert themselves to build trust and confidence in each other through serious efforts at joint exercises and other measures such as exchange of personnel etc. Ideal coalition operations with partners would be the delivery of humanitarian aid and disaster relief at the lower end of the military operations spectrum, rather than effective high-end warfighting, which may prove to be a bridge too far to cross. In actual warfighting, the creation of a common operating picture within a coalition will be difficult and time consuming since there will be only minimal interoperability. However, even with all the difficulties in conducting joint operations, coalition operations will enhance the stability of the security environment.

Allies on the other hand are nations that have dedicated mutual treaties and agreements, either bilateral of multilateral. Allies tend to have enhanced commonality at all levels of operations, from the strategic to the tactical, with a high level of interoperability achieved through long-term military interaction, exchanges and exercises. Since long-term friendships tend to create a high level of trust and confidence between nations, it will be relatively easier to create common operating pictures and greater mutual understanding.

Security relationships are increasingly important in a globalised world to ensure national security, and to a great extent these relationships are underpinned by the ability of the military forces to operate efficiently with partners and allies. The efficacy of such joint operations is basically dependent on interoperability. It is necessary to have interoperability at all three levels of warfighting to be able to conduct a successful campaign. At the lowest, tactical, level of operations, the military force will need to have mastered multi-domain integration leading to the ability to conduct seamless operations within it as well as with military forces of other nations. The operational level requires inter-agency jointness in order to put in place a whole-of-government approach to national security. The bringing together of all elements of national power in an appropriate balance of capabilities to address challenges contextually is an involved process and requires a great deal of practice and dexterity. The complexity increases when the outcome is dependent on elements of national power from different nations. At the strategic level, interoperability would mean functioning within coalitions and alliances with regional and international partners and allies to ensure collective security.

The foundation for interoperability is laid by the military forces of a nation rather than other elements of national security. This is achieved through carefully crafted interoperability. Interoperability with partners and allies is realised through creating and maintaining connections in terms of personnel, equipment, concepts and doctrine; and by jointly exercising to anticipate probable common challenges and risks. It is inevitable that the inherent flexibility of the military forces must always be maintained at the highest level to readily accept jointness, interoperability and integration.

A Whole-of-Government Approach to Security

In the prevailing multilateral world, the security environment is complex and uncertain. In such an environment, it is a strategic imperative to adopt a whole-of-government (WoG) approach not only to ensuring national security but also to all aspects of national governance that require external interaction and the development of international relations. Emerging and future challenges to the nation will not be restricted to being contained by one element of national power.

Many factors within a nation destabilise the society and could turn into security risks and challenges that spill over into the region, manifesting as violence and further destabilisation that vitiates the security environment. The destabilising factors could be as diverse as environmental degradation; breakdown in essential services within a nation; lack of employment opportunities for the youth, which could lead to criminalisation of some segments of the population; unsustainable population growth; skewed pattern of demographic growth; and many other unconnected and disjointed ones. A reasonable response needs to address the causes and not the symptoms alone in order to ensure that the instability is contained and then reversed. Military forces on their own can limit or even completely stop criminalisation and other such symptoms from spreading wider. However, the causes for instability can be eliminated only through a combined intervention that uses the capabilities of all elements of the national power base, employed in a contextually appropriate manner.

A WoG approach is not a new concept, although it has only been articulated in such a fashion in the past few decades. The process increases resource availability to face emerging crises and develops innovative solutions to complex security challenges that could emerge rapidly. In this holistic approach to ensuring security, military forces are normally the enabling power element that holds the different elements together, while ensuring appropriate level of contribution from each.

The Sword Arm – Military Forces

The military forces of a nation, with its inherent flexibility, remain the first-choice responders to face all challenges to national security. Once the immediate threat has been contained, the military forces will assume different roles—maybe continuing as the lead element or becoming an enabler—for further actions required to eliminate the threat completely.

Contemporary military forces of democratic nations face some major challenges in establishing themselves as competent forces. First is the difficulty in recruiting and retaining personnel with the necessary qualifications. Over the years, the main advances in military forces have been in the twin areas of technology and concepts—oriented towards creating a technological or knowledge edge over the adversary. These advances necessitate increased time for training and operationalising the personnel who form the sinews of the military forces and ensure that complex systems function optimally. Further, the demographic changes, most acutely felt in Western nations, mainly the challenge of an ageing population impinges on the ability of military forces to attract people of the right calibre.

The Western nations—within which reside most of the mature democracies—face the challenge of the 'baby boomers' retiring en mass, thereby reducing the central pool of qualified people from which the military forces, as well as other vocations are able to recruit and fill crucial positions. It has been calculated that in order to maintain the same availability of people the replacement birth rate will have to be 2.1 children per couple. This target has not been met for some years and is unlikely to be met in the Western nations well into the future. The result is a downward spiral in the number of people not only to support the functioning of high-end capabilities, but also the requirements of an enlarged welfare system. In a sort of a vicious and self-defeating cycle, industrialised nations with a static and ageing population are dependent on advanced technological innovations to maintain the balance between operators and capabilities. Military efficiency is also critically empowered by technological advances, making military force development a complex balancing act for most democracies.

Compounding the challenge that a changing demography places on military forces, the economic growth of most democracies indicate that individual growth opportunities are better outside the military forces of a nation. Military forces will have to fall back on their inherent flexibility in order to be able to attract, train and retain personnel of the right calibre. They will have to adapt to the changing times—creating flexible opportunities and carefully maintaining the balance between people and technology to ensure that the cutting edge competence that the combination brings is not diluted, both in application and in concepts.

Second challenge is the ability of military forces to assess the capabilities needed to ensure national security and create assured access to them. Thereafter it will be necessary to maintain the capabilities at the necessary level of competence needed to establish and maintain the 'edge'—technological, if possible and conceptual, in an assured manner—over potential adversaries. In doing so the military force of a nation should be able to contain all types of challenges to the nation.

Third challenge is the resource constraint that is faced by the military forces of all democratic nations, especially in times of relative peace. Nations are forced to enforce economic stringency through the curtailment of expenditure. In modern times, especially when available financial outlay is insufficient to meet all the needs of military forces, there is a fundamental question to be asked—is there a possibility of combining different domain-centric forces to restrict overlap of capabilities and thus wastage of resources? Is there substance in considering the creation of a core surface force and another 'envelope force' that combine the areas of space and cyber domains with air and maritime capabilities? These cannot be considered rhetorical questions but must be debated and analysed in order to either accept them, modify them or reject them as far-fetched. But debate them, all democracies must.

To start the process of an unbiased analysis of the military forces that even today carry the vestiges of World War II in its organisation, it is necessary to review, on a clean slate, the military budgets, modernisation plans and force structure within a top-down approach, starting at the highest levels of national security decision-making. In determining the future structure of military forces in democracies, the military strategy in its prevalent form and as it is being conceived for the future will be a critical influence. Only such a process, however involved it may be, will determine the capabilities needed to assure national security and ensure a predictable resource-stream necessary to acquire and optimally field them. The status and prestige of military forces in democracies in the 21st century depends on the success, or otherwise, of this involved process. No democracy of the 21 century can afford to post-pone this review if it is to safeguard its sovereignty.

*   *   *   *   *

The Book

This book explores, in a holistic manner, the status and role of military forces in 21st century democracies. It is felt that by concentrating on democracies—both mature and emerging—the true position of military forces, vis-à-vis the nation, its society and security needs can be critically assessed.

Some Unassailable Truths

While analysing the main thrust of the book some fundamental truths regarding military forces and their relationship with national security, that have stood the test of time, have been assumed.

It is the truth that military forces have remained a prominent and indelible part of the national power structure in all nations, irrespective of the type of government that is favoured. Their status and direct importance to national security have varied over time and is continuing to evolve; this fact is reflected in the waxing and waning of the prestige and acclaim given to soldiers as well as the rise and fall of resource allocation towards the upkeep of the military forces.

It is the truth that military forces have always been, and continues to be, at the vanguard of the national security equation. As the preferred first-responders to any challenge to national security, this is not a surprising situation. Even in modern times, when a WoG approach to security has become the accepted norm in democracies, military forces continue to be the core around which other elements of national power build and employ their specialised power structure. The enhanced importance of the other elements of national power has not diminished the primary position that military forces occupy in the security calculus.

It is the truth that military forces are the most flexible and adaptable element within the gamut of the elements of national power. The military forces have been the most altered in terms of contemporary evolution of the national power base. The willingness and ability of the military forces to adapt to emerging circumstances demonstrates the importance of leadership in maintaining a viable force. In fact, leadership has always been the strength, or weakness, of a military force. The undeniable strength of military leadership is the reason for the fact that the forces of democratic nations have repeatedly won numerous battles. It is also a fact that even after the military forces have won exemplary battlefield victories, democracies have lost the wars that were being fought. It is wrong to place the defeat in wars at the feet of the military forces and its leadership. In most cases the political leadership will be seen to be the blameworthy lot, even though in some rare cases a combination of the two could be held responsible.

It is the truth that military forces have been able to assure national security when the military leadership has been part of the security decision-making at the highest levels of government. The balance that military leadership brings to the process is critical to keeping the decisions contextual vis-à-vis the prevailing situation and circumstances. It is also a fact that whenever the military leadership has overreached in influencing the political leadership and the decision-making process, the results have not necessarily been advantageous to the nation. The involvement of strategic military leadership in the national security decision-making has therefore got to be nuanced but at the same time is crucial to ensuring that such decisions are even-keeled and compatible with the capabilities of the military forces. Only the military forces have a clear understanding of balancing the ends, ways and means equation, which is the bed rock on which assured delivery of national security objectives are based.

Structure of the Book

The book has been written as five independent sections: starting with a holistic analysis of national security, policy and grand strategy; then analysing the evolving geo-political environment and international strategic trends; the third contextualising war and examining the future of war; analysing the contribution of military forces to national security as an element of national power; and finally viewing the status of military forces in 21st century democracies. Essentially they have been arranged to look at the national strategic level first and then deductively narrow down to finally arrive at the examination of military forces and their role in 21st century democracies. Each section can be read as a stand-alone hypothesis and is argued individually. The hypothesis for each section is declared at the beginning of the section in a succinct one sentence statement and explained very briefly below the statement. The five sections are also written in such a way that they form a continuous narrative, the first leading to the second, almost seamlessly, and so on in a serial manner. When the sections are read sequentially, the book takes shape as a whole.

Each section contains several chapters. However, the chapters in the book are numbered sequentially, running from one to twenty through the sections. This process of numbering provides an external thread of continuity to the book, if one is indeed looking for it rather than continuity through content discussion.

The Sections

Section I analyses national security, policy and grand strategy. The premise being espoused is that the continuous evolution of the definition and understanding of national security has impacted and diffused the relationship between the concept of security and the development of policy and grand strategy. The chapters study the rise of nation-states through examining the model that emerged initially in Europe; and describes the abstract concept of national security as having evolved through the ages, tracing its development to its current broad understanding. The section looks at national security through the prisms of national military and economic capabilities that in turn provides insights which unravel some of the complexities that shroud this ephemeral concept. While highlighting the importance of creating a historical base to understand national security, the chapters investigate the inter-relationship between security, policy and strategy and studies the ends, ways and means equation.

Following from the discussions on national security and policy, Section II examines the evolving geo-political environment, emphasising international strategic trends that pertain to global security. The analysis in this section is consciously kept at the strategic level since the trends that manifest at the higher levels tend to have greater longevity and therefore deeper impact on the development of the broader security environment. A fundamental premise in this section is that the emerging challenges to geo-strategic stability, regional or global, could establish themselves either rapidly or in an evolutionary manner. However, their manifestation cannot be predicted. Inevitably such developments will create the right 'climate' and also provide the impetus for the emergence of new power centres. New power centres will invariably lead to the shakeup of the existing or traditional power balance, and event that will eventually be detrimental to stability and peaceful interaction between nations.

Section II goes on to argue that even though the Cold War period was considered to have been politically bi-polar, other semi-permanent power centres did emerge during that time. These temporary power groups managed to diffuse the supposedly clear cut demarcations of the security environment that is supposed to have been the hallmark of the bi-polar world. The section goes on to reason that the more important development has been the emergence of a multi-polar world that has led to the creation of alternative power centres even if their influence is restricted to particular regions. Even regional power have the capacity to dilute the influence of global powers, further underscoring the emergence of a multi-polar world. The culminating argument in the section is that there is an as yet universally not accepted trend in the global security environment that points towards the emergence of new international players who are capable of becoming regional and global power centres as they gather strength.

Section III delves into the core of military matters, discussing the future of conflict and contextualising war. Modern military forces face difficulties during contemporary conflicts in achieving traditional victory. To a great extent, for conventional military forces achieving any semblance of success in any military campaign is fast becoming a chimera. The section examines the development of these recent phenomena with the backdrop of the increasing proclivity of democracies to be involved in military interventions in the more destabilised parts of the world and also the fact that these tempo and intensity of these interventions vary spasmodically.

War is analysed through examining the Just War Theory and the principles that it espouses. Just War Theory is an independent area of study. However, in Chapter 8, the concept and principles have been paraphrased as a broad indicator of how the nature of war should be considered. It cannot be overemphasised that Just War Theory has to be studied in much greater detail to obtain a more profound understanding of its nuances and complexity. The section further examines the types of wars that are possible to be fought in the contemporary context with emphasis on the ones that are more probable to occur. The reasons and rationale for a nation deciding to carry out a military intervention in another sovereign nation are examined in detail.

The characteristics and conduct of war are, most of the time, changing in an evolutionary process and a number of factors affect both, making the process of change somewhat easier to fathom. Even so, the characteristics of war tend to remain more static with changes taking place in a gradual and long drawn manner. On the other hand, the conduct of war is especially prone to changes—at times rapidly—because of organisational, socio-politic, demographic and strategic factors, which are always evolving. The section elaborates on the noticeable trends and changes that are clearly visible in the conduct of modern wars. Chapter 11 looks at the current trend of non-state entities conducting asymmetric wars against the regular, conventional forces of nation-states. The characteristics and conduct of these 'Irregular Wars' (IW) as well as the qualities and features of the irregular forces involved are analysed. There are some conclusions regarding how a conventional force could adapt to the changing circumstances are drawn. Based on historical evidence of failures, some tentative recommendations and suggestions regarding how conventional forces could adopt is also made.

The section goes on to examine the challenges that face military forces with the emergence of a new era of warfare that has resulted in rapid changes to the conduct of war and the accompanying alteration in some of the fundamental characteristics. How these challenges could be addressed and ameliorated does not form a significant part of the narrative, the intention being to merely flag the trials that are bound to face the military forces of a nation as conflict evolves in unexpected ways. In Chapter 12 there is a focus on geo-political and geo-strategic issues that emanate because of the conflicts with particular reference to their regional impact. There is a noticeable thread that is drawn across the entire section. The impact of technology—on the evolving trends in the conduct of war and its characteristics, and how it dictates even the type of war that would emerge in a particular case—are seen as the visible commonality in the analysis.

Section IV examines the status of the military force in democracies as an element of national power, viewed and interpreted through the prism of the strategic interface between military forces and national security imperatives. Over the past few decades, the concept of national security has undergone perceptible changes and its definition continues to alter with time and circumstances while the military forces have also been subject to constant change in their characteristics and capabilities. It is only natural that the status of military forces will also alter with changing circumstances since the parameters for their judgement are in perpetual flux. However, they continue to be a primary element of national power.

Chapter 13 explains the hard power inherent in military forces and how it can be employed to further national security interests, needs and vision. In doing so, the chapter also briefly examines the various strategies that could be applied to achieve national security objectives without recourse to the actual use of lethal force. Thereafter competencies resident within military forces are analysed, taking into account the recent changes that have taken place towards giving an enhanced spread of responsibilities to them in democratic nations. This analysis is conducted through the prism of core and dynamic competencies that are considered to be unavoidably embedded within efficient forces. The chapter emphasises the fact that military forces themselves, while evolving and merging as new entities also face a plethora of challenges to both its development and further employment. This forms the essential core of the analysis of military power as a critical element of national power.

The effectiveness of military forces in a democracy is a direct function of the robustness of the civil-military relationship and the trust that exists between the civil and military leadership. This facet and its impact on military forces are examined a great detail. The importance of legitimacy in the application of force, and the legal aspects regarding the employment of military forces form a section of the chapter. The entire analysis regarding the employment of military forces has been consciously kept at the strategic level, particularly since the operational and tactical aspects are entirely contextual in modern war. They would be superficial in the framework of this book. The importance of concepts and ideas in creating a competent military force is explained in detail. This argument forms the conclusive part of the examination of the evolution of military forces and the unchanging nature of its core competencies.

Since the characteristics and conduct of war and conflict are continually in a state of evolution, their individual and combined influence is felt in all aspects of the development and employment of military forces. Chapter 14 considers these influences and is therefore important for the understanding of the military forces as a whole and to its on-going evolution. It examines how new ideas improve the competence and effectiveness of military forces and help them keep abreast of emerging challenges. The need for military doctrine to keep abreast of emerging concepts so that they can ensure that military forces stay at the cutting edge of capability and competence in order to contain security challenges is investigated. Section IV concludes that a flexible and agile military force, encompassing high-end technological capabilities, and functioning within the control established through a robust civil-military relationship is an inescapable and critical necessity for the well-being of a truly democratic nation.

Section V, the last in the book, is the core narrative of the *The Sword Arm*, explaining the status of military forces in the 21st century. It postulates that national security is best achieved through adopting a WoG approach, with the military forces in the vanguard. In elaborating on this hypothesis, Chapter 15 looks in detail at the evolution of threats and the ways in which they can be mitigated, while also exploring the connection between evolving and contextual threats. Further, their relationship with perceptions of national security is elaborated. In this analysis the vulnerabilities that face a nation—both long term and immediate--are examined and a clear distinction is made between them and emerging as well as existing threats. The chapter also looks at the role of government and international governance in mitigating the threats. The strategies that could be employed to alleviate recognised threats are then described in detail, with the employment of military forces within these strategies forming the core of the explanation.

Chapter 16 is dedicated to explaining the dynamics of national resources, the policies that control their allocation and how they directly affect the strength and status of the military forces. In analysing the influence of resources, the geo-politics of military budgets is considered an important factor and explained as such. The Global Financial Crisis (GFC) that afflicted most of the democratic nations of the world around 2008-10 is examined to emphasis the fact that even while there has been financial recovery of economies, the recuperation process has been much slower in the military forces of the nations involved. Chapter 17 concentrates on examining broad security strategies at the national level; the interaction of military forces within these strategies; and the place of military forces within the national security power balance.

Chapter 18 defines the position of military forces in 21st century democracies, placing them through the prism of the fundamental parameters and principles that guide their employment. This analysis provides an insight into the evolving and broadening roe of military forces vis-à-vis national security. While the chapter teases out the peculiarities of war and conflict in the information age, it looks at the increasing spread of responsibilities that are being shouldered by the military forces and how these changes are influencing the attributes of a 21st century military force, which in turn have been listed and explained. Chapter 19, the penultimate one, flows from the previous chapter, looks at the military force as an instrument of policy; a premise that is debated, explained and codified. There is particular emphasis in ensuring that there is a clear understanding of the relationship between the Laws of Armed Conflict (LOAC), military strategy and the conduct of operations. This understanding is necessary to explain how the strategic culture of a nation influences the highest level of decision-making regarding national security.

Chapter 20, the last one, attempts to provide a framework to strengthen the military forces within the constraints that invariably affect practising democracies. It emphasises the criticality of having a reasonably robust civil-military relationship at the highest levels of government; and its impact, both direct and indirect, on both the military forces and national security, viewed at its broadest. The chapter is brought to a close with a detailed description of the factors that determine the efficacy of military forces and the manner in which they directly contribute to national security.

And so here is the book...

That, in a nutshell, is what this book is about. Military forces have, from their very inception, been the bedrock on which the security of a nation has been built, even within the many and expanded definitions of national security that abound in the modern world. On the other hand, constraints in the availability of resources and conflicting demands for them in democracies pose a real dilemma to the elected representatives of a nation regarding the balance to be maintained in their allocation. It is within this somewhat murky circumstances that the tendency of democracies to neglect their military forces, in times of relative peace, must be viewed. Unfortunately this is a trend that is becoming more pronounced as the world is becoming more interconnected and information availability becomes easy. This book explains the reasons why it should not be so and why the military forces should be granted a status in keeping with their onerous responsibilities. After all, the security of the nation is not something that can be bargained with, especially in the current environment of borderless threats and unreliable alliances.

SECTION - I
NATIONAL SECURITY, POLICY AND GRAND STRATEGY
SHIFTING WITH THE SANDS OF TIME

THESIS: The continuing evolution of the definition and concept of national security has diffused the hierarchical relationship between national security, policy and grand strategy.

Ever since the Peace of Westphalia, the perception, concept and definition of national security have been in a constant, evolutionary state of change. In the contemporary geo-strategic environment, national security is directly influenced by the globalised economy as well as governance issues in fragile states that may be geographically distant to each other. As a result, the military forces of a nation have been compelled to extensively widen their ambit of operations to cater for the expanded and enlarged envelope of national security. At the same time national security policies and imperatives, the fountainhead of national security, have not been revised or articulated to accommodate the transformed realities. The strong, direct and tangible connection between national security policy and grand strategy, which is the foundation for the overarching security of the nation and from which the military draws its raison d'etre and strategic guidance, has become difficult to perceive.

INTRODUCTION

National security is the fundamental quest of all nations and states. The concepts of nation and state, and the nuanced difference between the two, have always been complex because the fundamental idea of a nation by itself is not always clearly understood. Nations can be consciously created, like the formation of the United States or they could have existed for millennia like some nations in Europe and Asia.[1] At its very foundation, a nation is a group of people who share an identity, which means that an individual must and does share a unique relationship with the larger community in which he/she lives. The International Webster's Dictionary defines nation as, 'a people as an organised body politic, usually associated with a particular territory and possessing a distinctive cultural and social way of life'.[2] It is difficult to understand national security without clearly identifying the status of nations within the international security system.

The state is much easier to define and understand—it is the political governance of the nation and the individual's legal relationship to the state. It is defined as, 'a sovereign political community organised under a distinct government recognised and confirmed to by the people as supreme, and having jurisdiction over a given territory; a nation'.[3] The interaction between nation and state can be varied, with some nations not having states or being divided between multiple states and some

---

1 Freedman, George, 'Geopolitics, Nationalism and Dual Citizenship,' in *Stratfor* 116/10, 21 July 2010, on-line version, accessed 22 July 2010.
2 *The International Webster's Comprehensive Dictionary of the English Language* (Deluxe Encyclopaedic Edition), Trident Press International, Florida, USA, 1996, p. 845.
3 ibid, pp. 1224-25.

states encompassing multiple nations.[4] States provide citizenship to their people. Therefore, from an individual perspective there could be a distinction between nationality and citizenship although in most cases this would coincide.

The world—international community of nations—has changed considerably in the past few decades, becoming a more belligerent place, as compared to the situation in the immediate aftermath of World War II. The post-colonial nations that for a number of years were tentative in their approach to finding their place within the international community have now authoritatively embraced nationalism. There has also been a noticeable drop in the belief in diplomatic overtures as a solution to emerging bilateral and multi-lateral issues. Another lingering, but unvoiced, issue is the lack of trust that post-colonial nations harbour against the Western nations. There is tangible, but again mostly unarticulated, sense of exploitation that makes the intervention by Western nations be viewed in a cynical fashion at best and actively opposed at worst. At least in the near term, this impasse is unlikely to change.

The basic issue that emerges is the question of how a nation defines its national security. Emerging from this understanding and inextricably linked to it is the ability of the nation to effectively pursue its national security interests. In something of a self-perpetuating cycle, the definition of national security is dependent on the nation's ability to ensure it and such abilities are developed based on the nation's understanding of national security. This is of course formulated within the bounds of national resources.

The end of the Cold War was considered as a point in history wherein the international community would lapse into a state of benign peace and nations would default to peaceful coexistence in some sort of a utopian world order. Nothing could have been further from the truth. The collapse of the Soviet Union definitely brought about a decrease in the chances of large scale conventional warfare between states. However, a number of factors, such as the unprecedented

---

4 Most of the European states are examples of a state and nation being one entity, while the linguistically and culturally divided states of India could be an example of a State encompassing multiple nations.

interconnectivity of the international system, combined to dramatically increase global instability. The most important fallout from this instability has been the increased instances of state fragmentation and failure, especially in the developing world.[5]

The post-Cold War situation demands answers to a set of new questions—what is a failed state? How does one recognise a failed or fragile state? Very succinctly, it can be stated that a failed state is one that does not have the attributes of a state and does not conduct itself like a state domestically and in its international dealings. In order to remain viable, a state needs to have effective control over the borders that delineate its territory; it must be able to provide at least the basic services to its citizens; and it must have the capacity to interact in a reciprocal manner with other states.[6] A failed or fragile state may not be able to achieve one or more of these criteria and depending on its failure would move up the scale of instability and failure.

Failed states become the nucleus for instability that could consume their immediate neighbourhood and spread rapidly across the region. Fragile or failing states have the potential to descend into similar chaos. The result has been that Western nations have felt the necessity to intervene with increasing frequency in destabilised states to protect their security interests. This trend has been particularly noticeable in the past two decades. When the reasons for such interventions are analysed, it becomes clear that Western nations have mostly responded to humanitarian crises brought about through the inability of the host nation to provide adequately for the safety and security of their citizens, by deploying humanitarian assistance forces including the military. Whether the breakdown of law and order within the borders of a sovereign state constitutes a direct or even indirect threat to the security of the intervening nation has remained a moot question.

The more developed nations tend to view security in a very broad manner and therefore consider failed states as a direct threat

---

5   Lauzon, Dru& Vine, Andrew (eds), 'Security and Governance: Foundations for International Stability', *Colloquium Brief*, Strategic Studies Institute, U.S. Army War College, Carlisle, PA, June 2010, p. 2.

6   Ashdown, P., *Swords and Ploughshares: Building Peace in the 21st Century*, Orion Books, London, 2008, p. 21.

to them, making intervention—in their minds at least—imperative. Such interventions, called variously stabilisation, peacekeeping and peace enforcement operations, attempt to foster effective governance strategies and capacity building in the failed or failing state. The primary intention is always to ensure that the instability does not wash-in to one's own shores with all the attendant risks to the economy, security and development of the nation. In a somewhat cynical manner this is seen as the manifestation of the pursuit of self-interest by the developed nations, in a different manner to earlier colonisation.

Irrespective of the underlying reasons for external intervention, stabilising a failing state is fraught with difficulties. State building is a nuanced process and no two efforts will be the same. The process varies with a number of factors such as the cultural ethos of the state, the infrastructure available, the reason for the state to have failed as well as the ability of the state to absorb the aid and assistance being provided. The common factor is that state building requires considerable time and resources. In fact establishing a functional government in a failed or even fragile state may take decades and the effort of both military and civilian expertise. Stabilising a state and providing the basic security for the population is indeed vital for further progress, but lasting peace can only be achieved through establishing a government based on transparency, accountability and the rule of law.

The strategy of the intervening nations must take these factors into account at the planning stage, failing which, even after efforts that last a number of years, the state will revert to its original fragile situation rapidly on the departure of the intervening contingent. From a military point of view, the strategy that builds up the military capabilities of the host nation must be carefully monitored to create sufficient safeguards to ensure that the military remains a legitimate arm of the fledgling government. Lack of such institutional safeguards will most likely lead to questioning of the governmental authority and further conflict. The strategy must be one of an incremental approach that builds up security. The drawback is that the success or otherwise of the strategy being implemented will only become visible after a considerable period of time.

Nation states—entities where the concept of a nation and state are superimposed amiably without any sign of conflict or dichotomy between the two concepts—can hope to develop and improve only if they are stable and the first requirement for stability is national security. The grand strategy of the nation must therefore provide a broad base from which to develop individual but interconnected strategies that secure the nation in a myriad number of ways—from military resolve and responses to trade, diplomacy and even the provision of humanitarian aid.

Chapter 1

THE RISE OF NATION STATES

The contemporary world is divided into numerous territorial areas—a clear expression of the geography of political power—which have internationally accepted and, at least conceptually, inviolable sovereign borders. Even at the end of the first millennium such clear and global geographical demarcations would have been impossible to visualise. The ambiguity regarding geographical boundaries developed mainly because knowledge regarding the world was restricted purely to the extent of the then 'known world' due to a paucity of information regarding other parts. This is evidenced by the historical fact that even in the early part of the second millennium the highly sophisticated ancient civilisations around the world — Chinese, Japanese, Indian and Islamic—developed in comparative isolation.[1] This isolation in the development of civilisations is all the more intriguing because there was a flow of trade and some exchange of ideas and technology as well as tenuous economic connections between the larger empires.

Even though trade was permitted, the levels and quantum of such trade was closely monitored and controlled in the larger empires. Further, territorial integrity of the nation was always zealously guarded. Two criteria stand out as common themes that the larger empires of the time considered to be fundamental requirements for the stability and security of the state in their dealings of with 'outside' world. First, primary importance was given to the protection of the geographic integrity of the empire, with any attempt at questioning it, even minor

---

1 Fernandez-Armesto, F.,*Millenium*, Bantam Books, London, 1995, Chapter 1.

border incursions, being ruthlessly put down. Secondly, these nations ensured that they maintained clear and visible sovereignty in dealing with 'outsiders', which was considered a primary requirement for the stability of the state. The greater empires were powerful enough to enforce this and their decline can be traced back to the decline in the power and authority of the ruler that led to an inability to enforce this criteria.

The concept of owning territory, and its defence when warranted, dates back to the times when human beings initially identified themselves as part of a group or clan and evolved from hunter-gatherers to cultivators and growers. This change in lifestyle initiated the necessity to claim a particular area within which they lived as their possession that needed to be protected for their survival. From these beginnings it was a natural and inevitable progression to delineate and claim an area as the sovereign territory of a particular group, clan or tribe. Human history thereafter is a long trail of the quest by these groups and tribes for assured integrity, sovereignty and security of their territory. With the advent of kingdoms with clearly demarcated geographical boundaries, the concept of such security became interminably meshed with the concept of a sovereign state.

The criticality of territorial security to the well-being of a sovereign state is clearly demonstrated by the single-minded pursuit of the concept by all national governments, from democratically elected ones to autocracies. The fact that this pursuit has often led to conflicts ranging from long-drawn wars to short skirmishes does not in any way detract from the importance of ensuring the territorial integrity of the nation. It also does not indicate that security of territory is an unobtainable goal. In fact territorial security is one of the foundational requirements to ensure the broader security of the state itself. It is an accepted fact that no nation, however powerful, can prosper for any length of time without the capability and will to ensure its security.[2] Therefore, it stands to reason that all independent nations must, and will, strive to ensure their own territorial integrity to the best of their ability. Historically this has been a fundamental source of confrontations and conflicts.

---

2 Collins, John M., *Military Strategy: Principles, Practices, and Historical Perspectives*, Brassey's Inc, Washington D.C., 2002, p.3.

Defining a Nation

The origin of the concept of a nation-state, as understood today, is difficult to determine. In its current form it is clearly a European or Western concept that started as the gradual articulation of the rights and responsibilities of the ruling princes and evolved into defining those of princely states. This was a long process starting from the fall of Rome in 476 A. D. and culminating in the Peace of Westphalia in 1648. The further development of the nation-state to its current position of sovereign primacy is paralleled by the development and institutionalisation of the legal premise for enforcing accepted norms in terms of international law.

Formation of Princely States

The medieval Christendom that mostly adhered to accepted legal norms was not a society of politically distinct states. However, the conquest of Constantinople in 1453 by the Ottoman Turks started a process of converting the horizontal feudal structure into vertical patterns of geographically defined territorial states.[3] This conquest brought about a change in the conduct of war and more importantly an infusion of scholarship and innovative thought into Europe through the forced movement of people out of ancient Byzantium. The creation of artillery to bombard and subdue towns under siege, adapted with increased mobility by Charles VIII of France in his invasion of Italy in 1494 is seen as the turning point in how states were perceived. It was realised that all the defences, so far considered impregnable were obsolete.[4]

The result was the adoption of the concept of a 'State'—a permanent infrastructure to organise logistical support, put in place command arrangements for the armies, and collect revenue to govern according to the will of the ruler. Gradually the State became the permanent fixture rather than the ruler, gaining wealth and power of its own. The modern state thus originated in this transformation form the rule by individuals to the concept of a geographical entity. This modern state is detached from the society it governs and from the

---

3 For a detailed analysis and explanation see Watson, Adam, *The Evolution of International Societies: A Comparative Historical Analysis*, Routledge, London, 1992.

4 Keegan, John, *A History of Warfare*, Knopf, New York, 1993, pp 320-322.

rulers who wield power, thereby providing it with the potential to be 'immortal'.[5]

The princely state combined the dynastic conventions of the feudal system with the distinct features of a secular state. However, the economically and geographically smaller states could not muster sufficient resources to wage war on the vast scale of open plains that became the norm after the effectiveness of artillery against fortified cities became evident. From early in the 16th Century to the middle of the 17th Century two conflicts intertwined in Europe: the religious struggle that commenced with the Reformation and the attempts by the Habsburg family to carve out an imperial state in Europe.

Although the conflicts were almost continuous for nearly 150 years, the essence of the complex upheavals that beset 17th Century Europe was manifest in the Thirty Years War (1618-1648) that culminated in the Peace of Westphalia. This can be considered the beginning of the modern sovereign state as perceived today. There is a viewpoint that the Thirty Years War was not one extended war, but a progression of conflicts that proliferated from separate regional disputes in different parts of Europe.[6] However, this point is not germane to the attempt at defining nation states.

The Peace of Westphalia

All the minor conflicts and major wars that had been fought in central and eastern Europe from 1609 were concluded by treaties of peace. However, these treaties were essentially *ad-hoc* in nature and did not solve or settle all the problems that led to the conflict in the first place. The Peace of Westphalia denotes a series of peace treaties signed between May and October 1648 in Osnabruck and Munster that ended the war between the Spanish-Austrian group and the French-Swedish-Dutch alliance. It was aimed at addressing all outstanding

---

5 Bobbitt, Philip, *The Shield of Achilles: War, Peace and the Course of History*, Penguin Books, London, 2002, pp. 80-81.

6 Some scholars view the Thirty Years War as part of a prolonged Bourbon-Hapsburg contest for European hegemony through a period (1609-1659) of intermittent warfare. For a detailed explanation of this view point see Steinberg,S. H., *The Thirty Years War and the Conflict for European Hegemony 1600-1660*, W. W. Norton and Company Inc, New York, 1966.

issues that had so far eluded resolution. This was a primary reason for the slow progress of the process—although the first step towards the peace was initiated in 1638, it was finally concluded only in 1648. The negotiations culminated in the signing of a treaty of peace between the Austrian group and Sweden and a treaty between Austria and France.

The treaties were the culmination of the first modern diplomatic congress and brought in a new political order in central Europe based on the concept of the sovereignty of the state. While the peace congress settled the territorial issues, it was only one part of the process. More importantly the Peace of Westphalia laid to rest— within a European context—the constitutional and religious problems that had for centuries plagued the region.[7] The congress addressed the issue of the relationship between the Church and the State. It declared the 'territorial superiority in all matters ecclesiastical as well as political'.[8] In essence the States declared their 'independence' from religious interference, publicly disregarding the authority of the Pope by ignoring a papal bull that was issued against the peace of Westphalia.

There were other provisions within the Westphalian Peace that confirmed its constitutional nature. For example, two new states—the United Provinces of the Netherlands and the Swiss Confederation— were recognised; war was recognised as a legitimate form of resolving conflicts but no state was allowed to be destroyed, and compensation was to be paid to those states that gave up strategically important possessions.[9] By the enactment and enforcement of a number of principles and rules that had far reaching consequences, the Westphalian settlement brought about a new constitution in the European state system. It imposed common restrictions on States underpinned by an underlying acceptance of sovereign equality of all, a concept that has endured over the years.[10]

---

7   Steingerg, S. H., *The Thirty Years War and the Conflict for European Hegemony 1600-1660*, W. W. Norton and Company Inc, New York, 1966, p. 81.

8   Bobbitt, Philip, *The Shield of Achilles: War, Peace and the Course of History*, p. 506.

9   ibid, pp. 507-508.

10 Randle, Robert F., *Issues in the History of International Relations: The Role of Issues in the Evolution of the State System*, Praeger, Westport, Conn, 1987, p. 53.

State Sovereignty

The understanding of the concept of sovereignty has varied throughout history and the term has been used in a number of ways in a contextual manner. However, the core of the terms has always been the belief of 'supreme authority within a territory'.[11] Fundamental to the notion is the state as a political institution in which sovereignty, its internal and external dimensions and its absoluteness, is embodied. Over the past half century the perception of 'supreme authority' has taken many diverse forms, but the fundamental idea has accommodated even the more extraordinary interpretations and has continued to remain central to the modern acceptance of a state and its associated responsibilities.

The other ingredient of sovereignty is territoriality, a principle by which members of a community are defined with membership being derived from their residence within borders. There is a subtle difference between territoriality and identity, in that, the borders of a sovereign state need not necessarily encompass a 'people' or even a 'nation'. On the other hand, it is possible for a sovereign state to include diverse identities purely by their being resident within a particular territory. The connection between territoriality and sovereignty is now an accepted fact and is a feature of authority across the globe.

Post World War II there has been a move to circumscribe the idea of a sovereign state through the strengthening of laws and practices to protect human rights. In 1948, the majority of states signed the Universal Declaration of Human Rights, although it was not legally binding, nor did it contain any enforcement provisions. Subsequent improvements to ensure that states were legally bound to adhere by the declarations—in 1950 and again 1960—did not infringe on the constitutional authority and sovereignty of the state. By the 1990s there was general acceptance that there was a need to circumscribe the sovereignty of a nation in cases where human rights abuses were taking place. Further, it was also realised that military enforcement of human rights practices was perhaps the only way to ensure that states met their declaratory obligations.

---

11 Stanford Encyclopaedia of Philosophy, http://plato.stanford.edu/entries/sovereignty, accessed 11 March 2011

A fundamental tenet of the Peace of Westphalia was the acceptance of non-intervention in the internal matters of a sovereign state. However, this was revised, in a gradual manner, by political and military actions endorsed by the United Nations and initiated by a group of nations in general consensus to remedy an injustice within the boundaries of a sovereign state. Normally this has lacked the consent of the government of the target state and is generally aimed at coercing the state to abide by the norms of international human rights. Such operations have been conducted in Iraq, the former Yugoslavia, Bosnia, Kosovo, Somalia, Haiti, Cambodia and elsewhere. This practice of intervention is likely to continue with the broad endorsement from the international community.

A fundamental change to the way sovereignty is viewed took place in 2001 with the writing of a document called The Responsibility to Protect. This was the done by the International Commission on Intervention and State Sovereignty, convened by the Government of Canada at the behest of the United Nations. This concept not only recognises the responsibility of the state to protect its citizens but more importantly states that this responsibility could be assumed by outside agencies when a state cannot protect its citizens or itself perpetrates injustice on them. This has put in place a concept of non-absolute sovereignty, conditional to the state meeting its obligations. This is a far cry from the absolute authority that was vested in the ruling hierarchy through the Peace of Westphalia.

The loss of absolute sovereignty through international declarations and obligations, enforceable through outside political intervention, that may take the form of military action, is in line with the concepts of some contemporary political philosophers. The validity of a government is almost completely based on its direct relationship to natural law. Absolute sovereignty is not commensurate with the development of international law and a stable world order; it creates a state centralism and is contrary to the democratic principle of accountability. Therefore, sovereignty of a state now is a much more nuanced concept, one that does not provide for absolutism and one that is interpreted within the internationally accepted norm of protection of its citizens.

The Origins of International Law

For nearly six centuries from the fall of the Roman Empire, its territories were successively attacked and subjugated by waves of barbarian invaders. Only by the end of the first millennium did a central core of the old empire emerge as a viable entity—mainly lands colonised by Germanic tribes in what is now France, Italy and central Europe.[12] Within this core two parallel power centres developed— the universal Church and the fragmented feudal system of the local princes. In principle the two were separate: the Church involved in religion, education and charitable work while the ruling nobility exercised military and proprietary prerogatives. However, in actual fact they were interdependent with the overlap more visible than the separation at times.

From a modern perspective it is difficult to imagine how such a system operates. The political society was organised into four co-existing functional sectors—the nobility or the ruling class, the clergy or the church, burghers and peasants—which were themselves rigidly vertical in organisation. However, the horizontal power of each of the sectors was severely limited with the merchants, artisans and others in urban conclaves functioning autonomously, completely independent of the nobility and the clergy. These urban centres—cities—developed the beginnings of the concepts of trade, banking, manufacturing etc., as it is known today.

The diversity of the commercial activities necessitated adherence to mutually accepted legal norms. Unlike in the Mediterranean region or Asia, which also had flourishing trade and commerce, the heterogeneous and fragmentary nature of Europe was more conducive to the development of regulatory laws. It can be seen that devoid of an overarching imperial hierarchy that subsumed diversity in dealings with 'outsiders' there is a high proclivity to engage in conflict. The contrast is evident in the case of China and India. China was able to deal with external influences for a long time through its centralised and homogenous imperial system whereas in pre-Moghul

---

12 Bobbitt, Philip, *The Shield of Achilles: War, Peace and the Course of History*, p. 75.

India fragmented societies prevented the development of a common culture. In both these cases, very advanced cultures failed to develop either a comprehensive state system or a broad legal system that was accepted by all.[13] In contrast the principalities in medieval Europe developed legal restrictions because there was recourse to appeal to the Church, which had already made inroads into governance, as an overarching higher authority to which feuding princes could appeal for the implementation of legal norms. It has also been suggested that the laws were enacted also to be used against the Church without rejecting the ecclesiastical authority per se.

Further, the universality of the Christian religion and community tended to impose constraints on an individual prince from initiating war. However, the princes of this period were not territorial, i.e. they were not princes of states and the population was too local to even think in terms of a national identity. This situation also fostered the development of legal rules since most of them had contractual relationships with each other, governed by the law of contracts. Similarly there were laws of crimes and laws of property. The current international law is based on this distinctly medieval pattern. The law of contracts formed the foundation for the international law of treaties; laws of crimes and torts among princes evolved into international laws of war; laws of property and inheritance produced the international law of territorial conquest; and the law of the society of princes became the law of the society of states.[14]

The Nation-State

The dictionary defines a nation as a 'body of people associated with a particular territory who are sufficiently conscious of their unity to seek or possess a government peculiarly their own.'[15] Based on this definition it can be argued that the concept of a nation has existed in an abstract form for centuries, perhaps with the formation of sovereign kingdoms

---

13 ibid. p.77.

14 ibid pp. 78-79.

15 Delbridge, A.& Bernard,J.R.L. (General Eds), *The Macquarie Concise Dictionary*, Third Edition, The Macquarie Library Pty Ltd, NSW, 1998, p.762.

as early as 1000 A.D.[16] However, there are certain common features that can be discerned from history as defining a nation-state. These are features that, if not clearly visible, will detract from the nation being a cohesive whole.

First, a nation must be willing and able to meet their full range of sovereign responsibilities within and even beyond their geographical boundaries. These responsibilities could wary from simple diplomatic and consular services rendered to its citizens to maintaining the capabilities to employ lethal force in the protection of its territories. The spectrum of responsibilities is very large. In the contemporary global order there are a number of nations that do not have the ability to shoulder their full responsibilities. However, international organisations provide the assistance necessary for them to retain their independent stature as nation-states.

Second, a clearly understood national identity—accepted by the people of the nation as well as by other states— is crucial to creating a national will to retain its sovereignty. A national identity that is accepted by those who carry it, as well as by others who view it, stems from a sense of national integrity. National integrity is a function of both geographic integrity and the cohesiveness of the population within the state. A fundamental requirement to have sufficient national integrity is the assurance of the rule of law within the nation. In effect rule of law is the centre of gravity around which national integrity forms. There are any number of instances from history that demonstrate the fact that failure to enforce the rule of law is the first step towards a nation sliding into failure and balkanisation. National will is also greatly influenced by the leadership. Ineffectual national leadership can become the weak link in ensuring the rule of law, leading to a loss of national identity.

Third, is the abstract concept of patriotism. Patriotism cannot be clearly defined but only explained for the fundamental reason that its interpretation is always influenced by history of the people concerned,

---

16 The ancient kingdoms in China and India have not been included in this analysis because they did not spread the concept of a nation but were based on the rule by force of an individual and his successors with the people being loyal to the regime to varying degrees. The build-up and the inevitable balkanisation of these large empires suggest that allegiances were not to the territory but to individuals.

prevailing tradition and most importantly their cultural ethos. Therefore, patriotism can be thought of as an intangible emotion, a feeling that come to the forefront and *in extremis* even engulfs a person when that person thinks about his or her country/nation in an abstract manner. This feeling could be generated by the successes and well-being of the state as well as troubles and tribulations that it may be undergoing and can manifest in a number of ways. Within a nation patriotism is nurtured in a myriad number of ways—direct and indirect. It involves visible symbols of the unity and sovereignty of a nation like the flag and national anthem as well as indirect methods like emphasis on the more 'glorious' part of the nation's history and martial traditions.

The fourth feature is of comparatively recent origin and is more applicable to the financial cohesiveness of a nation. There is no doubt that trade and commerce have always been important to the nation's prosperity throughout history. However, the interests of the nation vis-à-vis its security needs and commercial needs were always clearly prioritised with the security needs subsuming the commercial needs if necessary. This is not to say that commercial needs were not of any importance. They were, and a rising nation always manoeuvred itself to ensure the continued success of their commercial enterprises. A clear example is the British Government taking over control of the parts of India that were then controlled by the British East India Company after the Indian uprising in 1857. The loss of life and the questioning of British 'authority' in the Indian sub-continent was considered by the Government to be anathema to the solidarity and well-being of the nation in a broad manner and therefore action had to be instituted to safeguard the British Empire while not detracting from the highly lucrative commercial venture in India.

There are two other factors that also contribute, in a lesser manner, to the concept of a nation-state—the role of religion, ethnicity and the demographic distribution. While these factors played a vital role from the 16th to the early 20th Centuries, their relevance has somewhat diminished in contemporary considerations. The reasons are many, but primarily because of increased movement of people across the globe and the changed views of religious tolerance. However, the influence of these factors cannot be completely ignored when considering the status of nation-states. Demography, religion and ethnicity are major factors in the formation of a national identity that is crucial for the cohesion of a nation.

While the four features—fulfilling the state's responsibilities, having a clearly visible national identity, demonstrated patriotism and the primacy of national security—are fundamental to a nation-state's existence as an entity, there are three influences that detract from these time honoured factors. These detractors have become more pronounced in the contemporary international environment because of economic interdependence between nation-states brought about through globalisation of trade and commerce; the movement of people across the globe, for commercial purposes as well as the movement of refugees escaping from persecution or fleeing natural calamities; and the more open availability of the simple concept of migration to another nation to better individual prospects.

The first influence in weakening a nation's cohesiveness is socio-economic grievances. These can be brought about by corruption in governance, embedded historic inequalities within the broader society, lack of opportunities—perceived or actual—for the people to better their living standards and visible inequalities between the groups considered to be ruling elite and the common people. The acceptance of socio-economic inequalities is a function of historic, cultural and traditional factors and is as such non-quantifiable. Any of the situations that encourage such grievances can lead to political unrest and its attendant civil strife. The toleration quotient of a particular group of people to the grievances can and does vary, with some being very volatile and others very passive. Therefore, the tipping point for a nation to go into political turmoil will vary, although all nations will have a point beyond which the socio-economic grievances will not be tolerated in blind acceptance.

The second is a direct function of the modern trend of corrosive moral relativism brought about by the open availability of information and its rapidity of dissemination. Modern societies—especially in the more developed states—tend to steal away from the concept of patriotism and the inherent coherence of a nation. The greater importance being laid on the individual rather than the society as whole, which was almost the norm even a century ago, exacerbates this moral dilemma and corrodes the authority of the state. In extreme cases this leads to anarchy of a different kind, not brought about through socio-economic grievances, but through an excess of self-indulgence, which paradoxically was itself facilitated by the state. It is almost impossible to measure this influence or the beginnings of its onset making it difficult for the state to initiate remedial measures in time to stem this descend into relative ineffectiveness. The indications of the unseemly rise of individualism can be noticed by the gradual erosion of the importance being given to the symbols of nationhood that reminds the people of who they are and what they stand for as a nation. The relative status of the military forces within the broader society is one of the more visible indications of the overall situation in a nation.

The third influence is that of the relationship between commercial or corporate interests and that of the nation at large. In times of comparative peace, the two could be very close to each other. However, in times when the global security environment is in a state of flux the two interests cannot always be considered complementary. In the 17th and 18th Centuries the ruling monarch could, and often did, take direct action to secure the nation's commercial interests through military intervention. This situation does not exist anymore. Therefore, modern nations have to clearly delineate the relationship between corporate interests and national interests, based on the prevalent perception of security. In a world that is indelibly inter-linked through trade and finance this demarcation may not be the simplest action to initiate and conclude. There will always be an indirect influence of corporate interests that could, if not carefully ameliorated, impact national security calculations. Such a situation is more clearly visible in instances where the increasing power of multi-national corporations relatively eclipses that of smaller nation-states.

Summing Up...

Nation-states have evolved over a long period of time and this process is ongoing. However, the rate of evolution has slowed down in the past few decades and the process is gradually realigning to changed perceptions and ground realities. The constant factor in these changes is the steadfast belief of all nations—large and small, powerful and not so powerful, stable and flirting with instability—that their sovereignty is not questionable. On the other hand there is increasing belief in the more stable and developed nations that they must intervene in failing states to stabilise the nation, contain a potential escalation of instability, mitigate emerging security challenges and also to avoid humanitarian crisis that invariably accompany such failures. These two concepts are not compatible and lead to tensions between the smaller, fragile states and the intervening nations. In an overarching manner, the fundamental reason for most conflicts can be traced to the emphasis on the independence and sovereignty of nation-states.

Chapter 2

NATIONAL SECURITY

National security is an abstract concept and it has evolved along with the changed perceptions of the nation-state and its sovereignty. In fact, in a very basic manner, it is suggested that if a body of people owing allegiance to a particular nation-state is ready to defend their nation against any assault on its sovereignty, they are in effect pursuing their ambition to ensure national security. Therefore, the ancient city states of Greece, such as Sparta, Athens, Thebes and Corinth, were only exercising their inherent need for national security—defined within the understanding of the time—when they took up arms to protect the sanctity of their borders. Similarly, the defence that Troy put up against the invaders is also an expression of that nation's desire for national security.

As an academic concept, national security is a recent phenomenon and encompasses the earlier ideas that dealt with the states' efforts to neutralise both internal and external threats.[1] In very broad terms national security is the necessity to ensure the satisfactory survival of the nation-state through the appropriate use of political, economic and military power resident in the state and the employment of diplomacy to further its own interests. The initial focus of national security was on military capabilities that could maintain the territorial integrity of the state, although there was underlying realisation that security encompassed more than mere military security. Even though in contemporary terms national security assumes a broad range of facets it is still primarily concerned with the economic and military

---

1 Romm, Joseph J., *Defining National Security: The Nonmilitary Aspects*, Council of Foreign Relations Press, New York, 1993, p. 5.

security of the state. Further, governments have been reluctant to comprehensively define national security. This reluctance stems from the advantages of keeping it an ambiguous but powerful term to be evoked when the interests of the state are threatened in any way.

Essentially the traditional understanding of national security revolved around ensuring the inviolability of the geographical boundaries of the state and protecting the autonomy of the government, irrespective of whether the rule was autocratic or democratic.

There is a view point that suggests that the concept of national security as a philosophy to ensure international stability has been understood only since the Treaty of Westphalia. However, it is certain that the concept of national security was very clearly understood much earlier, although the actual term 'national security' was not in common usage even as late as the 1930s. While the direct connection between territorial security and prosperity of the state has not changed appreciably through the ages, the understanding and interpretation of the concept of national security has assumed a much broader context. The meaning of the term has undergone radical changes over time and is constantly being revised.

Changing Definition of National Security

There is no single universally accepted definition of 'national security'. Before the end of World War II, most nation-states were internally strong, meaning that there was only very limited internal dissention, and therefore the threats to a state almost always emanated externally. However, this changed after World War II with the newly independent post-colonial nations facing a plethora of internal issues that spilled over into the international arena.

Post-Colonial Nations. The security threats to a post-colonial nation are, more often than not, generated because of the linguistic, cultural and ethnic diversity within the geographical entity that the colonial power forged and then granted independence. The lack of cohesiveness and the inherent quest for identity within the population leads to internal strife and civil war in many cases, threatening the overall stability and security of the nation.[2] For these nations the understanding of national security will be very different to the accepted definitions in internally cohesive states.

National security as a concept originated from simple definitions that identified and emphasised the freedom from military attacks and political coercion. It has subsequently grown into a more sophisticated concept that includes non-military security in a contextual manner. At its broadest, national security is equated to 'human security', which is essentially an expression of the need for protecting the basic needs of a human being like access to clean food and water, protection from arbitrary violence from the state or other individuals and freedom from exploitation.[3]

One of the early definitions of national security was provided by Walter Lippman[4] in 1943. It said, "A nation has security when it does not have to sacrifice its legitimate interests to avoid war, and is able, if challenged, to maintain them by war".[5] It is obvious that the definition was strongly influenced by the war that was being fought at that time and reflects the conditions that started World War II in the first instance. It is also to be noted that there is emphasis on the legitimacy of the nation's interest, once again a clear indication of the impact of the conditions that prevailed before the outbreak of the war. In terms of a nation and war, this is an adequate definition. Although it does not take into account any other factor, the concept of legitimate interest can be interpreted to mean a broader understanding of national security.

---

2   Holsti, Kalevi J., *The State, War and the State of War*, Cambridge University Press, Cambridge, UK, 1996, pp. 25-28.

3   Sachs, Stephen E., *The Changing Definition of Security*, http://www.stevesachs.com/papers/paper_security.html, accessed on 25 November 2011.

4   Lippman, Walter (23 September 1889 – 14 December 1974) was an American intellectual, writer, reporter and political commentator and was among the first to introduce the concept of the Cold War. He was a philosopher who tried to reconcile the tensions between liberty and democracy in the complex modern world, famously in his book *Liberty and the News* in 1920.

5   Quoted in Joseph J. Romm, *Defining National Security: The Nonmilitary Aspects*, p. 5.

After World War II, the concept continued to be based on the ability to withstand coercion, with Harold Lasswell,[6] a political scientist, stating in 1950 that, " the distinctive meaning of national security is freedom from dictation." Very subtly Lasswell brought in the idea of freedom, although used in a slightly restrictive manner in terms of external coercion. This definition is broader than the ones perceived in the 1940s and moved away from being too prescriptive about how the necessary freedoms would be achieved or preserved.

It was not long before the subjectivity of the concept of national security was distinguished as being separate from the objectivity in terms of the actual threats and the elements within the nation they would be directed against. In 1962, Arnold Wolfers defined national security as, "An ambiguous symbol meaning different things to different people. Security, in an objective sense, measures the absence of threats to acquired values, in a subjective sense, the absence of fear that such values will be attacked."[7] The definition is noteworthy for two reasons. First, it acknowledged that the concept of national security was ambiguous and therefore, not completely definable in a universal manner. Since it meant different things to different nations, the differentiation in terms of objectivity and subjectivity was something that could not have common basis in all nations. Second, the need to protect the acquired values of a nation as being the foundation of a nation's security was articulated for the first time in an explicit manner. The interpretation of the term 'acquired values' can be very broad or parochially narrow depending on the context, adding to the ambiguous nature of the broader concept of national security itself. However, it also brought in a higher level of sensitivity to the concept by introducing the intangible ideal of protecting the values of a nation.

While it was not the first time that the elements of national power were brought into the equation, the 1996 definition that came out of a seminar in the National Defence College in India succinctly expressed the idea that national security was achieved through combining a

---

6 Lasswell, Harold (13 February 1902 – 18 December 1978) was a leading American political scientist and communications theorist who is ranked amongst the half dozen creative innovators in the social sciences in the twentieth century.

7 Paleri, Prabhakaran, *National Security: Imperatives and Challenges,* Tata McGraw-Hill, New Delhi, 2008, p. 52.

number of power elements. It stated that, "National security is an appropriate and aggressive blend of political resilience and maturity, human resources, economic structure and capacity, technological competence, industrial base and availability of natural resources and finally the military might."[8] The definition is also sufficiently broad to encompass all elements, but does not explain how a nation without sufficient recourse to all these elements can achieve security. Nor does this definition provide any conceptual direction regarding how this aggressive blend would enhance national security. It lacks a definitive and pragmatic thrust to explain what is to be achieved.

In 1983, Harold Brown who was the U. S. Secretary of defence from 1977 to 1981 in the Carter administration defined national security in a much broader manner in his book *Thinking about National Security: Defense and Foreign Policy in a Dangerous World*. He stated that, "National security then is the ability to preserve the nation's physical integrity and territory; to maintain its economic relations with the rest of the world on reasonable terms; to preserve its nature, institution and governance from disruption from outside; and to control its borders."[9] Along with the traditional concepts of protection of territory and physical integrity, this definition includes a number of other elements like economy. The more important factor is the inclusion of the need to protect the nature and governance from disruption, which opens up a completely new aspect of national security. The increasing breadth of the concept also brings about the need to have the wherewithal for a nation to protect these interests.

Around the 1980s, the concept of national power started to be articulated. While there is a distinct and palpable connection between power and security, they are not synonymous. In fact, national security cannot be achieved through the accumulation of power alone. This is so because the subjective sense of national security, the freedom from the fear of attack, cannot be achieved or the fear neutralised through the possession of power. Further, neither is the existence of

---

8 Definition from Proceedings of Seminar on 'A Maritime Strategy for India' held at National Defence College, New Delhi, 1996, quoted in Prabhakaran Paleri, *National Security: Imperatives and Challenges*, p. 52-54.

9 Brown, Harold, *Thinking about national security: Defense and foreign policy in a dangerous world*, Westview Press, Boulder Co, 1983, p.4.

such fear or freedom from it influenced by the relative power of a nation. However, it is possible to view national security, in an objective manner, through the lens of national power.

In 1990, Professor Charles Maier defined national security in terms of a nation's ability to control events and conditions. He stated, "National security is best described as a capacity to control those domestic and foreign conditions that the public opinion of a given community believes necessary to enjoy its own self-determination or autonomy, prosperity and well-being."[10] This definition directly indicates the necessity for a nation to possess the inherent power to determine and set the conditions that will ensure its security. This power is the nuanced application of national power and is derived from a broad range of elements, such as natural resource base, demography, education, scientific and technological capabilities, industrial development etc, that combine in different ways to produce it.

In contemporary interpretation, national security has evolved into an all-encompassing term, at times purposely kept vague to facilitate political manipulation of public opinion. Even purely academic definitions tend to take the cue from the actualities of day-to-day functioning of the state. This has led to the term 'national security' becoming one that is perhaps the most misunderstood and in a certain sense misused in discussions of what a nation stands for and the expectations of the people in regard to governmental responsibilities.

THE PRIMARY FEATURES OF NATIONAL SECURITY

Essentially, national security encompasses two distinct features—one, what a nation believes it needs to protect and two, creation of the wherewithal to do so. What a nation believes it needs to protect can be placed on a decreasing scale of importance. At the very base level will be the need to have physical security, for the nation as a geographic entity as well as the physical security of the people and their belongings within the state. This aspect makes domestic or internal security a prerequisite for external security. Physical security—of the people and their personal assets, national borders, national assets both inside and

---

10 Quoted in Romm, Joseph J., *Defining National Security: The Nonmilitary Aspects*, p. 5.

outside the sovereign territory of the nation—is the first and most important requirement to ensure national security. Only after assuring the sanctity of its borders can the nation move to consider more sophisticated aspects of security.

There is a corollary to this concept. History shows that there have been very few instances when national survival has been at stake, especially when considering middle level and major powers. Therefore, the indelible need displayed by nations to ensure national security, in whatever definition it is understood, must spring from some other ambiguous motive. A fundamental aspect of this motive, or compulsion, is a function of a collective national desire to defend and retain its wealth and values. It follows naturally that the efforts to secure the nation would be directly proportional to the amount of wealth and range of values that need to be protected.[11]

Much as in the hierarchy of human needs, the intangible quotient of values as national assets to be protected and, a nation's willingness to exert itself to do so, is dependent on its ability to physically secure itself. The definitions that have evolved over the years, while containing increasingly sophisticated nuances regarding what a nation must protect, do not take into account this basic factor. A nation in the throes of domestic upheavals will have no surplus capability to secure its value systems. Only when a nation is assured of its geographic sanctity, for a demonstrated period of time, can it prepare to secure the other more refined and normally intangible concepts and ideas that are distinctive to it.

Having placed values as a second tier issue in national security, to be contemplated after achieving what could be termed as base-level security, it is equally important to distinguish their impact. It must also be noted that geographic security and security of the value system cannot function separately, but are interlinked and influence each other. Values are abstractions. However, they have a salutary impact on the way in which a nation views its security. Values range from religious compulsions to common beliefs such as regarding the importance of

---

11 Wolfers, Arnold, 'National Security as an Ambiguous Symbol,' in *Political Science Quarterly*, Vol 67, No 4, December 1952, The Academy of Political Sciences, 1952, p. 489.

fundamental freedoms and the concept of human tolerance. A stable nation must have a set of base values that do not change contextually, irrespective of external influences. They must remain equally applicable in all dealings of the nation, in war and in peace. These values provide the measure for accountability of national leadership—both political and military—when security decisions are made and implemented. National values tend to get eroded when decisions are made for short-term political gains, whether domestic or international.

The second factor is the creation of the resources that will protect what a nation believes should be protected. This is an involved process and varies considerably between nations. Protection of national interests, that in turn ensures national security, is intrinsically connected to a nation discharging its obligations brought about through formal treaties and alliances as well as informal understanding; fulfilling its commitments to be a responsible international citizen and undertaking the actions necessary to contribute to the undefinable moral duty demands on a nation to protect its own interests as well as the ones that are common to its friends and allies. These actions lead to a viable national security enterprise having to be strategy led—matching the ends, ways and means—to use all the elements of national power to the best effect.

In this context, the strategy to be developed is at the highest level, focusing on the optimised use of both the soft and hard power of the nation and not merely the employment of physical resources to achieve laid down objectives. The resources necessary to protect the values of the nation will have to be drawn from the multi-dimensional strength of the nation. In contemporary analysis it is common to club the strength of the nation within the concept of DIME—diplomatic, informational, military and economic capabilities resident in the nation. However, there are four basic factors which affect the security resource development that do not fit in comfortably within these broad areas. First, the social structure of the nation, in terms of its cohesiveness and the spread of common awareness of national requirements that in turn is influenced by the average education level of the population; second, the legal aspects that not only cover diplomatic overtures and military action, but which will determine the actions that a nation is permitted to initiate within the constraints of domestic governance;

third, the technological standing of the nation vis-à-vis education, industry base, research and development capabilities, in other words the technological viability of the nation; and fourth, the political legitimacy of the government, which will have a direct impact on its ability to raise and distribute the resources.

A stable and 'wise' nation will always project and follow a trajectory of its own that caters for its unique requirements for development and security while simultaneously keeping a track of the trajectories of other nations, both allies and potential adversaries. This is essential to creating a viable national security strategy that will be flexible enough to accept even rapid changes in the security environment.

SECURITY, DEFENCE AND CONTEMPORARY ISSUES

Security and defence have been intrinsically meshed together since the very first nation-state was formed. In fact, the terms were almost synonymous for a long period of time, before other factors started to enlarge the concept of security. At their most basic level, both security and defence are concerned with the territorial integrity of the nation. Security is the ability of a nation to influence and contain political and military circumstances that could affect national interests into the future, even in geographically distant areas which could ultimately threaten political independence or territorial integrity. Defence has a more immediate nature to it and is the ability of a nation to adopt military measures to neutralise an actual violation or prevent an impending violation of its territorial integrity.

Security and defence interests do not diminish with the passage of time or with distance. They remain static unless there are changes to the overall circumstances of the nation brought about through domestic political or internal social convulsions.

Most nations attempt to create a viable security architecture through measures such as treaties, alliances, agreements, understandings and constructive dialogue, even if they have status of a major power. In the contemporary security environment it is not possible for a nation to create a setting that maintains absolute security by itself, irrespective of its resident power. The measures that nations adopt could be defence agreements that are bilateral, between two nations; mini-lateral, between a small number of nations; or multi-lateral, between a large group of nations.[12] Such measures define the relationship between security and defence.

Defence agreements, especially mini- and multi-lateral ones, carry within them some inherently uncertainties. These mainly emanate from economic considerations of abiding by the agreement. The contemporary international security situation indicates that such agreements would increase the chances of having to deploy military forces to distant theatres of operation with the cost to the nation of direct contribution to such deployments being difficult to fathom. Domestic sentiments are more likely to run contrary to such deployments and they would obviously be more expensive in purely financial terms. The political and economic impact may be higher than what a government is capable of containing effectively. Such a situation will place a great deal of strain on the agreement. The other aspect of defence agreements is that it necessitates a minimum level of interoperability between the military forces of participating nations. For a smaller nation this demand could be technologically too sophisticated and the costs associated with fulfilling this requirement could prove to be far too expensive. In a regional context this could make a small nation reconsider the relevance of such defence agreements with major powers and hold them back from entering into one.[13]

Nations also pursue the concept of security through the development of foreign policies that serve their unique needs. Most independent nations would like to maintain their neutrality, which gives them the maximum flexibility in ensuring the security of the state. However, smaller nations may not be able to base their security requirements on neutrality and could be forced into bilateral or regional alliances. This would negate the possibility of a region by itself being neutral and thereby may not provide the environment for any nation

---

12 Emmers, Ralf, 'The Role of Five Power Defence Arrangements in the Southeast Asian Security Architecture,' *RSIS Working Paper No. 195*, S. Rajaratnam School of International Studies, Nanyang Technological University, Singapore, 20 April 2010, pp. 1-4.

13 Thayer, Carlyle A., 'The Five Power Defence Agreements: The Quiet Achiever,' *Security Challenges*, Volume 3, No. 1, Kokoda Foundation, Canberra, February 2007, p. 95.

to pursue a neutral stance in security.[14] For these reasons—the high cost of defence capabilities and foreign policy imperatives—nations will always be influenced, in differing degrees, by enduring caveats to national security.

Governance

Internal security, within the state, is equally important to ensure national security. Internal disturbance issues would be more prevalent in nations that have autocratic or dictatorial governments than in democracies. One of the primary reasons for this would be the unfulfilled desire for participation and good governance, which may not be the norm in autocratic governments. This sense of deprivation is often aggravated by endemic corruption within the ranks of the ruling elite. While the state apparatus will try to enforce a sense of calm, in the contemporary international environment internal dissention and the accompanying security issues are becoming more common. Even in democracies, an elected government cannot consider public opinion as inconsequential. The connection between governance and security is indirect but very influential in the broader aspects of national security.

Another factor that has an indirect connection to good governance is the question of standard of living of the larger population. There are two aspects to this issue. First, the majority of the general population within the nation must have an acceptable standard of living. Second, this average standard of living must not be too far below the standard of living of the rich, elite and ruling classes. A very low average standard of living or a great disparity between the haves and the have-nots will invariably lead to internal strife of some kind or the other. It may appear on the surface that the poor and the underprivileged do not have any influence on the national agenda. However, this is never the case. It is the underprivileged population that will bring in radical changes to the society, as and when the divide becomes unbearably large and openly visible. This phenomenon is applicable both in democratic and dictatorial governments with even in very brutal autocracies being susceptible to it. Naturally national security will be the first casualty of such uncontrolled convulsions in the society.

---

14 Emmers, Ralf, pp. 3-6.

Natural Resources

In recent times reliable access to natural resources—in sufficient quantity and in a sustainable and affordable manner—is also being considered a part of national security. However, this move is mainly restricted to the more developed nations of the world because of the hierarchy of security needs that has been discussed before. A nation will not expend its security capabilities in the quest to ensure reliability of natural resources for its growth when its territorial integrity and geographic boundaries are being violated.

Of the natural resources that a nation would encompass within its national security umbrella, water is the most important. It has been predicted that Asia will start to suffer from water shortages from 2025.[15] Water scarcity has a cascading effect. It brings on depletion of food sources and associated issues of draught and famine that could threaten the very existence of the nation as a viable entity. In turn, this will create environmental migration with the associated cascading implications for neighbouring nation-states. Defending against this threat is complex, needing a whole-of-government approach, and may even need a nation to assume an offensive stance.

Assured availability of natural resources and energy has a direct influence on the way in which a nation pursues its security imperatives. Climate change bringing about drought and floods is perhaps the most easily understood in terms of natural phenomenon affecting security. These phenomena can increase the migratory impulses of people from the affected areas that could lead to issues of human security in terms of trafficking and human rights abuses. While these issues may not reach global proportions, it has the potential to create or exacerbate already existing regional security issues. When combined, these issues become threat multipliers that could prospectively subsume the security apparatus of smaller nations.

The demand for natural resources is already clearly visible across the world. It is also becoming apparent that states are willing to become aggressive and belligerent in their search for adequate

---

15 Laksmana, Evan A., *RSIS Commentaries 169/2010*, S. Rajaratnam School of International Studies, Nanyang Technological University, Singapore, 14 December 2010.

resources to ensure their own prosperity. Since the demand for natural resources will only increase into the future, it will also increase—in direct proportion—the probability of boundary disputes, especially in the maritime regions where the boundaries are not as clearly drawn as on land. This trend will also affect the operating environment of defence forces, as and when they are used to ensure natural resource security, and make it more complex.

Energy Security. Currently the world is dependent on fossil fuels for its energy requirements and therefore, energy dependence could be considered a part of natural resource security issues. This dependency will increase multi-fold by 2025 with disastrous consequences for states with smaller and more vulnerable economies. The possibility of regional conflict increases with this development. However, on the positive side, the same reasons that could perpetuate a conflict will also determine, and restrict, the duration and intensity of military operations or campaigns.

NATIONAL SECURITY THROUGH MILITARY AND ECONOMIC PRISMS

National security is an intellectually complex issue that must be dealt with, in a holistic manner, at the apex of governance. A robust strategic culture is important to maintain an unwavering long-term perception of national security. This cannot be cultivated in the short term but can only be built gradually through well-conceived security initiatives that have broad consensus within the nation. National culture, in terms of its history, ethno-centricity and perceptions of itself also has a significant influence in developing a strategic appreciation of long term security imperatives.

The culture and concept of national security must be built on long term strategic analysis. At the highest levels of government and strategic decision-making there must also be an overarching and common acceptance of the priorities that must always be maintained with respect to national objectives. Constant or short-term changes to this order of priority will almost always diminish the potency of a nation to meet its basic security needs. In the current global environment it is possible to lose sight of the long term national security requirements because of on-going low intensity conflicts. Sub-optimal awareness of long term security requirements will always lead to increased stress levels within the military and other elements of national power. This stress can, and almost always does, percolate into the strategic decision-making levels of national security and is a powerful motivator for a nation to adopt a short term view of its security priorities. Obviously this influence will tend to alter national objectives accordingly. Further, most of these conflicts involve long term deployments with rapid and irregular changes to their tempo and intensity, the combination of which erodes the strategic level priorities. Awareness of these pitfalls at the strategic level of national security policy making cannot be substituted with any other knowledge element.

National interests, national policy and political objectives must always be completely aligned and work in harmony for a nation to be secure. Political objectives, from which military objectives automatically flow, must only be developed after a whole-of-government input has been carefully analysed. This will avoid the chances of greater influence by one or the other elements of national power in defining the political objectives that must, as far as possible, be a projection of the nation's long term strategic objectives. There is an inviolable relationship between national security and political objectives which demands that these objectives be viewed in the long-term to ensure that the elements of national power are attuned to achieving them.

Limiting the Military Influence

Since the military is fundamental to ensuring national security it is but natural that military thinking, especially at the strategic level, will be a critical factor in analysing challenges to security. This could at times lead to military strategic ideas having an inordinately high influence on the strategic analysis and the formulation of national policies on security. Only the right balance between military imperatives and the inputs from other elements of national power will assist in the development of a broad and enduring national policy. Accordingly, there are a number of military factors that could be limiting factors in this process, all of which must be avoided. Failure to do so would result in the formulation of a national policy that will at best be inadequate and most likely will not be enduring.

Ethno-centricity. First, military thinking tends to be coloured through the prism of ethno-centricity. This can narrow the vision of national security from the perspective of one dominant element of the demographic mix. This aspect is particularly important in the current environment wherein most nations would have some amount of ethnic diversity in the constitution of their population. National security is based on the support of the population in terms of national beliefs and values, which alter with the changes that take place in the ethnic make up of the nation. As compared to the rest of the nation, these changes manifest at a much slower pace in the military forces leading it to be far more homogeneous in its ethnicity. Thus, the military forces of a nation usually tend to lag behind the nation in accepting a broader strategic vision of security.

Current Conflict. Second, any military force involved in long-drawn low intensity conflicts will over a period of time succumb to operational pressures of the here-and-now, shortening the vision required to develop robust strategic appreciation of security. This is particularly evident in forces that are small in size and capability, where the stresses of long-term deployment and combat will be felt much earlier and more intensely. This is a serious hazard that could gradually debilitate the force. The decline in the force capability could be so slow that it may not even be possible to identify the actual point at which it became incompatible with the strategic requirements of national security. Military forces need to be able to consciously extrapolate the present with the perceived future to avoid this calamity. The primary focus at the very base level should be to align constantly with long term national security requirements and priorities.

Preferred Threat. Third, military forces have a marked tendency to prepare for the threat that it is best suited to overcome than for what would actually emanate in the near-term. This is the combination of a number of embedded issues, the main one being the military forces' proclivity to self-perpetuate their capabilities, and in extreme cases, their invincibility. The focus on an unlikely threat will in most cases skew not only military preparedness, but also the national perception of threats to its security. While these military appreciations will often be at the operational level they have the potential to influence the strategic level debate and decision-making, even if such debates are led by 'strategic thinkers'.

Inevitabilities. Military planning is inherently pragmatic in nature. Therefore, it deals in a number of 'inevitabilities', especially at the operational level. While this is a positive attribute in purely military terms, when translated to the strategic level of national security planning it introduces an element of rigidity into the process. Rigidity in the planning process at the highest levels will always be detrimental to developing a durable security policy. Further, in international relations there are no inevitabilities as such and flexibility is the rule. Therefore, national security planning should embrace the pragmatism of military planning while carefully keeping at bay the military tendency to factor in 'inevitabilities'.

Soothsaying. All democratic nations normally have few groups of 'experts' who are articulate and more importantly consider themselves influential in matters concerning national security. More often than not these groups are bodies of mainly senior and retired people from government service, including the military, that try to influence the national policies towards what they consider as appropriate for the nation. They tend to be strategic soothsayers, who continue to mouth platitudes that have limited contemporary meaning other than in a vague and overarching manner. However, these groups are capable of muddying the critical issues, thereby making it more difficult for the incumbent national leadership to contribute effectively to national security debates. While these forums can, and do, have their positive influences, their negative impact on the security planning process very often outweigh them. These groups have to be dealt with carefully and sensitively, and not be permitted to confuse issues of importance or lead processes tangentially astray.

The military force is an essential and critical element in ensuring the security of the nation. There are a great number of factors that ensure the efficient functioning of the military that would have a salutary effect on the performance of other elements of national power. However, the military can apply some limiting influence on overall national security, especially at the conceptual level, which must be ameliorated to ensure the veracity of the nation's security policies.

Impact of the Economy

The concept of national security is indelibly connected to the economy, commerce and trade of a nation. The economic standing and viability of a nation directly affects its self-defence capabilities and overall security. While commerce and trade have historically been a regional and in some cases even international phenomenon, they have been rapidly globalised in the past few decades. From a purely commercial point of view, this has improved the overall economy of the world and brought increased prosperity to a large number of nations.[16] This globalisation of economy is a double edged sword. While it improves the standards of living of a greater proportion of the world's population as compared to earlier times, down turns in the larger economies also tend to become global in nature. In turn, it affects the security of a larger number of nations than would have been the case if global economy had remained divided into smaller regional groupings.

Interconnection. The global economy is today densely interconnected. The national and regional boundaries that doubled as economic insulation, even two decades ago, have become fragile if they exist at all. Therefore, the troubles and tribulations that convulse one economy tend to rapidly spread to other economies in a cascading manner, with the impact reducing as the ripple moves outwards. Even though economies connected only peripherally to the one that is faltering would normally not be affected greatly, there is the likelihood of other issues coming to the fore and creating a domino effect. Further, smaller economies, without sufficient fall-back options will succumb faster than larger and more resilient ones.

Imbalance. Financial and economic crisis in a nation, whether the result of external influences or self-induced, will always lead to an imbalance between security needs and availability of resources. As the imbalance becomes more pronounced the nation is likely to enter a vicious downward spiral of deepening crisis leading to increased imbalance that in turn creates an even deeper crisis. The security situation will also inexorably follow this downward spiral. From a security perspective this situation will always create the necessary conditions that will lead to alterations in the geo-political landscape.

---

16 The greater spread of prosperity has, at times, also been accompanied by charges of exploitation against the more developed nations. However, that aspect is not germane to the argument being proffered here regarding national security and economy.

Conclusion

A strong and resilient economy is necessary for a nation to put in place long-term security measures. In turn, assured long-term security is of cardinal importance in building a strong economy. Revival of emerging and developing economies into stable and dynamic entities that have the ability to withstand global pressures is essential to ensuring peace and stability. Globally, a greater spread of such economic well-being promotes the development of a multi-polar world, which is more conducive to stability than a bi-polar or uni-polar international geo-political environment. This will have a direct influential role in shaping the emerging global politico-economic architecture.

Summing Up...

Although national security was ensured from the very beginning of the creation of separate 'states', like in the case of Greek city-states, it remained an academic concept for a long period. However, the concept of national security started to get defined only in the last century, mainly after the end of World War II. The contemporary understanding of national security is very broad and encompasses a large number of factors that individually and in combination contribute to the stability of the nation. Even so, military and economic security still has primacy of place when national security is being discussed.

The definitions have evolved over time, keeping up with the prevailing global and regional security environment. In the contemporary scenario, where threats and challenges emerge at short notice and could be of disparate nature, the definition of national security is normally kept as broad and vague as possible to ensure that it has the depth and breadth to encompass these issues. Essentially, national security is about delineating the elements that a nation wants to protect and creating the infrastructure to do so. This in turn is based on the urge to protect the values and wealth that a nation holds dear, tempered with the overall capacity of the elements of national power to enforce the will of the nation when necessary.

National security imperatives and the capabilities of the military forces of the nation are interlinked and always influence each other—the development of capabilities is proscribed by the notion of national security and the nation's appreciation and demand of the security forces to ensure it. As a corollary, the capabilities resident in the military forces will tailor the concept of national security within a nation. The military forces have the primary responsibility for ensuring the sanctity of the nation's territorial integrity. The broader concept of national security—based on national interests and challenges—will not become redundant, although it will evolve and alter with the changes in the security environment.

National security is directly influenced by the stability of the nation's domestic governance. Any divisiveness within the nation that creates more than a token amount of debate will impinge of the veracity of national security. In addition, a nation must have assured access to the resources necessary to ensure an acceptable standard of living for its people. When this factor is denied, internal stability is bound to get disturbed, leading to a weakened national security stance. Therefore, national security should be carefully built on long-term strategic goals, arrived at after carrying out robust and honest analysis of the nation's requirements. This analysis should be devoid of opportunistic forward-thinking for it to stand the test of time. Any other projection will endanger the security of the nation.

National security imperatives in turn produce political objectives to be achieved. Political objectives must be developed based on the concept of a whole-of-government approach, which means that every element of national power must be taken into account when the priorities and imperatives are laid down. Such an approach will ensure that one or the other element does not become unduly influential in the process. Particularly it is necessary to limit the influence of the military forces in defining the strategic objectives, while considering the economic realities of the nation. It is vitally important to balance the resource availability with security requirements.

The viability of a nation to remain an independent entity is dependent on its ability to ensure national security at the appropriate level through all means at its command. National security is a multi-faceted concept that needs the optimised application of multi-dimensional capabilities. This is the fundamental responsibility of the government, which needs to ensure the availability of the required resources to achieve this aim. Ensuring stand-alone capabilities to achieve adequate and assured national security may not be an option in today's global scenario. Therefore, there is a clear role for alliances, especially in the case of middle and small power nations. The political aspect of national security gets further emphasised in this scenario.

Chapter 3

SECURITY, POLICY AND STRATEGY

From time immemorial, national policy, security and strategy have been interlinked. Explained in a different way, they represent the ends, ways and means construct of national security that is perhaps more relevant in the contemporary environment than ever before. Today, the belligerence of a nation will not be easily tolerated by the international community, irrespective of the stature and power status of the nation concerned. Therefore, the need to align national policy, derived from political aims that focus the nation's security needs and abilities, with the grand strategy to ensure national security cannot be overemphasised.

National security is the basis to develop political objectives that in turn form the basis not only for national policy but also to lay down the desired end-state (ends) when a nation has to enter into conflict to resolve issues that might challenge its sovereignty. Strategy (ways) thereafter is formulated to employ the resources (means) that are available to achieve the desired end-state. The challenge here is to make sure that there is no mismatch in this process. There are two ways that mismatches can occur—one, when the resources required to implement a strategy are more than resources available and two, when a strategy developed within the available resources falls short of achieving the end-state. Any solution to either of these challenges will impinge on the political objectives. Therefore, it is clear that a nation must be realistic vis-à-vis the national resources when laying down political objectives. Historically it is seen that when the ends, ways and means are not aligned, there is always the risk of challenges to national security that cannot be comprehensively addressed in most cases.

There are ample historic precedents for the understanding and formulation of strategy at all levels—from grand strategy to operational strategy. There are also ancient texts like Sun-Tzu's *Art of War* and Kautilya's *Arthasastra* that provide in-depth analysis of the influences on strategy and the inputs necessary to develop 'good' strategy. Historical analysis affords a significant insight into creating a process that develops national strategies and therefore an understanding of actual historical events and study of ancient and other historical texts assume great importance in formulating policies and strategies.

Relevance of Historical Analysis – A Case Study

The Peloponnesian War in Today's Context

National security, policy and strategy have always been interlinked—this comes out clearly even in cursory historical analysis. However, a careful analytical study of war and strategy that distils the 'lessons of history' is essential to develop successful strategies to counter contemporary challenges. Further, when such analysis is undertaken by all elements of national power, the chances of success in formulating a viable grand strategy for the nation increases dramatically.

The account of the Peloponnesian War by the contemporary general Thucydides[1] is a classic to study from a point of view of understanding this connection and how strategy works, or does not work.[2] The book deals with a war fought between democratic Athens and autocratic Sparta from about 431 to 401 B.C. It covers both the tactical aspects of the battles that were fought while also deals with the strategic aspects of the war. It is one of the most erudite strategic analyses of a long drawn war and highlights the role that politics, policy, idealism, civil-military relationship, alliances and coalitions play in the conduct of a war designed to ensure national security.

---

1   For a detailed analysis of the Peloponnesian War and Thucydides' account of it, refer; Strassler Robert B., (ed), *The Landmark Thucydides: A Comprehensive Guide to the Peloponnesian War*, Free Press; Touchstone Edition, New York, September 1998.

2   This analysis of the Peloponnesian War benefitted a great deal from a draft paper written by Rear Admiral Sudarshan Shrikhande, AVSM, IN (Retd), who was kind enough to share it with the author in its hand-written stage of a first draft. Some of the ideas put forward in the Admiral's paper have been expanded, adapted and refined in the following paragraphs.

The war provides numerous lessons, from the strategic to tactical, a number of which are relevant in a contemporary setting. First is the ability of a nation to adapt its strategies to emerging situations, especially when it is at war. In the face of initial reversals in the battlefield, Sparta rapidly adapted and evolved a much more cohesive strategy that guided the rest of the war. Second, is the necessity to have a civil-military relationship that is based on mutual respect for each other's professional competence. Athens, a democracy which entered the conflict with a good civil-military relationship, evolved an increasingly irrational policy as the war progressed leading to its adopting illogical strategies and a breakdown of civil-military relationship that finally resulted in its defeat.

Third, is the management of alliance and coalition partners. Both Athens and Sparta had allies and coalition partners. However, Athens had an almost master-slave relationship with its allies, making the allies hate them and wish them ill. On the other hand, Sparta had much smoother relationships with its own allies, making them far more loyal. For example Sparta had a small naval force and was reliant on its allies for naval power, which was readily forthcoming. Effectively managing the coalitions and alliances and the ability to influence possible partner-nations to support one's own course of action have always been the greatest challenges of grand strategy.

Fourth, the Peloponnesian War clearly showed that war is about politics. Therefore, the apex political establishment must focus on instituting a process by which the objectives that will achieve the final end-state required can be identified. A purely short term focus on objectives followed by realignment of priorities on a continuous basis is a recipe for disaster and failure at the strategic level of national security. A well-developed process which is entrenched, but retains sufficient flexibility to adapt to unforeseen circumstances—something that can never be ruled out in conflict—is a fundamental requirement to achieve success.

Fifth, Thucydides clearly explains the perils of empire overstretch. Military success is a major contributing factor to a powerful nation extending itself beyond its reasonable capacity and slowly going into decline. This is a self-perpetuating cycle; great power in a nation manifests in a powerful military apparatus being built, possession of a powerful military force increases the proclivity of a nation to employ it to achieve national objectives, military successes tends to make the employment of military forces seem the optimum solution to national security challenges, this in turn leads to preponderant military influence in the development and implementation of grand strategy and lesser political inputs and control. Military victory by itself is only a part of the overall success in achieving national security. Grand strategy therefore, must be controlled at the political level.

Re-thinking Grand Strategy

History provides a number of well documented episodes of strategic success that can be clearly seen as not being influenced by earlier thinking on the same subject, in other parts of the world. For example, the conquests of the great Genghis Khan and his progeny are legendary. However, the question can be asked whether he and his large army consciously executed a well-conceived grand strategy or whether the entire success emanated as a coincidence of the coming together of a tactically superb force and a vague idea of conquest, manifest in the fighting spirit of a people. That very little was recorded at that time does not in any way diminish the enormity or significance of the Mongol conquests, and only reinforces the fact that there must have been a grand strategic vision at the apex body of leadership of the army that conquered the world.

An analysis of the evolution of grand strategy is a necessity to obtain an understanding of national security and its intertwined relationship with military forces. Studying history for its own sake is perhaps a pursuit that will bring no tangible result, but historical analysis aimed at finding answers to contemporary challenges is a cornerstone to developing strategic concepts. Such an analysis will delineate the pitfalls that are likely to be encountered in the formulation of strategy. In fact throughout history a thread of wrong decisions that were contrary to the interest of the nation, but which were all the same ardently pursued by the governments can be discerned.[3] The list of failures is matched equally by successes that can also be studied to envisage the requirements to formulate appropriate strategies. Grand

---

3 Tuchman, Barbara W., *The March of Folly: From Troy to Vietnam,* Ballantine Books, New York, 1984, p.4.

strategy can be made to work, provided its subsets—the strategies that govern the application of individual elements of national power—are in consonance with each other and when combined create a whole that is larger than the individual parts. This means that grand strategy must possess sufficient inherent flexibility to align the application of disparate power groups.

Grand strategy is the national strategy that encompasses the war policy of a nation and other strategies to ensure a stable and enduring peace. Whenever a nation goes to war it should be with the aim of achieving a better peace than what existed before the war. If this is not the case, in fighting the war the state will have squandered its national power to no avail.[4] Essentially, grand strategy fully aligned with the broad national policy, should guide all actions of the state, not merely its military forces. This is of particular significance in a contemporary discussion of strategy. Up to the mid-20th Century, grand strategy was equated with the highest level of military strategy mainly because national security was defined in terms of the sanctity of national borders, which was primarily the responsibility of the military forces. However, the currently accepted understanding of national security also includes a holistic vision of the protection of national interests which is not limited within geographic boundaries. Under these circumstances, all elements of national power will have to work in cohesion to ensure national security. If this conceptis to be incorporated,the understanding of grand strategy will have to be revised. Grand strategy therefore will have to encompass the guiding principles for the application of all elements of national power.

Resort to the application of force—to go to war—has historically been accepted as a last resort and limitations have been placed on its conduct most of the time. Further, the acceptance that war can be a debilitating experience even for the victorious side has made nations, other than the more intransient ones, ready to accept negotiated settlements to disputes.[5] Over the centuries of warfighting there has emerged a grudging acceptance of the limitations of war as an instrument of ensuring national security in the long term. However,

---

4   Liddell Hart, B. H., *Strategy*, Second Revised Edition, Meridian Printing, USA, 1991, p.353.

5   ibid, p. 356.

the two World Wars obscure the wisdom that was gained over centuries and stand as moot testimonials to human kind's unwillingness to learn from the bitter experiences of history.

A comprehensive and articulated grand strategy is critical to the security of the nation. While warfighting is a physical act, its planning, execution and the conduct of negotiations are all mental activities. Strategic security thinking should form one of the fundamental bases for the development of grand strategy. A well-formulated grand strategy will make it easier to gain the upper hand and thereby make the ensuing peace more lasting.

The Primacy of Policy

National security policies govern objectives (ends), allocate resources (means), and lay down permissible courses of action (ways) to achieve the desired end-state. It shapes the politico-military strategies. In democracies, national policy will determine three fundamental principles that establish the security status of a nation—civil-military relationship; interaction between domestic and foreign policies; and the status of military power within the elements of national power.[6]

These policies broadly reflect cultural and other contexts and are relatively stable. Policies are different to doctrine, strategies and also commitments. Collective policies can link nations that have same or similar security needs, but are not inclined to any formal commitments. On the other hand commitments make it obligatory for a nation to initiate actions if the context of the commitment is violated. Fundamental national interests normally remain the same and evolutionary changes, as and when they occur, will be nuanced and take place at infrequent intervals. In contrast, national policies that support the same interests can be altered fairly quickly if need be while remaining within the same cultural context. Thus, the relative stability of policies must be seen within the broader cultural context of the nation and its abiding interests.

History clearly demonstrates that culture has always been a fundamental influence in the formulation of national security policies. In fact, nation-states adopt and alter general as well as security policy

---

6   Collins, John M., *Military Strategy: Principles, Practices and Historical Perspectives*, p. 47.

guidelines based on changing cultural circumstances. This creates a predisposition to reject or accept particular policies. The acceptance or otherwise of politico-military policies will in turn affect the attitude of the nation towards military forces and the circumstances of their employment. In what is a complex relationship, the security policies will be influenced by the three fundamental principles that establish the security status of a nation.

Civil-Military Relationship. The policy that guides civil-military relationship is fundamental to national security. One of the rudimentary principles of democracy is that the military forces must function under civilian control. Insufficient political control of the military is fraught with the risk of the military pursuing its own objectives that may not be aligned with national interests. However, civilian control of the military must be carefully balanced to avoid excessive political interference and control that will always be detrimental to military effectiveness. This is a delicate balance to maintain but is critical to the well-being of the nation. Most democracies therefore adopt different levels of decentralised civilian control over the military forces within the constitution. This not only legalises the hierarchy of control but also permits flexibility in the amount of autonomy that can be delegated to the command structure of the military forces. At the same time, incompetently managed application of decentralised civilian control over the military forces can have a detrimental impact on the effectiveness of their employment in the pursuit of national security. This could have an overall detrimental effect on the nation and should be guarded against. The issue stems from the lack of understanding of military matters amongst the elected representatives and the broad spectrum of political agendas that they represent. When appropriately balanced the system works well.

Interaction of Foreign and Domestic Policies. All nations have competing foreign and domestic priorities. While foreign policies are intricately connected to national security issues, domestic concerns—primarily political in nature—are removed from the security equation to a certain extent and are only indirectly linked. In most nations heavy investment in foreign affairs cannot be sustained indefinitely without it having a negative impact on domestic issues and economy. This directly translates to the outlay on military forces also having to be balanced with domestic financial requirements. Excessive concentration of effort on domestic economy will also create an untenable external security situation. It is necessary to maintain a reasonable balance between the two and to manage the balance in a contextual manner. This can only be achieved by adhering to a balanced national security policy. Neither of the two, foreign or domestic policies, should be given higher priority on a continuous basis, to avoid distorting the national security imperatives; a dynamic balancing act is of the essence.

Status of Military Power within Elements of National Power. It is the foreign policy that articulates a nation's self-perceived role within the international comity of nations. However, military capabilities determine the limits of a nation's power projection capability and are primary contributors to the international status and influence of a nation and therefore shapes the reality of a nation's 'self-perceived' role. This connection forces an interaction of the conceptual and the physical that in turn determines the nation's ability to ensure its security and protect its sovereignty. In fact, military forces have been predominant in foreign relations since ancient times in the civilisations of Egypt and Assyria, the Persian and Roman and Mongol Empires and the European colonial powers of recent history.[7] In a contemporary analysis however, there can be distinguished a noticeable trend to equate the contribution of non-military elements of national power towards national security with that of the military forces. This stems from the international tendency to resort to military forces only as a last resort when diplomatic and economic negotiations have failed. There is currently an appreciable and understandable reluctance on the part of democratic nations to employ military forces in a lethal manner to resolve crisis because of the unacceptability of even the barest of collateral damage that could lead to an unwanted result with strategic implications. Military forces will have to be used within a clear political policy that lays down the desired end-state as well as the limits of the employment of force. To achieve victory—the ends, ways and means must always be in absolute alignment.

---

7   See, for example, Ernest R. & Dupey, Trevor N., *The Harper Encyclopedia of Military History: From 3,500 B.C to the Present*, Harper-Collins, New York, 1993; Hildinger, Erik, *Warriors of the Steppe: A Military History of Central Asia, 500 B.C to 1,700 A.D*, Sarpedon, New York, 1997; Farewell, Byron, *Queen Victoria's Little Wars*, Harper and Row, New York, 1972.

National security objectives, derived from stable policies, underpin the development of military objectives. These objectives must be clearly expressed and consistent with national security interests and the resources available to achieve the desired end-state. Further, the formulation of these objectives should take into account a number of influences like domestic political stability, economic status of the nation, cultural ethos and homogeneity of the population and moral and ethical beliefs. All elements of national power have their own dedicated role within the broader strategy that ensures national security, especially in the contemporary politico-economic scenario wherein military victories by themselves may not be able to achieve political objectives. Strategic objectives have therefore to be well defined to focus the aims of elements of national power in achieving the objectives—national and subsets in terms of military diplomacy, economy etc.

The table below provides a depiction of the elementary relationship and hierarchy of policy, security and strategy.

Hierarchy	Source/ Derived From (Ways)	Desired Achievement (Ends)	Means
Grand Strategy	National Policy	National Objectives	All Elements of National Power
National Security Strategy	National Security Imperatives	National Security Objectives	Designated Elements of National Power
National Military Strategy	National Security Doctrine and Military Doctrine, Concepts & Capabilities	National Military Objectives	Military Forces
Theatre Military Strategy	Military Doctrine, Concepts & Capabilities	Campaign Objectives	Designated Military Forces

Security and Foreign Policy

A nation's relationship with its neighbours and the broader international community has a direct influence on its grand strategy, which in turn influences the very same relationships. The foreign policy of a nation significantly influences grand strategy. The ancient text of Kautilya and the comparatively more modern book of Machiavelli are quite explicit in drawing the connection between the two.

Although written more than two thousand years ago, the *Arthsastra* by Kautilya also analyses the indelible connection between grand strategy, security and foreign policy and brings out few enduring truisms vis-à-vis the security of the nation. He brings out six guiding principles—as relevant today as they were in ancient India—for the formulation and application of foreign policy in support of the national security policy.[8] The six principles are:

- A king shall develop his state i.e. augment its resources and power in order to enable him to embark on a campaign of conquest;
- The enemy shall be eliminated;
- Those who help are friends;
- A prudent course shall always be adopted;
- Peace is to be preferred to war; and
- A king's behaviour, in victory and in defeat, must be just.

If the word 'king' is replaced with the term 'government', all the principles are seen to be relevant even today. Kautilya elaborated on the role of allies and even went to the extent of declaring that allies are 'a constituent element of a State.'[9] In this case, allies do not have to be formal treaty partners, but any nation of influence in the region. Foreign policy should be such that the nations that have influence should be persuaded to support one's cause or at worst to maintain a neutral stance.

---

8 Rangarajan, L. N., *Kautilya: The Arthashastra*, Penguin Books India, New Delhi, 1992, p. 546.

9 ibid, p. 547

The Theory of Strategy

In order to achieve politico-military objectives, nations develop strategies that are designed to employ available resources to achieve the desired political ends. No one strategy can be applied to all contexts and it is also highly unlikely that different strategies would equally and optimally overcome a particular challenge. Inherent in the development process of strategies is the need for them to incorporate a number of variations in order to ensure that the applied strategy retains a certain amount of flexibility at all times. Good strategies optimise the employment of available resources, within the stipulated timeframe to achieve national objectives.

Primarily the success of a strategy is dependent on an accurate appraisal, calculation and coordination of the application of the means to achieve the end state. There is a two-way relationship between the end and means. In a holistic manner, the ultimate end must be in proportion to the means, and the means used to achieve lower level ends that contribute to achieving the final objective must be appropriate and not excessive.[10] Here the fine balance between excessive and deficient must be carefully considered.

Strategy should also be cognisant of the human element in conflict, which can never be predicted with sufficient accuracy under any conditions. However, it must not attempt to overcome this unavoidable factor through flexibility by constantly changing or adapting laid down strategies, but should be oriented towards diminishing the influence of the human factor on the conduct of battle, campaign or war. This can be achieved, to an acceptable degree, by exploiting manoeuvre and surprise. Manoeuvre of forces is in the physical domain while surprise is in the cognitive domain. However, both apply equally from the tactical to the strategic level of conflict and from the planning stage to the final execution. Further, there is a discernible connection between the two, each feeding off the other.

The fundamental understanding of strategy must be that the pinnacle is to produce a decision in one's own favour, as far as possible without having to conduct serious military operations. This has two further distinctions—the strategy to succeed in conquest would have

---

10 Liddell Hart, B. H., pp. 322-323.

to be very different to the strategy that is needed to ensure the security of the nation from external aggression. The earlier concept of a 'decisive victory' in battle to enhance the chances of victory in the war is perhaps not valid anymore in the calculations of national security. Strategy has to take into account this altered concept.

This leads to strategy having to concentrate on creating the effects that will neutralise adversary's actions or dissuade a potential adversary from initiating actions that are inimical to one's own interests. Essentially, in the contemporary environment strategy must be formulated to focus on the cognitive domain and should have to resort to the physical domain—actual warfighting through military operations—only as a last resort.

Pitfalls in Strategy Development

There are three major factors that must be scrutinised in the development process of any strategy:

- **Awareness of History.** Strategy can be formulated without any analysis of historical precedents or awareness of its evolution. However, such an approach is more likely to produce a less than optimum strategy than the ones developed after careful study of the mistakes that have been made in the past. Strategy development must always be informed by at least a working knowledge of previous strategies that worked or did not work and the reasons why a particular strategy failed.

- **Transparency.** National security strategy must be formulated with transparency that demonstrates its alignment with the declared definition of national interests. This will also ensure a higher level of accountability and involve all the elements of national power rather than being confined to few organs of the government. This is perhaps much more easily achieved in democracies than in autocratic or dictatorial governments.

- **Mistakes at the Highest Levels.** All governments, especially democracies, are prone to making mistakes at the strategic decision-making levels. The propensity changes contextually and some mistakes can be of monumental proportions. A majority of these mistakes might become apparent only in hindsight, although some of them could have been recognised at the time that the government was deciding on the course of action. It is vital to ensure that careful and, perhaps more importantly, honest appraisal of the ends, ways and means has been carried out before embarking on the formulation of strategy.

There are other factors that could derail the process of strategy formulation at all levels. For example, the lack of a collegiate approach will normally constrain the grand strategy that is developed from being overarching and effective. No one individual is capable of creating an impeccable strategy, but a team—with sufficient knowledge and functioning in a transparent manner—is more likely to succeed. This in turn is only likely in a democracy where more people and more institutions have the opportunity to exercise freedom of thought and expression.

Democracies, while having to deal with the challenges of governmental interference as well as the possibility of mistakes in decision-making, are more likely to produce better strategies. They also have better corrective mechanisms that allow errors in the development process to be corrected even mid-way, thereby making the final strategy robust.

Summing Up...

Throughout history, national security, policy and strategy have been indelibly linked. Historically, military conquests of significance—like the Mongol conquests of medieval times, mainly associated with Genghis Khan—have emanated from a Grand Strategy and clear guidance from an apex body, even if the conquering march looks to have been carried out without proper alignment with a national policy or security imperatives. In the contemporary security environment, national security has assumed a broadened remit, the concept itself evolving with the changes taking place in the global politico-economic and social conditions. It has therefore become important to ensure that the Grand Strategy of a nation encompasses all elements of national power, not the military forces alone.

In democracies, national security is based on the primacy of the Policy that governs the essential ends-ways-means calculus. This Policy is directly influenced by the culture of the nation and a number of other intangible factors that are unique to the nation. In a majority of cases the Policy guidance pertain directly to the military forces that retain the vanguard position in ensuring the safety and security of the nation. The military forces are controlled and guided by the civilian leadership at the Grand Strategic level. Therefore, civil-military relationship assumes great importance in ensuring that the strategy being adopted in any particular instance of conflict, and in general during times of relative peace, is appropriate to achieve national objectives. It is the responsibility of both the civilian and military leaderships to ensure that the relationship is maintained on an even keel.

National security and Policy are also products of foreign policy imperatives that are conditioned with essential domestic political compulsions. As a corollary, the development of foreign policy is normally done through the prism of Grand Strategy. In order to ensure the veracity of this complex relationship, military forces have to constantly fine tune its role vis-à-vis other elements of national power. In effect, the role of the military force in the multifaceted arena of national security is dependent on the status that it is given within the combined body of national power elements and within the broader national perspective. Only when this interaction is stable can it be ensured that military objectives are derived from national security objectives with tangible and direct alignment with the security policy, while being in consonance with the other elements of national power.

In a large number of cases, national policy and Grand Strategy influence each other in a mutual fashion. This influence is not so much in a cyclical manner, but in a linear process of give and take. Strategies are the vehicles that convert resources to achieve the desired end-state. This is so in all aspects of ensuring national security and need not have an element of warfighting in it. Good strategies optimise the use of resources and always achieve the imperatives of national security.

The development of military strategy, directly aligned with higher level guidance based on Policy takes cognisance not only of security objectives, but also of the human element in conflict. Since the strategy must take into account the fog and friction that accompany the application of force, it also needs to retain sufficient flexibility to permit adaptation in evolving situations. The aim of the strategy should be to create the necessary effects that target the cognitive domain. Military forces dominate the physical domain and are only partially influential in the cognitive domain. It does influence the behaviour patter, which is only one part of the cognitive domain, the other being the belief system. Change the belief system will bring the required level of stability and lasting peace, which cannot be achieved by the application of military forces. It requires a concerted whole-of-government approach.

National Security, Policy and Strategy are interconnected and work in tandem, influencing each other in a continual manner. Any dissonance in this combination will not be conducive to the well-being of the nation.

CONCLUSION

Three major events took place in 1989, which clearly demonstrated the connection between grand strategy, military means and the underpinning political purpose: the collapse of the east European Communist regimes as the massive Soviet military forces became incapable of supporting them; the Chinese military actions that crushed the fledgling democracy movement in Tiananmen Square; and the US overthrow of Panama's dictator Manuel Noriega. These were events that had global political significance and could be said to have influenced the development of the international security environment for the next two decades and more. In fact, some of the repercussions are still being felt across the world.

National strategy must always be aligned with political objectives, irrespective of the type of government that is in power. Further, strategy should not only be for the here and now, but should take into account the possible future trends in security and the needs that could arise. It must also be cognisant of the means that are necessary to effectively implement a strategy, for the duration desired. A majority of instances would be open-ended, without a definitive timeframe for completion, which would make resource requirement predictions a challenge.

Grand strategy, since it is derived from national policies cannot be reactive. It must be the clear base from which the nation should be able to not only mitigate threats but also find the flexibility to exploit the emerging threat to its own advantage. At the next level, military forces functioning within the ambit of grand strategy should be able to adapt at a sufficiently rapid pace to confront the unexpected. At this level, slow adaptation may not be sufficient to neutralise threats. The demarcation between the grand strategic level and the military strategic level cannot always be clearly designated. Therefore, in this slightly grey area, there is always the danger of operational ideas and concepts being directly linked to political objectives thereby becoming grand strategy. Awareness that such a situation can develop and watchfulness to avert such progression amongst the higher planning staff is the only remedy.

There is another facet of grand strategy that needs a mention. Every nation does needs a grand strategy and, as a corollary, not all nations are capable of formulating one. This means that some nations that have strong and legal alliances with more powerful nations may be able to adopt the grand strategy of the ally and formulate their national policies accordingly. On the other hand, formulating and implementing grand strategy requires a certain amount of strategic preparation as well as access to a minimum critical amount of resources. This may not always be the case with all nations, leaving some in the unenviable situation of not having a grand strategy. This situation could make the nation unable to respond to threats and begin a slow decline into a fragile state. Once again the solution is perhaps to seek an alliance with a more powerful nation with shared values and interests to stem the decline in strategic security ability.

While there is an indelible connection between security policies and strategic concepts, they are totally independent of each other. Security policies are guidelines that regulate the application of national power to achieve national objectives and are directive in nature. Strategic concepts are options that can be employed to neutralise threats through the proportionate synthesis of elements of national power and are applicative in nature. However, they cannot be evaluated in isolation as one feeds off the other and their combined output secures the nation.

Similarly, a nation-state, national security, policy and strategy are all beads in the same necklace; they are interconnected and propagate a total value far in excess of the sum of the individual beads. A nation-state needs to meet a bare minimum number of conditions to be considered a sovereign entity; national security is becoming far more broadly defined than ever before with even the protection of values being considered national security; from this belief of what is national interest, the national policy and strategy are developed; and the elements of national power are optimally employed to achieve the end-state dictated by political aims. On the face of it, the above progression would seem fairly simple and uncomplicated. However, to draw a thread through the four critical areas and keep them in alignment at all times, while also ensuring the availability of adequate resources is a Herculean task—something that a number of nations may find very challenging.

SECTION - II

THE EVOLVING GEO-POLITICAL ENVIRONMENT

INTERNATIONAL STRATEGIC TRENDS

THESIS: New challenges to global geo-strategic stability are altering the traditional international power balance and creating space for the emergence of a new multi-polar world.

The contemporary concept of national security brings about a dilution of state sovereignty as well as an increase in the proclivity to use force on the part of the more developed or industrialised world. However, the global strategic environment is noticeably moving towards greater instability brought about by enhanced international connectivity and the increased diffusion of power to smaller states. Issues of democracy and governance are emerging as critical issues in the developing world where the aspirations of the people are not fully understood by the local regime or internationally and therefore are unlikely to be met. On the other hand, the power gap between the current global powers—predominated by the United States and its Western allies—and the rising powers of Asia, Africa and South America, represented by the BRICS alliance, is rapidly reducing. The outcome will be the creation of a new multi-polar world where middle powers will be able to switch allegiances from one great power to another at their convenience, creating a global order that is in constant flux.

INTRODUCTION

The collapse of the Soviet Union in the mid-1990s was considered to be the harbinger of a peaceful and coexisting world order, since the primary issue—that of antagonistic ideology—that divided the world into two groups had been removed. However, with the abrupt removal of the discipline that had held the world firmly in two parts the long suppressed ethnic, religious and nationalistic tendencies of nations and individual groups re-emerged. Disputes over the possession of natural resources and the earth's riches have been historically the reason for conflict and wars. For the nearly 50 years of the Cold War the two super powers held the economic conflicts in check by creating an artificial division of the world's resources between the two groups. The end of the Cold War brought to an end the validity of this expedient, throwing open the door for smaller nations to exercise their own power in pursuing national objectives.

The current geo-political environment is firmly multi-centric and also in a state of constant flux. The manipulation of the environment by individual nation states for their own benefit and manoeuvrings within the politico-economic and strategic-security surroundings increases the sense of uncertainty regarding international stability. The result has been the evolution of an asymmetric environment that is being superimposed on an evolving state-centric world order. Further, when combined with the absence of a collective alignment in terms of national and regional objectives, this state-centric order tends to be a strong divisive force that works against long-term geo-political stability. The superimposition of a discernible asymmetry creates an environment that is conducive for the growth of non-state entities pursuing disparate agendas that often manifest in violent action. The current strategic environment is extremely fragile.

There is evidence of the increasing importance being placed on the growth of individual nations. At the same time there seems to be less than clear understanding of the need for nation and state building, especially in newly independent and emerging democracies. Nation building should be aimed at developing national cohesion and pride through economic development, improving the functioning of the civil society and emphasising the primary role of education. State building on the other hand should be concentrated on establishing institutions of government that increase stability through improving basic governance and the provision of law and order. In combination this process will empower the people of the nation and create a stable and growth-oriented state. Unfortunately there are large parts of the world which remain outside this ambit, the nations within which form an 'ungoverned' and grey area of lawlessness and instability. These nations are disruptive, unbalancing and fragmenting the geo-political and security environments of the region. The stable nations of the region, and even globally, understand that if allowed to percolate without interference, the instability can gradually encroach on their shores and envelope them. In these circumstances the only available option is direct intervention—however unpalatable it may seem.

The geo-political environment—regional as well as global—has to be viewed and analysed through a prism that provides commonality of criteria being examined to ensure that a baseline is established to compare and understand evolving changes. This is important because of two fundamental reasons. First, it is difficult to distinguish the different relationships between nations as well as the interactions between individual nations and the international political and economic systems. Second, national interest is constituted by three primary elements; economy, security and politics. However, when viewed at the highest strategic level the economic policies, security objectives and political imperatives of a nation overlap each other to an extent where their individual impact on national interests is difficult to fathom. However, the national interests of every nation and how they are pursued has direct implications for regional stability and the development of the geo-strategic environment. It is, therefore, important to set common criteria for such an analysis in order to measure the significance of events that influence the geo-political environment. For an event—economic, political, military or diplomatic—to be considered significant, it must result in a noticeable, if not decisive, change to the international system or must fundamentally change the behaviour pattern of a nation. The measure of significance would be the amount of change the event makes to the regional or global balance of power or the quantum of impact it would have on the external and domestic interaction of a major power.

The stability of the global strategic environment is being challenged by a large number of disparate issues, some of which emanate from domestic issues within nations that they are unable to contain and some that are regional or even global in their origin or rapid spread.[1] Some of the major domestic issues are the inability of the government to respond adequately natural disasters; easy access to rapidly flowing information in a global context that could strain governmental control; the diminishing support in democracies for established political parties and the slow move towards alternate people's groupings and environmental or ethical themes; the unimpeded rise of nationalism in some nations; and the depletion of natural resources, necessitating the reorganisation of national finances and possible economic downturn. Generic threats to stability could stem from uncontrolled environmental changes that could impact a number of areas; competition for limited regional resources; the extended reach of terrorism facilitated by technology; the on-going, albeit gradual, global financial redistribution that could lead to an unsustainable imbalance; non-availability of adequate conflict resolution mechanisms short of war; and the proclivity of the more stable nations to intervene in the affairs of less stable nations.

There are four major areas that must be analysed to understand the reasons for the current complexity and volatility of the geo-political environment. They are:

- the fundamental reasons for the continually on-going change in the world that leads to constant and certain instability;

---

1   Development, Doctrine and Concept Centre, Ministry of Defence, UK, Strategic Trends Program, *Global Strategic Trends – Out to 2045*, Fifth Edition, London, 2014. https://assets.publishing.service.gov.uk/government/uploads/system/uploads/attachment_data/file/348164/20140821_DCDC_GST_5_Web_Secured.pdf accessed between March and June 2015.

- the impact of the increasing interdependence of nations on the global strategic environment;

- the challenges, present and emerging, to regional and global geo-political stability; and

- the changing international power equation with the emergence of new regional powers with a penchant to influence global events.

Chapter 4

THE EVER CHANGING WORLD

On hindsight it seems that until the collapse of the Soviet Union that brought about the end of the Cold War there was a sense of stability within the world order, even though the spectre of a nuclear war was always tangible in the background. The end of the Cold War in the early 1990s coincided with the explosion of information technology that brought about a number of rapid changes to the global geo-political and security environment. One of the major changes that by itself has cascading effects is the diminishing importance of geography, brought about by the speedy dissemination of information. In one sense this contraction of geography was achieved almost casually and not through any concerted effort. Today events taking place in any part of the globe are visible simultaneously in real-time to the entire world. When these events are of strategic nature—like the fall of a government, or the invasion of a state—their repercussions in other nations are almost instantaneous. Geography—predominantly physical distance and differences in climate and culture—is less of an inhibiting factor in the spread of strategic changes than ever before.

An analysis of the global geo-political environment is never an exercise that brings out clearly defined strategic trends. Even the visible trends will tend to be vague and broad, creating a sense of the unknown. However, a number of major strategic changes taking place internationally can be recognised. However, the fact that these changes are taking place at different paces and have independent trajectories as well as global implications, make it extremely difficult to discern, let alone understand the emerging international strategic trends. As these changes tend to percolate from the national or grand strategic, down into the operational and tactical level of diplomacy, economy and the military, the process of mapping and analysing the effects they create become lengthy and arduous. Even so, they can be discussed under a few broad elemental themes that bring together similar trends that, although widespread, are in alignment. The themes are the decline of state sovereignty, the rise of ethnicity and nationalism, the deteriorating security scenario, the Middle East imbroglio, the proclivity to use force and the strategic role of the United States (US) especially in the Asia-Pacific region.

Decline of State Sovereignty

Over the past few decades three trends that are not always in alignment have become discernible within nation-states. The first is the spread of national interests beyond the borders of the nation and the dichotomy of national prosperity being a direct sub-set of these broad national interests. Second, is the decline in state sovereignty, in an absolute sense, with most democratic nations tending to disperse power to inter-state networks that are more flexible and adaptable than centrally controlled systems of state power. Third, there is a visible trend that points towards the rise of mega cities that control the trade, finance and economy of a nation from a few hubs. These hubs at times function as independent entities with a narrow focus outside the orbit of national interests.

The formation of the European Union was meant to be an innovative and path-breaking development in consolidating the sovereignty of the state. This initiative by the more developed nations of the world, if it functioned efficiently, would have created a template for other groups to follow for global and regional governance.[1] However, this enactment of a unified trading bloc by the stable democracies of the world is almost rife with vulnerabilities. In fact, the very question of national sovereignty, which the Union was supposed

---

1 For a detailed analysis of the formation, functioning and challenges of the European Union read, Calleo, David P., *Rethinking Europe's Future*, A Century Foundation Book, Princeton University Press, Princeton, March 2003; and Drozdiak, William, *Fractured Continent: Europe's Crises and the Fate of the West*, W. H. Norton and Company, New York, September 2017.

to uphold, has become a stumbling block to its cohesiveness. Europe has been the crucible for the development of modern day democracies and therefore, its decline in terms of real and virtual power as compared to what used to be termed the developing world is all the more important to appreciate. The reasons for the decline are many, the main ones are—a shrinking workforce and an increasingly aged population, the failure of attempts to reverse the demographic trend through immigration, and the inability of the governing bodies to carry through social reforms necessary to ensure the stability needed to retain at least the barest minimum growth rate. In essence, issues that originate as societal concerns very rapidly manifest as national economic challenges. Here both the state and society have come under threat simultaneously with a number of nations not having the wherewithal to counter threat to either.

The past two decades have seen an increase in the political turmoil in different parts of the world with a steadily increasing number of states moving closer to becoming failing states. The decline from a fragile state to failing and then failed state can be very rapid and almost impossible to stop once the fall has started. This situation will lead to forced migrations and in extremis to demographic invasions of neighbouring states that may themselves be fragile or close to failure, thereby initiating a domino effect. This situation automatically threatens the sovereignty of all nations within the region through the risk of unwanted interference that could even lead to armed conflict.

Instability in a region—that leads to the declining veracity of national sovereignty—can also be brought about by proliferation of technology. It is becoming relatively simple for nations, even ones who do not have a proven track record of responsible international behaviour, to acquire sophisticated weapons. Indiscriminate weapon acquisition by one nation will almost always lead to a regional arms race that may not be economically sustainable for some nations. While the repercussions may not be immediately apparent, this situation has the potential to spiral out of control and create fragile states that would otherwise have continued in a more or less stable state. Further, some less stable nations have been able to acquire nuclear capabilities through dubious means. While the means of becoming a nuclear state is not in debate in this discussion, the overall instability of such nuclear states is a concern. They not only threaten the stability of the region, but bring about ambiguity regarding their own as well as the neighbouring nations' sovereignty through expansionist designs and open belligerence.

RISE OF ETHNICITY AND NATIONALISM

The post-colonial world has seen an explosion of ethnic strife, brought about mainly as a spontaneous rebellion against so far suppressed ethnic aspirations. There are two independent, yet interconnected elements to the question of ethnic identity. First, the colonial powers imposed arbitrary geographic borders that fractured common ethnicities, forcing the separated parts to reside in different states. Second, the creation of nations that contained different ethnicities, either fully or in part led to some nations having ethnic minorities. Into this difficult situation was superimposed loyalty towards religion and the increasing nationalistic spirit of newly independent nations. In these circumstances internal conflict in a nation-state is bound to occur, with the strong possibility of intervention from immediate neighbours who share an ethnicity with some people in the affected nation. Conflict between two ethnicities has the potential to escalate into medium level conflicts between nations if one of the parties straddles international borders.

Nationalism is a more intricate trend to track and comprehend[2]. There are differing explanations of nationalism. George Orwell, in his classic essay *Notes on Nationalism* defined it as, 'the habit of identifying oneself with a single nation or other unit, placing it beyond good and evil and recognising no other duty than that of advancing its interests.'[3] He also clearly distinguished between nationalism and patriotism. Patriotism is explained as devotion to a particular place and/or a particular way of life, which one believes to be the best in the world but has no wish to force on other people. In other words, patriotism is inherently defensive, both militarily and culturally. Nationalism on the

---

2 Encyclopaedia Britanica, Hans Kohn, Nationalism, https://www.britannica.com/topic/nationalism accessed on 10 March 2015.

3 Orwell, George, *Notes on Nationalism*, First Published by Polemic, London, Great Britain, May 1945, accessed on line at 'http://orwell.ru/library/essays/nationalism/english/e_nat' on 23 August 2011.

other hand is inseparable from the desire and pursuit of power. The sole purpose of all nationalists is to secure and increase the power and prestige of the nation or unit that subsumes their individual identity. Therefore, it is inherently an offensive stance.[4]

It was only during the 18th and 19th Centuries that nationalism became recognised as a distinctive force. In the contemporary environment, the inherent devotion, pride and loyalty towards one's own nation has become an effective and pervasive force in politics and governance. While the Orwellian definition is still applicable, it can now be further refined to state that it is the sentiment of a group of people united by powerful bonds of religion, ethnicity, language, a common way of life and shared history. It is immediately apparent that such nationalism can, and often does, flow across the geographic borders that territorially define nation-states. The essence of nationalism is its unifying and integrating quality—bringing together the people or peoples of a particular area with allegiance to a single nation. Historically it can be seen that the empires that comprised a number of nations ultimately disintegrated because of the lack of a common nationalism. The decline and break-up of the Roman and Moghul Empires are unambiguous examples.

In the post-colonial and Cold War era, the manifestation of nationalism is patently obvious. In fact nationalism has been a major contributor to the unification and elevation of independence struggles across much of the developing world leading to liberation and the formation of a large number of 'nationalistic' nation-states. Herein lie the seeds of conflict. While nationalism inspires self-confidence in a newly independent nation, when it is carried to extremes, the potential for abrasive nationalistic behaviour that could lead to conflict is very high. Even within a nation, nationalism can become a divisive factor that accentuates the differences between intra-national groups who have differing and divergent opinions about the future shape of the nation. The effect of this could be the increased manifestation of separatist tendencies leading to the fragmentation of an already fragile state or the manifestation of a civil war.

---

4   ibid.

Modern capitalism has given a fundamental twist to the concept of nationalism by superimposing economic realities on it. Complete economic self-sufficiency is not a possibility in the contemporary inter-connected world, which automatically leads to nationalism being underpinned and reinforced by the desire to exploit less developed and vulnerable nations for economic self-fulfilment. The rapid growth of multi-national concerns in developing countries—which is gradually being seen in those countries as economic colonialism for exploitation—is an expression of aggressive economic nationalism. This is the new reality. The fallout from this form of nationalism is that it creates hostilities between groups within the same nation, promotes militarism and is detrimental to progress and stability. By extrapolating rampant economic nationalism to the next level it can be seen that it leads to the imposition of alien civilisations and laws on politically and economically weak nations—a different form of imperialism that always brings with it the seeds of conflict and strife.

DETERIORATING SECURITY SCENARIO

Traditionally the world was divided into the more developed and developing nations, based on economic growth, robustness of governance, rule of law and other factors such as human rights issues and political stability. In a different manner, the international standing of a nation was also looked at in terms of political, military and economic alignment to separate and distinguish different levels of development. However, since the end of the Cold War such divisions have become less relevant, with the inter-connected global politico-economic environment creating groupings that are temporary. Such arrangements do not contribute to long-term stability and create an environment that is inherently unstable and more conducive to the development of crises that may erupt suddenly without notice. History demonstrates that this could happen even after long periods of peace and stability. Even with a range of prediction tools and methods, such as Bayes's theorem[5] and structured thinking, available to predict

---

5   Bayes's theorem, devised by Reverend Thomas Bayes and published in 1763 two years after his death, can be used to work out complex problems involving probability distributions. It is a way of arriving at statistically reliable probabilities based on partial information. The theorem is considered a milestone in modern mathematics. Bryson, Bill, *At Home: A Short History of Private Life*, Transworld Publishers, London, 2010, pp. 19-20.

occurrences with minimal data availability there is not sufficient guarantee of correctly predicting on-coming security challenges.

Economic changes that disenfranchise fragile nations, cultural incompatibility within a nation-state and in an inter-connected region and political instability that can rapidly spread across the borders into neighbouring states can create an uncontrollable deterioration of the overall security environment. Such convulsions are difficult for any one nation to contain and require concerted effort by the more stable nation-states of a region to alleviate. Acceptance of pre-emptive intervention to stabilise failing states is the result of a tacit acknowledgement within the international community that such actions are necessary to prevent regional instability. However, the absence of effective conflict resolution mechanisms in some of the global hot spots increases the potential for conflicts while simultaneously reducing the chances of stopping them, thereby permitting them to escalate of their own accord. The international community's inability to intervene in certain situations contributes to a challenging and volatile security scenario.

The world is also going through a period when there are open and very clearly visible divisions over a number of issues between Western and non-Western nations. Most of these are ethical or economic issues that have direct influence on the security of independent nations and indirectly on regional stability. The economic turmoil that is currently engulfing the European Union and the United States has turned the focus to Asian nations, comparatively untouched by financial troubles, to take up the mantle of leadership in a number of traditional issues. This situation is further exacerbated by the United States being preoccupied with two simultaneous wars and its reduced capacity for international leadership. When the two situations are combined it is likely to bring about changes to the accepted international norms and values—away from the western world, towards the Asian continent. Even the slightest shift in the existing international balance will create a ripple effect on all aspects of bilateral and multi-lateral relationships between nations.

Equally important as the shift in economic focus are the differences in the basic thinking, understanding and acceptance between the East and the West regarding ethical issues. These issues range from the acceptance or otherwise of climate change and the ability and/or willingness to reduce the impact; the enforcement of international human rights norms; the medical challenges of cloning and allied research; the understanding of the concept of individual citizens privacy; adherence to the laws of armed conflict; dealing with multi-national companies; participation and leadership in world bodies that have international ramifications; and the acceptability of nuclear power; to the perceived role of the United Nations in an ever changing world. Any of these issues, and many other minor ones, could become a point of contention because of a cultural divide and other nationalistic tendencies that cannot be fully bridged at any given time. Under these circumstances the international community will have only limited capability to reconcile differences, even between small nations. Precarious volatility and a pervasive sense of insecurity are likely to prevail for the foreseeable future.

Middle East Imbroglio

The Middle East has been an area of conflicting interests and of deep concern for the international community since the end of World War II. From the late 1950s, when the region settled into a state of uneasy co-existence after the initial hiatus regarding the formation of Israel and the confrontation over the Suez Canal, the nations of the region have largely been governed by autocratic rulers—either hereditary kings and princes or military strong men. Whether or not such governance was benign and beneficial to the state or otherwise is a moot point in this discussion. The fact is that these rulers did bring about some amount of stability to the region during the later part of the 20th Century. The strategic significance of the region, emphasised by its energy resources and lately the rise of Islamic fundamentalism, made the international community turn a blind eye to the excesses and human rights abuses that were committed within the nations.

The Arab nations of the region have been united in their overwhelming antagonism towards Israel. While this has led to a number of conventional wars, there is also tacit agreement within the ranks of the more stable nations that a long-term solution to the on-going insurgencies against Israel has to be found. In addition to the long-standing Palestine issue, most of the nations of the Middle East suffer from a demographic conundrum. The increased prosperity of the state—brought about through the export of oil and associated energy resources—has led to a disproportionate increase in the number of educated youth. There is now a large proportion of the population who are below the age of 30, are educated but do not have the opportunities to be gainfully employed.[6] In the 1990s governments were able to contain the frustration of the population through welfare programs that provided a fairly high standard of living to even the unemployed and unemployable groups. The rapid increase in population and the gradual radicalisation of the Islamic religion made this a difficult balance to maintain. A stage was reached when only the oil-producing nations were able to 'buy off' the population to ensure comparative stability. At the same time, the non-oil-producing nations faced uncertainty regarding their future and started a slow descent into social disorder. The so-called 'Arab Spring', which erupted in 2011, is the tangible result of this trend.[7]

The world is critically dependent on the Middle East's reserves of oil to meet its energy needs, although steps are being initiated to find an alternative source of energy. Therefore, the stability of the region takes on added importance in the global context. The trend in some of the less prosperous Middle Eastern states towards becoming fragile was noticeable as early as two or three decades ago. Similarly, a simultaneous and gradual shift in these same nations towards religious fundamentalism was also clearly discernible. For a number of reasons, some of them extraneous to these events and some brought about through the preoccupation of the Western nations with their own prosperity, these warning signs were either not analysed or ignored. There have been two outcomes. First, a number of fragile states went on to oust the autocratic governments and their rulers through popular revolts and second, fundamentalist religious groups, so far banned or kept under check, emerged into the mainstream political activity. The entry of religious fundamentalism into the governance equation could

---

6   Gelvin, James L., *The Arab Uprisings: What Everyone Needs to Know*, Oxford University Press, New York, 2012, pp. 19-21.
    For a comprehensive and journalistic analysis of the Arab Spring, read Worth, Robert F., *A Rage for Order: The Middle-East in Turmoil, from Tahir Square to ISIS*, Farrar, Straus and Giroux, New York, 2016.

7   Kalha, R.S., 'Is the Arab spring over?', IDSA Comment, *Institute for Defence Studies and Analyses*, New Delhi, 26 June 2012.

have grave consequences for the broader stability of the region, which in turn will echo in the international environment. So far Western policy has been the fundamental deciding factor in the Middle East and within a status quo it is likely to continue for at least the mid-term future. However, if religious fundamentalist governments come to power, this could change rapidly, a situation that may not be acceptable to Western nations. Under these circumstances the possibility of conflict erupting without much warning is very high. There are strong possibilities that the Middle East region itself could become broken, rather than a few states being fragile, with disastrous consequences for global stability.

A large number of fundamentalist groups have emerged, some merging with each other to create larger bodies, some being defeated and then morphing into some other form but continuing a similar pattern of violent terrorist activities. In the past decade the latest iteration, the Islamic State (IS), has made great inroads into Syria and Iraq. Its success was such that it was able to declare the formation of a Caliphate headquartered in Raqqa in Syria. The foreign intervention aimed at 'defeating' the IS has been haphazard and without a resilient and focused strategy. The fight against the IS is not the only challenge that the Middle-East is facing. The Kurdish demand for autonomy and even a separate nation for themselves is bound to continue with now solution in sight. In the Syrian Civil War, now in its sixth year, the direct intervention of Iran has facilitated its rise as a counter-balance to Saudi Arabia's ambition to be the regional hegemon. This change in the balance of power led to a tense stand-off.

The infighting between the various factions and countries involved in the conflict, primarily against the IS, has reached a stage wherein it is difficult to delineate who is supporting whom and who is fighting whom. The current state of the Middle-East is by far the most complex geo-political situation that the world has witnessed in history. The complexity is further increased by the religious sectarianism that is endemic to the region.

Proclivity to Use Force

During the Cold War the smaller nations of the world were more restrained in their dealings with neighbours and more often than not, even border disputes were amicably settled. This may have been because of the bipolar character of the world and the control imposed on the actions of smaller powers by both the super powers. In the past two decades there has been a visible shift in the behaviour of nation states when dealing with challenges, both externally and in quelling dissent internally. There is an increased proclivity, even in democratic nations, to use force in support of national interests.

There are three major reasons for this. First, the easy availability of fairly sophisticated weapon systems without any attached political caveats. Unlike in the Cold War era, military-industrial complexes of developed nations now sell weapon systems of almost all denominations to anyone who can afford them. This has created a situation wherein immature nations stockpile weapons and use them at the slightest provocation. Second, the Western nations are going through a phase of self-examination and emphasise the need for restraint in the application of force—in effect, they do not dominate the application of force as before. This creates a feeling within the newly independent and developing nations that the possibility of international intervention is low. The implicit belief is that the international community will be unwilling and may not have the capacity to protect the interests of the smaller nations. This is a far cry from the time when the onus of responsibility for maintaining 'world order' was considered to rest fully with the Western nations. There is a tangible diminishing of the Western dominance in the application of force and ability to intervene to enforce peace. There is a sense of being left to themselves that brings about an attendant feeling of insecurity, increasing the paranoia of threats to national interests.

Third, in the post-colonial developing world there are still unresolved issues of borders, sharing of natural resources and above all else, a confused sense of patriotism and nationalism. In combination with a heightened sense of insecurity these issues can rapidly degenerate into disputes and conflicts. The inclination to use force is also increased by the improved weapon effectiveness in terms of precision and range. Their use in the pre-emption mode also becomes a viable option under these circumstances. All these factors increase the probability of a conflict breaking out without much notice and escalating at a very fast pace. A corollary is that with the removal of economic checks and balances that come with independence, poor nations also have the ability to purchase effective weapon systems, even if they are few in numbers. When such a nation has a particularly aggressive culture and feels that it has 'nothing to lose', the modern weapon systems can be exploited to become extremely influential in diplomatic negotiations even with stronger and wealthier nations. This is particularly so if the wealthier nation has a low threshold of pain tolerance.

While not directly in the realm of application of force, the issue of weapons of mass destruction (WMD) is a spin-off from it. In the past few decades there has been a proliferation of WMD. The trend has been for smaller states that feel marginalised by trade, ideology, religion and even through rogue governance to strive to obtain WMD in their attempt to become more relevant in the international order. Such actions by themselves are fairly harmless, but the fact that most of these nations, and their rulers, suffer from a sense of delusion and self-importance makes their acquisition of WMD a dangerous development that threatens the stability of the region and could even have a global impact. The result could once again be pre-emptive attacks by nations that have concerns regarding how these WMD would be employed in the future. Historically, the Israeli air raid on the Iraqi nuclear facility at Osirak is an illustrative example of this process. In this particular case the fact that there was no Iraqi retaliation diffused an otherwise volatile conflict situation.

GLOBAL STRATEGIC ROLE OF THE UNITED STATES

Contrary to predictions, the collapse of the Soviet Union and the end of a clearly demarcated bipolar world did not automatically propel the United States (US) into the position of unopposed leadership of the world. In actual capabilities it did remain the only super power, but it was not openly granted that status by majority of the international community. The envisaged unipolar world, with all nations living in a stable and peaceful world overseen by a benign US, did not emerge. The period between the end of the Cold War and the attacks on the World Trade Centre on 11 September 2001 was perhaps the window of opportunity for the US to push for world leadership in an assertive manner—not through the employment of its powerful military force, but with innovative use of the considerable soft power that the nation had at that time. However, in a sad commentary of the leadership of the most powerful nation in the world, this opportunity was not grasped and optimally employed to further US interests in a bipartisan manner. In a charade reminiscent of the Roman Empire, during this entire period the US continued to be self-indulgent domestically and arrogant in the evolution and implementation of its foreign policy.

The aerial attacks on the twin towers in New York and the Pentagon changed the complexion of the US view of itself and the world[8]. The only good thing to come out of these attacks was the spontaneous and almost universal feeling of good will towards the US, which was clearly expressed by most of the nations. However, the subsequent actions of the US, which belied its claim to world leadership and even to maturity as a nation, quickly dispelled any notion that the rest of the world had regarding the stabilising influence that the US would play in the 21st Century. The international community is still being affected by the repercussions of the two wars that the US initiated, one—in Afghanistan—with UN approval and the assistance of a large number of nations and the other—in Iraq—unilaterally with the assistance of nations that joined the 'coalition of the willing'. Between September 2001 and about the end of 2005, the US had effectively squandered every bit of international good will that was apparent in the aftermath of the September 11 attacks. The actions of the US in these four years had long-term impact and irretrievably altered the global strategic security environment.

The US started what was termed the 'War on Terror' in late-2001. There is debate whether or not the current engagements, legacies of invasions in 2001 and 2003 in Afghanistan and Iraq respectively, are still part of this so called war. However, under the current circumstances that is a moot point. At least in the beginning this was an open-ended conflict with the US playing for word domination, although this strategic objective was never stated as such. The conduct of this 'war', especially the invasion of Iraq and its aftermath which is still on-going, exacted a very high price in human lives lost on both sides, a great deal of destruction of Iraqi infrastructure and the extra-ordinary amount of resources expended. The increasing burdens on the US military

---

8 Basevich, Andrew J., *The New American Militarism: How Americans Are Seduced By War*, Oxford University Press, New York, April 2005, pp. 36-42, 112-117.

power and the economy has resulted in gradually wearing down the once mighty power of the US into a quagmire of international loss of status, domestic economic challenges and a deficit of global good will—in combination these point towards the rapid decline of US soft power.

The US administration is now more willing to listen and engage in frank talks with allies, partners and even recalcitrant opponents, as compared to its stance up to 2008. There is a perceptible effort at trying to restore the moral authority of the US in dealings with all nations. Its success or failure will however be evident only in the long-term. Further, there is also a concerted effort being made to reinvigorate US cultural and diplomatic acumen that was not prominently used during the first decade of the 21st Century when the nation was heavily committed to two separate military campaigns. There is understanding at the highest levels of the US administration of the loss of soft power and the need to combine diplomacy, economy and cultural aspects in order to regenerate the lost power. Once again, the result of this effort will not be apparent in the short-term. The current US predicament is difficult, and the efforts being made to change the situation will have a ripple effect globally, irrespective of their success or failure.

United States in the Asia-Pacific

The US faces a number of challenges as well as clear possibilities in the Asia-Pacific. How it deals with these issues and opportunities as well as the initiatives that will be put in place will to a great extent determine the strategic security environment for the region. Within the region there has been a tendency to write off US influence, especially after the global financial crisis and the domestic economic turmoil that it went through in July-august 2011. This would be a mistake. While there are clear indications as well as reasonable proof of the rise of China's economic, military and diplomatic power, at least in the medium-term—three to four decades—the strategic primacy of the US in the Asia-Pacific is unlikely to be questioned. In its calculations, China would have factored in this situation—a belief confirmed by the abnormally soft Chinese approach to the Taiwan issue. Even during a period of extreme diplomatic belligerence with most of its neighbours in mid-2011, China was careful not to create intransigent issues regarding Taiwan that could have led to an unwanted stand-off with the US. If there was even the slightest doubt regarding US ability to contain emerging challenges in the region, it is certain that China's actions would have been different.

Even though US strategic primacy is accepted, there are a number of issues that create a sense of constant change in the region, especially for the smaller nations. The first issue is the strategic resurgence of Russia and its penchant to interfere, even peripherally, in the Asia-Pacific region at moments that are opportunistic. The intent may only be to keep engaged and to create discomfort for both China and the US, but its effect on the smaller nations of the region is significant. This contributes substantially to the diplomatic and trade calculations of the regional nations as well as in the collective bodies of the region like ASEAN and APEC. Russian initiatives in the region are often cloaked in secrecy, as far as their intent is concerned, which makes them all the more important to monitor. The US continues to be wary of Russian involvement, especially at a time when it is continuing to struggle with two unfinished military campaigns.

There is no doubt that the Asia-Pacific region that in its widest definition includes even the Indian Ocean, shapes the US identity as a maritime trading nation. The US continues to harbour grand designs of advancing democracy as a panacea to the ills of bad governance that leads to fragile and failing states. The US wants to envelope a democratic Asia as a critical player in this global design to advance democracy, a move very strongly opposed by China. The manoeuvrings in this respect is still very circumspect, but visible in any analysis of the strategic environment of the region. US grand strategy in the Asia-Pacific is built on creating and fostering a network of allies and partners. Towards this end there have been dedicated moves to engage with almost all nations in the region, through military exercises, economic support and diplomatic overtures. As the focus on the Middle East and Afghanistan is gradually reducing, there is increased convergence of US soft power elements in the Asia-Pacific. The ebb and flow of US-China interaction—something that cannot be accurately predicted—will create a sense of uncertainty in the region that is not conducive for stability.

There is a gradually emerging wariness regarding the divergence—perceived or actual—of US interests from the strategic interests of allies, which creates a great deal of discomfort within the region. In the past few years the US administration has made very appreciable attempts at changing this perception through a number of high level visits and diplomatic initiatives. The economic turbulence in the US has also made the region somewhat cautious, especially since it is difficult to predict the time or style of recovery and also the immediate and medium-term impact a downturn, or worse another recession, will have on the US focus on the region. This circumspection is further stressed by the debate regarding the US ability to stay the course in its engagement with the region. However, there is tacit understanding that the sovereignty of the nations and the regional stability needed to ensure it can only be assured through the active engagement of the US in the region. In essence, the region would like the US to be a benign and largely reactive power that would play a critically pivotal role as and when required in the interest of regional stability.

Summing Up...

The global strategic security environment is in a state of flux, it is constantly changing, the only variation being the pace at which it changes and the effects that these changes create—rapid and reactionary or evolutionary and gradual. Under these conditions all nations—from the most powerful to ones emerging as sovereign states—have to undergo a process of continuous realignment of their resources to ensure that proportionate allocations are made to ensure the safety, stability and security of the state. The primary need is to balance the resource requirements for adequate external defence, the domestic political compulsions that are especially important for democratic nations and the necessity to cater for the changing regional equilibrium.[9]

In trying to cope with the global uncertainties and strategic upheavals a majority of nations have adopted measures to ensure that the freedom of action to safeguard their national interests is not forfeited. This means the ability to retain the freedom to trade and develop the economy of the nation without undue external interference. The most

---

9 Emmers, Ralf, 'The Role of the Five Power Defence Arrangements in the Southeast Asian Security Architecture', *RSIS Working Paper No 195*, Nanyang Technological University, Singapore, 20 April 2010, pp. 9-12.

visible outcome of this fundamental requirement is the tendency of almost all nations to engage in bilateral discussions and agreements as far as possible in the sphere of trade and economy. This is however likely to reinforce only short-term advantages. To compliment bilateral agreements most nations also enter into multilateral alliances to protect their long-term goals, especially in relation to the security of the nation. In a democratic nation this results in a move from maintaining a pure balance of power to creating a concert of power with other like-minded nations. A combination of the two is most likely to succeed in strengthening the institutions within democratic nations through free exchange of ideas and concepts, thereby creating the necessary resilience in a nation to withstand the vagaries of an ever changing world.

Chapter 5

GLOBAL STRATEGIC ENVIRONMENT

THE INTERDEPENDENCE OF NATIONS

Over the centuries, a number of institutional changes have been the foundations from which a new world order emerged. The technological innovations of the 19th Century laid the foundations for what is now termed as the industrial revolution, which is viewed as one of the primary factors in improving the world in terms of its broad prosperity and providing the impetus for exploration that in turn created a greater understanding of global wealth. The downside was the conquests and colonisations that at times destroyed highly evolved civilisations and more importantly sowed the seeds of what would become an east-west divide.

Post World War II, the world order has been influenced by the improvements of transportation and information technology that have led to two distinct but yet interconnected phenomena. First, it has brought about an as yet unparalleled integration of production and distribution of goods and services bringing together national economies and leading to 'globalisation', a term that has been perhaps overused. Second, information transfer almost in real-time has made events that take place in one part of the world have an almost immediate impact on another physically distant one, virtually shrinking the geographic distances between nations—another type of globalisation. The combination of the two has made the contemporary world move towards being a much more interrelated global community than even a few decades back.

The contemporary world is becoming increasingly interconnected because of the ramifications on trade and economic stability brought about by the technology-enabled ability to move massive amounts of data almost instantaneously to any part of the world. This interdependence of nations also manifests in the politico-economic stability of individual nations. Although the explicit trigger for the event was rooted more in geopolitical issues, the so called 'Arab Spring' that swept the Middle East from early 2011 was greatly aided by quick information sharing demonstrating the influence, in a visible manner, of its crucial influence on broader political developments. The basic fact is that irrespective of the type of government in power—autocratic or democratic—there is an indelible connection between popular opinion and political leadership that cannot be ignored. This goes to the very root of national stability and wellbeing.

There are seven fundamental issues to be considered when analysing the evolving international geo-political environment through the prism of an unavoidable interdependence between nations— challenges in international relations, globalisation, the impact of the on-going global financial crisis, demographic changes, the on-going power diffusion and its effects on smaller nations, the contest for global shared areas and legal aspects of international relationships.

Resolving Challenges in International Relations[1]

International relations are the basis for ensuring global stability, if that can be considered an attainable goal. Relationships between nations can be multi-lateral and bilateral and all relationships are not the same, in fact each relationship is unique. The relationship between two nations, whether through a multi-lateral forum or bilaterally will determine the way in which emerging issues are resolved. There are two fundamental factors that must be borne in mind at all times during interaction and negotiation between nations. First is that each issue or challenge is

---

1 There are a large number of books available that study the subject of 'International Relations.' The following analysis has benefitted from a number of books and articles, a few of the books are listed below: Waltz, Kenneth N., *Man, the State, and War: A Theoretical Analysis*, Columbia University Press, Columbia, April 2001; Kissinger, Henry, *World Order*, Penguin Books UK, 2014; Lamy, Steven L., Masker, John S., and others, *Introduction to Global Politics*, Oxford University Press, New York, First Published 1997, Fourth Edition, 2017.

unique and must be dealt with accordingly. There are no overarching solutions to all challenges or issues. Second, each state or nation is unique and therefore will have its own interpretation of the best way forward to solve or address challenges. Attempts to superimpose one nation's opinions on another will almost always lead to break down of discussions and negotiations.

In international relations, the apparent success or otherwise of a nation plays an important role in its ability to influence the stability of the region; or in the case of global power, international stability. In this context, although there is open speculation regarding its capacity to be the de-facto world leader, at least for the immediate future the United States will influence, and its interests guide, all decisions that have global consequences. As a corollary, decisions made within the US will have international impact and repercussions.

At the macro level of international relations, there is a difference between recognising an issue or problem and accepting it; between such acceptance and formulating a solution that is agreeable to all parties concerned; and between formulating a solution and successfully implementing it. The process from the beginning of negotiations to achieving a solution is almost always lengthy and fraught with the potential to fail at all times from beginning to end. However, dialogue and negotiations are the only way through which lasting solutions can be achieved even to extremely vexed issues between states. There are some common factors that influence the resolution of challenges that arise in international relations.

First, in the contemporary strategic environment, no one nation—irrespective of its power base and influence—can solve an international issue on its own. Multi-lateral forums normally provide greater strategic depth than individual or bilateral initiatives. However, multi-lateral forums, if they are regionally restricted could have its own unique weaknesses that could constrain the initiatives to solve the issue. On the other hand, bilateral partnerships could also be limiting in its scope, especially if third party initiatives become necessary to progress negotiations. There is also a contradictory aspect to this. It is possible to reduce all issues to a regional status and reduce the number of nations involved, making it possible for regional forums to create the environment to resolve emerging challenges. The intractable fact is that international problems are best settled multi-laterally.

Second, it is easiest to solve an issue if it is addressed at the earliest. This is primarily so because of two reasons. One, at the very emergence of an issue the positions of the states involved are not rigid or entrenched, providing a reasonable amount of flexibility to all concerned to come to amicable terms. Two, domestic compulsions that make finding common ground through a process of give-and-take difficult will be least at the beginning of a crisis. As negotiations proceed domestic issues within a nation will become more influential in defining the stand of a nation on particular issues. Failure to nip the problem in the bud will invariably lead to long-drawn and resource-intensive processes that will only produce solutions of lesser veracity.

Third, international challenges only get resolved when there is tangible trust between the personalities involved. This is particularly important because institutions can breakdown in a crisis, leading to breakdown of communications and the attendant increase in tensions. Forceful personalities with demonstrated integrity and moral courage are required in such times to ensure that relationships between nations do not become fragile and tenuous. Trust between personalities involved would be the redeeming factor in an otherwise downhill slide in the strategic and security environment.

Fourth, all solutions are political in nature. Even if the resolution of a challenge is arrived at through the employment of military forces, the final solution will have to be political if it is to be long lasting. The legitimacy of power—military, diplomatic and economic—and its application is underpinned by political acceptance. Legitimacy of power projection is the most important factor in making all actions acceptable to all the parties involved. Further, the solution that is finally adopted must take into account the interests of all nations that are involved so that no residual ill-feeling is left. In implementing a political strategy to resolve emerging challenges, intervention is a forceful tool. However, for effectiveness it must be at the cutting edge of the overall strategy and cognisant of domestic political influences of the recipient nation. In fact, domestic political compulsions will always restrict what is possible to be achieved in addressing challenges in international relations.

Resolving challenges to international relations is essentially about agreements on a whole array of issues from political participation, borders and military movements to humanitarian minimums and economy and trade. This can be the only basis for developing a stable regional and international environment.

Globalisation

The effects of the process of globalisation on the international strategic environment can be clearly demarcated into two distinct, but interrelated groups. The first group contains the benign effects that lead to integration of economies, flow of trade and commerce and the strengthening of international institutions. The other group is formed of the disparities that arise from globalisation—the weakening of smaller economies, exploitation of resource rich but non-industrialised nations and the socio-economic collapse of fragile states. There are a number of sub-factors that contribute to and influence the process of globalisation—both in improving and distorting the international environment. The balance between the two determines the state of the world in terms of the broad security environment. Further, there are three developments that arise from globalisation that impact the strategic environment.[2]

First, the developing economies of the world have benefited from globalisation in terms of increasing their industrialisation, with its attendant advantages. Second, regional and global interaction has forged new links between nations and made geographical borders more open. In some cases this openness along with the increase in trade and commerce, has led to the formation of new regional economic and security groupings. Such groupings obviously have positive as well as negative influence on the security environment of the region. The robustness of the group will determine how well the negative impact can be neutralised. Third, the open economic situation could have both beneficial and detrimental effects on the economy of a nation. Once

---

2 Forbes, Dean, 'Regional Integration, Internationalisation and the New Geographies of the Pacific Rim', in Waters, R. F., & Mcgee, T. G., (eds), *Asia-Pacific: New Geographies of the Pacific Rim*, Crawford House Publishing, Bathurst, NSW, 1997, p. 14.

again, the strength and resilience of the national economy will be the deciding factor in shaping its trajectory under these circumstances.

In a generic manner, therefore, globalisation has both negative and positive attributes. This dichotomy is particularly visible in the areas of economic, environmental, energy and food security challenges. A nation must take stock of its own situation and then act to ensure that the negative influences are mitigated to the extent possible in order to derive the full benefit that accrues through benign globalisation. It is in this context that the question of the viability of smaller economies comes into focus. As much as an economy can be boosted by interconnected trade it can also become stagnant and declining, a possibility that is much greater in the case of smaller and developing economies. This could happen because of the non-viability of smaller enterprises to compete against much larger international conglomerates with the capacity to even absorb large initial losses if necessary. Essentially it comes down to the staying power of the economy in the long term. Therefore, a nation must be vigilant to ensure that it gets its fair share of the relative prosperity that globalisation brings.

There are three major consequences of significance that stem from globalisation, which are not strictly only economic in nature. First, internationalisation of trade will have political fall outs that may not even be envisaged as the interaction progresses. In the quest for increased trade and new partners, traditional allies could become competitors and temporary commercial adversaries. Considering that nations remain friends with each other essentially out of self-interests, economic competition has the potential to stretch all but the most robust of alliances. A secondary effect of such a situation will be the increased dynamism in international relationship that could lead to strategic volatility.

The second consequence flows from the first—the more developed and stable economies would vie with each other to influence and gain the allegiance of smaller nations. This increased competition could vitiate international diplomatic relations, especially when the need for cohesion in international bodies like the United Nations is paramount to ensure stability in the more precarious regions of the world. A corollary to this situation is the high probability of increased requirements for the international community—meaning the developed economies—to provide humanitarian assistance in response to both natural disasters and man-made calamities. The necessity to build relationships and the interconnected nature of contemporary trade and commerce underpins this requirement. In these conditions, the military forces are invariably expected to take the lead, even if they are not trained or equipped to undertake humanitarian relief efforts in a global context.

The third consequence is that the volatility in international relations, brought about fundamentally through economic competition, will place extra strain on international agencies involved in bipartisan and charitable activities. To a great extent these agencies serve a critical role in containing the knock-on effects, particularly of civil wars and other conflicts. While providing humanitarian aid to smooth over natural calamities is comparatively easy and can be done by a hastily gathered group, dedicated organisations are required to create the infrastructure necessary to ameliorate—to some degree at least—the ravages of armed conflict. The international institutions that have the ability to do this may need to develop greater built-in flexibility to increase their ability to adapt to the rapidly altering world scenario if they are to avoid collapse—to perform at a level that would make a fundamental improvement to the situation on the ground.

Increasing Economic Interdependence of Nations

The foremost effect of globalisation is the loss of independence of national economies, including the major ones. In the contemporary scenario the movements within one national economy always create a ripple effect on the economies of its trading partners and through them secondary or tertiary effects on other economies, in an ever widening circle. The spread of this ripple is dependent on the size and strength of the economy that is undergoing the convulsion with larger economies having greater and longer effects. In addition, the effects are felt not only in economic activities, but they also influence other strategic trends and security issues—nationally, regionally and globally, relative to the size and the rapidity of the changes taking place.

Even though economic interdependence is already a global phenomenon, there are nations that still exist on the poverty line. These nations affect the upward mobility of economies that are connected to them and even have the power to drag down less robust economies that deal directly with them. The issue of poverty has another aspect that must be carefully monitored. In emerging nations that are trying to establish economic stability and subsequent growth, pockets of poverty can expand very rapidly into uncontrollable sizes that could eventually engulf large swaths and destabilise the nation. This trend must be carefully watched and analysed, with remedial measures being initiated by the nation itself as well as its economic partners. The spread of poverty, if unchecked initially, can overwhelm smaller economies of the entire region.

Globalisation has brought about another observable trend—the increase in the virtual power of non-government organisations (NGO) and multi-national companies. In turn both these entities reinforce the emerging tendency towards global economic interdependence, irrespective of the size and volatility of a particular economy. These non-state actors, some of whom control budgets that are larger than the combined budgets of a number of nations combined, exercise significant clout in economic matters. The strategic security environment is never far from the influence of the economy and therefore, almost by default, the NGOs and multi-national companies have the ability to manipulate the security equation in a nation or region[3]. The fact that they do not owe allegiance to any nation or set of principles other than their own commercial or altruistic interests makes this situation somewhat out of step with the requirements for national and regional stability. In extreme cases the impact can even be felt globally. While private entities with global authority, without the responsibilities inherent in a government, have so far been able to function to safeguard their own interests, there is growing understanding, and reluctant acceptance, regarding the need to curb their manipulation of economies and other environments. In democratic nations reliant on broadly based capitalistic economies, curbing the spread and influence—both in the national as well as international economic development—of large companies, which are critical to the prosperity of the nation as a whole, will be a difficult task. The steps that nations adopt to achieve this will be interesting to watch for their effectiveness and repercussions.

---

3 Ward, Thomas J., 'The Political Economy of NGOs and Human Security', *International Journal on World Peace*, Vol 24, No 1, March 2007, pp. 43-64, https://www.jstor.org/stable/20752764 accessed on 15 March 2015.

Another factor that necessitates economic interdependence is the growing resource scarcity. The demand for raw material and basic energy resources is now at an all-time high, and unlikely to reduce in an appreciable manner. The situation is complicated by the fact that a large amount of these resources is found in emerging nations who have developing economies and are comparatively less stable. There are three primary issues that stem from this situation. First, the need to fulfil the domestic resource requirements will gradually become a primary preoccupation for small and medium economies. This will adversely affect the growth potential of the economy, and in extreme cases, lead to unsustainable negative growth. Such a situation is a major contributory factor in destabilising a nation.

Second, the quest for resources and energy could lead to bitter rivalry and competition between nations that would otherwise have peacefully co-existed. Between nations that have natural resources the necessity to secure them could lead to territorial disputes that could escalate depending on the perceived value of the disputed resource as well as the prevailing international environment. Third, the competition for resources by the more developed nations could irrevocably lead to the destabilisation of the supplier states. This could happen through unwarranted influence being brought to bear on the government, clandestine support of rebel elements that could lead to insurgency and even civil war and the unscrupulous exploitation of natural resources leading to unresolvable environmental challenges. Due diligence by the more stable and developed nations of the world in the exploitation of natural resources of the less developed parts of the world has not been a strong point till now. Global energy needs have a direct bearing on the geo-strategic environment, a situation likely to become more acute in the future.

There is another aspect of interdependence that needs to be considered in understanding the evolving international strategic environment—the economic rise of Asia. In the past three decades there has been an appreciable increase in Asia's share of global wealth. This is not only because of the steady growth of the Chinese and Indian economies, but also based on the relative stability of the other middle level economies of the region. However, as Asia is becoming richer than before, it is also becoming more difficult to manage from an economic perspective. The dynamism that encourages economic growth is predominantly based on a multilateral approach to resolving economic challenges. The increased prominence on multi-lateral dealings tends to bring about more volatility in trade and commerce, which could at times lead to unmanageable developments. Thus for example, the rising wealth of Asia could itself become a challenge to overall regional stability and produce cascading global ripples.

In the past decade economic dynamism has visibly shifted to Asia and there is a discernible stagnation and decline in the economic well-being of the 'First World' nations. The developed world is struggling with a relative erosion of power brought about by the economic downturn. This economic slowdown has given impetus to a number of other factors—that otherwise would not have been of any great significance—that reinforce the decline in the power status of these nations. There is a gradual change in the global order established after World War II and further strengthened by the collapse of the Soviet Union, with a shift in strategic focus towards Asia becoming perceptibly evident. Whether this process will accelerate and the repercussions of the shift when it is completed are difficult at best to predict. However, it is certain that a shift in economic and power balance, one that may not be possible to reverse, is underway.

Impact of the Global Financial Crisis

> Divergent threat perceptions within Europe and the likelihood that defence spending will remain uncoordinated suggest the EU will not be a major military power by 2025.
>
> National Intelligence Council Report,
>
> 'Global Trends 2025: A Transformed World'[4]

The global financial crisis (GFC) is commonly believed to have begun in July 2007 with a credit crunch and the loss of confidence

---

4 Quoted in Skinner, Tony, 'US Power 'likely to wane', warns NIC Report', *Jane's Defence Weekly*, London, 26 November 2008, p. 9.

by investors, predominantly in the US, that caused a liquidity crisis. By September 2008 the stock markets around the globe crashed and became volatile to the extreme. The crisis resulted in the collapse of a number of financial institutions, some of them very large and influential, and the bail out of banks by national governments. It also led to failure of key businesses and a significant decline in economic activity and finally a global economic recession by late 2008. The crisis by itself is deemed to have ended by mid-2009 although a number of aftershocks continue to buffet global economy. It still has a profound effect on much of the world.

The US has been particularly affected by the crisis, which originated there, and its aftermath. In June 2009, the Brookings Institute reported that between 2000 and 2009 US consumption accounted for more than a third of the growth in global consumption. The recession in the US has directly impacted and slowed growth across the world, in some places rather dramatically.[5] There is a belief, as explained by Paul Krugman that currently the US is in the early stages of a third depression—a third period of economic stagnation, the first two being in the 1870s and 1930s respectively. Further, he contends that 'this third depression will be primarily the result of a failure of policy'.[6] The advanced capitalist economies are now caught up in a stagnation brought about through industrial maturation and financial accumulation. The shift in the centre of gravity of the capitalist economy from production to finance has only compensated for the stagnation at the cost of increased fragility.[7]

Whatever the detailed reasons for its onset and the on-going international struggle to overcome the financial challenges, the GFC has directly influenced the strategic environment in a noticeable

---

5 Baily, Martin Neil & Elliott, Douglas J., *'The U.S Financial and Economic Crisis: Where Does it stand and Where Do We Go From Here?'* The Brookings Institution, http://www.brookings.edu/papers/2009/0615_economic_crisis_bailey_elliott-aspx?p=1 accessed on 29 August 2011.

6 Krugman, Paul, 'The Third depression', *New York Times,* New York, 28 June 2010.

7 Foster, John Bellamy, &Magdoff, Fred, *'The Great Financial Crisis—Three Years On,'* Monthly Review, Volume 20, Issue 5 (October), http://monthlyreview.org/2010/10/01/the-great-financial-crisis-three-years-on accessed on 30 August 2011

manner. The first consequence was the exposure of the European Union as an institution that could only manage prosperity, with almost no ability or power to initiate the necessary concerted corrective action in times of economic adversity. This was compounded by the reluctance of the larger, more stable European economies to directly intervene, at a sufficiently early stage, in nations within the Union that were experiencing financial difficulties. Intervention, however well-intentioned and deliberate, after the onset of a challenge will need to be much greater and for longer periods that if it was undertaken earlier.

Another observable reaction was that from the beginning of the GFC all nations acted independently in their own individual interests without considering a collective response. This made the containment difficult for nations whose economies were more susceptible to the volatility of the economic market, making some of them, like Greece, reach the breaking point. The reaction from most governments was to intervene financially in an effort to stop the downward economic slide that would bring socio-economic challenges such as unemployment with it. The result was that the global financial institutions and some multi-national companies were 'rescued' by the government to avoid the fallout from their closure. This brought about a change in the balance of power, with the State exercising more financial power than private financial institutions—a gradual reversal of roles in open market economies. Yet another outcome from this situation was an almost immediate stop to the, till then, increasing importance of sub-national groups that had slowly started to exercise a disproportionately broad influence within society and the state at large.

Until the onset of the GFC most democratic nations favoured a multilateral geo-strategic environment, fearful of the global influence that the US wielded. This trend was further emphasised by the approach that the US took in opposing global terrorism and the unilateral, but informal, declarations of war in the Middle East. However, nation-states watched the interaction of multilaterism in times of financial adversity and observed what they viewed as its inadequacies in being able to protect the sanctity of the nation-state. The question being actively debated is whether or not there can be global stability in an enlightened multilateral world. The perceived drawbacks of multilaterism, laid bare in the onslaught of the GFC, have led to a more inward looking analysis that has brought about a slow but certain resurgence of the sovereignty of nation-states. In the past few years a number of initiatives have emerged that may or may not lead to fruition. The most noticeable is in the altering of international relationships, with like-minded nations forming informal groups to regulate trade and thereby exercise a modicum of control over economic manoeuvrings.

Global geo-strategic stability has always been underpinned by the strength and resilience of nation-states to weather overarching challenges. However, the strategic reshuffle of the international environment during the last decades of the 20th Century and the early 21st Century have gradually made this basic truth less than obvious. The need to have strong foundational institutions with sufficient stable dynamism for growth and development and adequate governance based on well laid out policies was highlighted and strengthened by the GFC. The direct connection between the economy and security of the nation was the primary lesson that emerged.

Long-Term Implications of Demographic Trends

The total population of the world is increasing mainly because of increased longevity, the drop in infant and child mortality and the increase in global birth rate. However, this creates a lopsided growth from a geo-strategic perspective because the growth is not uniform across the world, which produces aberrations in the national and regional demographic spread. In fact in the past few decades the world has transitioned into demographic instability. It has been suggested that the visible increase in population is more the result of an on-going momentum which will slow down and eventually lead to a levelling off in population growth.[8]

There is a direct connection between the age structure of a nation's population and its economy. The ratio between the available work force and the age-retired people in a nation will determine its economic development trajectory. Indirectly therefore, population growth trends

---

8 Bloom, David, & Canning, David, 'Global Demography: Fact, Force and Future', *PGDA Working Papers No 1406*, 2006, http://ideas.repec.org/p/gdm/wpaper/1406.html accessed on 30 August 2011.

will affect the economy and the global strategic environment. From a national viewpoint the primary impact of population growth and the demographic structure will be felt on the socio-economic policies of a nation. Policies related to labour, trade, retirement, welfare systems and investments in health, education and social security networks are all dependent on a comprehensive understanding of demographic trends.[9]

World Population Trends.[10] While the world population continues to grow there is evidence that except in the least developed countries, overall population growth has slowed in both developed and developing nations since the 1970s. In terms of distribution, the proportion of the world population that is from all developing countries increased from 68% in 1950 to 82% in 2010.[11] In 1950, the 10 largest countries were 62% of the total world population. That dropped to 59% in 2010.[12] China and India together increased from 36% of total world population in 1950 to 37% in 2010, while the US dropped from being 6% in 1950 to 5% in 2010.

Demographic trends that can already be predicted with reasonable accuracy will have a significant influence on the global strategic environment. The changes that will come about will also create the necessity to develop new alliances and foreign policy initiatives, even for the current major powers. This is predicated on the fact that the region that was the centre of gravity for most of the 20th Century—Europe and Russia—will become relatively unimportant, with nations

---

9 ibid.

10 Shackman, Gene, Xun Wang & Ya-Lin Liu, *Brief Review of World Population Trends*, http://gsociology.icaap.org/reprot/demsum.html accessed on 31 August 2011. The statistics provided in the two footnotes below have also been obtained from this report.

11 Asia increased as percent of total world population from 54% in 1950 to 56% in 2010; Sub-Saharan Africa from 7% to 12%; Latin America and the Caribbean from 6% to 9%. Western Europe and North America decreased as percent of total world population from 18% in 1950 to 11% in 2010; the Commonwealth of Independent States from 10% to 6%.

12 10 largest countries in 1950 were (in descending order) China, India, US, Russia, Japan, Indonesia, Germany, Brazil, UK, and Italy; in 2010 they were China, India, US, Indonesia, Brazil, Pakistan, Bangladesh, Nigeria, Russia and Japan.

that were till now operating at the periphery of global economy taking centre stage.

There is no doubt that the demography—in its broadest definition—of the world is undergoing a number of changes. There are many and varied reasons for these changes but they are not of direct significance in this analysis and therefore have been left unsaid. This analysis concentrates on the impact of these global demographic changes on the international geo-political and strategic security environment. In this respect, demographic changes can be studied under five broad groupings—their influence on national power, the ageing of the industrialised world, the increase in youth population and its distribution, the significance of migration and urbanisation.

Influence on National Power

There is sufficient historical evidence to support the theory that the rise and fall of civilisations have been closely linked to demographic changes. Decreasing populations have often been seen to be overwhelmed either militarily, culturally or economically by groups with growing and expanding populations. There have also been other geo-strategic consequences of population growth. Population growth, especially if the nation perceives itself to be geographically constrained can lead to expansionist foreign policies, which could in turn alter the strategic environment. In extreme cases this could also lead to conflict over territory, resources and cultural individualism. Increase in population can also create state sponsored incentives for innovation and technological breakthroughs. The Industrial Revolution was partly the result of a widespread conviction in Great Britain in the 18th and 19th century that the large population growth was unmanageable.[13]

Unprecedented population growth can lead to economic volatility and social unrest. If the situation cannot be controlled by the State through financial and welfare intervention it could deteriorate to anarchy and even revolution. National power is fundamental in stabilising the state when demographic changes become significant, whether to ease domestic pressures through expansion—both physical and economic—or to contain external pressures that may themselves

---

13 *Long-Term Global Demographic Trends: Reshaping the Geopolitical Landscape*, July 2001, CIA Report, USA, https://www.cia.gov/library/reports/general-reports-1/Demo_Trends_For_Web.pdf accessed on 31 August 2011, p. 13.

be brought about through regional or global demographic changes. Further, national power itself is affected by the changes, perceived and actual, that are brought about in the socio-economic status of a nation. There is always a nexus between the political movements and the actual age-spread of a nation's population. A greater percent of the population being within the 18 to 30 age group will make a nation more susceptible to fundamental changes in its policies that could affect international relations and thus significantly alter the strategic landscape.

There is also a limiting factor in the influence of demography on national power—the ability of a nation to convert the advantages of a large population into conventional power. Large and increasing population can be both an advantage and a challenge. If the strength in population is not actively harnessed into creating a comparative advantage for the nation in relation to its neighbours and competitors, it can become a resource sapping challenge that could slowly debilitate the nation. Converting the advantage of greater population to conventional power will require astute management of the available resources and the focussing of national manpower to projects of national interest. This focussing in turn would require a basic core of assets and a minimum of skills being already available within the nation. An economically poor nation may not be able to achieve this synergy, in which case the large population will become a burden with the potential to make the nation an economic failure.

Forced migration, ethnic clashes and rivalry, religious fundamentalism and intolerance, extreme nationalism, resource depletion and even environmental degradation directly influence the power structure of nation. These same factors also directly affect the political and economic stability of a nation. In effect, these demographic factors act as a bridge between national power and the geo-strategic environment within which it operates. Demographic attributes of a nation are so intertwined with its power structure that the two cannot be fully separated.

Ageing of the Industrialised World

It has been calculated that the industrialised nations of the world will face a crisis of having a predominantly aged population by 2020. In fact many of the indications are already visible. As many as 19-

20% of the population will be elderly by 2015-2020 in almost all the industrialised nations of the world[14] putting an increasing burden on the taxpaying working populations of these countries. The effective labour force contraction will directly affect the economic output and could be the catalyst for greater inflation. In the current financial environment wherein a number of these nations are struggling under large debt burdens this additional load could be the proverbial last straw that would force them to reduce their international economic leadership roles.

In combination with a reduction in the growth rate, an increased percentage of national population being in the aged group would translate to a decrease in numbers that are in the working and home-building age. Any noticeable reduction in this age group will create a reduction in demand for everything from real estate to consumer goods that could lead to falling returns within all financial and manufacturing sectors. The cumulative effect could be a drop in national GDP and the resultant drop in standards of living that together will alter the overall strategic environment.

This situation will create a number of geo-strategic ramifications. One: currently there is an implicit belief that international military intervention to stabilise a region—irrespective of the reason for having to do so—is the moral responsibility of the 'west'. The demographic changes will lessen the ability of the industrialised nations—through a forced reduction in military numbers and decreased resource availability—to manage the global hotspots. The moral imperative to intervene but the lessened capacity to do so could lead to a certain amount of friction between traditional allies within the developed world in terms of the distribution of responsibilities. More importantly, this decreased ability to initiate and sustain stabilising interventions will lead to either a gradual change in global leadership if another group of nations assumed the mantle of intervention. If such a shift in responsibility does not take place it is likely that an international apathy towards the conflicts that have no direct bearing on the security of one's own nation could develop. Such a situation in its turn could lead to escalation of conflicts as well as lesser overall ability to alleviate humanitarian suffering for the most vulnerable people.

---

14 ibid, p. 7.

Two: if the more stable nations of the world are forced to assume a hands-off attitude to simmering issues across the world with the potential to destabilise whole regions, the chances of rogue states pursuing their own agenda, even with the overt employment of military forces, will increase. Any discernible shift in this direction could lead to unexpected and challenging reorientations of the strategic environment, both regionally and globally. In an indirect manner, the gradual demographic changes taking place in the developed world will make the overall security situation more delicate and unbalanced.

Three: in the long term, nations that are now concentrating on improving their own economic status will tend to assert their will in an expanding circle, initially on matters within the region and then in international forums. The demographic changes and its secondary effects on the current industrialised nations will quicken the pace of this change. This will entail a definitive change in the centre of gravity of global events—in all probability—to Asia. Associated with this will be the shift in the leadership of the United Nations and its associated institutions that have so far been controlled by the developed, western nations. Together, this will create a dramatic change in the global geo-strategic and socio-economic environment and directly affect the security balance.

In democracies the size of the military force and its supporting civilian enterprise is a practical percentage of the total work force. Considering that this situation is unlikely to change, the combined effect of the pressures of an ageing population, especially in the European nations will be a palpable reduction in the size of their defence establishments. This will have far reaching consequences that will alter the geo-strategic balance globally. The international diplomatic and security environments in 2030 and beyond will not even have the slightest resemblance to what prevailed at the turn of the century.

Youth Population Growth

A number of nations in the developing world have a large youth population, much larger as a percentage of total population than three decades ago. By 2020, the world's poorest and politically most unstable countries—including, but not restricted to, Afghanistan, Pakistan, Gaza, Iraq and Yemen—will have the largest youth populations. The inherent political instability and lack of proper governance in the poorest of nations directly translate to their inability to provide the economic and institutional resources to effectively integrate the youth into mainstream society. This alienation in turn will perpetuate the cycle of instability, ethnic strife, anti-government activities and finally lead to civil wars and revolutions. Economic growth, necessary to generate jobs and contain youth unrest is almost a direct function of political stability.[15] The poorer nations will find it impossible to break this cycle and in all likelihood go into a spiral of instability and failure. In the past 'youth bulges' have produced political upheavals in places like Algeria and Northern Ireland. In contemporary times, the on-going Arab Spring uprisings of 2011 in the Middle East are demonstrable manifestations of the frustrations of a large youth population.

The disgruntled youth population, concentrated in the poorer nations, provides fertile recruiting grounds for terrorist organisations. In a number of cases it is seen that these youth groups harbour hatred of the more stable nations—mainly western democracies—that are seen as anathema to their cultural, religious and ethnic beliefs. They are also generally anti-government, generating conflict between the population and the legitimate government. The positive aspect of this situation is that these activities normally weaken authoritative regimes and can pave the way for a more liberal and democratic government to be installed. However, in practice it has so far been seen that the transition to true democracy in most of these cases is not easily achieved. Free society is an elusive goal—irrespective of ethnicity, religion and culture of the people—when brought about through violence. Stability can only be brought about by the steady hand of democracy, that itself needs long-term solutions, temperance and magnanimity from the 'victors' to be sustained.

From a political perspective it is possible that even senior leadership of some youth bulge nations will adopt anti-west positions in an attempt to pacify the volatile youth population. It is also possible that governments, especially in the Middle East where religious activism is on the increase, that have so far been aligned with and friendly to western democracies will find it increasingly difficult to cooperate openly for fear of domestic repercussions. In this context, if military intervention is undertaken it is certain to lead to rapid loss

---

15 ibid, pp. 38-40.

of support for the action and active and virulent insurgencies, at times condoned by the supported government itself. The interdependence of global economy makes it imperative for the developed world to ensure improvement in the economic status of the youth bulge nations in order for their own economies to prosper. When analysed in combination with the demographic changes taking place in the industrialised world and its fallouts, it becomes immediately apparent that there is no way that these nations can be sidelined if the world is to continue on the path of global economic development.

Significance of Migration

One of the significant fallouts from the youth bulge in developing nations is the boost it will provide to both legal and illegal migration of people to nations with more established and stable economies. Migration provides partial solutions to some of the issues that developing nations are confronting while also posing equally complex challenges. Either way, the one certainty is that migration will significantly change the socio-economic balance of both the out-migration nation, normally in the developing world, and the recipient nation, almost always a developed western country. Such changes will have international significance.

There are a number of factors that will contribute to increased global migration levels in the coming decades. The primary ones are increased globalisation of the economy and interdependence of national economies, decolonisation and the subsequent democratisation of large parts of the developing world and the increasing disparity in the standard of living and income of individuals between the developed and the developing world.

Developed nations will need a large influx of skilled immigrants to stabilise their economies. Selective acceptance of migrants from poorer economies is perhaps the easiest solution to the issue of labour shortage in developed nations. This will benefit the developing nation's economy through expatriate reimbursement to their home countries and the host nation through an increase in tax and consumer base, thereby assisting to alleviate budgetary challenges associated with the ageing population base.[16] However, it must be accepted that there will

---

16 ibid, p. 42.

be an inevitable influx of unskilled migrants who would be less likely to add value to the host nation and could even become liabilities. A balance in the migrant intake therefore becomes a necessity. Migration in the scale required to balance the demographic unevenness will bring to the fore two issues that will increasingly become politically controversial and divisive. One, for the host nation, there will be strong public resistance to immigration since it is almost certain that the ethnicities of the migrant population—with its attendant differences in religion, culture and societal norms—will challenge the ethnic and cultural homogeneity of the accepting nation. This will fuel political controversy. Second, the sending countries will over a period of time resent the drain of high-skilled workers and professionals because in the long-term it will affect their own developmental options.

Perhaps more important than the changes and challenges that will be faced by individual nations is the fact that large scale migrations can very rapidly alter the ethnic balance of the host nation, causing instability. In addition, as they settle down and feel part of the national ethos over a period of time, immigrants will increasingly seek to influence both domestic politics and foreign policy. If the immigrant population feels that they have no opportunities to influence the political process, they will succumb to a sense of disenfranchisement. Either way, this issue has the potential to divide the nation into an 'us and them' political confrontation.

The global communications network smooths migration by enabling the diaspora to facilitate the movements of their geographically distanced compatriots by lobbying the host country. It is also possible that an immigrant community will try to influence the decisions of the government regarding its dealing with their original country, especially if there is political, social and economic upheaval there. However, illegal migration facilitated by crime syndicates has already become a security challenge for the host nations. Further, forced migration as a result of military conflict, civil wars, economic crisis and natural disasters has also become a common occurrence that has a distinctly destabilising effect and has therefore become a critical issue in security considerations.[17]

---

17 ibid, pp. 44-57.

Impact of Urbanisation

It has been calculated that by 2015 the majority of people will reside in urban centres rather than in more rural settings. This is driven by many factors. Urban centres have resurged as the economic hubs in most nations registering greater growth potential, which makes them attractive to upwardly mobile younger generations. Productivity of rural agricultural land could gradually become marginal leading to the loss of its economic viability and forcing migration. This could be further compounded by an increase in the density of population in rural areas. Internal conflict or natural disasters also create an inclination in the population towards migrating to urban areas in search of relative stability. This trend could evolve into a mass population movement beyond the control of the state and bring with it its own peculiar challenges—such as unemployment, increased crime, breakdown of civic services—to the urban centres.

The noteworthy factor is that such urbanisation is taking place more in the developing rather than the developed nations. This could be a direct result of the inability of developing nations to provide the economic and physical infrastructure to sustain minimum living standards outside the cities, creating the conditions for an internal migration pattern towards the cities. This is further emphasised by the fact that the majority of cities that have already reached 'mega city' status—cities that have population in excess of 8 million people—are located in the developing world.

The trend towards urban living will make the cities grow at a rate higher than planned and predicted by the government and poses a number of challenges that most of the developing nations may not be able to overcome. First, the increase in urban population will lead to greater atmospheric pollution and lack of adequate basic amenities like drinking water and hygiene facilities. This could lead to the overcrowded areas becoming breeding grounds for disease that could grow to epidemic proportions. Second, there will be very clearly apparent disparity in the income distribution that could lead to social upheavals. Third, the social services, as they are at a low level of efficiency in most developing nations, will become saturated and become failing institutions. All these factors can be the primary causal factor for urban conflict in the guise of anti-government protests that could very rapidly evolve into civil war. Uncontrolled urbanisation is certain to lead to internal destabilisation of fragile nations.

The most significant impact of urban migration, which is predominated by the younger generation, is the emergence of societal problems. The youth moving away from rural families into the city, which lacks a cohesive society and community support, breaks up the traditional family as well as social and religious structures, that otherwise provide guidance to individual behaviour. This invariably leads to violent and anti-social behaviour in the youth group and in some cases can lead to ideological and/or religious extremism. This decline in positive behaviour can alienate entire generations of people and create broad and significant challenges to geo-strategic stability.

Natural Resources Scarcity

The economic strength of a nation is dependent on the availability of natural resources to feed its manufacturing sector and provide adequacy of food and shelter to its people. Sufficiency in resource availability strengthens security, further reinforcing the importance of natural resources to national security. In the past few decades, environmental issues that affect resource availability have assumed greater importance in security considerations and influence the development of governing policies in most stable democracies. Water and oil are the two primary resources whose availability will become contentious in the near-term future.

The ready availability of water is likely to be the most volatile resource issue of this century. Global water consumption is increasing rapidly and is being exacerbated by unchecked population growth in the areas where the challenge to obtain water is most acute. In the more arid regions of the world; the Middle East, Sub-Saharan Africa, northern China; governments will face difficulties over the procurement and allocation of water. This will lead to regional tensions that will only be heightened with the passage of time. The United Nations Environment Program has calculated that at the current rate of per capita consumption of water as many as 20 countries in North Africa will face acute water shortages by 2025. This is a daunting prospect that is fraught with the real danger of disputes that could rapidly erupt into armed conflict.

The sources of water are normally large rivers and lakes that need not be contained within one nation. This creates the possibility of a nation being able to control the water resources of another situated downstream. In terms of leveraging this situation to one's own advantage, the options are many. As the scarcity becomes more acute, it is not unimaginable that water could become a coercive 'weapon' that can be wielded to create the necessary effect on a neighbour. Such actions can create a volatile geo-strategic environment that can be extremely destabilising.

Power Diffusion to Smaller States

An uneven mix of geo-political, socio-economic and strategic security developments in the international environment has culminated in the diffusion of power making the world move inexorably from the unique unipolar situation in the 1990s to an evolving multi-nodal one with very unclear boundaries and definitions of power. It is easy to state that there is a shift in the balance of power from the Atlantic and Europe to the Pacific and Asia, which in any case seems to be happening. However, the real situation and the probable progression into the future are much more complex than that.

The US is still the predominant power in the world, despite its current financial and political difficulties. Here the understanding of power is at its most basic in relation to a nation—the ability of a nation to act, unilaterally if required, to secure itself and to assert its will at any place and time of its choice. Currently, and at least for the next three decades, the US would be the only nation capable of such power projection. However, while the power of the US has remained in an almost *status quo* situation, its global status as a benign democratic nation and the champion of the downtrodden and oppressed has been damaged in the past decade. This has largely been the result of poor judgement and strategic mistakes that were committed by its leadership and the irrationally assertive manner in which it has pursued the wars that it started. When this loss of status is combined with the financial troubles that the US is going through, it becomes a contributory factor in the on-going international power diffusion. The trend will be for the redistribution of power to move away from its concentration with the US.

The current trend is for small and medium power nations to search for like-minded countries to create purpose-built partnerships that do not impinge on other matters of national interest[18]. This is a far cry from the grand alliances of the past and has distinct advantages. It creates a situation in which smaller nations can craft interest-driven coalitions that could function on an as required basis without tying down a nation to a limited number of predetermined options, especially in the realm of national security. When a number of such coalitions are formed and function without encroaching on other aspects of governance and foreign policy of the nations involved it would be the start of an evolution towards a multi-nodal world. While a multi-nodal world need not immediately diminish the concentration of power in the larger nations, it will provide greater power to the smaller interest-driven coalitions and lead to a greater amount of power diffusion towards smaller nations.

Along with the trend to form smaller coalitions wherein all partners have equal parts to play rather than creating a major power led coalition, there is also a noticeable move towards fashioning politico-military alliances of convenience. Like the interest-driven coalitions these groupings are also, to a great extent, interest-driven, but the politico-military alliances have a longer life span. A nation normally does not involve itself in alliances that do not have the promise of longevity. Therefore, politico-military alliances, generally considered more binding and perhaps the most important from a national security perspective are preferred. However, under the prevailing global socio-political and economic environment they are less frequently formed.

Another phenomenon of comparatively recent origin is the emergence of non-state entities, as both threats to security and in the form of NGOs and multi-national enterprises that exert economic and social pressures on smaller nations and can, at times, even dictate state policy. In some small and economically struggling nations the slow diffusion of governance functions from the state to non-state

---

18 Long, Tom, 'Small States, Great Power? Gaining Influence Through Intrinsic, Derivative and Collective Power', *International Studies Review*, 19(2), June 2017, Published by Oxford University Press, pp. 185-205, https://www.researchgate.net/publication/311765016_Small_States_Great_Power_Gaining_Influence_Through_Intrinsic_Derivative_and_Collective_Power accessed 09 August 2017.

entities is clearly visible. In some cases—even if rarely—such a situation may have its merits but in a majority of cases it will lead to the loss of state authority and will be the beginning of a slow decline of the state apparatus towards failure. There is an inherent risk of the extraordinary financial powers of some international NGOs and multi-national companies inhibiting economically weak states from effectively exercising legal authority over their own resources. Further, such states may not have the cohesion and robustness of state apparatus to resist the initiatives of these non-state entities, even if they wanted to. The economically stable powers will have to assume a more proactive role to stop this diffusion of state power within their areas of influence.

The diffusion of power to smaller nations and their coalitions is a double-edged sword. On the one hand it will provide a visible modicum of power to these smaller states and thereby increase their ability to be more assertive in matters that concern the wellbeing of their own nations. This will be all the more important to nations that are considered large in the regional context. Such assertiveness will lead to a greater sense of nationalism and will bring greater stability to the region. On the other hand, assertiveness that crosses a certain bound of normalcy will almost certainly bring about confrontation with other regional powers and also with the smaller nations of the region who would resent the overbearing approach. This situation is inimical to stability.

Irrespective of the repercussions of the slow diffusion of power away from the major powers and into groups of smaller nations, this process is unlikely to stop. The reactions of the larger powers to this slow diffusion of influence and power as well as the formation of regional groupings will be very different to those of the smaller powers because their own power will diminish while the smaller powers will gain in terms of their influence regionally and as groups, even in international debates. This is likely to lead to situation wherein the smaller powers will be more enthusiastic to embrace power diffusion through the formation of regional groups to the chagrin of larger powers. The reality is that even though the US will retain its primacy as a global power, its ability to intervene and change the course of events will diminish. However, even robust coalitions of small nations will not have the expanse of power necessary to enforce their writ even in regional contexts. The net result will be a global situation of uncertainty that will in turn create instability because smaller nations will tend to hedge their bets and create alliances to form a sort of 'great power' that would ensure their security. Such alliances may not always be homogenous in their outlook and therefore will not be robust enough to withstand the stress of ensuring even regional stability. The pointers are that a multi-nodal world will function erratically from a stability point of view, with unforeseen results and unpredictable actors taking centre stage.

GLOBALLY SHARED DOMAINS

Even though there are a large number of issues that bring about complete disagreement between nations, some of them almost irreconcilable in terms of the absolute basic principle of the challenge, there are three major areas that have been internationally recognised as shared environments. For centuries the international waters of the oceans have been considered accessible to all nations without prejudice, except in time of declared war. The process of defining the Exclusive Economic Zone (EEZ) of a sovereign state came about mainly because of the need that was felt by nations to protect their own coastal areas and the wealth contained in the immediate vicinity. In more recent times, the international community has made very serious attempts to create a similar situation for the use of space and cyberspace. In fact, in these domains there is an on-going attempt to establish the limitations of a zone similar to the EEZ in respect of the user nations. At an altruistic level this is an objective that the international community of nations should aspire to achieve. However, the realities are far removed from this.

Use of the Oceans[19]

The definition of EEZ and its acceptance by all nations are also becoming increasingly contested. The situation is complicated in areas where the EEZ of two nations overlap to some extent. Further, in recent times explorations have indicated that there could be valuable

---

19 Buck, Susan J., *The Global Commons: An Introduction*, Earthscan Publications, Abington, UK, 1998, Chapter 4, 'The Oceans'.

resources available on the seabed for exploitation, making even smaller nations reluctant to relinquish their claims or withdraw from contested areas. In some cases there have been attempts to extend the EEZ far more than what has been delineated in the international agreement. Again, such moves threaten the stability of the region, especially when the nation concerned is perceived as having regional hegemonic ambitions. Even though the oceans have been the pathways for development, conquest and globalisation of trade and commerce, their unimpeded use by all nations of the world is by no means assured. The control of the seas and attempts by a number of nations to gather a larger share of the oceanic wealth by contesting EEZ demarcations and also trying to extend their limits has introduced an element of instability in the use of the seas.

Seaborne Trade. International trade is almost completely dependent on commercial shipping capabilities. Even with the advent of much faster modes of transportation, movement of goods through the sea lines of communications remains the primary artery for almost all nations. The industrial might of most of highly developed nations of the world is critically dependent on the movement of raw material and energy resources across the seas. There have been threats to sea-going commercial vessels from the beginning of such trade activities. However the disruption of movement of goods along the sea lines can now become a critical failing point in the economy of a nation. The increase in piracy at the choke points in the global seaborne trade and commerce has now reached a stage wherein it is considered a global risk. However, there is only very limited consensus regarding the steps to be taken to ameliorate the risk that these activities pose to international stability.

Activities in Space

The space domain became active only in the 1950s and even then it took a number of years before its direct influence on security and defence issues of a nation became clearly apparent. In a short span of few decades space has become so important to the effectiveness of military forces and the functioning of almost all commercial and governance activities of the state that the loss of space capability is now considered catastrophic to national security. Space is now a vital domain that has to be defended for one's own security and as a corollary is also a critical vulnerability. The outcome has been that space has become a contested domain in spite of an international understanding that space should not be used to store weapons and that space assets must not be targeted.

There is a dichotomy in this situation. All modern military forces are almost completely dependent on space-based assets for communications, surveillance, targeting and for the precision of the weapons being employed. Considering that these assets are perhaps the centres of gravity for the performance of a military force, it would seem that they are legitimate targets to be attacked in times of war, much like the other assets of a military force. The belief that space-based assets should not be attacked or disrupted therefore is perhaps a naïve notion when weighed in reality.

Even then various attempts are on-going to develop globally acceptable governance norms on the use of space. Mechanisms like the Outer Space Treaty in 1967, the Moon Treaty of 1979, as well as UN initiatives like the Prevention of Arms race in Outer Space are examples of such initiatives. In 2008, the European Union suggested an explicit Code of Conduct (CoC) regarding space activities and on 6 June 2012 launched a multilateral diplomatic process to negotiate an International Code of Conduct for Outer Space.[20] While this CoC is gradually gaining acceptability, it is non-binding and its conceptualisation is essentially premised on the belief that states are ethical and responsible actors. In reality, there is no verification protocol and these initiatives have extremely limited relevance.[21]

Irrespective of the formal or unwritten rules that govern the use of space, it is clear that space is becoming congested with more nations attempting to become space powers. Even today, space exploration is

---

20 Lele, Ajey, 'Space Code of Conduct: Inadequate Mechanism', *IDSA Comment*, Institute of Defence Studies and Analyses, New Delhi, 18 June 2012, http://idsa.in/idsacomments/SpaceCodeofConductInadequateMechanism_AjeyLele_1 accessed on 25 June 2012.

21 ibid.

an extremely expensive activity and also needs a highly evolved and sophisticated technology base to succeed. These two factors somewhat restrict the number of nations that are able to actively participate in space activities, but do not limit the use of space-based assets by nations through partnership arrangements and commercially available applications. The commercial applications are very lucrative for the vendors, leading to high levels of competitiveness in the utilisation of space. Activities in space will continue to increase and the utopian goal of peaceful coexistence in this domain is unfortunately not obtainable. There is almost a resigned acceptance that space will become the next battleground when the technologically advanced nations come into direct confrontation with each other. The results could be extremely damaging to the international community and the prevailing fragile stability.

Cyberspace

Cyberspace is the latest environment in which nations are testing the competence of their rivals and competitors while also monitoring their allies' capabilities. In a very short period of time, much less than even the time it took for space-based systems to become invaluable, cyberspace has become an all-encompassing domain that envelopes almost all activities of any consequence. The information revolution that is constantly happening as an on-going phenomenon is the product of cyberspace activities and capabilities. Cyberspace provides almost instant global connectivity. Almost like a testimony to the base level of human nature, there has been a simultaneous rise in the efforts to disrupt the harmony of cyberspace.

For reasons that are not immediately apparent, the international community has not tried, more than in a token manner, to establish some basic protocols regarding safeguarding the cyber activities across all nations. Therefore, intrusions in the cyber domain have become fairly common with some of them becoming alarmingly disruptive to the conduct of normal financial and commercial dealings. The question that is now being debated is whether or not such intrusions have been state-sponsored or the work of rogue elements and individuals. There is speculation that the ability of nations to intrude offensively in a rival's cyberspace through the use of state-sponsored agencies is one of the main reasons for the lack of international consensus in regulating the use of cyberspace. The reality is that both state-condoned/sponsored and individual cyber-attacks have been taking place in the past few years. This brings out another trend that has come into predominance only in recent times. While disruption in space required a great deal of resource availability, cyberspace is open to any individual with sufficient expertise and does not require elaborate infrastructure to establish a disruption. As a result, nations are now expending an unnaturally large proportion of their resources in ensuring cyber security.

Commonality

Global shared environments can bring about both stability and confrontation. The need is for responsible nations to ensure that the rights of every nation, irrespective of size, status or capability, to use these spaces to improve the lot of their people is protected and assured. The current geo-strategic environment is not conducive to such a situation. In fact the very opposite seems to be the case, with the major economies of the world attempting to ensure that their own access to these environments is trouble free, irrespective of the broader accessibility issues.

More than this self-serving attitude, which should not be a surprise in the global political arena, it is the development of policies and capabilities aimed at denial of access to shared global areas that is a matter of concern. It is also not surprising that anti-access and area denial capabilities are being developed by the larger nations. It is conceivable that these capabilities will be put to use against equally strong nations in a contest for control of areas and environments that should naturally be shared. However, such use could also raise the potential for direct confrontation and therefore may not happen very commonly. On the other hand it is almost certain that these capabilities will be used against smaller and less powerful nations to deny them access or in a deterrent manner. In the long term these activities will tend to create instability regionally that will culminate in international destabilisation.

Status of Combating Powers

> Aggression grows in unsettled or disorderly times and explodes in a power vacuum.
>
> Bevin Alexander[22]

Conflicts of different hue have become commonplace in the world. The reasons for two parties entering into conflict spread across a very large spectrum, from invasion to human migration necessitated by natural disasters or man-made calamities. Conflict between two sovereign states is by itself a complex issue that can only be resolved through intense and intricate negotiations. In the past few decades there has been a noticeable increase in the number of non-state entities—individuals and groups—perpetuating acts of violence against well-defined states. Resolution of conflict in which one party is a non-state entity, or at times covertly state sponsored groups, requires a much greater amount of effort and more importantly a longer period of time.

The negotiations are complicated by the lack of accountability of non-state groups for their actions, that could at times be fully against the norms built into the international law of armed conflict. This creates a very delicate situation during the negotiations, especially when one party is a state that has adhered to such laws. In these circumstances it will also become difficult to place the responsibility of the actions of the group. While this by itself may not be a stumbling block to negotiations, the issue of responsibility assumes far greater importance in the implementation of the negotiated peace. It is more than likely that such negotiated peace may not be long lasting, especially if the non-state entity concerned has ideologically splintered groups operating at the fringes of the mainstream.

There are two factors to be considered when considering the status of the combating powers and its influence on the stability or otherwise of the politico-strategic environment. First, the power of deterrence

---

22 Alexander, Bevin, *The Future of Warfare*, WW Norton & Co Inc., New York, 1995, p. 19.

is greatly reduced in the case of non-state entities because they do not respond to any traditional levers or inducements. This complicates the pre-conflict reconciliation process and reduces the chances of its success since one option; that of deterrence; is effectively removed. Second, is the question of the legality of the non-state entities. In a broad manner, members of non-state groups do not have the protection that is inherently applicable to the members of a sovereign state's defence forces. In a tangential thinking process, this could also be the reason why they do not feel the compulsion to operate within the existing laws. However, the result is that this situation complicates the manner in which the state's defence forces can and do conduct operations against such irregular groups.

This brings about the need to debate the intangible issue of morality and ethics. The questions of morality and ethics are further obscured by the fact that, more often than not, such diffused conflicts will be the result of external intervention into a failing or failed state in order to stabilise it. For that reason, it is vital for any nation attempting to stabilise a failing state to have, as a minimum, the moral high ground that is only gained by international approval for the intervention through the United Nations. The UN is considered by a number of nations to have lost its authority, but in a world that is gradually disintegrating to a state of comparative lawlessness, this is the only body that carries a modicum of moral stature. Physical prowess and the capabilities to enforce its will reduce in actuality in direct proportion to the lack of moral authority to undertake the actions being contemplated by a nation. Destabilisation of a region is a certainty when a nation applies its power without the backing of sufficient moral standing and ethical correctness in its actions.

Summing Up...

The global strategic environment is in a state of constant flux for a number of reasons—some minor, with effects that are short lived and some more influential in altering the relationships between nations in a bilateral as well as multi-lateral manner. One of the factors that was initially considered to be of short term consequence but has proven to be of much greater impact has been the national debt crisis that is currently debilitating the US. The political stalemate that has developed inhibits the ability of the Government to initiate direct measures to overcome the issue and has slowly turned a financial situation into a security challenge for the nation. Nevertheless, the US has the inherent capability to not only confront and get over this challenge but also to regain its global leadership status that has been somewhat diminished in the past few years.

In this context, China's continued economic growth; its on-going military modernisation program that has been recently given a further impetus; and more importantly its expansionist stance in terms of political influence, resource assimilation and the determination to offensively negotiate disputed geographic boundaries have to be analysed to obtain a true picture of the global strategic environment. The extreme combative swings in the China's foreign policy initiatives and its proclivity to automatically negate or veto any move that is initiated by the Western nations to enhance global stability creates a volatile environment. Smaller nations will find it difficult to function within such an environment. This situation is actually a borderline case for smaller nations and the more fragile nations could, in an extreme case, become a failed state fairly rapidly. Regional stability envelopes an added factor under these circumstances.

Chapter 6

CHALLENGES TO GEO-POLITICAL STABILITY

Nation states are the basic and dominant units that determine global stability. All changes to the status of nation states bring in an element of uncertainty, even if only at the national domestic level, and uncertainty regarding anything is the first step towards instability. These changes could be short-term, with the state reverting to its original status swiftly and with relative ease or long term wherein the change may have extended repercussions and could even be permanent. Further, changes can be rapid and revolutionary or manifest in an evolutionary manner over a long period of time. Irrespective of the type or rate of change its significance has to be measured purely through the effect it creates in terms of impact and longevity. In this regard, permanent changes obviously have the most enduring impact on regional and international geo-political stability.

There are a number of factors that could initiate changes to the manner in which a nation state views itself and also the status accorded to it by other nations. In addition some factors could also directly influence the internal status of the nation in terms of its stability; both economic and political; and future prospects[1]. One of the major factors that must always be considered in this context is the overarching security environment in its prevailing situation

---

1   National Research Council, *Understanding the Changing Planet: Strategic Directions for the Geographical Sciences*, The National Academies Press, Washington D.C., 2010, Chapter 9, 'How Are Geopolitical Shifts Influencing Peace and Stability', pp. 91-96.

and also the predictable future. Security challenges are ever present hazards to geo-political stability and can be broadly classified into three categories. The first is state-driven threats, which means that the threat originates and is actively supported by another state who would become the adversary. These threats could be classified as the most dangerous to the survival of the state and are the ones that could cause the maximum disruption and instability. Guarding against such threats require the build-up and maintenance of a robust military capability well-supported by other elements of national power, functioning within a broad whole-of-government approach to national security. The second is non-state-driven threats, like terrorism and insurgency, which could originate within the state or be perpetuated or directed by groups outside the borders of the state. These threats could also become equally dangerous to the state in terms of its existence if they are allowed to gain support and permitted to grow unchecked. However, containing insurgencies, especially the ones generated from within the state, requires a very clear and comprehensive strategy that goes beyond the employment of military forces and into the realm of socio-political and economic reform.

The third category is events-driven threats, which could emanate from natural disasters in the nation or the region, or man-made disruptive events in a state within the region needing humanitarian intervention of some kind. Any such event could generate security challenges through human migration, creating failing states or simply by straining the nation's ability to respond effectively. Normally the effects of events-driven threats will be comparatively short-lived although they could have long-term impact. These challenges are also more difficult to predict in comparison to the state or non-state driven threats which can be envisaged through proper analysis and intelligence gathering. The security apparatus of the state needs to retain a more than normal flexibility to cater for and contain events-driven threats. However, all three threats enumerated above will produce consequential sub-challenges to security that can have a domino effect. These sub-challenges will also have linkages—mostly indirect but at times very clearly direct—to each other that go across the categories, making the distinction between them somewhat diffused.

Challenges to the geo-political stability, global or regional, can emerge as a result of one significant event or can be the culmination of a number of congruent events of lesser magnitude. Therefore, it is difficult to list all the events and factors that could lead to geo-political instability or become a challenge to the even flow of international relations. In an overarching analysis the challenges being faced by a large number of nations—ones that are not unique to a particular nation state—and which would in the long term become issues that would affect the stability of all nations and regions can be brought together under three broad groupings. The groupings are, the restructuring of the strategic landscape; issues of democracy and national governance; and the significance of the Islamic geography.

Restructuring of the Strategic Landscape

When the Cold War began at the end of World War II it was believed that the world had become a more dangerous, and by implication, a more volatile place. However, hindsight in the second decade of the 21st Century clearly indicates that the era of the Cold War was a time of certainties and an assured stability, although the potential for it to degenerate into catastrophic instability was always visible. The current strategic environment is more volatile than it has ever been in world history. The reasons for this volatility are many and they are not being analysed in detail here as such. However, this volatility compels all nations to rethink the future and since the future is far from predictable with any level of assurance, the security strategies and capabilities need to be reoriented on a continuous basis[2]. This increases the resource burden on all nations, with the smaller nations struggling to keep up with the basic demand. As compared to even a few decades ago, the chances of nations with average stability sliding into a fragile state is much higher now. This trend will only exacerbate into the future. The strategic landscape in most regions of the world is in flux.

Another post-World War II development that influences and changes the strategic landscape is the gradual erosion of the once distinct division between war and peace. In the past sixty years the status of war has gone from open declaration of war, to undeclared

---

2 Davies, Robert, 'Strategy and the New Uncertainty', Chapter 3 in Verity, Julie (ed), *The New Strategic Landscape: Innovative Perspectives on Strategy*, Palgrave Macmillan, New York, 2012.

but clearly visible state of war, nations have now reached a stage where even when they are in a state of war they tend to openly state otherwise. The common understanding of 'war' and the term 'a state of war' themselves have been transformed. This diffusion in the demarcation between a state of war and of peace—irrespective of whether the disruption is internal or external—has necessitated the restructuring of the strategic environment for most nations even if comparative stability exists within their borders. Two more reasons compel this change. First, challenges that emerge in the contemporary scenario are more dynamic and complex than ever before, making the development and implementation of appropriate strategies extremely difficult. Second, the strategic context and operational characteristics of war have altered considerably, one being defined by a broader appreciation of global interdependence on a number of issues; and the other being influenced by factors inimical to the conduct of an 'orderly' war fought within the internationally accepted norms of its conduct. The predictability of the strategic environment is currently at its lowest and likely to remain so at least into the medium term future.

Small power states tend to treat nuclear- and conventionally-armed greater powers with a certain amount of respect. Even so, it is seen that provoking smaller states beyond a point could be dangerous since their reaction cannot be predicted. A minor conflict could erode relationships that are in the process of being built-up and are not formalised. On the other hand, smaller nations cannot take great power support for granted, even in cases where formalised and endorsed treaties exist. In all cases, intelligence gathering at the strategic level is never fool proof and therefore strategic predictions tend to be faulty.[3] Following on from this challenge, even in minor conflicts the achievement of the desired end-state is not possible for a single domain-centric military force. An integrated approach to security becomes absolutely necessary.

Contemporary Issues

There are three major issues that necessitate the continuous restructuring of the strategic security environment and also dominate

---

3   Cohen, Ariel & Hamilton, Robert E., 'The Russian Military in the Georgia War: Lessons and Implications', *ERAP Monograph*, Strategic Studies Institute, US Army War College, Carlisle, PA, 2011, pp. 70-73.

the process[4]. First is the inability of almost all nations to distinguish the large strategic security threats that need a whole-of-government approach to nullify from the lesser threats that could be neutralised by the military forces alone. The reaction to almost all threats to a nation will involve the employment of its military forces in some form or the other. This is a historically proven fact and is unlikely to change into the future. The requirement therefore, is for a nation to be able to differentiate the threats that the military alone cannot diffuse and require a concerted effort by all elements of national power to overcome. The inability to do this effectively could bring about a situation wherein the military is required to achieve objectives that will be difficult if not impossible to accomplish on its own. The concept of integrating all elements of national power to create a stable security environment is now well developed. However, currently there is no single nation that can actually conduct a comprehensive whole-of-nation campaign to achieve national objectives. The acceptance that military forces alone can very seldom ensure national security in all its guises has brought about a restructuring of the security equation both domestically and externally for most nations.

Second, is the increasing economic interdependence of nations and its foreign policy ramifications. From a security perspective, the influence of economic aid is even more important than traditional policy inputs in structuring the strategic landscape. In comparison to the mid-20th Century, currently a much larger number of 'independent' nations are reliant on foreign economic aid to meet more than 50 percent of their domestic requirements. There are many consequences that stem from this situation. It means that a larger number of nations are dependent on donor nations, of which there are not many, for their well-being. The economic downturn of a donor nation can almost immediately affect a number of recipient nations, creating an unfortunate domino effect where the ripples increase in effect as they travel further from the nucleus. Normally such instability would be regional, but in the contemporary context of global trade and commerce it could spread to other regions as well.

---

4   Richards, Julian, *A Guide to National Security: Threats, Responses, and Strategies*, Oxford University Press, Oxford, UK, 2012, pp. 32-35, 48-50, 70-72, & 116-128.

The third issue that creates instability, within a region as well as globally, is the constantly debated question of global justice. Uncontrolled refugee flow caused by civil wars, natural disasters like floods, famine and earthquakes, calculated genocide and/or poverty is a humanitarian issue with profound security implications. This in turn increases the pressure on more stable nations to intervene in the troubled areas and brings with it the issues of legality and the attendant moral and ethical issues of external intervention. The absence of a universally accepted legal baseline for intervention and the limited power that the UN wields further complicate the process for all nations. As a corollary, the democratic nations of the world are increasingly trying to bring the perpetrators of war crimes, such as genocide, to justice in the international court of justice. While this is a relatively recent development, it has far reaching consequences for the conduct of war and armed intervention. It is not far-fetched now to conceive that the leader of a nation that has intervened externally on humanitarian grounds could face criminal charges in the international court—justly or unjustly. The absolute moral high ground from which interventions in the second half of the 20th Century were launched is now shaky and uncertain. The strategic landscape is altering abruptly and in ways that were not thought possible even two decades ago.

Challenges of Immigration

Flowing from the unintended flow of refugees is the issue of immigration. All members of the United Nations have an obligation to accept a laid down quota of genuine refugees and assimilate them into the larger society of the nation. Most of the flow however will be directed towards the more mature, developed and stable nations some of whom are less than willing to accept an uninterrupted flow of immigrants. The reason for this unwillingness is mostly rooted in economic pragmatism, since the national economic outlay to fully integrate immigrants into the host nation can at times become prohibitive, even for comparatively affluent nations. There is also an underlying reason that is gradually becoming more apparent for this reluctance to accept immigrant population in any great numbers.

Most stable nations have an already established and homogeneous cultural, and in majority of cases, a cohesive ethnic identity. Dependent on the size of the population, mass immigration could quickly alter the ethnic make-up of the nation and almost immediately make the society multi-ethnic. Such a change will always bring with it the challenges of integration of the migrant into the already established cultural ethos that will tend to foster a sense of 'us and them'. The issue is double sided in that, the migrant must be willing to assimilate and the host society must be willing to accept. In a majority of cases this is not the case and minor incidents of confrontation will be the beginning of a divisive force that has the power to break up a nation. The reluctance of established nations to accept large migrant population stems from these concerns, which have not been assuaged by the challenges being faced by the bigger nations of Europe who had accepted large numbers of immigrants in the immediate post-colonial time.

Although it is difficult to make generalisations based on only half a century of evidence, two trends can be clearly noticed in the immigration and assimilation process of the post-World War II era. First is that a majority of immigrants are inclined to group together in the host nation, physically and socially—only a natural tendency considering the fact they have been replanted in an alien environment. This however could have the unfortunate consequence of their being segregated from the mainstream and becoming alienated almost on a permanent basis. There are instances of even third generation immigrants in European nations being unable to speak the language of the host nation. Such alienation will always create a separate religious or ethnic state within a state with all the issues—social, economic, political and legal—that come with such informal but rigid divisions.

The second trend is the broader political changes that are bound to take place when the first trend of isolation rather than assimilation becomes clearly visible. Political changes in stable nations are normally gradual. Violent revolutions that have replaced established ruling elite in a number of cases in history, as well as in the 2011 'Arab Spring' uprisings are the result of growing instability in the nation, generally brought about through blatant misrule. The primary political change that has taken place in the democratic nations that have accepted immigrants in significant numbers is the emergence of politics based on religious convictions. For a number of centuries the Western nations, and by extrapolation most other nations following the same or similar models of democracy, have consciously kept religion and the state separate. The advent of Islam challenges this very concept. Over a period of time the immigrant populations, predominantly of the Islamic faith, have started to demand the joining of governance and religion. Nations who have a large immigrant Muslim population find that there is a demand to change their political system to bring religion and governance closer. In some nations this is taking place in a multi-ethnic manner with other religious denominations also opting to create an overlap between religion and politics.

It is a fair statement that a majority of immigrants, particularly the ones that arrive as refugees fleeing persecution, civil war and/or natural or man-made calamities, tend to make the best of the opportunity made available to better their lives. However, there is a high probability that there will also be some subversive elements that arrive as immigrants. A particularly challenging issue for the host nations is the manner in which they have to deal with these embedded subversive elements within the migrant community. The need in all cases is assimilation and not segregation—something that can only be achieved by concerted effort that has to come from both the host nation and the immigrant community. Failure of this process will bring about the break-up of the social fabric of the nation. The security implications of such a break up are both domestic and external.

Immigration of people from the less fortunate places to the more stable and economically established countries will continue. By default the Western democratic societies are more prone to be the target of aspiring immigrants from developing nations. These movements will be both through the established legal process and through illegal channels. The security implications of such movements will be far-reaching, creating a constant pressure on the strategic landscape of the developed world and making it change in hitherto unforeseen ways. Fault lines within the broader society of a nation—because of the arrival of a new culture, ethnicity or religion—create new security challenges that the nation may not have forecast and is therefore unable to withstand. Governments across the world have to understand and come to grips with the paradigm that fractures in the socio-economic, religious, ethnic and cultural makeup of the nation, primarily the consequences of unassimilated immigration, are the new frontiers of national security.

Issues of Democracy and Governance

A democratic form of government is universally considered as the optimum to meet the aspirations of the people of a nation. This is not to say that this form of government is flawless or that it cannot be corrupted, but that it provides the people of a particular state a sense of participation in determining their own destiny when the process is carried out with a modicum of honesty and directness. However, the progress of the democratic process, as well as the quest for increasing individual freedom for citizens have started to create negative overall influences in the governance of the nation. Even the stable and established democracies of the western world are facing issues with the concept of an open democracy that guarantees certain unassailable fundamental freedoms to all its citizens[5]. The exercise of a particular freedom, which may be enshrined in the constitution of the nation, by one individual or a group is now very often being indicated as impinging on another individual or group's guaranteed freedom. Tolerance—religious, ethnic, cultural and political—which is the cornerstone of a democracy is gradually waning, being replaced with vociferous demands for individual freedoms as interpreted by narrow viewpoints. Governments are now besieged with the plethora of opinions that a single issue raises within a state.

Diminishing Decision-making Ability

A large number of democracies in the world practice a multi-party oriented democratic system. This provides a platform for even peripheral concepts and ideas to be represented, which in itself is a positive influence on governance. However, it is increasingly being noticed that multi-party governments are being constrained in taking decisive action even on matters that are of great importance to the well-being of the nation. In certain cases governments have reached a sort of a grid-lock in their decision-making process, creating situations wherein the country is almost at a standstill in all aspects. Multi-party governments normally have diminished decision-making abilities purely because of the need to cater to varying political requirements

---

5   Martell, Luke, 'National Differences and the Rethinking of Social Democracy: Third Ways in Europe', Chapter 5 in Munshi, Surendra, & Abraham, Biju Paul (eds), *Good Governance, Democratic Societies and Globalisation*, Sage Publications India, New Delhi, 2004, pp. 93-109.

of the constituent members. This is not conducive to creating clear developmental strategies for the nation and detracts from providing focused guidance at the strategic level.

The democratic system of governance has been in existence for a long time. During that time there has been a visibly increased tendency in all democracies to incorporate greater checks and balances on the actions of all elected representatives, partly because of the abuse of power that has taken place in a number of instances. Over a period of time this has become a constraint to open decision-making and led to a dilution of power at the executive level. There are occasions in the development of nations where decisive and purposeful leadership is the primary requirement to overcome challenges to the development of the nation. In contemporary democracies such leadership is only possible in times of great crisis for the nation when a strong leader is essential to provide clear forward guidance. In most cases, the decision-making will be a meandering process that detracts from optimising the nation's potential for development towards greater prosperity.

Another factor that diminishes the decision-making ability and the veracity of decisions itself is the public apathy that is apparent in a majority of the established democracies. One of the main reasons for this is the general lack of trust in politicians, who are often caricatured as corrupt and self-serving. While they are elected by the general public, the lack of trust displayed by the same people is at times unfathomable, and is a negative influence in the acceptance of government actions, even if they have been well-thought through and could be broadly beneficial to the state. This is a vicious cycle that can become self-perpetuating if not carefully addressed and contained. Ideally an elected representative should have proven himself/herself to be a person of integrity and able to contribute to the larger good of the society. Becoming politically active should not be seen as a profession, but as an extension of service the nation. However, the current trend in most democratic nations is for the political leadership to be 'professional politicians' without any other professional experience. This also contributes to the lack of trust of political leadership. The erosion of moral authority of the democratically elected representatives is one of the primary issues that, by itself, could bring about the fall of democracy in a nation. A further outcome is that a strong democratically elected leader is always viewed with an appreciable amount of suspicion regarding the reliability of his/her democratic credentials. The overt strength of a leader creates the fear of such a leader becoming autocratic. A fine balance of being a forceful leader without seeming to be autocratic is difficult to achieve, but is the hallmark of an effective democratic leader capable of guiding a nation through a crisis. Such a balance would also have to be tempered with the public perception of the 'right' combination of democratic and autocratic leadership.

A nation must have clear agendas and a focused approach if it is to improve its economic, security and political stability. This can only be achieved through transparent and correct decisions in all aspects of governance. The negative influence of the democratic process on the decision-making of a government can become a challenge to the progress of a nation, which in turn will impact on both domestic and foreign policies of a nation and affect the broader regional geo-political environment.

Threats to Stability

Throughout history, no nation has been able to function effectively in complete isolation. However, in the contemporary environment, this interdependence has evolved into a vital aspect of the well-being of a nation. Today, a threat to one nation will invariably influence others in the region and depending on the size of the nation involved, can even have global repercussions. There are a number of issues that could spill over from and into democratic nations purely by virtue of the openness of the society associated with democracies. Transnational crime[6] and the challenges that come with humanitarian catastrophe—through natural causes or man-made—will almost always spread across nations, irrespective of borders. The issue will be even more acute when the nation that is most affected is unable to contain the problems, almost immediately escalating the threat to a regional level.

New democratic sates or the ones that are progressing towards democratisation—being formed even now as an aftermath of the colonial era—are often fragile both economically and politically. Therefore, they are more prone to failure when faced with even a

---

6 Albanese, Jay S., & Reichel, Philip L., (eds), *Transnational Organized Crime: An Overview of Six Continents*, Sage Publications India, New Delhi, 2014.

minor challenge that an established democracy would have been able to weather without much trouble. Such states, if they fail, can serve as global pathways that facilitate the relatively easy movement of criminals and terrorists as well as the proliferation of weapons of all kind. They can rapidly become havens for international illegal activities that threaten the stability of the entire region. In these circumstances the more stable nations would have to intervene to ensure regional stability. However, an inherently democratic nation will find that recourse to such intervention will have to be a last resort, which may result in too little action initiated too late to neutralise the challenge.

Democratic governments are affected by the electoral cycle of the nation—every government has to be elected back to power by the general public. A great deal of effort is therefore made to ensure that the perception regarding the government across the nation is positive. This leads to an extraordinary situation wherein the media wields an unnaturally high level of influence on the functioning of the government, especially closer to the end of the election cycle. In less stable democracies the government may even be inclined to initiate short-term populist measures to placate the media as well as the voting population. In economically strained conditions this will contribute to making the state more fragile and make it less able to withstand the consequences. While the influence of the media may not be very high in all circumstances, in some conditions it can evolve into a critical factor that could produce far-reaching effects.

To a large extent most nations rely on the military forces to ensure their sovereignty and independence. This has been the case traditionally and continues to be so, even if in a somewhat more nuanced manner. Even the contemporary concept of a whole-of-government approach to national security, which is based on the employment of all elements of national power in a contextual manner, is underpinned by the ability of the military forces to secure the theatre of operations. The military forces of democratic nations continue to operate within the laws of armed conflict (LOAC) as accepted through the Geneva Conventions and follow-on articles. However, the threats to national security have altered considerably and now consist of groups perpetrating acts of violence and terrorism without any regard for the established norms of combat and international law. The consequence has been a decrease in military effectiveness to counter and contain threats that emerge at random and tend to be non-traditional in a majority of cases. Democracies struggle to neutralise physical challenges to the nation while keeping within the accepted norms of LOAC and also retaining the high moral ground necessary to ensure the legitimacy of all actions that are initiated. The rigidity of the LOAC as applicable now can become a destabilising force by restricting the actions that a nation could legitimately undertake to protect its interests.

Democracy by itself is the best available form of government that meets the aspirations of people to be able to exercise basic fundamental rights. However, its implementation can at times create issues that tend to create more instability than stability. This is particularly apparent in newly independent nations attempting to establish democratic rule. Under these circumstances it can be suggested that a benign 'directed democracy'—under a powerful and forceful leadership, in a context-driven manner—would suit the conditions better and avoid a nation being pushed to a fragile state because of democratic processes going awry. This might seem almost heretical to the advocates of the democratic process, but seems to be a solution to the ills that are becoming apparent in almost all democracies to a greater or lesser extent. The question is whether or not this sort of governance is sustainable without the rise of autocracy. In determining this, the culture, education, established institutions like the military and judiciary and their capacity to provide stability will be vital. What is clearly visible is that irrespective of the stability or otherwise of democracies, they are all under some kind of pressure that if left unattended, will increase the likelihood of strategic instability.

Significance of the Emerging Islamic Geography

Followers of the Islamic religion account for 23 percent of the world's population, although 69 percent of them are geographically concentrated and live in nations that are more than 87 percent Islamic.[7] Further, of the 31 percent of the world's Islamic population that does

---

7 Libicki, Martin C., Shatz, Howard J., & Taylor, Julie E., *Global Demographic Change and Its Implications for Military Power*, RAND Publications, Santa Monica, CA, 2011, p. 40.

not live in Muslim-majority countries, almost half live in India, making them also geographically concentrated.

The revival of the Islamic identity has been in progress for nearly half a century. However, it is only in the past two decades that the revival has seen greater impetus and a more focused approach. There is a palpable move towards cultural and religious assertion in all Muslim countries and among the adherents of the faith at large, greatly facilitated by the ease with which global communications can be extensively used for almost instantaneous networking and information transfer. There are two fundamental differences between Islam and most of the other major religions. First, Islam is a borderless ideology with its followers considering themselves first Muslims and only thereafter anything else in terms of nationality and ethnicity. Second, it combines the three arms of the government—executive, judiciary and parliament—which is consciously kept separate and above religion in democratic states, into a religious code. In effect, the Islamic code of governance directly challenges and overrides the separation of the state and religion which is a fundamental principle of the western concept of nation states.

The Islamic nations, mainly in the Middle East, face two basic issues that challenge the ability of their governments to exert sufficient control over their populations. Until the uprisings of the 'Arab Spring' took place in 2011, most of the nations were ruled by autocratic leaders or by hereditary monarchies with almost no vestige of democracy to link the government to the general population. The population within the country is kept under control through a calculated process of state-delivered largess to ensure an acceptable living standard and repression through efficient policing capabilities, creating a sort of autocratic welfare state. The wealth that can be distributed to keep the people on-side in this context is generated through energy resources. The depletion of these resources would essentially lead to a diminishing capability to undertake welfare activities. This will mean that both the nations who do not have such resources and those that deplete their resources rapidly will almost certainly face unrest, instability and ultimate collapse.

The second issue is one of population distribution, interlinked to education. There are concerns that most of the Islamic nations face a youth bulge in their population with a significant percentage of the population being in the age group of 15 to 35.[8] By and large, this bulge group is educated within a state-sponsored system that is primarily based on religious education but does not normally create adequate awareness of global issues. Nor does the system prepare the youth to undertake advanced studies in the international academic sphere. Unemployment because of lack of opportunities within these nations—which normally do not have a developed industrial base—and difficulties in obtaining employment in the international market breed frustration that opportunistic reactionary groups channel to their own needs. These nations are fertile breeding grounds for the recruitment of frustrated youth to revolutionary movements.

Third is the issue of radical or extreme religious doctrine that is propagated—at times with state approval—to expand Islamic religious influence. The world-wide revolutionary Islamic social movement, articulated by the Wahabi doctrine that originated in the 18th Century in Saudi Arabia, adheres to a particularly strict form of Islam. A less than complete understanding of these beliefs, their apparent contradictions with other religions and its in-built intolerance of other belief systems makes this doctrine one that polarises people purely on the basis of their religion. This is anathema to most democratic nations and makes Islam stand apart from the accepted norms of these societies. The discomfort felt by a large number of Muslim immigrants in western democracies is partially because of this reason. The result is the creation of destabilising forces within the broader society of the nation in question.

The inability or unwillingness of a significant percent of the immigrant population to assimilate and the recent increase in global terrorism perpetuated by persons of the Islamic faith combine to create a less than complementary image of the people and the religion. This is further exacerbated by regional Muslim separatist struggles—normally manifest as acts of wanton terrorism—which have been on-going in a number of nations. These struggles have created a need for individual nations to deal with both separatism and terrorism on their own, at great expense, in order to maintain the sovereignty of the state. Since these separatist movements are mostly driven by the

---

8   Howe, Neil, & Jackson, Richard, 'Battle of the Youth Bulge', *The National Interest*, July/August 2008, pp. 33-40.

desire to create an 'Islamic state' as opposed to the more religiously tolerant ones, there is increasing belief that people who practice the so called moderate Islam are only the ones who do not want to fight for their religion and that there is really no moderate Islamic doctrine. This development is detrimental to better understanding of the religion and improving religious stability regionally and globally. There is a need for cooperation between nations facing the divisive forces that stem from religious extremism to ensure that the geo-political stability is not adversely affected.

International terrorism is now a fact of life, however discomforting it may be to accept as such and is the favoured tool of most terrorist activities. That such terrorist activities are mainly led by Islamic movements is again uncomfortable for the people of the religion to accept. The Western nations have also underestimated the extent to which the 'jihadi' theology has spread among the religiously inclined, making it easier for the tangential groups to operate. There is also increasing decentralisation of the organisation and constantly innovative operational concepts are being developed, making the groups effective systems with in-built flexibility to survive through adaptation.

The primary effect of these changes is to destabilise the geo-political environment and create fissures through dividing even traditionally homogenous nations on cultural, ethnic and religious grounds. Extremism, within any religion, is extremely difficult to counter and neutralise, especially in tolerant and democratic nations. Governments need to develop and institute long-term measures to avoid giving the divisive forces sufficient traction to gain a foothold within the fabric of the society.

Summing Up...

For nearly half a millennia, global stability has been built on the bedrock of the concept of nation states, which has been held sacrosanct in international politics. All global interactions stem from the premise of the inviolability of a nation state. Therefore, it is only natural that any change in the status of a nation brings with it uncertainty and accompanying instability. The status of a nation is determined primarily by three factors—the perception of other nations; internal domestic stability; and the ability of the nation to ensure its own strategic security, using all its power elements.

Ever since the end of World War II and the beginning of the Cold War, the global strategic landscape has been continually altering at a rate that is faster than witnessed before. The restructuring of the geo-political environment has become an on-going process, thereby keeping it in a permanent state of flux. The volatility of the global security scenario is demonstrated clearly by the fact that the distinction between war and peace has almost become non-existent. Another indicator of the prevalent uncertainty is the proclivity of nations to employ the military forces to address any emerging challenge. The larger threats must always be dealt within the concept of a whole-of-government approach, whereas minor threats could be contained by the employment of military forces. However, they have been brought together for the military forces to solve, even in cases where the military may not be the optimum tool.

The strategic security environment of a nation upon which the security policies are based are affected by three factors—in unison or independently, but on a regular basis. These are—the economic interdependence of nations; the lack of ability, or the unwillingness of the so-called developed world to ensure global justice; and the unintended flow of refugees that could overwhelm the host nation. It is believed that only a democratic form of government will be capable of containing rapid changes in the strategic security environment.

It may indeed be true that a democratic form of government is the optimum, relative to other forms of governance, if practised altruistically and meets the aspirations of the people. However, democracies have deteriorated in their delivery of governance, because of the necessity to form multi-party coalition governments and also the gradual encroachment of personal corruption amongst the lawmakers. Such a situation could lead to a paralysis of the government. In other cases, the flaw is in the proclivity of the incumbent to move towards an autocratic form, because of the democratic majority that he/she has won. In turn, this trend could manifest as a de-facto dictatorship under the veneer of 'staged' elections. This is a dichotomy. Post-colonial nations have been particularly vulnerable to becoming fragile democracies and a number have succumbed to being dictatorships.

These nations tend to have an over-reliance on the military forces to ensure stability, often at the cost of diminishing democratic values.

The revival of the Islamic identity that is being witnessed across the world is really not a new phenomenon. It has actually been in progress ever since the end of World War I and the break-up of the Ottoman Empire. However, in the last three decades there has been a noticeable trend towards an exaggerated assertion of Islamic religious identity, even in nations where they are only a minority. This trend has further led to both overt and covert support for the propagation of radical religious doctrine, which invariably culminates in violent terrorism. This is now a global malaise that brings instability to the nation and region. The current global instability is primarily a product of this one factor.

Challenges to global geo-political stability are many and new ones are emerging at multiple levels. They have to be also dealt with at the appropriate levels to ensure that the challenges are contained. However, there is a palpable tendency, particularly within democratic nations, to use military forces across the board and at all levels to address these challenges. Such a strategy is unlikely to bring full closure to the challenge and therefore will not bring about a restoration of stability. In fact, there is a likelihood of an impetus being provided to destabilising forces.

Military forces are only one of the elements of national power. In order to convert its battlefield successes into tangible victory for the nation, it is necessary to adopt a whole-of-government approach to dealing with security challenges. A holistic approach based on this concept is difficult to achieve, especially when some elements of national power do not fully understand the nuances of national security in the modern context. Military victories can only be converted to political success when a concerted effort is made by all elements of national power.

Chapter 7

EMERGENCE OF NEW GLOBAL PLAYERS

In the past few years a great deal of discussion has taken place regarding the rise of China and the apparent decline of the power of the United States and its imminent fall from a position of primacy in the world order. However, the decline of the US, if it does happen at all, will not be radical but gradual with sufficient number of opportunities for the nation to arrest the decline and reclaim its position of primacy. At least for the mid-term future, if not the foreseeable future, the US will continue to be the only global power. This situation does not mean that other nations are not improving their inherent capabilities and progressing towards becoming active global entities. In fact, the capability and capacity gaps between the US and a number of rising powers are gradually narrowing. When the gap closes to a stage when it can be deemed to be of limited significance, the global strategic balance will also start to change. It is not possible to predict the direction of such change since it will depend on a number of factors, primarily the intention of the rising powers and their domestic compulsions. The change in the balance could range from the benign to a situation of confrontation and the ensuing instability.

The fundamental indicators of a nation's rise—regionally and then globally—are its economic growth and stability, the availability of a large and skilled working population, appreciable growth in its political power that transcends its geographic borders and visibly expanding military power. Even if three of the four indicators are demonstrated it can be surmised that the nation is on an upward trajectory. The rise of a nation is also indicated through increased assertiveness in foreign policy issues as well as by its willingness to engage in areas that are relatively unstable. In addition these nations will also display greater interest in the functioning of international organisations like the United Nations and also in the provision of humanitarian assistance as a display of their 'soft power' with their gradual increase in maturity and confidence. By these tokens, China, India, Brazil and possibly Indonesia can be considered emerging powers that will be able to exert considerable influence in the regional and international geo-political environment over a period of time. In view of their current socio-political, economic and security situation their rise is a virtual certainty, barring unforeseen and significant upheavals.

FACTORS TO ACHIEVE GREAT POWER STATUS

Even if a nation is considered to be a rising power, it may not have the impetus or essential elements to become a 'Great Power'. Historically, great power status could be equated to an Empire, defined by geographic span of control and the ability to enforce total authority, like the early Roman Empire or the British Empire in the 19th Century. In more recent times, especially during the Cold War, the term Super Power was applied to the two nations that at that time had global power projection capabilities, and more importantly, the demonstrated will to use them if necessary. Great power refers to any nation that has strong political, economic and cultural influence, both regionally and globally, and the demonstrated ability to mobilise its power and normally succeeding in employing it as required for its own benefit as well as for the advantage of the larger comity of like-minded nations.[1]

Great power status can be claimed or conferred on a nation only if it fulfils a number of criteria and displays certain characteristics, some of which are not even tangibly visible and cannot be quantified easily. However, these characteristics and criteria have often been considered self-evident to the assessor and therefore suffering from the disadvantage of subjectivity.[2] Early considerations of great power status were based purely on the ability of a nation to prevail in war.[3]

---

1 Herd, Graeme P., & Dunay, Pal, 'International Security, Great Powers and World Order', in Herd, Graeme P. (ed), *Great Powers and Strategic Stability in the 21 Century: Competing Visions of World Order*, Routledge Global Security Studies, Routledge, Abington, UK, 2010, pp. 12-17.

2 Waltz, Kenneth N., *Theory of International Politics*, McGraw-Hill, New York, 1979, p.131.

3 Taylor, Alan J. P., *The Struggle for Mastery in Europe 1848-1918*, Oxford Press, Clarendon, 1945, p. xxiv.

This has subsequently been expanded to encompass a number of other elements of national power. There are five major criteria to be considered when assessing the capacity of a nation to become or be a great power. They are considerations of geography in terms of territory, population and sphere of influence; economic capacity and potential for growth; stability and competence of governance; power projection capability; and external acknowledgement of a nation's great power status.

Considerations of Geography

There are two aspects to geography that must be considered. The first is purely in terms of the integrity of the nation and the second in terms of its geographic sphere of influence. The territorial integrity of the nation must be unquestioned with all borders well established. In addition, the nation must be able to resolve any border disputes with neighbours in an amicable manner. The other aspect of territorial integrity is a population that is homogenous in its commitment to the nation. Internal strife that divides the population along lines of ethnic or religious confrontation always detracts from a nation becoming a great power. The cohesiveness of the physical geography of a nation is critical to its progress towards great power status.

The second aspect involves the geographic sphere of interest and the ability to influence it. This is a distinguishing factor between regional and great powers, with the influence of a regional power being confined to its immediate neighbourhood. A great power must have the ability to influence the prevailing international system, extra-regional interests as well as the necessity and the capacity to directly engage outside of its region to protect its interests. This ability to go beyond the regional order to influence and if necessary alter the global order is a prerequisite for a nation to aspire to great power status. The exercise of such abilities, to create and preserve global or regional geo-political stability and ensure an equitable strategic security, could be termed as the 'burden of great power status'.

Economic Capacity

In order to be a great power, a nation must have economic stability and an inherent potential for growth, at least into the mid-term future. In addition, the national financial institutions must have adequate checks and balances to ensure growth within the boundaries of the national legal system. It is also necessary to have a state-decided system of taxation that is stable, equitable and enforced across the board. The national economy must also be able to compete favourably with other similar economies as well as undertake significant roles in the international monetary system. The economy of a great power will be strong enough to significantly influence global financial systems.

From a domestic point of view, the nation must be able to maintain a minimum per capita income threshold that is internationally accepted as being sufficient to maintain a reasonably good standard of living. Similarly, a great power should have eradicated poverty within the nation. While poverty eradication calculations are normally based on less than 10 percent of the population being below the international poverty baseline, a great power will have to establish a higher baseline and lesser percentage of population below it in order to claim eradication of poverty. In fact poverty should not be a factor that has to be considered within the economic structure of a great power. A great power must also be able to maintain a positive human development index at all times.

Governance

The term governance is used to describe the manner in which a country is governed and is derived from the Latin verb *gubernare*, meaning 'to govern'. It covers the full spectrum of political, economic and administrative decisions made by the nation—government, business entities and the civil society—in managing the country's resources and other affairs. There could be many types of government, such as monarchy, dictatorship, democracy, oligarchy, plutocracy etc,. The ultimate aim of any government should be the provision of good governance of the state. Good governance should have the following eight major characteristics as a minimum: it should be participatory, consensus oriented, accountable, transparent, responsive, effective and efficient, equitable and inclusive and follow the rule of law. It should also ensure that corruption is minimised, minority rights are taken into account and it is responsive to the present and future needs of the society.[4] These are the minimum norms that a nation must adhere to at all timesto be considered a great power.

After evaluating the requirements for good governance, it can be surmised with assurance that democracy is the most effective form of government. In a circumspect manner it can therefore be stated that a great power must be a democracy. This is also validated by the fact in order for a nation to be great, the people of a nation must 'own' its greatness. This is most easily achieved in a practicing democracy. A great power will have good and stable institutions supported by an informed and active citizenry who are able to exercise their political and civil rights. This in turn requires the education system within the nation to be of a high calibre and also available to all the citizens at least up to a minimum level—primary education at the very least. A democratic form of government is the most suited to provide this. Nations are ruled by a succession of different governments, each successive one composed of a body of people.[5] In democracies there is a clear distinction drawn between the state and the ruling regime, with the interests of the state being always of the primary interest. A great power cannot have this distinction blurred even a little bit and therefore a democratic form of government becomes a prerequisite to attain great power status.

Power Projection Capability

A great power needs to be able to shape the environment within which it functions—essentially it needs a system that makes use of its capabilities to shape the intent of other nations. This can be achieved through creating a synergy between the material power of the nation and its socio-cultural ethos. In other words, the social structure of the nation—its cohesiveness, resilience and underlying belief in what the nation represents and stands for—must resonate with its power production and projection capabilities. An added factor, as important as the material power generation capability, is the moral principles that form the foundation for the nation's actions, which must always be beyond reproach. In effect a great power must always retain the moral 'high ground'.

---

4 As defined by United Nations Economic and Social Commission for Asia and the Pacific (ESCAP) in *Global Education*, on http://www.globaleducation.edna.edu.au/globaled/go/pid/17 p. 1, accessed on 14 September 2011.

5 Flint, Colin, & Taylor, Peter, *Political geography: World Economy, Nation-State and Locality*, Prentice Hall, New Jersey, 2007, p. 137.

Power projection—both hard and soft power—is an inherent capability necessary for a nation to be considered a great power. Hard power, most often, is the ability of the nation's military forces to achieve national objectives. Great powers need to have the capacity to project military power across the entire sphere of their interest, which automatically translates to a global capability. This capability must also be defined in terms of time, in that a great power must be able to sustain this power projection for a significant period of time without adverse effects to the national economy. This is a critical requirement to be fulfilled. In this context, whether or not a great power must possess nuclear weapons capability can be debated. It is felt that, in the current and emerging security strategic environment, a great power needs to be also a nuclear power, failing which its influence will tend to diminish. Further, 'non-great powers' who possess nuclear weapons can create a certain amount of leverage although not in the scale of an established great power.

Soft power, a term that has come into common usage comparatively recently, is all the ways in which a nation can expand its influence without using the lethal power resident in its military forces. However, all non-military power projection, such as the imposition of economic sanctions, does not automatically fall under the concept of soft power. The exploitation of soft power is an indirect way to exercise power by being a nation that others want to emulate—getting others to want what the great power wants.[6] The primary inputs to soft power are the nation's values, culture, policies and institutions. Essentially a great power must be able to create an impact on other nations and influence them purely through its perceived 'goodness'—of its overall culture, the way it does domestic business and the way it conducts itself in all its external dealings. This will always be a slow process and a great power needs patience and the ability to sustain the gradual injection of influence for soft power to work.

External Acknowledgement

Great powers must have the ability to project the aura of power. They must be able to give the appearance of stability and strength

---

6 Nye Jr, Joseph S., *The Paradox of American Power*, Oxford University Press, New York, 2002, pp. 8-9.

under all circumstances, which will further stabilise the geo-political situation both regionally and globally. However, the corollary to this is that appearances, especially self-proclaimed, can be deceiving. Great powers, actual or aspiring, tend to overestimate their ability to influence the course of events and their capacity to enforce their will on nation's they consider to be less powerful.[7] It becomes necessary that great power status is therefore acknowledged by other nations that critically examine the great power and the intricacies of its functioning.

Formal or informal acknowledgement of a nation's great power status, by other stable nations, is an essential criterion for being a great power. The status of great power is at times confused with that of a super power, with some analysts tending to consider the terms synonymous and using them interchangeably. There is a nuanced difference between the two. A super power nation is in a condition of being powerful, especially in the realm of hard power, whereas a great power nation attains and retains that position through the exercise of a number of unwritten rights and responsibilities.[8] Since there is no formal process of recognising a great power, it becomes all the more important that this status is conferred through a tacit judgement of the nation's behaviour and relations with other powers.

The assessment of a nation's behaviour or conduct in international affairs is perhaps the most important process. This requires not only examining a nation's willingness to act as a great power but also a retrospective analysis of its actions when it has initiated actions that have implications for itself and other nations alike. The other important criterion in the same area is to examine whether or not a nation has sufficient influence to be automatically included in discussions of contemporary regional and global political, economic and diplomatic challenges and whether the final outcome and resolution has been influenced by its contribution. If the answers to both are positive, it can be safely assumed that the nation already has great power status or is progressing towards becoming a great power. This test has historical precedence to it when great power conferences settled vexing issues

---

7 Quiggin, John, 'China's Imminent Collapse', *The National Interest*, http://nationalinterest.org/commentary/chinas-imminent-collapse-5880 pp. 2-3, accessed on 15 September 2011

8 Modelski, George, *Principles of World Politics*, Free Press, New York, 1972, p. 141.

of the day, before the advent of the United Nations and other world bodies of distinctly democratic nature.

Summing Up...

The world has always been led by nations that have exhibited a penchant for exercising their power to influence lesser states—through conquest, trade, cultural influence and the sheer magnificence of their own state. It is also true that along with such a status and the adulation of a majority of other nations, there has always been the growth of adversaries to the great power who attempt to diminish its influence. This is a historically proven fact.

History also provides a clear road map—the why, how, where and when—of the decline and fall of great powers. However, it is not as forthcoming in providing answers to questions of how a nation rises to great power status, how long it takes and how it retains its position of ascendancy. In addition, there are no clear indications that can be drawn out regarding the recognition of the onset of what seems to be the eventual decline of great powers. Only the criteria that must be met for a nation to be conferred great power status can be clearly delineated and adapted to contemporary times.

In the past two decades China has emerged as a possible counterpoint to global US hegemony, although it still has not gathered the power necessary to make the world bi-polar again. On the other hand, its internal divisions, both political and racial, detracts the US from furthering its progress to retain the international primacy that it has so far enjoyed. Even so, it will continue to be the most powerful nation at least for the mid-term. Other nations, notably the group referred to as BRICS (Brazil Russia, India, China and South Africa) have the capacity to become regional powers, and China has already achieved this position. Their ability to work cooperatively is, however, in doubt. Bilateral bickering, for example the complex India-China relationship, holds back progress in all spheres in these nations.

New global players have already emerged in the post-Cold War security environment. Their individual and collective stability will determine the emerging global power equation.

CONCLUSION

The global environment of social, political, economic and international relationships has always been changing. The noticeable difference in the contemporary situation is the greatly increased rate at which this change is taking place in comparison to even a few decades ago. Nations that are unable to adjust and align their national trajectories to this altered momentum face the uncomfortable likelihood of becoming fragile and failing. In addition, the older alliances that ensured stability and provided assistance to the less powerful members of the group have mostly unravelled under the pressure of this rapid change. This becomes a challenge to stability when no new alliances are forthcoming to fill the gap that has been left with the dissolution of the old ones. With the number of nations of limited calibre increasing, this challenge now assumes dire proportions.

Tensions between nations, ethnicities and religions are increasing almost on a daily basis. In parallel, instability also increases primarily because in the post-colonial world the number of nations that have mixed ethnicities and religions have also increased. While a majority of the tensions are internal to particular nations, the spread of ethnicities across borders tend to make these tensions assume regional importance and also influences the relationship between nations. The post-colonial world should have settled down by now—since most of the independence movements finished by the 1990s—but the repercussions of the arbitrary laying down of borders are being acutely felt only now. This is particularly visible in Africa. Further, the newer nations create a greater demand for political and economic equality in the international arena that the ex-colonial and now more stable nations are unlikely to meet. The scene is set for rising tensions that could very easily boil over into intransient stand-offs. In this context, the availability of recourse to a nascent international legal and justice system might serve to temporarily mitigate the situation, but it is unlikely to have a lasting and significant influence in settling issues.

A combination of three factors further destabilise the international geo-political environment—the diminishing influence of the great powers on the rest of the world; the willingness of nations to support, even overtly, non-state groups who operate at the fringes of legality; and the immaturity of emerging powers in their international dealings. In terms of security and stability, so necessary for the progress of human kind, the world is at its most volatile and the fear is that the volatility has still not reached its nadir. There is worse to come.

The breakup of the Soviet Union and the accompanying end of the Cold War culminated in the geographical separation of nations becoming less pronounced in a virtual sense. Events taking place in faraway places started to have influence on nations on the other side of the world. The world has always been evolving, but the rate of change in the past few decades have been much higher than ever before—and more importantly, the world is changing interminably. These changes have also led to the dilution of state sovereignty, as understoodtraditionally. In fact, the concept of a 'state' as an entity, is itself under siege; while the lure of ethnicity and overt nationalism is on the rise. Although the trend started in the 19th century, nationalism became a defining force during the early part of 20th century. In the past few decades, nationalism has assumed an economic hue. The developing world has started to view the economic overtures of the more developed world with scepticism and equate it to economic colonialism. The recent actions of China is seen as a classic example of such activities.

There is fear of a deterioration of the global security environment for a number of reasons. A majority of them are connected to economic issues, which create fragile states that are prone to becoming regional, and in extremis, international security challenges. Further, religious fundamentalism—that manifests in violence, civil war and broader conflict—mostly emanating from the Middle-Eastern region further vitiates the global situation. In addition, the proclivity of the Western nations to employ force in attempting to contain the bubbling destabilising forces creates circumstances that are conducive to the development of groups bent on creating further challenges to global security. The combined effect is one of destabilised regional and international environment, devoid of a sense of control.

Changes that are taking place in international relations, both rapid and evolving, challenges the status quo and have the capacity to alter the international strategic environment. Globalisation, which has a number of consequences of its own, acts as a catalyst for this movement. The primary impact of globalisation is the increased interdependence of national economies, which manifests more on the smaller nations with economies that are more prone to external influence in relation to the more mature and robust economies. Similar to the intertwining of economic development, world population trends also have a direct impact on the security environment. These trends alter the perceptions of national power in a holistic assessment. The differences in demographic trends between the more developed and the developing world is becoming starker than at any time before. While the more developed nations are struggling to contain the challenges created by an ageing population, the emerging nations are faced with a recognisable youth bulge with its advantages as well as challenges.

The strategic security environment has entered a phase of flux that has increased the unpredictability of all aspects of international security. In an unbiased appreciation of contemporary security environment, it would seem that the US still has strategic primacy. However, it is also equally evident that this primacy is being increasingly challenged and that the US is unable to enforce its will to the extent that was possible even a mere decade ago. Other than the diminishing stature of US power, the assured use of global commons for all nations is also becoming contested in many regions. Added to this quandary, a larger number of smaller nations are facing issues of governance with lessening emphasis on the doctrine of democracy. Under these circumstances, instability is bound to increase.

Instability, whether regional or spread over a broader area, also brings with it the development of alternate power centres. Such developments invariably lead to increased competition for influence and status between both emerging and established powers. Although great power status is outside the grasp of most nations, each nation aspires to creating its own sphere of influence in an effort to create its own security sphere that could withstand troubles and tribulations that could buffet it from the outside. Fundamentally, the quest by individual states for stability is the major factor that contributes to regional, and through it, global instability.

SECTION - III
THE FUTURE OF CONFLICT
CONTEXTUALISING WAR

THESIS: In recent times the characteristics and conduct of war have altered to an extent that contemporary conflict does not follow the principles of just war theory and conventional military forces of sovereign states find it increasingly difficult to prosecute military campaigns successfully to a 'victorious' end state.

Military interventions have become increasingly common in the past few decades while at the same time the Laws of Armed Conflict are being adhered to by the combatants more in the breech than in the observation. A number of factors affect the conduct of war irrespective of the identity of the participants and there are clearly visible trends in its conduct that directly affect the characteristics of a conflict. Unfortunately most of these trends tend to be detrimental to the effectiveness of conventional military forces and emphasis the asymmetric advantage or irregular and insurgent forces. Irregular warfare is at the asymmetric core of this development making it necessary for conventional forces to adapt to the new realities of operations while also retaining the traditional ability to carry out their fundamental role of defending the nation in a state-on-state conflict. This requires greatly increased flexibility that has to be achieved within a finite resource base and a fiscally strained national economic environment.

INTRODUCTION

Wars and battles have always caught the imagination of human beings. A significant amount of study is still devoted to ancient battles because they seem to be the antithesis of modern day conflicts which are litanies of ethnic massacres, suicide bombings, counter-insurgency operations, destruction of infrastructure and loss of life of non-combatants. In contrast, ancient battles were clearly defined state-on-state conflicts with well understood rules of combat that both sides adhered to and lasted a short period of time within which the victors and the vanquished were determined. There is a certain romanticism attached to the ancient conflicts although they were unimaginably traumatic and bloody. Hannibal's butchery of Romans at Cannae, twice as many as British casualties on the notorious first day of the Battle of the Somme from a much smaller overall population is an example.[1] However, in spite of the visible differences in the conduct of wars and battles, there is an ageless quality to the nature of war. War in its broadest definition is unchanging.

War is organised violence in the ultimate pursuit of political gain, whether perpetuated by a recognised state or by a group that do not have a clearly identifiable geographic sovereign identity. The political dimension will determine the aims and purpose of war, a fact that is unchanging and enduring. This is the factor that gives war its ageless quality. Extrapolating this reality, it will be a fairly accurate to state that future wars will be born of future politics.[2]

---

1 Lazenby, J., *Hannibal's War*, Warminster: Aris & Phillips, Oxford University Press, Oxford, UK, 1978, pp 84-85.

2 Owen, William F., 'The War of New Word: Why Military History Trumps Buzzwords', *Armed Forces Journal*, Virginia, November 2009.

While the unchanging nature of war can be demonstrated through a number of examples, it is equally necessary to accept the evolving nature of the character and conduct of war. In the contemporary geo-political scenario security is a global phenomenon and geography does not provide the protection that it did even a few decades ago. Geographic boundaries that were sacrosanct in terms of ensuring the sovereignty of a nation have lost the primacy they held. In fact the past two decades have seen the political-military map of Eurasia, one-third the earth's land mass, change radically. These changes, primarily based on the break-up of large and non-homogenous nations, have also altered the focus of a nation vis-à-vis its perception of security. An element of self-centredness has entered the calculation of possible courses of action that could be adopted in given situations. The foundation of a viable polity is now almost completely based on its ability to protect its own interests without considering the cost to other entities in doing so. It can be said that responsible global citizenship is gradually losing its appeal even to established democracies.

Under these circumstances nations that have a low tolerance threshold to direct attacks to its sovereignty or indirect pressures to its independence in terms of decision-making will be fragile. Fragile states can very rapidly transition to failing states with all the attendant security implications that such failure brings not only to the state itself, but also the ripple effect that it creates both regionally and globally. The irony is that there need not be an act of overt war to make a functioning nation deteriorate rapidly to a failing state. However, a viable and non-political military force is an instrument of state that enforces stability and therefore its presence can often stem this decline, especially in democracies.

In terms of the conduct of wars, the willingness to commit suicide in order to advance a cause—as opposed to the concept of a soldier's willingness to risk his/her life in the course of performing what is generally accepted as their legitimate duties—is a very powerful asymmetric advantage and extremely difficult to counter. While this method of taking the fight to the unwary public and creating a sense of fear and helplessness is not a new development, its widespread use is a more recent phenomenon. In combination with political or religious ideological aims that are not compatible with the modern concept of democracy, the ease with which lives are taken in such operations makes the conduct of such irregular warfare a complicated undertaking for regular military forces. The response to this situation requires a nation to deal with a wide and complex range of factors—in both the physical and cognitive domains of the adversary—that the military forces alone will not be able to address. Therefore, most nations have evolved their security strategies to one of a whole-of-government approach wherein all elements of national power have some role to play in securing the nation's interests. While the lead status and amount of contribution of each of these elements will vary with circumstances, this concept does provide a holistic response to irregular and diffused threats.

In discussing the broader meaning of warfare,[3] it must be understood that combat operations—primarily the application of lethal force by the military—is only one of its many components. From the perspective of a nation, warfare encompasses all actions that it undertakes to ensure the security of all its national interests. Since war itself is a political action, this means that combat is complementary to warfare and the actions required to secure a nation must not be confused as synonymous to combat operations. In recent times the term 'winning the peace' has been used to indicate activities other than combat operations, but it does not provide a clear indication of the involvement of all elements of national power in the endeavour to secure a nation. However, the focus at the highest levels must always be in safeguarding the national interests in which the military has a role, albeit a vital one.

Even though the broader aspects of national security are well understood, most nations have not been able to create a working model of a whole-of-government approach to security—a bringing all elements of national power to be applied in a focussed manner to achieve the desired end-state. The reasons for this situation are many: a lack of clarity at the highest levels of government regarding what constitutes national security; a lesser than required understanding within the government of how each element of national power contributes to national security as well as the implications of not achieving the necessary synergy between them; a belief that the military must always

---

3   For a detailed study of warfare and its historic evolution read, Keegan, John, *A History of Warfare*, Vintage Books, New York, 1994.

be the lead element in ensuring the safety and security of the nation; a reluctance within each of the power elements to surrender certain amount of control to the lead element in a contextual manner that is necessary for a joint approach to solving challenges.

This gap in what should ideally be an unbroken protective stretch of interwoven capabilities emanating from all elements of national power makes nations vulnerable to a host of threats, particularly so when they are unconventional in nature. A reflexive response has been an over reliance on the military forces of the nation—the traditional protectors and also the most organised for 'warfare' amongst the elements of national power. This situation impacts directly on the military forces in two ways. First, the national stance regarding security—whether offensive or defensive—will determine the orientation of military strategy in that it translates to the military forces either being ready to absorb a first strike from potential adversaries or being able to initiate offensive action, pre-emptively if required. The second impact flows from the first. The force structure, capability development, concepts of operations, training and acquisition patterns will all be determined the accepted security stance of the nation and biased towards either offence or defence.

Irrespective of the ability of modern states to accept that necessity to have a whole-of-government approach to national security, the character and conduct of war is evolving, as it always has been, whether driven by technological advances or because of changing attitudes brought about by an increased awareness of differences in life styles and standards of living.

Chapter 8

ANALYSING WAR

War, in its traditional form and broad understanding as a series of declared combat operations between two sovereign states, has become an anachronism. While armed conflicts abound around the world in a continuous manner, wars have ceased to be fought. This situation brings forth a large number of complexities when international laws regarding the conduct of wars/conflicts have to be enforced on the warring parties. In these circumstances analysing war is a complicated task and fraught with the danger of arriving at totally wrong conclusions regarding the correctness or otherwise of actions initiated by the participants. In the contemporary scenario, this difficulty is further exacerbated by at least one side of the conflict operating as loosely formed coalitions without any formalised alliances. Interpretation of objectives and activities therefore become extremely involved and can lead to wrong assessments with the clear possibility of arriving at impossibly wrong conclusions.

A few years ago the United Nations passed a resolution that provided legal sanction for third country interference in conflicts if it could be proved that the interference was aimed at protecting people from the effects of the application of lethal force. However, this concept or principle has until now been evoked and applied only in a selective manner by the more stable nations of the world. Therefore, it is only natural that the perception of the developing world is that the larger world powers will only interfere under this concept if there is a viable element of gain for them from undertaking such interference. Whether or not this perception is correct is a moot point. The point here is that the application of force, whether to protect or to conquer is in itself an act that must not only actually be, but also seen by an unbiased observer to be just. Consequently the international community discusses the application of force normally within the precepts of what is commonly called the Just War Theory.

Just War Theory

The application of force—war or conflict—is directly contradictory to some of the most fundamental principles, both moral and ethical, upon which human civilisation is built—do not kill others, contribute effectively to minimising the suffering of others, do not deceive others, treat everyone fairly with justice and a few more equally all-encompassing ones.[1] However, the consequences of going to war are enormous in terms of lives lost, damage and suffering and therefore the reasons for going to war needs to be such that the moral principles can be set aside without any serious doubt.

The horrors associated with war have always concerned humans. The dissertations of great philosophers from ancient China,[2] Greece[3] and India[4] invariably debate the matter of ethics and morality in the conduct of conflict and are recurring themes in their works. Although these were more in terms questions regarding the 'correctness' of actions taken by opposing armies, they paved the way for more robust discussion and the eventual formulation of the universally accepted

---

1 Fotion, Nicholas, *War & Ethics: A New Just War Theory*, Continuum International Publishing Group, London, 2007, pp. 2-6.

2 For more information on Chinese thinkers' views on the morality and ethics of war read: Confucius, *The Analects,*trans. by Dawson, Raymond, Oxford University Press, Oxford, UK, 2008; Mo Tzu, *The Basic Writings,* trans.by Watson, Burton, Columbia University Press, New York, 1963; the early chapters dealing with the writings of Mencius in Legge, James, (ed), *The Chinese Classics,* Adamant Media Corporation, Boston, 2000, (First published in 1894).

3 Information on ancient Greek philosophical thought on the subject can be obtained in: Plato, *The Republic,* trans. by Jowett, B., The Modern Library, New York, 1941; McKeon, Richard, (ed) *The Basic Works of Aristotle,* Random House, New York, 1941.

4 Further information on ancient Indian writings on ethics and morality is available in: Geutsh, Eliot (trans), *The Bhagawad Gita,* Holt, Rinehart and Winston, New York, 1968; Doniger, Wendi, & Smith, Brian K. (trans), *The Laws of Manu,* Penguin Books, New York, 1991.

Just war Theory. The contradiction here is that in a majority of cases the theory is more visible in its non-adherence than in it being followed by nations or groups involved in conflict, irrespective of the reason for the conflict.

Just War Theory primarily deals with two aspects of war—justice of the war (*jus ad bellum*) and justice in the war (*jus in bello*). The theory elaborates the reasons that should be fulfilled before a nation can enter a state of war and thereafter the norms it must comply with in the conduct of the war or conflict.

There are six primary principles that must be satisfied for justice of the war, the reason for a nation to go to war, to be satisfied. They are: just cause, last resort, proportionality, likelihood of success, right intentions and legitimate authority.[5] Resisting acts of aggression, imminent or actual, against one's own nation or an ally or countering humanitarian catastrophes satisfy the need for a just cause. A perceived necessity to annex foreign territory or resources for one's own benefit does not count as justifiable reasons to initiate actions that would lead to war. The principle of last resort requires all participants to exhaust every avenue possible to avoid going to war thereby increasing the chances of avoiding war.[6] In the context of justice of the war, proportionality means that the at all times the benefits of going to war must outweigh the costs that must be borne in order to succeed in achieving the desired objectives. A war should not be entered into unless there is a reasonable chance of it attaining some degree of success. There is a subtle difference between intentions and motives. In Just War Theory the analysis is regarding the intention of taking action and not the motives for doing so. As long as the intention is right the principle is satisfied if actions are not continued to further exploit the results. The last principle of legitimate authority requires that only those who are legally designated to decide about going to war should have taken the decision to engage in war.

The Just War Theory separates the principles that must be considered before entering a state of war and those that must be

---

5   Fotion, Nicholas, pp. 18-20.

6   Regan, Richard J., *Just War: Principles and Cases*, The Catholic University of America Press, Washington D.C., 1996, p. 64.

adhered to during the period that actual war is conducted. There are two primary principles that elaborate on the conduct of war within the bounds of justice—proportionality and discrimination.[7] Proportionality in the context of justice in war is concerned with the actual conduct of individual campaigns and battles. The principle distinguishes the very thin line that separates the use of excessive force and overwhelming force in achieving campaign or battle objectives. Essentially it advices that in selecting an option for action, the one that is likely to cause the least damage to adversary and own forces must be chosen. However, whether or not this principle is being adhered to, is difficult to measure especially during the actual conduct of the campaign or battle, since it is almost completely dependent on perceptions of both the importance of the objectives to be achieved and the necessary force to be applied in order to achieve it.

The principle of discrimination is perhaps the most important one in Just War Theory.[8] It demands that participants in war should at all times distinguish between legitimate and non-legitimate targets in the conduct of the war. However, the distinction between the two is not easy to maintain at all times, especially in modern conflict where the battlefronts are not clearly defined and tend to be obtuse at the best of times. The other side of the coin is that even though it is difficult to clearly distinguish targets, it is easy to analyse whether or not the principle of discrimination has been broken, almost immediately after—or at timed even during—the conduct of a battle. Further, indiscriminate war violates the rights of people far more than what is required to pursue victory in war.

Just War Theory is only a theory and does not have any official status as such. The most important aspect is that in its purest form, Just War Theory does not cater for the changes that have taken place in the characteristics and conduct of modern war. These changes have been brought about through two major developments. The first development is at the strategic level of governance. Over the past few decades political developments have altered the relationships between nations and have also brought into mainstream consideration a number of non-state entities. The non-state entities normally pursue

---

7   Fotion, Nicholas, pp. 21-23.

8   Regan, Richard J., pp. 87-95.

very narrow agendas which however defy geographic boundaries that have long been the accepted as the basis for national sovereignty. This in turn directly impacts on the application of lethal force by a nation, as opposed to it declaring a state of war, and further, the way in which a conflict is conducted. Wars are no longer fought between nations alone, but between a mix of actors, some of whom have legitimacy and some do not. Under these circumstances, adhering to the principles within the Just War Theory becomes even more difficult. The second development is at the operational level of the conduct of a campaign. Technology now permits a nation to attack a target anywhere in the world almost instantly. A combination of these two developments does not permit the Just War Theory to be fully endorsed in the conduct of most modern conflicts. There is a need to further refine the theory to ensure that nations can defend their sovereignty within acceptable moral and ethical considerations.

The Vagaries of War

War, a phenomenon that has existed all through human history, is full of contradictions. The reasons for nations going to war have varied from the frivolous to the sublime; its conduct has been determined more often by the ruthlessness of its participants rather than displays of human kindness; its inherent characteristics have continuously evolved to an extent wherein the a contemporary conflict would be unrecognisable as such to an ancient warrior where he to be transported in time; the role of the military forces in its conduct has changed over time from one of primary and only participants to being one more element of national power to enforce its will; the moral, ethical and legal aspects of that have been arrived at as a baseline for its 'civilised' conduct is no longer a yardstick to measure right or wrong; the concept of national security has evolved into an all-encompassing one, a large umbrella under which all actions of a nation can be conveniently placed. In short, war displays more vagaries than any other human endeavour.

The reasons for a nation to go to war, declared or undeclared, are many and varied.[9] However, the basic objective in all cases is to destroy the adversary's ability to wage war. The reasoning as to why

---

9   Ibid, Chapter 3, 'Traditional Just-Cause Considerations', pp. 48-68.

such a state of affairs must be achieved could be once again varied, the character and conduct of the conflict can take many shapes and it is even possible that the final objective may not be achieved. Under all circumstances the final aim, the destruction of the adversary's capabilities to apply lethal force advantageously, is almost a constant. This is unlikely to change. The political objectives for going to war can only be realised after this military necessity has been achieved. Before the commencement and after the end of hostilities, diplomatic and other endeavours will have primacy in the application of national power in achieving political objectives, even if the ability to use military force is carefully displayed as a forewarning. The physical aspects of war are about neutralising the adversary's military capability, but in the overall picture they constitute only a contributory part to achieving the desired final end-state. In discussing war there is an often stated belief that a nation goes to war to ensure justice. This is not true because justice is for the punishment of criminals; wars are entered into to destroy the warfighting capabilities of the adversary—potential or actual. By their very nature, war and justice are incompatible concepts.

Even a superficial analysis of wars that have been fought over the years brings out the fact that even carefully planned campaigns seldom go according to plan. In fact almost all successful wars are built on miscalculations and setbacks that have been identified in the course of the conflict and remedial measure instituted. This is because events, even within a well planned and executed campaign, are not completely predictable. Wars occur at unpredictable times, take unforeseen courses through its conduct and very often have unexpected consequences. The result is that the participant that has the best ability to adapt to fast changing circumstances will have a better chance of being successful, even if the conflict was commenced with some amount of disadvantage.

In the past few decades, the need to ensure that basic human rights of non-combatants are not violated in conflict has become a compulsory requirement that can only be violated at the cost of the loss of popular support both domestically and internationally for the nation concerned. Simultaneously, the characteristics of contemporary conflict has changed very rapidly with the military forces of nations being employed to overcome irregular adversaries who do not subscribe even to the basic moral, ethical or legal norms of its conduct. Irregular warfare is almost completely outside the conventional laws that govern war. The existing laws are mostly reciprocal obligations for the conduct of conventional conflict between nation states. They do not address the conduct of contemporary conflict in unconventional asymmetric settings.[10]

Contemporary conflicts pit conventional armed forces against networks of insurgents, terrorists and supporter personnel who do not adhere to the agreed approaches to military engagement and humanitarian protection. In these conflicts the irregular force typically shelters within the civilian environment and do not adhere to the laws of armed conflict. However, they are also the first to evoke the same laws when conventional forces are operating or when they are captured. Similarly they operate outside the civil laws of the country within which they function, but evoke the same civil laws to claim their rights to protection by the law enforcement system of the nation. Effectively they claim a one-way street approach to the legality of their actions. The effectiveness of this approach is amplified by the sensationalist media which tends to demoralise the conventional forces and erode their democratic support. Human rightsadvocacy organisations, whose very existence is dependent on the same conventional forces' protection, is in strategic alignment with the modus operandi of these irregular forces. Two questions need to be urgently asked. First, what human rights apply in a conflict that is a dynamic mix of guerrilla warfare, terrorism, law enforcement, humanitarian assistance and the reconstruction of social order? Second, if human rights norms are to be adhered to, who or what agency is going to ensure that all participating entities will in real terms adhere to them?

The continuous and on-going attempts being made to regulate the conduct of conflict through international legislation is perhaps the most important factor that must be considered in any analysis of war. This is indicative of three absolute realities. First is that the existing international rules are ill-adapted to irregular warfare and open to one-sided manipulations. Second, that since all kinds of war are traumatic events, they need to be regulated to ensure that some undefined

---

10 Rose, Gregory, 'Irregular warfare blows hole in Geneva rules', *The Australian*, 26 August 2011, p. 33.

baseline 'correctness' in its conduct is maintained by all participants. Third, this necessity to regulate its conduct stems from the acceptance that war itself can never be fully and completely avoided at all times. Further, a fourth reality, not often articulated but equally important, also can be derived—war is based on brutal reality and international legislations are unable to deal with it. However, war in an undefinable form will remain the focus of human activity.

Discretionary Wars

Wars can be logically divided into divided into ones that a nation enters into out of necessity and those that are fought at its discretion. While wars of necessity are easily understood in terms of the reasons why they have to be fought and the repercussions of not being successful, wars of discretion are more complex to explain and understand.[11] Further, wars of necessity can only be avoided at the risk of surrendering some amount of national sovereignty, which in turn will always be detrimental to ensuring the nation's security. The very concept of discretion is open to debate in any issue, since it is an intangible idea. This underlying fact leads to the common perception that a nation enters a war of discretion only to gain some amount of benefits for itself. This may indeed be true. However, with the increasing complexity in defining national security, wars of discretion have become a source to strengthen the security envelope around the nation.

Exercising the option to enter into or keep away from a war of discretion has more advantages than disadvantages to ensuring the nation's security. Three major advantages can be envisaged. First, it is obvious that if there is a direct and immediate threat to the survival of the nation, there will be no discretion to be exercised—it will be necessary for the nation to go to war. The corollary is that when the threat to the nation is marginal, it has the luxury of trying to contain it through all other means at its disposal before having to resort to war, in other words there is an opportunity to exercise discretion. Second, wars of discretion need not have any treaty or alliance obligations. This works in two ways. One, a nation need not automatically enter into

---

11 Freedman, Lawrence, 'On War and Choice', *The National Interest*, The Centre for National Interest, Washington D.C., 20 April 2010, https://nationalinterest.org/article/on-war-and-choice-3440 accessed on 25 March 2015.

conflict purely because an ally or a treaty partner has done so because the conflict may not be covered within the treaty obligations; and two, the nation by itself can enter into a conflict without evoking its alliance partners to do so. There is some amount of discretionary flexibility that is available to a nation in this context.

Third, the extent to which a nation has to be involved in a conflict can be regulated on an as required basis when involved in a war of discretion. Involvement can be tailored to suit the demands of domestic politics and international obligations, which could at times be conflicting. The advantage is that a nation can scope its involvement to suit its available resources and subsequently scale it up or down as necessary through the duration of the conflict. Further, a war of discretion lets a nation retain the ability to withdraw at its convenience, especially if its involvement has been predominantly in the non-combat spheres of the conflict.

The most important disadvantage in entering into a war of discretion is the debate regarding the moral right of a nation to do so that invariably follows such an action.[12] The very fact that discretion has been applied opens the decision for further analysis and disagreements. The issue is that however robust the decision to involve a nation, there will always remain some element of doubt regarding the need to have been involved. This will be more apparent in nations with long democratic traditions that tend to have fairly vociferous anti-war movements. Further, the gains that come to a nation from its involvement in a conflict will always depend on the bias of the analysis. Since each of them would normally subscribe to different viewpoints, there will be only limited chances of consensus. The fact is that, in a democratic nation, entering a war of discretion will always lead to rigorous scrutiny of the decision to do so in relation to prevalent socio-political compulsions.

In the contemporary security environment nations are more likely to enter into wars of discretion unless there is a direct threat to its survival as a sovereign entity. This is mainly because such an action provides the government with the maximum options to respond to a challenge to national security thus retaining greater flexibility. The

---

12 Regan, Richard J., Chapter 1 'Justifying War', p. 3.

likelihood of state-on-state conflicts, which could a force a nation to enter into conflict out of necessity, is very low. Under these circumstances nations will have to formulate clear policies regarding how, when and in what form they will subscribe to wars of discretion. This is necessary to have a thread of consistency in the decision making without which the perception of arbitrary involvement in conflicts that are perceived as not being directly connected to national security will prevail.

Limited Wars

Limited wars can be defined in a broad manner as those whose objectives are less than the unconditional defeat of the enemy, one that is not general or total war but involves the military forces of two or more nations. There is a fundamental factor that determines the scope of limited wars—essentially they do not involve the use of catastrophic force, like nuclear weapons, with the belligerents deliberately avoiding its use even if they possess the means to apply such force. Limiting the aims of the conflict, a political process, will also ensure that the threshold to catastrophic force is not breeched.[13]

In all wars the military dimension is always subservient to the political dimension; this truism being especially valid in limited wars. Even though the military dimension can never gain pre-eminence, there is a noticeable trend to gloss over the political dimension in the conduct of limited wars. This could lead to laying down an unachievable end-state thereby committing the nation to a war that cannot be won. All wars are politico-military enterprises. It begins with delineating the strategic aims of the war and then defining the limiting parameters within which the military will have to operate. Defining the military parameters is indispensable in limited wars.

Limited wars should normally have limited political objectives. They should not be so extensive as to compel the conduct of long drawn campaigns of great magnitude that finally expend more resources than can be obtained from the political value that is derived

---

13 Ahmed, Ali, 'Political Dimensions of Limited War', *IDSA Comment*, Institute of Defence Studies and Analysis, 29 March 2010, http://idsa.in/idsacomment/PoliticalDimensionsofLimitedWar_aahmed_290310?q=pri accessed on 1 April 2011.

from victory. Therefore, the political dimension has both external and internal facets to it. Limiting the external aspect requires a great deal of political maturity and wisdom and shaping the context is an exercise in domestic politics. The most important fact in planning a limited war is that the political dimension, which in turn determines whether or not a conflict stays in the realm of limited wars, is completely outside the military domain. This puts the onus of responsibility of going to war as well as ensuring non-escalation into a broader conflict clearly on the civilian leadership in democratic nations. However, in a majority of cases, only the initial direction is seen to be forthcoming from the political leadership with the further deliberations on the conduct of the conflict—whether or not to escalate its area and/or intensity—is almost always confined to the strategic military domain. This situation has the inherent danger of diffusing the focus on achieving the strategic political objectives and the military forces striving to achieve a lower level military oriented end-state.

Limited wars should be considered and conducted for what it essentially is meant to be—a war conducted to obtain limited objectives when all other attempts to resolve issues that are of paramount importance to a nation and its security through peaceful means have failed. Two conditions must be met for a nation to initiate a limited war. One, the issue or challenge that is to be mitigated must be such that if it is not addressed the overall security of the nation will be directly jeopardised almost immediately with long-term residual effects. Two, the fundamental objectives to be achieved should be clearly articulated and must be within the capacity of the military forces to achieve without excessive strain to the nation's economy and future well-being.

Since limited wars are restricted in their aims and conduct, clear winners and losers may not always emerge. Consequently, there is a distinct and greater possibility of limited wars deteriorating into guerrilla warfare and insurgencies than the chances of it escalating into a broader war. This is a scenario that will have further implications for the overall security of the nations involved and has the potential to impact the stability of the regional security environment. Policy and decision-makers will have to be cognisant of these follow-on ramifications of entering into limited wars.

Military Intervention

In the past decade, the more developed world has militarily intervened in different parts of the world in order to prevent mass murder and genocide to avert these conflicts from becoming humanitarian crises and to enforce law and order.[14] There are two aspects of the rationale for such interventions that need to be analysed. First is the evolution of the principles upon which such interventions are sanctioned and then conducted. The concept of 'right to protect' is of fairly recent origin and it has been further expanded in its application in the NATO intervention in the civil war in Libya. The UN mandated intervention in Libya was initiated against a suspicion of intent to conduct mass murder, rather than as a response to the actual conduct of such a deed. This precedent opens the door to the development of a doctrine that prescribes unlimited intervention against any regime suspected of planning oppressive measures within their sovereign territory. The fact that such interventions have till now been conducted against regimes that have been inimical to the West has cast a shadow over the legitimacy of these actions. There is a growing perception that this doctrine is being propagated to conduct military interventions for political and economic reasons against any regime that the West disapproves of, rather than because of a genuinely felt need to avert human catastrophes.

The second part of the rationale to intervene is in the case of failing or fragmenting states becoming a source of global instability. The compulsion to intervene in these cases is more deep-rooted in the broader security imperatives of neighbouring states and therefore could also be conducted in a unilateral manner by a regional power to contain the situation. There is a school of thought that considers military intervention to stabilise a fragile state as a foreign policy initiative. Irrespective of the mandate or the rationale, such interventions are complex operations. Complete break-down of law and order is perhaps the last phase of the descent of a state into instability and failure. Failing states become the centres for weapon proliferation and transnational crime, havens for terrorist organisations, and invariably generate a refugee crisis for the neighbouring states.

---

14 Evans, Gareth, *The Responsibility to Protect: Ending Mass Atrocity Crimes Once and For All*, Brookings Institution Press, Washington D.C., 2008, pp. 11-19.

The difficulty in intervention is that there are no standard answers to a number of questions that needs to be asked and answered before the intervention can succeed. The main issues that must be addressed are—what are the criteria that determine that a state has become fragile or is failing; even if a state is failing, should external intervention be resorted to; if intervention is being considered, what considerations should be examined; after the decision has been made to intervene, what is the optimal time to do so; and defining the objectives to be achieved and the desired end-state.[15] Conflict erupts in fragile states through a cycle that starts with a weak administration that cannot perform the fundamental function of providing basic safety and security for the population which in turn generates civil conflict that the administration is unable to control. In these interventions the military conflict phase could be short-term or degenerate into low intensity conflict conducted through insurgencies or guerrilla warfare. In all cases, lasting peace and stability can only be created through accountability and rule of law, which itself will be a lengthy process. The military component of these interventions while comparatively small, could be long-drawn and violent to the extreme.[16]

Summing Up...

Wars, armed conflicts, insurgencies and terrorist activities invariably involve the lethal application of force. In addition, recently the United Nations has passed a resolution that provides legal sanction for a third country to intervene in an on-going conflict to protect non-combatant civilians from the possibility of being subjected to attacks by military or other attacks that would endanger their lives. This concept is termed the 'right to protect' and was used as the legal permission for the

---

15 Lauzon, Dru, & Vine, Andrew, *'Security and Governance: Foundations for International Stability'*, Colloquium Brief, based on Kingston Conference on International Security, 21-23 June 2010, conducted in Kingston, Ontario, Canada, published by Strategic Studies Institute, US Army War College, Carlisle, PA, 2010.

16 There are differing viewpoints regarding the entire concept of military intervention and the debate regarding the 'correctness' or otherwise of such actions is on-going. In order to obtain a balanced view of both sides of the narrative two books are recommended reading here. Snow, Donald M., *The Case Against Military Intervention: Why We Do It and Why It Fails*, Routledge, New York, 2016; and Seybolt, Taylor B., *Humanitarian Military Intervention: The Conditions for Success and Failure*, Sipri, Oxford University Press, Oxford, UK, 2007.

Western intervention in Libya in 2011. The concept, although passed in the UN General Assembly, received a mixed reaction from the international community when it was applied in Libya. The lukewarm response, especially from the so-called developing nations could have been because of the manner in which the Western nations interpreted the resolution to effect a regime change that finally led to the 'murder' of Muammar Gadhafi, the ousted dictator of Libya at that stage.

Going to war is considered acceptable if the actions fit within the ambit of the Just War Theory. Since the consequences of a war or armed conflict are enormous, in terms of both blood and treasure, it is critically important to ensure that the decision to go to war is morally beyond reproach. The ethics and morality regarding going to war, as well as its conduct, has been debated over millennia and eventually led to the development and formulation of the Just War Theory. This theory separates the principles that must be considered before entering a state of war and the ones that must be adhered to during its conduct. However, the Just War Theory is just that, it is merely a theory with no official or legal status. There are no mechanisms in place to enforce compliance to the theory. Further, the theory only caters in a marginal way to the continuing evolution of the characteristics and conduct of war. If the Just War Theory is to gain importance and be considered the baseline for entering a war and its subsequent conduct, it is necessary to refine it further and bring it to contemporary relevance.

Wars are brutal and merciless affairs, the ruthlessness determined only by the culture, ethos and morality of the participants. Unlike in ancient and pre-modern times, wars now engulf the entire nation and is the ultimate activity conducted by a nation to enforce its will on another. Ever since wars and armed conflicts became an integral part of the political process, several attempts have been made to establish a baseline regarding the moral, ethical and legal aspects of its conduct. Establishing the minimum acceptable pattern in the conduct of war has not been an easy task, and even today is an incomplete task. Further, the 21st century, even the accepted norms have been ignored. The dividing line between 'right' and 'wrong' is not clearly visible any longer and there is an all-pervasive ambiguity to all aspects of war. The situation is more conducive to the development of vagaries, rather than moving towards a conscious display of moral and ethical 'correctness'.

Most modern combat takes place between the forces of established nation-states and non-state entities and are irregular in nature. Under these conditions where the irregular force is disadvantaged from a military perspective, human rights violations are becoming increasingly common. On the other hand, the regular military forces of a nation are becoming increasingly constrained in the application of lethal force and even in initiating action against irregular forces. The situation is further exacerbated by the irregular forces sheltering within the non-combatant civilians, which in turn increases the possibility of collateral damage. The attempts being made by international agencies to regulate the conduct of war, while being a tacit acceptance on the fact that wars cannot be avoided, is unlikely to achieve any significant breakthrough in the near, or even mid-term future.

Wars can be divided in a very broad manner into wars of necessity and wars of discretion. Wars of necessity occur when the security of a nation is threatened beyond a point where there is a reasonable chance of a negotiated settlement. Anything but a victorious result in any war of necessity would have grave implications for the nation. Wars of discretion, limited wars and military interventions create different levels of involvement by a nation that can be tailored to suit the circumstances. In such wars, the objectives are normally connected to national security imperatives only in an indirect manner. In the contemporary security environment, nations are more likely to be involved in these kinds of wars or conflicts, which are restricted in aim and conduct. Since the aims are normally restricted, it may not always be possible to clearly identify the winners or for a nation to declare victory. The diffused understanding of victory on the part of the irregular forces further confuse the appreciation of winning and losing. Wars and armed conflicts cannot be wished away, they are part and parcel of the global political process. Understanding war is a fundamental input to national security.

Chapter 9

FACTORS AFFECTING THE CONDUCT OF WAR

The conduct of war is in a state of continuous change, although it may not seem so to a casual observer. While the ultimate objective to be achieved is always political, the actual conduct of a conflict, the lethal employment of military forces irrespective of the status of the adversary, evolves through the influence of a number of factors that include the physical capabilities of the force enhanced through technology on the one end and intangible concepts such as friction in combat and the human dimension at the other. However, it could also be said that at a very base level of combat operations, very little has changed over the centuries of warfighting. It has always been, and remains, an intensely human endeavour that brings into focus the terror and fear inherent in violent acts that imperil the very existence of human beings. In contrast, the tools that are used to wage war and the methodologies and concepts for their optimal employmentare in a process of continual evolution. This is a subtle distinction to make, but is necessary to be understood in order to grasp the underlying implications and impact of major factors that affect the conduct of war.

Contemporary trends in the conduct of war are considerations at a slightly level lower than the factors that are being discussed. These trends straddle the strategic and operational level of conflict and have immediate and long-term impact not only on the actual conduct of a war but on the overall national security. They also affect the chances of success of a military force engaged in any type of war. Emerging trends tend to change the conduct of war both in an evolutionary manner as well as inputs that create step changes in their conduct, mainly at the operational level. Monitoring the trends that seem to shape the conduct of war in terms of potential adversaries and thereafter adapting one's own forces to the changes being brought about is of cardinal importance to maintain the effectiveness of a military force. This process of adaptation has to be done for both the physical aspects such as equipment and weapon systems as well as concepts of operations and employment strategies. Failure to do so will invariably find the military force in question being compelled to go into conflict situations with an undeniable disadvantage that would invariably lead to failure.

The fundamental nature of war remains unchanged over the years—in a broad manner it has always been a violent struggle for political legitimacy.[1] The understanding or explanation of political legitimacy could be nuanced in different ways, but it does not change to an extent that it can mean something completely different in different parts of the world or in changing circumstances. While this factor is the constancy of war, its conduct has been continually changing. In other words, the strategic purpose of war and therefore its nature is constant, while the operational part of war, its conduct, is in perpetual flux. In order to analyse war and understand its complexities, it is necessary to study the conduct of war and the factors that influence and bring about the changes. The actual conduct of a war, although at the operational level, has a direct impact on the strategic level of decision-making and therefore, on achieving the desired end-state.

There are a number of factors that affect the conduct of war, all of which can be clubbed together under seven broad areas—organisational factors, socio-political underpinnings, support of the population, technology, contextual elements of change, permanent operating factors and friction.

Organisational Factors

Primarily organisational factors refer to the issues that stem from the organisation of the military force that percolate downwards into the

---

1 Shaw, Martin, 'The Legitimacy of War Today', *E-International Relations*, 26 July 2008, https://www.e-ir.info/2008/07/26/the-legitimacy-of-war-today/ accessed on 26 March 2015.

combat elements of the force. However, there are also certain elements of higher level organisation which could both directly and indirectly influence the conduct of a conflict.[2] The primary organisational factor that needs to be analysed is the command structure of the force involved. The viability of the command arrangements will directly affect the outcome of every war, campaign and battle. Military forces are primarily hierarchical organisations and tend to be rigid in their command alignment. This is conducive to good order and discipline and was a necessary trait during the times when the outcome of conflict was primarily decided by physical combat between two armies.

Contemporary conflict demands the delegation of combat related decision-making to the lowest level of command in all three arms of the military to optimise the effectiveness of the force. On the other hand, modern technology permits commanders at the highest strategic level to oversee tactical action in real-time if they so desire. The urge to be involved in actual combat is very high and can become insurmountable when a soldier is viewing combat actually taking place. This becomes even more difficult in circumstances wherein the responsibility for ill-considered decisions that could lead to failure at the tactical level could be placed at a higher level of command. The tendency to intervene must be balanced within the new realities of the conduct of combat operations and is an urge that senior strategic leadership must carefully control in a contextual manner. Further, in contemporary conflict, tactical failures can very often have strategic repercussions. Delineating the tactical conduct of combat operations and providing strategic guidance at the appropriate time is critical to the overall success of any campaign. This is a major organisational factor that affects the conduct of war.

Socio-Political Underpinnings

At the strategic level it is easy to understand that war or conflict always has a political underpinning in that the end-state that is desired by all the participants will have a political undertone. However, the conduct of the war is directly influenced by the social and cultural ethos that

---

2 Feld, M. D., 'Information and Authority: The Structure of Military Organization, *American Sociological Review*, Vol 24, No 1, February 1959, pp. 15-22. https://www.jstor.org/stable/2089578?seq=1#page_scan_tab_contents accessed on 26 March 2015.

is ingrained in the military or non-military personnel actually carrying out combat functions. Obviously the social ethos would be aligned with that of the broader population and could play a decisive role in the manner in which the military force conducts itself. The socio-political factor is fundamental to a nation's acceptance and adherence to the laws of Armed Conflict as well as to how morality and ethics in war are viewed and pursued.

In contemporary conflict, this factor has increasing relevance, especially if one of the antagonists in a conflict is a non-state entity. Non-state entities that have entered into armed conflict will almost always have a different view of morality and ethics in the conduct of combat operations, invariably at odds with what is considered international norm. However, such differences may not be fully in tune with the accepted norms of the society that they belong to, although their actions will be visible to the larger population and in a peculiarly detached manner also condoned by them. This is a dichotomy in that the larger population, on whose behalf the non-state entities are waging the conflict, more often than not, tend to disassociate with them in matters that concern morality, ethics or LOAC. Irrespective of this dissonance, the conduct of conflict will always be dependent on the national ethos regarding the actual conduct of combat operations and the combatants' willingness or otherwise to carry out actions that are considered improper by the international community.

Support of the Population

For a nation to conduct a successful campaign it is necessary to have the support of the population, particularly in democratic nations. Going to war must be a considered decision taken at the apex of government and also must have majority support from the people, which is essential to maintain the morale of the forces in combat and to back the government through the national impact of having entered into war. Instances where this has not been the case or where the support dwindles over a period of time through the conduct of the campaign have almost always resulted in the failure of the campaign. The corollary to this is the criticality of popular support for the functioning of a non-state entity conducting an irregular war against the military forces of the nation and/or its allies. Unless the people support these clandestine activities there can never be a chance of success in these conflicts. The conduct of any warlike operations, whether within the state or far away from its borders, whether conducted as insurgency, counter-insurgency, limited or all-out war, the support of the people is a fundamental factor that affects the conduct and the outcome of a conflict.[3]

Technology

Technology—the availability or the lack of it—is an important element in determining the conduct of any conflict. In the event that the opposing forces are evenly matched in terms of current capability, technological innovation and the ability to absorb higher level of technology at a faster rate than the opponent can become the deciding factor. While technology is undoubtedly an important war-winning factor, the non-availability of sophisticated technology to a force does not automatically translate to defeat in a conflict. It is a combination of technology, concepts of operations and innovation along with some other intangible factors that makes a military force efficient and successful.[4] However, technology will affect the manner in which a campaign is conducted.

In contemporary irregular wars, non-state entities would generally be operating at a lower level of technology and therefore would resort to asymmetry in order to neutralise the technological edge of the adversary, who would normally be conventional military forces. An innovative military force combating such adversaries will be able to leverage off their technological superiority to create asymmetric advantages of their own. However, there has been a noticeable trend in recent times for the irregular or non-state entity to also acquire and employ sophisticated weapon systems, thereby reducing the technology gap and edge between them and conventional military forces. In all kinds of conflict, technology, to a large extent, determines the conduct and influences the final outcome. Even though this may be true in a number of contexts, some military forces tend to be over-reliant

---

3 For a contrary view of popular support for the insurgency or the Irregular force read, Davies, Richard, *Hamas, Popular Support and War in the Middle East: Insurgency in the Holy Land*, Contemporary Terrorism Studies, Routledge, Abington, U.K., 2016.

4 Van Creveld, Martin, *Technology and War: From 2000 B.C. to the Present*, The Free Press, New York, 1991, pp. 235-284 & 311-321.

on technology for their effectiveness at the cost of innovation, a trait that can become a vulnerability when faced with an astute adversary. Technology can be a double edged sword.

Contextual Elements of Change

The context and environment within which a conflict is joined does not stay the same throughout the duration of the conflict. In fact, the duration of the conflict itself can never be predicted with any accuracy which lends itself to the uncertainty regarding the context and environment become even greater. In this case the environment encompasses the physical as well as the intellectual—meaning the political, ideological, religious—aspects of the conflict space. Further, the support base of the contestants is also likely to change with the progress of the conflict, especially in long-drawn ones. While in most cases of irregular war, the physical aspects might not change during the conflict, the intellectual aspects will continually change with the progress of the conflict. Such changes will be more pertinent to irregular wars as opposed to state-on-state conflicts because of the on-going search for innovative ways to create asymmetry as conventional opponents adapt.

The conduct of a conflict in all its aspects—intensity, tempo and modus operandi—is influenced by the ideology and doctrine that is pursued by opposing forces. In turn the progress being made by either party will affect the steadfastness with which a particular ideology, political or religious, is adhered to during the conflict. In essence, the physical conduct of combat operations will be a direct indication of the changes being brought about in the cognitive domain—behaviour pattern and belief system—of the participants. Contextual changes to the cognitive domain can be brought about by a number of factors both internal to the military or non-state combat forces as well external influences in varying degrees.

Permanent Operating Factors

Conventional military forces operate within a laid down standard concept that is refined and changed in very limited ways. This makes them fairly predictable in a given situation and therefore makes them easier to counter than a force that operates in unconventional ways.

The disadvantages of predictability have been recognised in most modern armed forces, but only selected small units are permitted to operate outside the standard operating procedures. This restriction is a permanent operating factor that directly influences the conduct of a war or conflict. While adherence to procedure does bring in rigidity in combat, it can also be a source of strength in times of uncertainty even at the tactical level. The training required to inculcate extreme flexibility in operations is very high as are the risks associated with accepting completely independent concepts of operations to be put into combat operations. Therefore, even modern military forces operate within a set of standards and procedures, even though they may have sufficient in-built flexibility.

The challenge that conventional military forces, with their limited flexibility in operations face is the high level of freedom enjoyed by the tactical sections of insurgents and irregular forces. Centralisation in the case of irregular forces would only be in terms of the basic ideological belief and not even in defining the desired end-state. In fact the desired end-state is normally in an amorphous condition within these non-state entities. While such a situation can have tremendous advantages in the conduct of operations, the very same diffusion in command and control that brings them about, tends to negate the focus required to ensure that all the elements of a fighting force is acting in cohesion towards a recognised goal. Historically this has been a weak link in irregular forces' ability to achieve their objectives. Even in contemporary conflict this drawback is clearly visible and conventional forces can and should exploit the lack of operational cohesion within the irregular force.

These operating imperatives, whether resident in conventional military forces or within irregular forces and non-state entities, directly influence the conduct of operations. Further, an indirect influence on the conduct of conflict is the issue of the laws of Armed Conflict (LOAC) as accepted by the majority of nations.[5] Adherence to

---

5   For a holistic appreciation of the contemporary laws of armed conflict read, Green, Leslie C., *The Contemporary Law of Armed Conflict*, 3rd Ed, Manchester University Press, Manchester U.K., May 2008, which has been acclaimed as one of the most significant works to appear on the subject in recent years. There are also a number of other texts available on the subject for detailed interpretations and different views.

international law in the conduct of war was not a major issue as long as wars were fought between the forces of two sovereign nations. In fact breach of the laws was an uncommon occurrence that was condemned. However, circumstances have radically changed with the emergence of non-state entities that wage 'unconventional' war to achieve their objectives. The warfighting forces of these entities do not, as a general rule, adhere to the accepted norms of combat. At the tactical level this gives them an asymmetric advantage over conventional military forces that have a responsibility to scrupulously follow the LOAC and even more restrictive rules of engagement (ROE) that may be imposed on them. The conduct of war will obviously be affected by these vagaries in the makeup of the forces in combat and these remain permanent operating factors throughout the conduct of a campaign.

Friction

Friction—the intangible element that brings about uncertainty in all aspects of war—is a constant factor in the conduct of any conflict. While this has been so since the beginning of recorded history, it was first identified and articulated by Clausewitz in his work, *On War*. He contended that real wars are different to the abstract concept of war and the academic analysis of them, essentially because the idealised conditions that are used in the calculations and planning are never achievable in actual conditions. Both physical constraints and psychological factors impinge on the thought process and are important determinants in decision-making at all levels of the conflict. The various factors that are both physical and cognitive have been placed by Clausewitz under the concept of 'friction'.[6]

War does not start and finish in a discernibly finite time frame, but is a contest between powers that develop, generate and project force in different ways and rates. This disparity brings about a situation conducive to uncertainty even when adequate information is available to the decision-makers and they have a clear picture and understanding of the situation. Again, such uncertainty creates friction in the actual conduct of the war. At the physical level, the intrinsically dangerous nature of war frequently makes the exercise of sound judgement

---

6   Rapoports, Anatol, (ed), *Clausewitz On War*, Penguin Books, Middlesex, England, 1968, p. 4.

extremely difficult and even impossible in some cases. The immense physical effort required to carry out actual combat activities also has a detrimental effect on judgement and affects decision-making directly.[7]

In war, petty circumstances, disappointments, tactical setbacks, the lack of cohesion, the intricacies of logistics and any number of other factors create enormous friction—against the forward movement or manoeuvre of the force—which then becomes a permanent factor that must be considered from the planning stage itself of any battle, campaign or war. Every conflict is different and will have individual traits and character; therefore, identifying the factors that can contribute to friction in each instant is important. Fundamentally, the conduct of any conflict will be directly influenced by friction and the ability of the concerned commanders to overcome or mitigate its effects. The lesser this capability in a force—more the chance of its failure.

Summing Up...

Through the history of humankind, the nature of war has remained unchanged—it remains a violent struggle for political legitimacy. However, the conduct of war has remained in a constant state of volatility. War and armed conflict is fundamentally a human endeavour and therefore is subject to the caprices of human nature, perhaps more so than any other human activity. Even so, its conduct is altered by the tools available for the lethal application of force and the evolving concepts of operations. Both these factors are continually being refined because of the increasing availability of technology-enabled capabilities. The conduct of war is also influenced by a number of extraneous factors that may not be directly associated with the actual application of force.

The organisational ethos of the military force and the socio-political factors within the nation affect the conduct of war. In recent times, the arrival of non-state entities in the battlefield have also brought about visible changes to the context and conduct of war. Under these conditions, the non-military factors that impact its conduct assume added importance in war. Support of the population also become an important factor to be considered when a nation is at war with irregular, non-state entities. Further complications are added when

---

7 ibid, pp. 118, 160, 163-167.

these conflicts are driven by religious and sectarian strife. Ideological struggles can never be won by military forces alone and therefore the support of the general population has a direct impact on the outcome.

The conduct of war is also influenced by the Clausewitzian friction, which is unavoidable. Both physical and psychological factors add to the friction of conflict. The fact remains that the strategic purpose of war has remained a constant for centuries. However, with the rapidly changing global security environment, its conduct is becoming increasingly complex and ever-changing.

Chapter 10

EMERGING TRENDS IN THE CONDUCT OF WAR

It is human nature to use force to obtain something that may not be easily available through any other means and as a corollary to resort to the use of force to safeguard coveted assets. When this proclivity is transferred to the realm of national security and prosperity, the result is armed conflict or war. This is a historically proven fact. Through the progress of human civilisation, wars have become better defined and analysed as well as having international agreements and laws put in place to regulate its conduct. Upholding the accepted moral and ethical standards in its conduct is both a challenges and a constant source of concern to the forces involved.[1] This is further complicated by the necessity to adhere to the LOAC and ROE as applicable, often in a context where such adherence is not common to all participants.

The increasing restrictions being placed on the use of force have made the conventional military forces seek other means to increase their effectiveness, mainly through innovative use of technology. However, sophisticated technology has its own peculiar challenges to be overcome before it can be effective. First, it requires a very broad level of scientific development within the nation to develop, maintain and operate efficiently. Even if a nation were to resort to acquiring sophisticated technology from external sources, it would require a well-educated and extensively trained cadre of people to operate it optimally. Second, even considering that a nation has such

---

1 Smith, Dan, *Trends and Causes of Armed Conflict*, Berghof Research Centre, Berlin, 2004, pp. 7-10.

a capacity, the process—whether indigenous development or foreign acquisition—is extremely expensive. The situation is compounded by the fact that weapon systems are normally single-use items, making them recurring expenditures.

A combination of these factors and the truth that war as such will be an on-going phenomenon in international relations has in turn spawned a number of new trends in the conduct of conflict. These trends have developed from both conventional military forces attempting to optimise their effectiveness and irregular forces operating at a lower technological threshold trying to neutralise the advantage that technology provides to the military forces. These developments are cyclic in terms of threats, counter moves and counter moves to that and so on. However, it is important to understand the emerging trends in the conduct of warfare in order to be able to analyse the efficacy of the application of force in a given circumstance as well as to cast forward to see the direction that war is likely to take.

The emerging trends in the conduct of war are predominantly at the lower strategic and higher operational level—some of them dealing with the planning aspect and a majority with the actual concept of operations that is directly influenced by the availability of technology and the ability of the force to be innovative in its use.

Changes in the Intangible Sphere

War has always been complex and could perhaps be classified as the most complex human activity. However, in the contemporary context, this complexity has become even greater because conflict has moved away from certainty to the arena of unpredictability mainly because it has become more unstructured than ever before. In the battlefield, this unpredictability is further increased by the use of both sophisticated and rudimentary weapon systems—tools of war—simultaneously and by all participants. In this sense, wars have become 'hybrid' in their conduct. This is a trend that is likely to continue for the foreseeable future with the only change being the sophistication levels of the equipment and systems being used.

The next intangible factor that is becoming more apparent is the mix of conventional and unconventional concepts of operations that is selectively employed. This translates to carrying out physical operations while simultaneously mounting innovative non-kinetic attacks on dual-use or even purely civilian infrastructure, rather than the military alone, in what can be termed as a multi-pronged attacks on the entire power structure of a nation. Cyber-attack on the financial infrastructure of a nation is a prime example of innovative non-kinetic attacks. This mix between the physical and virtual can be at the strategic, operational or tactical levels of combat or even conducted simultaneously in two independent levels.

Cyber-attacks can be clubbed into three broad areas. The first are attacks that physically destroy equipment, which means that even if the attack is subsequently countered or stopped, the capability cannot be recovered without replacing the hardware that has been destroyed. The only option available is to replace the damaged equipment. The second are exploitation activities more commonly termed 'hacking' which is an enduring challenge. Exploitation is resorted to for subverting secure networks and to obtain information—mining for data—that can then be used to diminish the efficacy of the adversary's warfighting capability. Hacking can also be undertaken to temporarily disable the state computer network to exploit the ensuing confusion. Third is the use of internet as a weapon system to influence the cognitive domain of the adversary; to change the will of the people of an adversarial nation to one that is more conducive to one's own; and to subvert the morale of the adversary through spreading misinformation.[2] Each of these areas is crucial in the broader consideration of national security.

Visible Trends

There are a number of very clearly visible trends that are gradually changing the conduct of war, and along with it challenging the traditional methods of capability development, force structuring, concepts of operations and training. The debate whether to alter the time-tested methods and cater for these trends or to assume that these emerging trends are only of short term importance, has not produced any viable answers. Conventional wisdom however tends to fall on the side of treating these contemporary trends as short term phenomena

---

2   Alexander, Keith, General US Army, Commander US CYBERCOM (established May 2010), *Interview*, Jane's International Defence Review, November 2010, p. 4.

with the distinct possibility of other trends developing in the near future. Care must also be taken to ensure that the trends that could have long-term impact are identified and attempts must be made to even try to predict some of them.[3]

Civilianisation. One of the most obvious trends, noticeable in the past two decades, is the civilianisation of conflict. This is manifest in two distinct ways. First is the entry of non-state entities into combat operations employing their own militias who are not traditional, uniformed conventional forces of a sovereign state. These groups challenge the till-now accepted norms of the conduct of war and can be considered to be functioning outside the LOAC and other internationally acknowledged and customary ways of waging war. The second flows from the first in that these groups—irregular forces—almost always operate in the close vicinity of civilian population and blend with non-combatant population easily. In these circumstances there is a distinct possibility of collateral damage to purely civilian infrastructure and even loss of innocent lives which are then used by the irregular forces for propaganda purposes.

Urbanisation. Another noticeable trend, flowing from civilianisation, is for combat operations to be conducted in urban areas rather than in the more rural and less populated parts of the theatre. This is a conscious attempt by irregular forces to take advantage of the complexity of operations, particularly against conventional military forces reliant on superior firepower for success, in built-up areas where the margin of error is very limited. By operating in urban, populated areas, the irregular forces effectively neutralise the sophisticated technological capabilities of conventional forces, who are bound to operate within the LOAC and further restrictive rules of engagement, and thereby compel them to fight on an equal footing. Such operations also provide propaganda opportunities to the irregular forces whenever the military forces commit errors in targeting that lead to damage of civilian infrastructure.

Issue of Prediction. From the perspective of democratic and stable nations, who carry most of the burden of intervention, one of the

---

3 Rupy, Kendra, &Rustad, Siri Aas, *Trends in Armed Conflict 1946-2017*, Peace Research Institute, Oslo, 2018.

biggest challenges is to predict with reasonable accuracy the geographic location of the next challenge.[4] While it is possible to monitor the politico-economic progress, or otherwise, of developing and fragile states to a certain extent, the actual descent into chaos may come without any warning. This situation will obviously create a disadvantage for the intervening nations and their forces. However, in the emerging global politico-security environment, stabilisation and security operations assume far greater importance because of the disruption—security and/or economic—that can be caused by the failure of even small states. Further, international approval for such intervention, usually through the United Nations, will also add to the time required to initiate appropriate action. Delay in stabilising a deteriorating situation will always make it more difficult to stabilise, leading to the stabilising force having to enforce peace through the lethal application of force although the application of force is something that stabilising forces would want to avoid. Another factor that directly affects the concept of intervention is the critical necessity to have domestic public support for the success of such operations. Unfettered support for intervention could be a challenge, especially if such intervention is not in the immediate neighbourhood of the nation concerned. Successful predictions can enable proactive intervention and can reduce the need to apply force as well as lessen the essential requirement to seek public support for such actions.

Small Force Elements. Even the biggest war will require small war capabilities. Any campaign is a combination of smaller engagements, at times conducted simultaneously, that together create the decisive impact necessary to overwhelm the adversary. Special operations, irregular warfare tactics and dispersed operations are becoming defining characteristics of the modern battlefield. This dispersed and dynamic characteristic of contemporary conflict requires that sufficient autonomy be given to small operations and point towards an increasing independent status being bestowed on small force elements. While this is possibly a necessity in contemporary circumstances, it would be far more efficient to create a command infrastructure that is contextually

---

4   Hughes, Dr Geraint, *Predicting Future Trends in Warfare*, Defence-in-Depth, Defence Studies Department, King's College, London, 2018, https://defenceindepth.co/2018/02/21/predicting-future-trends-in-warfare/ accessed on 01 October 2018.

adaptable but one that functions under a set of enduring traditional command guidelines without it being altered unconditionally.

Conventional Military Forces

Most of the conventional military forces of the world—those of democratic nations as well as autocratic ones—are structured to carry out combat operations against forces like themselves, military forces of other sovereign states. However, the experience of the past decades have challenged this traditional construct and forced military forces to adapt their capabilities and force structure to cater for an altered combat environment that attempts to reduce the effectiveness of conventional forces. Today all efficient military forces, although structured around conventional capabilities to defeat other conventional forces, are designed with the necessary flexibility built into them to be able to rapidly adapt to even severe asymmetric challenges and overcome initial setbacks. To a large extent the ability to leverage of inherent flexibility will depend on the effectiveness of the force's leadership—honed through experience in various contexts and overcoming challenges of decision-making in dynamic circumstances—across all levels. Multifaceted experience of the officer cadre will be a distinct advantage in these conditions.

Even under conditions that are more advantageous for irregular forces, conventional forces have certain inherent capabilities that can be leveraged to their advantage. First, these forces have the ability to move swiftly into multiple theatres of operations through employing air mobility—a rapid force projection capability through the employment of expeditionary forces that cannot be matched by even the best irregular force. Second, they have the ability to carry out high-end operations as a matter of course, which could be tailored to overwhelm an adversary with far lesser firepower and staying power. Third, at the operational level conventional forces have the ability to manoeuvre rapidly while continuing to be engaged in contact with the adversary through managing effective communications and leveraging the larger mass available to them. The ability to carry out deep precision strikes is the fourth advantage that can create an advantage. In combination with the ability to conduct time-sensitive targeting—that could pre-empt or even prevent conflict and will definitely have direct and immediate impact on the on-going combat operations—the strike capability of conventional military forces is one that should be tailored to emerging operational conditions.

Integration of Effects. The fifth advantage that conventional forces can create is the integration of effects, although such integration has still not been optimally achieved. This is a complex process.[5] Operational effects can be purely in the physical domain and need not have any impact on the cognitive domain of the adversary. However, the ultimate objective should be to influence the highest level of the cognitive domain—the belief system. In order to achieve this, the connection between kinetic action and the cognitive domain must be clearly understood and it may be necessary to go through a number of stages to make the link in an indirect manner. The focus will have to be targeting the cognitive domain with increased fidelity and sophistication.

Summing Up...

The use of force to enable individual and collective security is as old the beginning of human interaction and stems from basic human nature that demands physical safety at all times. In the broader context, this requirement translates to wars and armed conflicts. In parallel to the urge to use force to achieve one's objectives, the altruistic nature of human beings also attempt to move towards upholding moral and ethical bindings within the accepted norms of the time. In turn this move has restricted the use of force in the conduct of war to some extent. The fact that the complete force available to a military force cannot now be unleashed on an adversary without international condemnation has led to the quest for increasing the efficiency of military forces. Improvement in efficiency has been achieved through the innovative use of technology.

These trends in the conduct of war affects the actions at the lower end of the strategic level in a noticeable manner. The trends are also becoming tangibly more complex because of the increasing uncertainty in the conduct of war. In effect wars have become unstructured activities that cannot be predicted with accuracy. The situation is exacerbated by the addition of two more domains to warfighting activities—that

---

5   Gompert, David C., 'Preparing Military Forces for Integrated Operations in the Face of Uncertainty', *Rand Issue Paper*, Rand, San Francisco, 2005, pp. 9-12.

of cyber and space. When these two domains are superimposed on the three conventional domains, the complexity in the conduct of war increases exponentially. Initiating action under these circumstances will require a robust and sophisticated command and control structure.

In recent times, wars are increasingly being fought in urban areas because of the proclivity of irregular forces to merge with civilians for shelter and to seek support within the non-combatants. This trend escalates the chances of creating collateral damage that has become politically unacceptable to the democratic nations of the world. However, the trend to merge with civilians in the urban environment is becoming common making it difficult to clearly demarcate the battlespace. Inevitably the battlespace of modern conflict has a mix of combatants and civilians in it. Further, there is also a trend in modern conflict that tends to employ civilians as combatants. This is achieved by the creation of irregular militias, insurgents and other non-state entities. In most cases the status of these combatants vis-à-vis the LOAC is uncertain, which introduces another complication to the equation.

Instability in volatile regions of the world brings about the need for focused intervention by the more developed and stable nations of the world. The situation is further exacerbated by the difficulty in predicting the region where a future instability will evolve. The United Nations Resolution on the 'responsibility to protect' (R2P) has unambiguously created an altruistic moral responsibility for the democratic nations of the world to step into extremely complex geo-political situations. The trend is for the onus of responsibility to contain deteriorating geo-strategic and politico-economic situations to be shifted to the developed world. As a corollary, any such intervention however well-intentioned, will invite the criticism of the UN concept of R2P being selectively applied. The situation is vexed, to say the least. There is no doubt that in order to be successful in modern combat situations, the inherent capabilities of the military forces—upon which rests the ultimate responsibility for the protections of the sovereignty of the state—will have to be contextually adapted. Only well-developed flexibility of the conventional forces will be able to cater for the evolving trends in the conduct of war.

Chapter 11

IRREGULAR WARFARE: THE ASYMMETRIC CORE

Leveraging asymmetry in conducting irregular warfare is not a new concept; it has been used all through history by forces that are inferior either numerically or in overall capability as compared to the adversary. It has also been the favourite method employed by a conquered people to resist a more powerful invading force. The primary principle is to neutralise whatever advantage the adversary has through the employment of innovative strategies and tactics that are different to the commonly used ones and at times do not even adhere to the accepted norms of the conduct of combat.

Insurgencies and Guerrilla Warfare

Insurgency and guerrilla warfare are not the same kind of conflict, but form the nucleus of irregular warfare. However, the differences between insurgencies and guerrilla wars are delicately nuanced and of interest only when clear distinctions are to be made in terms of the origin of an on-going conflict and to distinguish the adversary in each case. Insurgencies are normally conducted against the incumbent government by indigenous groups in an attempt to redress perceived or actual grievances and persecution—political, ideological, economic or religious. However, dependent on a number of factors, the insurgency could start to get support from outside the nation and/or the government could also ask for and receive external assistance to contain the insurgency. Further, if the conflict is of a magnitude that could affect the broader regional stability, other nations of the region—as yet unaffected by the conflict—might decide to intervene unilaterally to manage the issue. In most cases when external agencies get involved, the pattern and intensity of the insurgency tends to change for the worse, with the chances of it developing into a guerrilla war and further into a full-fledged civil war increasing considerably with any kind of external interference.

Guerrilla wars are typically efforts to get rid of unwelcome occupiers of the nation.[1] Although insurgencies can deteriorate to guerrilla wars, they do not normally start for the same reasons. Guerrilla wars span a broad spectrum of conflict. At the low end are small-scale raids, ambushes and attacks by small groups acting independently to achieve localised objectives and to harass the occupying power. These could also be at times classified as insurgent operations, if the reason for the attacks is not clear. The high end of the spectrum is mobile warfare conducted both by small groups as well as large formations, equipped with modern arms and pursuing a fully integrated politico-military strategy.[2] While insurgencies can develop and become low end guerrilla wars, it normally does not develop into the high end, dedicated big formation mobile warfare. However, insurgencies and guerrilla wars share some distinct similarities, especially in their broad characteristics and conduct. Both rely heavily on asymmetric concepts of operations to obtain and retain battlefield initiative, and the use of asymmetry in most cases is restricted to the operational level of conflict.

In a similar manner to distinguishing insurgencies and guerrilla wars, it is also necessary to understand—from the perspective of the conventional military forces—the fundamental difference between counter-insurgency operations, commonly termed COIN, and a traditional military campaign. The basic difference is in the desired end-state to be achieved. Accepting the fundamental truism that all conflicts or wars are essentially political in nature in relation to their ultimate end-state, the difference is obviously in the military end-state to be pursued. A military campaign—one that is conducted against another sovereign military force—will, or should in ideal circumstances, have

---

1 Weir, William, *Guerrilla Warfare: Irregular warfare in the Twentieth Century*, Pentagon Press, New Delhi, 2009, p. ix.

2 Sirohi, Captain R. K., *Guerrilla Warfare*, Prashant Publishing House, Delhi, 2009, pp. 2-3.

a clearly articulated military end-state, the achievement of which will end combat operations. Thereafter it becomes the responsibility of other elements of national power to leverage off the military 'victory' to ensure that political objectives are achieved. This continuum of objectives is easy to visualise and conceptualise effectively.

In contrast, COIN operations undertaken by conventional military forces, by their very nature, are difficult to understand in a conventional construct.[3] In COIN the purely military objectives can only be laid-down at the tactical level in most cases. The strategic objectives are normally a complex mix of socio-political and economic imperatives that a military force can at best derive only very diffused strategic objectives for their operations involving the application of force. COIN is essentially about meeting primarily social, political and economic expectations of the larger population of the affected nation. In this space the role of the military becomes peripheral, in creating a safe environment for other government agencies operating to mitigate grievances. While this fundamental aspect of insurgencies and the concepts for countering them seem straightforward and simple to understand, the normal reaction of governments to insurgencies seem to be devoid of any rational thinking on these lines. The initial reaction is always military. This may indeed be necessary to stabilise the insurgent region, but it also begs the question as to how the insurgency was allowed to develop to a stage wherein the domestic policing and internal security mechanisms are unable to deal with it. Further, there is also the question of the objectives that a government requires the military to achieve when employed against insurgencies, which in a majority of cases are never clear. All governments have to accept the fact that insurgencies cannot be defeated or contained through the employment of military forces alone.

There is also a very clearly discernible tendency in democratic nations to turn to the military forces to carry out operations that are meant to improve the socio-economic status of the people who support insurgencies. Once again, this is a misuse of military forces since they are not trained for these duties. The corollary is that this inappropriate

---

3 Rid, Thomas, & Keaney, Thomas, *Understanding Counterinsurgency: Doctrine, operations, and challenges,* Routledge, Abington, 2010. (Particularly the introductory chapter 'Understanding Counterinsurgency' by the editors)

use of military forces creates a tendency for a government to not invest in alternative and more suitable organisations to carry out such operations. This trend is becoming more pronounced as the developed world is becoming increasingly involved in countering destabilising insurgencies in the less developed regions of the world. Such a trend is fraught with the danger of diluting the military forces' warfighting abilities required for them to be effective in their core responsibility of securing the sovereignty of the nation and protecting its interests. As the 21 century progresses, democratic nations have to be cognisant of the pitfalls of over utilising the military forces on peripheral duties.

Irregular Forces: Characteristics and Conduct of Operations[4]

All non-state entities, insurgent groups and guerrilla forces are clubbed together under the term irregular forces. The very term, 'irregular', indicates that these forces are the opposite of regular or conventional forces—in dress, concepts, modus operandi, warfighting ethos and in not being accredited to a sovereign nation. In a very broad manner all these groups, whether insurgents or guerrillas, share some common characteristics as well as similarities in the conduct of their operations. The scale of activity may vary in different cases, but they operate in a narrow band within the spectrum of conflict, that is between peace keeping and enforcement and conventional military conflict. More often than not irregular forces support an ideology or concept rather than the notion of a nation and can be spread across a number of nations, at times even transcending ethnic and linguistic homogeneity.

A primary strength of irregular forces is that they are living, evolving entities that thrive with the support of complex adaptive networks. They are in a state of constant evolution fundamentally to ensure their survival since conventional forces can overwhelm a static irregular force through the use of superior capabilities resident in them. They are idiosyncratic in nature, drawing strength and sustenance from dynamic concepts, both in their ideology and operations. The same dynamism provides irregular forces with varying levels of resistance, redundancy and recuperative capabilities, making them extremely difficult to totally eliminate as entities. This is further emphasised by

---

4   Thornton, Rod, *Asymmetric Warfare: Threat and Response in the Twenty-First Century*, Polity Press, Cambridge, U.K., 2007.

their ability to operate without leaving any clear foot print to follow or track, making the task of countering them extremely hard.

Irregular groups can be completely homogenous in their makeup, in terms of ethnicity, religion, language, customs and all other aspects that distinguish one human being from another. However, they can also be an eclectic mix of societal groups, political parties and religiously motivated terrorist groups that are in combined manner singularly focused on one particular objective. A common factor in all these groups is their common and unusual understanding of victory. For most of these groups not being defeated is considered victory, which is contradictory to the popular belief that victory in conflict starts with the defeat of the adversary.

Asymmetry. One of the primary characteristics that define irregular forces is their proclivity to resort to asymmetric warfare when confronted with the greater power projection capabilities of conventional military forces. The concept of asymmetry is essentially the strategy of the weak, aimed at eroding the greater power and control of a nation. Under these circumstances the effectiveness of the traditional strategy of deterrence—the show of force and demonstrated capability and willingness to employ the force—will be diluted considerably. In most cases irregular wars start with minor disruptive activities that cover limited geographical areas and then gradually escalate to envelope larger swaths as the irregular force gains ground. The transition from minor operations to full-fledged irregular war may or may not take place and is dependent on the support that it receives and the actions initiated by the government. While embarking on an irregular war itself is an overarching strategy, it does not follow any formalised strategic plan towards which lower level activities are directed. The entities perpetrating insurgencies are normally self-organising, in that they grow from outside support and splinter at will into separate entities with only very tenuous connection between the splintered elements. This ability to morph into new forms is a primary strength of irregular forces. An irregular force must have the capacity to transform and adapt to emerging situations and changing environments in order to survive. This is the built-in resilience of such forces. This resilience also provides the group with the ability to respond to external stimuli in an expedient manner, in most cases making them even more effective.

Command Structure. Irregular forces generally have a vague and diffused command structure, making it impossible to identify the leadership, although large guerrilla groups may have a more hierarchical command ethos. This in turn creates a situation where the operational objectives and its connection to the ideological end-state are difficult to clearly map out and understand. Further, the diffused operational ethos prevents the identification of the centres of gravity of the insurgents or non-state entities making it difficult to clearly target them. These forces mount operations from purely civilian bases, which inhibit the unrestrained use of force by the opponent in an attempt to avoid unnecessary collateral damage to non-combatants and even dual-use infrastructure. Another factor complicates the command structure further. A majority of irregular forces will be cellular in their organisational structure because of the diverse sources—religion, patriotism, ethnicity, political ideology etc.—from which they emerge. Therefore, it is not impossible for one irregular entity to be comprised of diverse cells interacting at different levels, but very loosely bound to an ultimate objective. This facilitates operations to be controlled at different levels in a contextual basis, further complicating the understanding of their chain of command. Irregular forces tend to be a broad network rather than centrally controlled.

Modus Operandi. Irregular forces fighting in support of an ideology are extremely difficult to define, since ideology is not a physical entity. Their strength, against more conventional forces, lies in their diffused state of existence that makes it difficult to define them as an entity. This is further aggravated by the geographical fluidity that irregular forces cultivate by operating within the population and moving away from contact with the adversary at a time of their choice. This also translates to a battlefield not being geographically defined which is a distinct disadvantage to conventional forces that tend to adopt traditional concepts of operations. These forces will almost never enter into a set-piece battle and nor will they face off with other forces directly. In all instances they will shy away from direct confrontation, even with numerically inferior conventional forces. Irregular forces almost always resort to hit and run raids, use of booby traps etc., to create asymmetric advantages. This permits them to choose the battlefield of engagement, set the objective to be achieved in a particular skirmish and choose the optimum tactical action to do so. The success of initial actions will determine the long-term operational concept that they adopt.

International Norms. Another aspect that distinguishes most irregular forces is their calculated ruthlessness in the actual conduct of combat that is contrary to any internationally accepted norms as well as the callous and inhumane treatment of prisoners. This is possibly adopted as a means of making the conventional forces apprehensive about their status both in combat and as prisoners if they are captured and thereby lowering the morale of the force. It is also reasonable to assume that these tactics are adopted because of the underlying belief that conventional forces will always adhere to LOAC and other international conventions. As an extension of this belief, the irregular force generally considers adhering to LOAC, ROE and humanitarian considerations by the conventional military forces as weaknesses to be exploited.

Local Support. The success or failure of an irregular force is almost completely underwritten by the local support it can generate because of their lack of strategic depth and limited resource availability. In a majority of cases, some amount of local support will be willingly offered, especially if the fight is against an unpopular regime or foreign occupier. However, the issue of local support is much more complicated than it seems on the surface. The availability of support will depend on the socio-economic circumstances of the area, with active resistance being offered by civilians in certain cases. This will be the case especially if the government forces tend to enforce their writ on the same areas with the use of force. In these circumstances irregular forces have been seen to resort to the use of force to intimidate all who oppose them and to gain support of the local population for their activities. While this may not be the ideal way to win the 'hearts and minds' of the local population, there are any number of instances of irregular forces using coercive means to obtain resources from local areas. The upside, from the irregular forces' perspective is that, the willingness of local support—even through coercion—tends to increase with the overall success of the insurgency or guerrilla war.

Long War Strategies. Irregular forces conducting asymmetric warfare will try to develop and employ unconventional anti-access strategies to deter intervention by international forces. These strategies could include the capture or destruction of access infrastructure like air ports, roads and railway lines, indiscriminate attacks on innocent civilians as well as incumbent government authority and the covert encouragement of anti-social activities. They will also attempt to prolong the engagement in the belief that the political will of the intervening nation or coalition of nations will be short-lived and that the conventional forces will be withdrawn sooner rather than later. This 'long war' concept is based on the willingness of the irregular force to continue sporadic engagements for a long time and the belief, based on historic examples, that democracies tire easily of war and attrition.[5] The lack of will to ensure staying power, compounded by the high costs or prolonging a conflict, is considered a weak link and vulnerability to be targeted. In addition, this belief is taken further, not without some amount of justification, in viewing the western nations' aversion and low tolerance towards own casualties as another complimentary centre of gravity that can be exploited to influence a speedy withdrawal. Resorting to indiscriminate killing through the use of 'suicide bombers' and improvised explosive devises is probably a tactic based on this belief. Suicide terrorism is also an effective psychological tool that can create a sense of helplessness in the civilian population, turning them away from supporting government forces.

Unconventional War. The conduct of an unconventional or asymmetric war has two fundamental defining characteristics. First, the battlefield appears empty and fragmented because of the adversary's dispersal and concealment. This means that the irregular combatants blend with the population easily, and by being amongst the people, leave the fighting space empty. It is fragmented because by employing the tactics of diffusing into the population, the irregular force denies any recognisable fronts in the conflict, ensuring that the battlefield is effectively fragmented but can come up anywhere at the time and space of their choice. Second, asymmetric conflict is almost always characterised by very high tempo and intensity, which is controlled by the irregular force and not the conventional force opposing them. However, it can also be observed that the tempo and intensity peak and wane in irregular patterns, adding to the complexity of forward planning in countering these operations. Further, battle is joined

---

5   Morrissey, John, *The Long War: Centcom, Grand Strategy and Global Security*, University of Georgia Press, Georgia, 2017, pp. 49-70.

abruptly and the duration of each engagement is dependent on circumstances and almost always controlled by the irregular force. A combination of these factors, that give the irregular force the initiative in most encounters, is a challenge to overcome.

Technology. A subsidiary factor to be considered is that with the easy availability of sophisticated technology in the covert arms market, the gap between traditional high-end conventional conflict and the lower-end irregular wars is reducing. Today, irregular forces that have sufficient resources operate highly technical anti-aircraft missiles and other capabilities. In this equation, conventional military forces will have to be extremely adaptable to change their modus operandi after deploying into theatre when the presence of high-end capabilities within the irregular force becomes apparent. Unawareness of such capabilities can very rapidly lead to tactical defeat for the conventional force. While a tactical defeat can easily be overcome, in the case of these conflicts, it could as quickly bear influence at the strategic level leading to grave consequences. As a corollary, even without being defeated tactically, it is possible for the conventional forces to suffer strategic set-backs. The employment of conventional military forces in asymmetric warfare should be a carefully considered and exercised option.

DEFEATING IRREGULAR FORCES

Defeating an irregular force is an involved process, but not outside the capability spectrum of a well-trained conventional military force. Even if the initial phases of a campaign are conducted in a reactive manner, it is possible to turn the tide and seize the initiative from the less organised adversary who also has to cater for inferiority in firepower and manoeuvre. The characteristics resident in conventional forces have to be optimised in a contextual manner to cater for individual circumstances.[6] No two irregular wars or insurgencies are totally alike. There may be similarities, but each of them needs to be analysed and counter strategies developed to suit the particular requirements. The

---

6 White, Jeffrey B., *Some Thoughts on Irregular Warfare: A Different Kind of Threat*, Centre for the Study of Intelligence, Washington D.C., April 2007, https://www.cia.gov/library/center-for-the-study-of-intelligence/csi-publications/csi-studies/studies/96unclass/iregular.htm accessed on 30 March 2015.

failure of conventional military forces to prevail against non-state entities can be traced to their inability to adapt and optimise their superior capabilities.

Isolating Networks

Countering and containing irregular forces is far more difficult than conducting a campaign against conventional forces of another nation for a number of reasons. Fundamentally this is because an irregular force is diffused and does not present a viable centre of gravity that can be targeted to debilitate the force. In most cases they are intentionally splintered into many parts to ensure survival even in case some parts are neutralised. Therefore, an irregular force normally operates as a group of independent networks, loosely connected to form a coherent whole, which is one of their primary strengths. As a corollary, the responses have to be multiple and simultaneous for effectiveness. However, this strength can be carefully targeted and gradually turned into a weakness that can then be exploited. Success will require a multi-pronged strategy that simultaneously attacks an individual networks ability to operate, its internal capacity to generate power and at the same time isolates the network from the broader force. This will target the fitness of a particular network contribute to the irregular force and will gradually erode its overall capability to continue the conflict.

A conventional force that operates in a network enabled manner will be able to take the initiative in a more comprehensive manner than a force operating with a traditional focus. The other factor in pursuing a multi-pronged strategy is that the necessity and criticality of the human beings in implementing such a strategy will always slow the system. When the strategy is to be applied to a dynamic irregular force, there is the chance of the human element slowing the process to an extent wherein the irregular force is able to extricate itself from the attack without suffering much damage.

Expeditionary Capabilities

From the perspective of a conventional military force encountering an irregular force that adopts asymmetric warfare strategies and tactics, there are two facets of its expeditionary capabilities that can be used to advantage.[7] First, the expeditionary capabilities resident in conventional forces can be adapted to create the capability to concentrate force in different areas of the theatre as required. The inherent ability of conventional forces to respond swiftly to geographically distant areas is a clear advantage that facilitates a numerically small force to cover a large geographical area. This also reduces response time thereby curtailing the adversary's ability to prepare and creating an element of surprise. Rapid response capabilities create greater real-time capacity to intervene that when combined with increased lethality and range of conventional military forces produces an increased capacity to contain emerging security challenges of all kinds. When the challenge is asymmetric in nature, this capability is extremely valuable.

Second, to overcome irregular forces it is necessary to engage them as far out in time and space as possible. This means that a nation must possess force projection capabilities that have excellent range and reach and are imbued with sufficient expeditionary capabilities. Terrorism—that resides at the lower end of the spectrum of irregular warfare—should almost always be combated in an expeditionary manner, other than in cases where it is generated from within the nation itself. In addition to being expeditionary, these operations will entail increased overseas deployments for both military and civilian agency personnel and will bring with them complex management issues. By its very expeditionary nature, these operations will generate engagements with their own unique characteristics as well as the necessity for involved diplomatic initiatives.

Pre-emption[8]

There is another strategy that could be used to counter the proliferation of asymmetry. It may not be politically acceptable in all circumstances, but the strategy of military pre-emption—neutralising the emerging threat before it can develop into a full grown insurgency

---

7   Dorman, A., Smith, M., &Uttley, M., (eds), *The Changing Face of Military Power: Joint Warfighting in an expeditionary Era*, Cormorant Security Studies Series, Palgrave Macmillan, UK, 2002, pp. 15-43.

8   Gupta, Sanjay, 'The Doctrine of Pre-Emptive Strike: Application and Implications', *International Political Science Review*, Vol 29, No 2, March 2008, Sage Publications, California, pp. 181-196. https://www.jstor.org/stable/20445135?seq=1#page_scan_tab_contents accessed on 310 March 2015.

or irregular war—is an option that must be considered at the highest level of national decision-making. This strategy can be effective in circumstances where other whole-of-government-approach forms of intervention have failed. There are two fundamental advantages of pre-emptively countering a possible threat and containing its escalation. First, it is much more cost-effective than having to carry out a full-fledged intervention to fight an irregular war that includes the deployment of ground forces into hostile territory. Second, it provides a clear demonstration of a nation's intend and willingness to use its power projection capabilities in a proactive manner to secure its interest. From such demonstrations flows the concept of effective deterrence.

Information Warfare

Conventional military forces have technological advantage over the irregular forces that would permit them to disseminate information and intelligence at a faster rate than the adversary. This is critical at the tactical level of the conflict because the irregular forces have the inherent capacity to disperse swiftly after initiating an offensive action. Rapid information dissemination that creates an opportunity for obtaining decision superiority is crucial to winning battles and campaigns in any kind of war. Decision-making capacity at all levels of command and conflict—its speed, veracity and applicability—directly affect mission effectiveness.

Adaptive usage of communication superiority can create an asymmetry by itself for the conventional forces that can be exploited to great advantage. This can create both strategic and tactical advantage through exploiting the element of surprise. In the case of irregular forces, information dissemination has an added importance. Normally knowledge of the adversary is obtained at the higher levels of command and then disseminated into the lower levels on an as required basis. This process works well when the adversary is a conventional military force. In the case of an irregular force—where an adaptive command and control model is the optimum—it is necessary to provide commanders at all levels with the necessary information because combat decisions in most cases would be taken at the lower levels of command without sufficient time available to obtain information. Only with sufficient information will a small unit of the conventional force be able to target the core structure of the irregular force, which is one of their few appreciable centres of gravity.

Containment

Irregular wars can be countered at different levels depending on the capability of the government to take decisive action. The actions can be scaled in stages from prevention to pre-emption, followed by containment and management and after that to instituting recovery. Options available to the incumbent government continually reduce as the scale moves towards management. Prevention—the optimum solution in all cases—can only be achieved through having sufficient intelligence gathering capacity, both technology-enabled and human collection, and the civilian and military means to enforce compensatory measures. Pre-emption has already been discussed in detail.

Containment, while requiring military measures, should also be combined with providing legitimate alternatives to the irregular force to wean them away from adopting violent means to achieve their objectives. Military action should be aimed at exposing and neutralising key elements of the irregular force, suppressing loosely coupled liaisons between its elements and identifying, isolating and attacking fundamental dependencies of the force. At the same time, military responses should be precise and discriminatory to avoid any collateral damage that could have unintended consequences. The primary aim should always be to maintain support of the local population by protecting them form intimidation by the irregular forces and ensuring that no damage is done to civilian infrastructure. In most cases this would entail having a robust border protection system so that the irregular forces do not receive any external assistance and also are unable to seek sanctuary outside the nation's borders and sovereign control. These are all short-term solutions to contain an irregular force.

Long Term Solution

Management of insurgencies and irregular wars requires that the incumbent government take a long-term view of it. The primary cause for the development of these conflicts is dissatisfaction within the general population with the conditions of their regular day-to-day living. Such grievances could stem from political repression, religious prosecution, suppression of basic freedoms, endemic poverty perceived to be the fault of the government and even gradual societal changes that reach a critical point. In the long term, only initiatives to change the belief system will have any effect in subduing the unrest within the population. This could take the form of providing opportunities for political participation and freedom, moving towards an inclusive and tolerant religious framework, ensuring the basic human rights and freedoms for the population and development of institutions and processes that will provide education and improve the employment prospects, especially of the younger generation.

Investing in the overall development of the nation to provide opportunities for the people to achieve their aspirations and engaging in public diplomacy to influence their belief system—where both initiatives are interlinked and one cannot succeed without the other—is perhaps the only long term solution.[9] Widespread individual prosperity that increases collective economic stability is best achieved in democratic nations. In a roundabout manner, it can be surmised that since individual economic growth and political and religious freedoms are more readily obtainable in democracies, the chances of irregular wars or insurgencies taking place in them are lesser than in autocratic states. In other word, individual prosperity is foundational for stability.

Other Factors

There are a number of other factors that should be carefully analysed and acted on to defeat irregular forces. Countering insurgencies may have to be a bottom up process, especially after it has taken root and the government has moved to a containment stage. This would mean that the highest level national strategy for defeating the irregular forces will have to emanate from the tactical appreciation of the lower level commanders and soldiers regarding the best way to contain the spread of insurgency. Such an approach however, must be the exception rather than the rule since influencing the belief system of a disgruntled part of the population will have to be a strategic initiative employing all elements of national power.

---

9 Baille, Mark, 'Know your enemy: Not just terrorism,' *Defense News*, Virginia, 11 April 2005, p. 21.

The all-pervasive nature of science and technology normally provides the conventional military force with an edge over the less developed irregular forces. However, in the contemporary security environment, irregular forces also have access to technologically sophisticated weapon systems and the technology gap is not as pronounced as it used to be even a decade ago. Therefore the pervasive nature of technology in contemporary battlefields does not provide a complete answer to the challenges that emerge when containing irregular forces. It will also be necessary for the government to control the easy availability of dual-use technology when an irregular war is being conducted.

Terrorism is normally placed at the lower end of the spectrum of irregular wars. Terrorism is an extreme form of asymmetry—especially the suicide bombing tactics—and will almost always create an element of surprise in favour of the irregular force. However, a stable democratic nation will not be undermined by even a number of acts of suicide terrorism since it goes against the foundation of democracy, that of individual freedoms. The unexpectedness of such attacks, at least in the initial stages, may not always lead to an advantage for the irregular forces. If the response to such acts that create surprise is nationally coordinated and strategically focused, the impact will be greatly diluted and will dissipate faster than if the response originates at the operational and tactical levels.

Defeating terrorists, insurgencies or guerrilla forces—irregular forces of all kinds—will always have to be a whole-of-nation enterprise. The military forces have a definitive and critical role to play in this, but the responsibility to contain and manage these conflicts and then recover the nation to stability cannot be abrogated to the military. Such an action by the government is bound to fail with perhaps disastrous consequences for the sovereignty of the nation.

Summing Up...

The concept of irregular warfare is as old as warfare itself and is fundamentally dependent on asymmetry. It consists of insurgency, unconventional warfare, counter-insurgency—in effect any kind of armed conflict other than conventional military-on-military war.[10] Insurgency and guerrilla warfare are at the core on irregular warfare, but are not the same. There are nuanced differences between the two even though the modus operandi of both may be the same. The similarity also goes down to the base level where, in both cases, the political and/or religious ideology is the point of conflict.

Similarly, COIN is different to the normal, conventional campaigns, although both are conducted by traditional military forces. In COIN operations, only the armed conflict, the application of lethal force, is the responsibility of the military forces. Insurgencies can be contained only by adopting a whole-of-nation approach and there are no purely military solutions to such conflicts. In a majority of cases the insurgency is started and fuelled by economic and social disparity within a nation and the extreme deprived state of the poor people. This fundamental cause, socio-economic in nature, cannot be addressed by the military forces and needs a concerted effort at the national level to alleviate.

Irregular forces, a term that encompasses all fighting forces other than the constituted military forces of a sovereign nation, are evolving entities. Their ability to evolve on a continuous basis, dependent on the context, is their primary strength. They are dynamic because of necessity and the more successful irregular forces adopt their dynamism to become an inherent characteristic. Irregular forces embody resilience and redundancy, making it extremely difficult to eliminate them fully. They have a fundamental advantage in that not being fully defeated is counted as victory.

Irrespective of whether an irregular force is engaged in insurgency, guerrilla warfare or some other kind of armed conflict, they share some common characteristics. First, all of them rely on asymmetry—the strategy of the weak and numerically inferior forces—for success. The strategy of asymmetry relies on a distributed action-oriented concept of operations. Second, these forces normally have a diffused command structure. Even though there is an accepted commander of the forces, the rank and file are not centrally controlled but operate

---

10 For a holistic understanding of modern counterinsurgency read, Kilcullen, David J., *Counterinsurgency*, Oxford University Press, New York, 2010.

under a general guidance that indicate the strategic goal. Third, irregular forces and their composition are difficult to define, since they are normally supporting an ideology—political or religious. Flowing form this ambiguity, it becomes difficult to pinpoint their strength and it is difficult to identify and target their centres of gravity.

Fourth, most irregular forces do not adhere to the accepted norms of the conduct of war and pay no heed to international laws that guide the use of lethal force. Therefore, they demonstrate a propensity to exploit the regular forces' instinctive adherence to the LOAC and other rules of engagement. In the eyes of irregular forces the LOAC is a distinct weakness in the operations of regular military forces. Fifth, irregular forces lack strategic depth and is completely dependent on local support for success. Their success and local support form a self-perpetuating cycle—the more local support that irregular forces get, better their chances of success and their increasing success brings them more local support. Sixth, most irregular forces have a long-term strategy meant to tire the opponent and dilute the political will of the opponent. They develop anti-access capabilities for the territories over which they may have tenuous control and carryout continuous and long-tern disruptive activities.

Defeating an irregular adversary is not an easy task and needs specialist training that is very different to the traditional training imparted to regular military forces. The skill sets required of the military are very different to the ones needed to succeed in conventional military operations. Irregular wars are most long drawn affairs and therefore military forces engaged in such conflicts run the risk of being tempted to alter their force structure and concepts of operations to cater for it. Such adaptations will be detrimental to the forces' capacity to conduct successful conventional campaigns. The ideal situation would be to create a separate force to conduct irregular warfare, while retaining the regular army for high-end combat. Defeating irregular forces will always remain a whole-of-nation long-term endeavour where all elements of national power contribute to the conflict.

In the 21st century, there have already been more irregular wars than at any other comparative timeframe in world history. The regular military force, thrown into the fray at random, have been struggling to adapt to the ever-changing and intelligent adversary. It is certain that only military forces that are agile and sure-footed in a completely flexible manner will be able to succeed, without succumbing to the onslaught.

Chapter 12

CHALLENGES OF A NEW ERA

Conflict is at the heart of human interaction—individual, across groups and between nations. The disparities in living standards—the product of a number of sub-sets that are fundamental to development—between the haves and the have-nots within a nation and between nations will continually erode the progress towards a stable, all-inclusive and peaceful strategic environment. This has been an eternal challenge to global security with only the catalysts for confrontation changing with time.

The contemporary environment faces a number of challenges, some far greater than what has been faced before.[1] However, the capacity of the more stable nations of the world to intervene even in faraway places have also increased manyfold in the past few decades. The ethos of the international community has evolved into one that is largely intolerant of nations where basic human rights are abused and other regimes that oppress their own people in brutal ways. The United Nations has become a vociferous advocate of the need to protect human rights and also supports the concept of 'right to protect' that is a contemporary attempt at legalising external interventions needed to create a safe environment for people in volatile areas. While these are laudable developments, the implementation of this good intent has not come up to the lofty ideals and is seen to be biased in its application. Therefore, the world remains unstable in an overarching manner with a number of areas in a state of low level but continuous

---

1 Camilleri, Joseph A., 'The Competition for Power and Legitimacy in an Age of Transition', in Solomon, Hussein, (ed), *Challenges to Global Security: Geopoliticsand Power in an Age of Transition*, I.B. Tauris & Co, London, 2008, pp. 27-54.

volatility with the potential to boil over very rapidly if the right catalysts come together. The more concerning aspect is that these areas cover a large swath of territories and nations starting from southern Europe, eastern Mediterranean, the Middle-East, South Asia, all the way up to the northern mountains of North Korea.

There are also other emerging challenges for which no adequate solutions exist and which will continue to evolve along with the attempts to contain them. Therefore these challenges have to be viewed and dealt with as long-term issues that have the potential to create catastrophic destabilisation within a region and at times even globally. The main ones are the issue of weapons of mass destruction, breakthrough technologies and the constraints faced by nations to act in unison to neutralise global threats.

The major challenges to global stability at the beginning of the 21st century are: the financial crisis enveloping the older democracies that were supposed to be stable and 'developed'; the on-going spread of radical Islam combined with the developments in the Middle-East that has been termed the 'Arab Spring'; national governments, mostly in the developing world, that do not have the capacity to govern properly leading to the state either failing or becoming a rogue state; and the rise of nations without sufficient maturity to positions of international power. While the global impact of these challenges, at least for the present, seems to be minimal, they have the potential to spread in uncontrolled ways with disastrous consequences to stability. It has been seen repeatedly that stability—economic, governance and societal—are fundamental requirements to ensure security, with in a nation, region and by extension the world.

A Declining Europe

The end of the Cold War could be also equated to the end of the European Era—the waning of European dominance in world affairs.[2] The collapse of the Soviet Union while bringing new hope of a peaceful world order also brought about a loss of focus on foreign policy to the more developed nations, perhaps because of a false belief that good will alone will suffice to secure national interests. The balance of

---

2 Bongiovanni, Francesco M., *The Decline and Fall of Europe*, Palgrave Macmillan, UK, 2012, pp. 189-220.

power that was ensured because of the equilibrium maintained by the two Super Powers was lost, without the balance shifting in a convincing manner to the United States. In a world where only one Super Power exists, the balance of power theory assumes that this leading power will intervene only when a clear imbalance occurs. The measure of imbalance is a matter of perception and the proclivity of regional and global powers to intervene or not tinged with pragmatism. Therefore, it is difficult to have any assurance that the status quo would always be maintained in international affairs.

The disappearance, at least for some time, of the principal adversary was also accompanied in Europe by a concerted thrust to improve the economic and trade prospects of the nation, even at the cost of ignoring geopolitical realities. The European nations placed geo-economics above geopolitics and created the European Union by surrendering a great deal of economic and political sovereignty in order to compete with the United States and China in the economic sphere.[3] In recent years, the European Union has been unnerved by a resurgent Russia's moves to re-establish its influence over the erstwhile Soviet States that are now independent, but whom Russia considers its 'near abroad'.[4]

To add to the challenges that face Europe, the global financial crisis has brought the European Union to the point of collapse. Europe today is a long term threat to global stability for a number of reasons— it cannot be managed militarily; its citizens have the right to travel to a large number of developed nations without the need for regulatory checks like visas, which could spread the financial crisis further than otherwise and destabilise the host nations; it has an ageing, and in some cases declining, population that needs to be carefully managed through open immigration policies; a primary source of immigrants is the sub-Saharan region and an influx of people from there is bound to bring to the fore racial, religious and cultural tensions that already plague a number of nations; and their military forces are slowly decaying

---

3 Kagan, Robert, *The Return of History and the End of Dreams*, Atlantic Books, London, 2008, p. 21.

4 Popescu, Leonard and Nicu, *A Power Audit of EU-Russia Relations*, report by the European Council on Foreign Relations, Brussels, November 2007, p. 21.

because of lack of adequate resource allocation to maintain even the bare minimum capabilities.

Turmoil in the Middle East

The first decade of this century has been blighted by the rapid rise and spread of violent Islamic extremism, a trend that is unlikely to subside in the near future. In the contemporary security scenario, radical Islam is now centre stage and a factor in the security calculations of all nations, both domestic and global. This global phenomenon has now been given a new impetus with the on-going turmoil in the Middle East, the home of radical Islam.[5] One factor that must be considered in the recent upheaval in the Middle East is that analysts across the world completely failed to predict the so-called Arab Spring.

Even in late 2010, the Arab nations were peaceful with authoritarian regimes ruling most of the 22 member states of the Arab League. Although poverty and unemployment rates were high, they were not considered to be any great impact to the overall stability of the state. In fact, the 'Failed State Index' published by the Foreign Policy magazine—that categorises countries into five different states: critical, in danger, borderline, stable and most stable—did not place any of the Arab states in the 'in danger category. The social unrest brought about through dire economic situation, lack of freedom, rampant unemployment within the educated youth and the collective use of social media that brought regime change to four autocratic states was unforeseen. Equally unforeseen was the instability that followed each of the uprisings.

Instability needs three elements to become a movement that changes the face of a nation irrevocably: conditions, catalysts and triggers.[6] Conditions are by nature long term issues that only evolve gradually like societal changes, whereas catalysts tend to increase the

---

5   There are a large number of books that have been written on the rise of radical Islam and its spread across the globe. Jason Burke, a well-known journalist provides a list of ten books in his article 'Jason Burke: the key books on Muslim extremism', 7 November 2012, in https://www.theguardian.com/books/2012/nov/07/jason-burke-key-books-muslim-extremism accessed on 31 March 2015.

6   Gaub, Dr Florence, 'Predicting the Arab Spring: What we got wrong', *Jane's Defence Weekly*, 8 February 2012, p. 22.

tension brought about by such changes and are short-term in nature. Catalysts are distinctly different to the root cause of the problem and by virtue of their inherent dynamism are more difficult to identify and monitor. Triggers that start social dislocation are one-off events that coalesce the pent up and accumulated feelings and make them cross the tipping point. Triggers are almost impossible to predict. Rapid changes in perceptions, demography and institutional structure are all disruptive catalysts that indicate the move towards more radical instability within a nation that could bring about regime change.[7] The unfortunate issue is that a metre regime change does not always bring about a peaceful aftermath since the very conditions and catalysts that augured the change will continue to exist for a reasonably long period of time thereafter. Therefore, the instability in the Middle East brought about by the Arab Spring is unlikely to subside in the near term.

Weapons of Mass Destruction

Weapons of mass destruction (WMD) are traditionally thought to be nuclear in character. Nuclear weapon proliferation is an issue that is internationally debated, with sanctions being imposed on recalcitrant nations pursuing the development of such weapons. However, the resources and technological expertise needed to produce even a very small yield nuclear weapon is enormous and beyond the capacity of most nations to support. Therefore, there are only a few nations that are pursuing the development of nuclear weapon capacity even in the face of international condemnation. North Korea and Iran are two such nations. North Korea is already thought to possess basic nuclear weapon capability while Iran is continuing the rapid development of weaponisation capability within its nuclear facilities. The challenge for the international community is to ensure that sanctions imposed on these states do not reach a stage where they are forces to tip the security balance by using these devices even as a demonstration of intent. This is a fine balancing act, and if the history of sanctions against autocratic regimes is anything to go by, then sanctions are not likely to have the desired effect.

There is a school of thought that supports pre-emptive military action against these so-called 'rogue' states to destroy their nuclear

---

7 ibid.

facilities. Such action is not likely to create the necessary effect of ensuring that the target nation thereafter desists from undertaking such development. In fact, it is more likely to spur them to further development and use of the weapons when they are ready. In the broader global security equation, while the possession of nuclear weapons by unstable and volatile states is a source of constant concern, it might still be a better option to contain the fall-out through stringent sanctions that are enforced through an international agency.[8] Such measures, could further lead to gradual disarmament initiated by the intractable state itself. Even though nuclear weapons in the wrong hands is perhaps the most potent WMD threat, the probability of such an event happening is very low. That does not, however, preclude doing away with a constant vigil against such developments.

In the contemporary security scenario the challenge of WMD is not restricted to nuclear weapons alone; in fact, the threat is more from the employment of other systems that could create mass destruction. Biological and chemical weapons can also have disastrous effects on very large areas and population, when used effectively. For example, uninhabited aerial vehicles used for crop spraying can be very easily converted to spread biological weapons across urban areas. The actual damage caused may be limited, but the panic that would ensue would itself become such that the government would be hard pressed to contain it. The loss of public morale and loss of faith in the incumbent government are intangible cascading effects of such attacks.

WMD attacks need not in reality cause a great deal of physical damage. It is only necessary to attack one high-value target in a very visible manner to create the effects that will debilitate a nation. A catastrophic attack on a symbol of national power has the potential to paralyse the leadership for at least a short period of time, which can be exploited by an intelligent adversary with well-laid plans for further actions to destabilise a targeted nation. The uncontrolled proliferation of missiles has made it possible for even minor non-state actors to acquire sufficiently sophisticated missiles capable of

---

8   Russell, James A., 'WMD proliferation, globalization, and international security: whither the nexus and national security?', in Russell, James A., &Wirtz, James J., (eds), *Globalization and WMD Proliferation: Terrorism, transnational networks, and international security*, Routledge, Abingdon, UK, 2008.

long range targeting. This facilitates missile attacks with biological or chemical warheads from difficult to monitor locations, making them a distinct possibility. WMD attacks are challenges that the world has to be cognisant about, but with very limited capability to provide any assured and credible counter-measures in a pre-emptive manner.

WMD proliferation is a critical international concern, but an equally worrying tend is the widespread proliferation of advanced military and dual-use technologies. Further, this proliferation is mostly taking place through a range of legitimate activities with only limited illicit conduits also being used. There is increased demand within the developing world for transfer of sensitive and sophisticated technology as an inclusive part of the legitimate purchase of high-technology weapons.[9] The potential for dual-use technology being used for clandestine purposes by state-supported entities is much higher today that it was a decade ago.

Breakthrough Technologies

The world is witnessing the rapid development of massive computational capacity, the ability for real-time global information exchange through a number of readily available and comparatively cheap technologies and the capacity to connect directly to the desired node anywhere in the world at will. While these developments have been effectively used to improve the quality of life of millions of people across the globe, they have also been adapted to more sinister purposes. They have facilitated the faster development of disruptive technologies that have the capacity to create negative effects on the well-being of a nation and its population.

Breakthroughs in directed energy systems and nano-technology have the possibility of creating potent weapon systems built around their individual characteristics and, more importantly, upon their convergence in the very near future. Directed energy weapons are already in their trial stages and will be fielded within the next few years by the major military forces. Their use will bring to the fore the vexed issues of LOAC, morality in the employment of force and ethics regarding the use of non-lethal weapons. Since the cutting edge

---

9   Nurkin, Tate, 'Getting Creative to Fight Future Battles', *Jane's Defence Weekly*, 23 November 2011, p. 25.

technology required to develop such capabilities are resident only in a few nations, these weapons will invariably be used to create an asymmetry of their own for the conventional forces of those nations. Whether their use in combat or otherwise is right or wrong in a moral sense will be a point of debate for a very long time.

Research and development is creating quantum improvements in sensor technology, information transmission, miniaturisation at the molecular level, robotics, biotechnology and cyber operations. All these developments are dual-use, in that they are used for peaceful purposes such as to create improvements in medical care while also being efficiently adapted to create disruptions or challenges to the traditional notions of national security. These challenges may not seem to have great potential in terms of creating high levels of security threats, but in the contemporary scenario can become debilitating to the normal functioning of the state apparatus. The difficulty once again is not so much in countering the effects created by the use of these technologies, but in being able to prevent such attacks from taking place. There is no fool-proof method that can be employed to safeguard national assets from attacks using disruptive technologies.

Another aspect of the impressive developments in science and technology is the impact that these developments have on the conduct of wars. The quantum improvements in information technology when effectively combined with the greatly enhanced precision of contemporary weapons have reshaped the manner in which even short and limited wars are fought. However, ensuring that the benefits of such technology is maximised in a military force is almost totally dependent on its ability to access and adopt new technologies. This requirement could become a stumbling block to the growth of overall efficiency of the force itself with the associated constraints in its application. Further, the inability to access state-of-the-art technology can increase the gap between advanced military forces and the middle level ones to an extent wherein coalition operations could be hampered because of lack of interoperability.

In cases where the military forces are sufficiently technologically advanced—in training and education—availability of sophisticated technology could permit the force leapfrogging some stages of the development and inducting high-technology weapon systems without having to go through all the stages. This is a distinct advantage that can be leveraged to transform a middle level force into one that operates at the cutting edge in a short period of time.

Constraints on National Military Forces

The contemporary security environment has deteriorated to an extent where the more developed and stable nations feel the necessity to intervene in the unstable and volatile areas of the world to ensure that the instability is contained within a reasonable timeframe without it spreading further and creating a domino effect. There has been an unforeseen effect of such actions—the developing world now has an expectation that the developed world will intervene to stabilise any precarious region, subtly shifting the onus of responsibility for creating a stable and peaceful global community to the developed world. As a result, the developed world—which should be read to mean the more stable Western democracies—has been forced to intervene, mostly through military deployments, in regions in turmoil through civil war, ethnic cleansing, insurgencies and political violence. The 19th century cliché, 'the white man's burden' has assumed a completely new meaning in the 21st century.

The employment of military forces however, has been constrained for a number of reasons.[10] First, even in case of an all-out war, the contemporary environment restricts the targeting capabilities of a nation. This is primarily a direct effect of globalisation because of which the destruction of an adversary's economic nodes—both direct and indirect—will have a cascading detrimental effect on one's own economy. Targeting to create the effects necessary to successfully subdue an adversary and stabilise a region is now an involved and complex task. In most cases it is not possible to achieve complete effectiveness within the constraints that military forces have to function vis-à-vis unrestricted targeting.

Second, most nations do not have the capacity to carry out unilateral actions to secure a destabilised region. The norm of the day now is to operate as coalitions that have been brought about to achieve

---

10 Gompert, David C., 'Constraints of military power: Lessons of the past decade', *The Adelphi Papers17-133*, International Institute for Strategic Studies, London, 2008, pp. 1-13.

a certain laid down objective. However, recent experiences in forming coalitions have shown that the process of creating a cohesive and focused entity is extremely difficult. Even within traditional alliances, political and strategic influences hinder seamless operation of coalitions. When multi-national partners with differing priorities in achieving objectives and indifferent to the need for unified command and control are brought within a coalition's overall calculation, the process of decision-making and decision-implementation become ponderous. Further, when pitted against an agile and intelligent adversary this 'heaviness' could transform itself into a great disadvantage capable of inflicting self-defeat. The agility of decentralisation within a complex but flexible command structure is still to be completely mastered by conventional military forces. At the operational level, interoperability will always remain a stumbling block to effectiveness of the application of force in coalition operations, further exacerbated by restrictions, both conceptual and technological, to information sharing.

Unity of purpose, unity of command and unity of effort are the three pillars on which coalition operations build their success.[11] Dichotomously, these are also the three issues that challenge the effectiveness of coalition forces. The fact that a coalition has been formed is indicative of unity of purpose at the strategic level. Unity of purpose, articulated by the national leadership of coalition member nations at times does not get translated to unity of purpose at the strategic level of military planning, which almost completely negates the possibility of achieving unity of purpose at the operational level. Even more difficult to achieve is unity of command. For obvious reasons of sovereignty, perceived or actual, nations almost always insist on retaining command of their military forces and are extremely reluctant to allow dilution of command authority. All coalition forces operate under a unified command structure, but the nuanced manner in which such command can be exercised is at best a diplomatic juggling act. The impediment to decision-making can be such that very powerful coalition forces may not be able to achieve even a limited modicum of success. Unity of effort is again superficially visible at the strategic level, but the differences in rules of engagement and

---

11 McInnis, Kathleen J., 'Lessons in coalition warfare: Past, present and implications for the future', *International Political Review*, December 2013, Vol 1, Issue 2, Palgrave Macmillan, UK, 2013, pp. 78-90.

capability spectrum of the deployed forces normally create a gap that is visible to all members of the coalition. This is detrimental to the cohesiveness of the coalition.

A coalition operating without adequate cohesion will gradually fall prey to the malaise of command indecision. Indecision at any level of command is a downward spiral for a military force. In the case of coalitions, the indecisiveness will be normally manifest at the strategic level of command because of the very nature of the force and can actively make it dysfunctional very rapidly. By the same token, there will also be an increased tendency at the higher levels of command to micro-manage operations even to the tactical level. While not the same as indecision, micro-management can lead to indecision at the lower levels of command when the junior commanders try to second guess the decisions of the higher commander. Both these situations sap the efficiency of a force very rapidly and can be debilitating unless remedial action is initiated at an even quicker pace. These two factors are peculiar to conventional forces since irregular forces do not follow a set line of command in a rigid manner.

As the spectrum, intensity and scope of security threats increase along with the unit cost of conventional weapon systems, the resources available to counter/procure them are reducing or staying static in most nations. Austerity measures and forced budget cuts, brought on because of the global financial crisis, is affecting the Western world's ability to fund even current commitments let alone prepare for a spreading spectrum of security threats. These tensions have also started to impinge on the efficacy of traditionally strong alliances like NATO. Resource constraints superimposed on a security environment that is complex and demands rapid decisions and actions place a premium on the optimisation of available forces, achieved through developing and implementing methodologies that are at once both innovative and flexible.

The Denial of Victory

Till the end of World War II, wars were fought to achieve outright victory over an adversary culminating in unconditional surrender. The whole concept of victory and defeat has undergone a radical change. Unlike in traditional wars, contemporary conflict does not provide any prospect for victory in any of the campaigns for conventional military forces. In fact victory does not seem to be an objective any longer.[12] The perception has shifted to weighing the improvement or otherwise of the security situation brought about through the actions initiated by the security apparatus of a nation.

The foremost thinkers on war have concluded that the only legitimate reason for going to war was the improvement of the human lot. This has been adopted and adapted in various forms, including the famous expression 'making the world safe for democracy'. In recent times this has been evoked in the United Nation's concept of the 'right to protect', or the need to end oppression. Military forces are now considered a vital, if imperfect instrument for alleviating humanitarian distress,[13] a concept of employment that cannot and does not include victory as a fundamental objective. Further, military forces are today being deployed for state-building, which is considered a norm. Although some amount of pacification of the local opposition as a prelude may be required, such deployments are aimed at ensuring the safety and security of the deploying nation.[14] Victory as such does not fit into this broad spectrum of responsibilities being shouldered by the military forces.

Future Wars – Continuity and Change

Future wars and conflicts will retain a number of constant factors that act as the thread of continuity while a number of evolving changes will make it further complicated and dynamic. The violence and unpredictability associated with battles will continue to characterise even small skirmishes. Because the conduct of battles will ultimately be based on imperfect information, the fog and friction that accompanies all employment of military or other forces capable of applying lethal force will continue to baffle commanders at all levels. Irrespective of

---

12 Spiller, Roger, *An Instinct for War: Scenes from the Battlefields of History*, Harvard University Press, Cambridge, 2005.

13 Edmunds, Tim, 'Shifting Military Roles in Europe', in *International Affairs,* Vol. 82, Issue 6, 2006, Royal Institute of International Affairs, London, 2006, pp. 1061-1073.

14 Coker, Christopher, 'The Future War: What are the New Complexities', in Olsen, John Andeas, (ed), *On New Wars*, Oslo Files: On defence and Security – 04/2007, Norwegian Institute for Defence Studies, Oslo, 2007, pp. 89-92.

the complexity associated with war, the warrior spirit of soldiers—the warrior ethos—will always remain a constant source of strength at all levels of command and operations.

There are two more factors that have not changed in a very long time and are unlikely to do so in the near future; the principles of war and the human dimension in all conflict. The principles of war have been articulated in different ways over millennia and there has been an underlying continuity in the fundamental principles, making them almost 'timeless'. Essentially the principles are foundational pillars on which any military campaign is built, from the planning stage through to its conduct and successful culmination.[15] The principles of war, perhaps more than any other factor, embody the unchanging nature of war and conflict, even while the conduct and characteristics of war are constantly evolving. Therefore, they are the primary guiding elements in the conduct of any conflict, across the entire spectrum.

The human dimension is one of the primary factors that affect the conduct of war as well as create the uncertainties associated with the employment of force. Wars are fought to create the desired effects in the cognitive domain of the adversary, essentially to alter their behaviour pattern. However, it is not possible to have complete assurance that the actions initiated by one's own forces will make the adversary behave in a particular manner because of the difficulty in predicting human reaction. Therefore, the human dimension is the most dynamic element to be considered in analysing wars. This very dynamism can also be considered a constant factor in the conduct of war and conflict. From a military perspective the human element encompasses the leadership, soldiers and the relationship between them, as well as the overall ethos of the nation and the civil-military relationship. Even in the technologically most advanced military force, ultimate decisions are all made by human beings, which mean that the vagaries of the human mind will always impinge on the conduct of war.

While there are factors that have remained constant over the years, and are likely to stay so with very minor variations of little

---

15 Kainikara, Sanu, *Principles of War and Air Power,* Working Paper No 31, Air Power Development Centre, Canberra, June 2011, p. 2.

importance into the near future, there are some aspects of the conduct and characteristics of war that have continually evolved. The first is the recent adoption, by most nations, of an effects-based approach to national security. For military forces, creating effects to achieve the desired end-state is not a new concept. The subtle change is in defining the end-state and refining the manner in which the effects to achieve it are created. Until the later part of the 20th century, the military forces were left to themselves to achieve an end-state, which was essentially military in character. Achieving military end-states was the culmination of all wars, after which negotiations brought an end to the conflict. Today, the end-state is determined by the desired national security outcome that will, of necessity, always have to be political. This change makes the military force only one element, albeit a critical one, in the broader application of force in the pursuit of national security. The military forces in contemporary conflicts have to design their campaigns to achieve national security objectives with the military objectives assuming a lower order of precedence as contributing factors to the overarching whole-of-government approach to the conduct of a national effects-based campaign.

An effects-based approach can also be adapted to become a key factor in threat avoidance through the employment of both deterrent and coercive strategies. In some ways, this approach to national security could be viewed as the conduct of parallel warfare, even if the implementation of these non-invasive strategies involves the use of lethal force in punitive attacks. The developments in weapon capabilities that ensure precision and proportionality of such attacks make it easier to execute these strategies effectively.

The second is the increased size and complexity of the battlespace. Battlespace used to be defined in olden days by the distance a cavalry force could travel in a few hours, but even this was built around a core fighting area of a few kilometres. Mechanisation of the army, long-range guns and more importantly the advent of air power increased the size of the battlespace into a vast area. In this situation, although the frontline, where the two surface forces met, was still defined, there was a tacit understanding that the battlespace was now measured in areas instead of the forward edge of surface battle. In more recent times, over the past few decades, the battlespace has become amorphous with no clear line of contact and no defined battlespace as such. The battlespace is now indistinguishable from the normal cities and villages of a nation and truly encompasses the entire geographic areas of the competing states. No place and no individual are safe from direct or indirect attacks as a result of a confrontation. The expansion of the battlespace into the cities and other built up areas makes manoeuvre and accurate targeting very difficult for the military forces. This complexity is further increased for conventional forces by the necessity to adhere to rigid laws of armed conflict and rules of engagement and the all-important need to avoid any kind of collateral damage.

The third change is the clearly visible improvement in the agility of conventional military forces. From static battles of ancient times, conflict now encompasses very rapid movements of both personnel and materiel and their quick employment. This trend has been further emphasised in recent times in the conduct of irregular warfare where the adversary more often than not does not engage in static battles but is more prone to employ hit-and-run tactics. Such actions increase the chances of success for an irregular adversary who does not have the capacity to win a direct battle against conventional forces. The aim is to inflict as much damage as possible, both in terms of casualties and infrastructure, with minimum risk and then to blend with the general population. Such tactics are asymmetric in nature. While asymmetry by itself is not a new concept, the sophistication of its application has increased considerably in the past few decades. Agility—the inherent capability to actively adapt rapidly to emerging challenges—therefore becomes a fundamental requirement for conventional forces to successfully counter irregular forces operating in small and dispersed groups and employing a hybrid concept of asymmetry. Modern military forces are adapting to this reality and moving away from the traditional heavy, but ponderous, forces reliant on superior firepower for success. The evolution from static formations to light, agile forces that can be rapidly deployed and extracted has been a step change from the traditional military forces of a sovereign nation.

The fourth change is the critical importance of information in all aspects of warfighting. Information has always been a vital requirement for decision-making. However, technological advances in its collection and, more importantly, its dissemination have now increased the impact of information on the decision-making process from the strategic to the tactical levels. Collection methods have now reached a level wherein the collected information far outweighs the capacity to analyse it. At the same time the dissemination process has been quickened to be as near real-time as possible to meet the demands of information-dependent operations. The two are at odds and will remain so until the capacity for collection and the capacity to analyse the collected material are evenly matched. Exploiting information is now a science and specialisation as opposed to the process being resident in the commander in earlier times.

This situation has both advantages and disadvantages. The main advantage is that the decision-making individual is provided sifted and focused information, avoiding the potential for superfluous information to cloud the decision-making process. Availability of critical information in a timely manner is a fundamental building block to having decision superiority. While decision superiority by itself is a comparative state, without adequate information input it will be impossible to compete with the adversary to obtain the necessary superiority. The downside is that the process of weeding out information is done at the staff level and therefore there is the possibility of critical information being left out of the commander's brief by junior personnel who may not be aware of the entire strategic picture. Having evolved into information hungry organisations, modern military forces struggle to balance this dichotomous situation.

Summing Up...

From the beginning of history, the world has always been affected by destabilising forces that tend to bring disparate groups into conflict. It is also a fact that some of these forces bring nations into confrontations that leads to conflict and war. Today, the world is facing more such challenges than have been faced before. In the contemporary scenario, instability in vulnerable regions of the world tend to increase very rapidly and with very little warning time. As a corollary, the ability of more stable and better developed nations to intervene to stabilise a deteriorating situation has also increased manifold in the past few decades. This increased capacity has created a tendency for nations to intervene at their choice. The developments in ensuring human rights in a global manner and the no-tolerance attitude towards human rights abuses have further made interventions a common occurrence in the 21st century.

Challenges to global stability are many—some are established and some are emerging; some may have no solution to contain them; while some will continue to evolve even after being contained and become ones that defy attempts at containment. This chapter has examined the major factors that challenge global stability. The chapter discusses the decline of Europe as a globally influential group of nations; the ongoing turmoil in the Middle-East; the proliferation of WMD; the wide availability of cutting-edge and emerging technologies; the constraints placed on the employment of conventional military forces; and the conduct of future wars.

The nations of Europe were the world leaders in the 20 century, but in the past few decades their influence on global affairs has reduced for a number of reasons and is only very limited at the moment. Europe now faces a number of challenges that it may not be able to ameliorate even in the mid-term. The nations have contracting economies, an open immigration policy that strains the domestic infrastructure and increases racial, religious and ethnic tensions that tend to fracture the society and diminishing military capabilities. The European nations can barely contain internal turmoil and the economic downturn and now has become part of the problem rather than their usual position of being stable democratic nations.

Ever since the US-led invasion of Iraq in 2003, the Middle-East has been a bubbling cauldron of sectarian violence and religious extremism. The region creates and harbours 'jihadi' elements who resort to indiscriminate terrorist activities. The virulent Sunni-Shia divide, autocratic and/or theocratic governments and concerted anti-Semitic activities aimed at Israel complete the chaotic picture of the region. Terrorism has been exported world-wide from the Middle-East and has now become one of the major destabilising forces in what used to be the more stable regions of the world. Western intervention has not been able to contain or remediate any of the long festering wounds in the region. The bias of Western actions have only managed to make the situation worse. The Middle-East is also home to a large population of educated but under-employed youth who are restive. They perpetuated the so-called Arab Spring in a number of autocratic nations, which were ruthlessly put down. However, the population is still simmering beneath the surface in most of the region. While there are no short-term solutions for the problem, even long-term solutions seem complex and difficult to achieve.

Biological and chemical weapons are more likely to be the ones employed, if at all, with nuclear weapons an extremely unlikely contender. Biological and chemical weapons are easier and cheaper to acquire or manufacture and their proliferation seems a certainty in the near-future. However, the existence of such weapons is difficult to ascertain with assurance. Proliferation of such weapons is a critical international concern. There is also an appreciable trend to create dual-use technological facilities that military forces are reluctant to destroy. Rogue nations take advantage of this restriction placed on the conventional military forces to further their research and development of weapons of mass destruction.

Cutting edge technologies, especially information related, have changed the conduct of war. Quantum improvements are taking place in the fields of sensor technology, miniaturisation and artificial intelligence. Alongside, there is also an on-going moral and ethical debate questioning the veracity of the use of such systems in warfare. Even so, the technological improvements are continuing without any let up, and the more mature improvements are being inducted into the military forces. There seems to be little doubt that emerging technology will be used in wars as and when they become available. Acquiring cutting edge technology is looming as a challenge to middle powers of the world. As the cost of development of such technology continues to go up, availability of such technologies to be procured is becoming more politically based that ever before. It is highly likely that in the future technology would be made available only with political caveats placed by the providing nation.

More developed and stable nations tend to place extraordinarily strict rules of engagement on their military forces when they are deployed for campaigns. At times these restrictions make it difficult to carry out appropriate targeting to create the necessary effects, Further, the globalisation of trade, commerce and the economy also interferes in the ability of the military forces to neutralise selected targets as it would adversely affect the economy of the region. In the 21st century, most nations lack the capacity to deliver military results on their own. The solution has been to create coalitions to initiate military action when required. Coalitions have the added advantage of bestowing some amount of political legitimacy to the military actions being initiated. On the other hand, coalitions tend to lack unity of purpose and even unity of command in certain cases. The situation leads to dispersed unity of effort and dilutes the military focus in a campaign.

Future wars will have some continuities with the contemporary characteristics and conduct of armed conflict. The principles of war, bedrock of the employment of military forces and the human dimension in conflict that brings in the unpredictable will remain a constant. There have been some evolutionary changes to the conduct of war and this evolution will remain a constant with only the pace varying. The changes that are noticeable have been the increasing size of the battlespace that is not delineated by geography anymore, brought about by sophisticated technology; the military becoming one element within a whole-of-nation/government approach national security; and the addition of two more domains, space and cyber space, to the three already existing ones in terms of warfighting.

Every era produces new challenges for the military forces to overcome. In every era, military forces evolve and adapt to neutralise the challenges that are not only evolutionary but also revolutionary and emerge without warning. Creating step changes in the concept of operations and accepting quantum changes in military capabilities to contain the evolution of conflict has been a never-ending and continuous cycle, ever since human beings went to war.

CONCLUSION

Throughout history warfare has never been purely about combat operations conducted by the military forces of a nation against its actual or perceived enemies. They have only been one part of the actions that a nation initiates, overtly and covertly, to secure its borders and more broadly its vital interests. Within the contemporary global political and security environment, the protection of national interests has become as important as the fundamental need to defend its geographic borders to retain the necessary sovereignty. This situation has led to the articulation of the far-reaching concept of a whole-of-government approach to national security, within which the military plays only one critical part. In such a overarching approach, the other elements of national power—economy, diplomatic and informational capacities—will also share the burden of securing the nation, in differing ratios contextually.

All wars are replete with uncertainty from beginning to end. It is full of suffering for all involved—victor and vanquished—and at times very unreasonable both in its cause and conduct. History shows that wars and combat operations tend to bring out the worst character traits in human beings. In a majority of cases wars do not go according to well-laid out plans, making an already complex enterprise even more so. Perhaps because of the suffering that war inflicts on even the non-combatant population of the participating nations, there is an international effort to lay down the minimum required human rights assurance from all parties in the conflict. However, this demand has to be balanced with the contemporary change in the status of combatants because of the increasing number of non-state entities that are participating in combat operations of one or the other kind. These non-state groups have only limited sanctity, if at all, in international laws and therefore increase the complexity for conventional military forces in dealing with them.

There is a continuous debate within the international comity of nations regarding the legality of going to war as well as its conduct. The consequences of war are enormous and therefore it is definitely necessary to set widely acceptable moral principles to guide the path to going to war as well as its conduct once war has commenced. There are primarily two aspects that are considered in analysing war: justice of the war (jus ad bellum) and justice in the war (jus ad bello). The first looks at the causes that a nation can reasonably assume as sufficient to go to war while the second aspect analyses the 'correctness' of the conduct of the war in terms of morality, legality and ethics. In effect, the international community believes that wars, if they must be fought at all, must be conducted in a reasonably humane and civilised manner. This just war theory demarcates the principles that must be satisfied before a nation embarks on a war and those that must be adhered to in its conduct.

In the prevailing political, economic, social and security environment it is possible to distinguish between a war of discretion and a war of necessity, even though an overlap and therefore a grey area could exist between the two. Importantly, the recent proclivity for military intervention can be regarded as residing in the grey area of this spectrum. More than a decade into the 21st century, the international community has still not managed to find consensus on the need or otherwise to intervene in parts of the world that are volatile and destabilising for different reasons. The United Nations has approved the broad concept of intervention within the ambit of the notion of 'responsibility to protect' and used it selectively in the past few years. However, there still remain different opinions about the employment of this concept. There is no doubt that the processes and mechanisms that stabilised the international system are changing, with the agents of such change clearly visible in some cases and obscure in others. These factors are not always complimentary and therefore could intersect at random creating further strains on the stability of the international system.

Irrespective of these differing opinions, there is clear evidence that the international community is more prone to consider intervention than was the case two or three decades ago. Within this paradigm, the developed Western world is more prone to attempt military intervention as compared to the Asian nations. This may be a throw-back to the colonial era when the Western nations intervened and annexed a large portion of the globe with hardly any thought of the needs or aspirations of the existing local regimes. On the other hand, Asian nations by and large have been historically reluctant to be seen as the aggressor or interventionist, except in extreme cases. In today's post-colonial environment the developed nations' proclivity to intervene has brought about two distinct developments. First, there is an implicit belief within the rest of the world that the onus of responsibility to carry out a military intervention rests squarely on the western world. Second, there is cynicism in a large part of the world regarding the public reasons, mainly in terms of national security interests, that the intervening nations provide for the actions being initiated. So, while intervention can indeed be altruistic, the recent history does not support the acceptance of it being a selfless act on the part of the developed world.

In resorting to military intervention there must always be a clear distinction between 'what not to do', which are policy decisions, and 'how not to do' which is concerned with the military implementation. In all interventions there must also be differentiation of making peace, through diplomatic or other means and enforcing it, which is primarily a military function. Further, interventions must be aimed at repairing failed or failing states and if necessary to fight the spawning of terrorism. In fighting terrorism, even though a large number of forces may be on the ground, it must not be equated to occupation or even state-building. The commencement of insurgent activity normally has its roots in such actions that cross an invisible line. Fundamentally great powers must use restraint as a tool of national security, especially when considering military intervention.

A number of factors, most of them applicable historically across all conflicts, influence the conduct of war and increase the complexity and unpredictability associated with it. There is an indelible connection between complexity and the unpredictability of war, one feeding off the other in a self-perpetuating cycle. Further, the widespread prevalence of irregular wars, making them almost the norm, makes the employment of conventional military forces complicated. Irregular wars, guerrilla wars and insurgencies being the nucleus, can only be effectively countered through a whole-of-government approach. A military campaign in a counterinsurgency mode can never succeed on its own, since the military objectives will only support the achievement of a tactical level end-state. Counterinsurgency campaigns have to involve all elements of national power, with the non-military elements being able to leverage off the military successes.

The emerging trend in security challenges could be divided into geographic areas and issues that are common across the world. Europe and the Middle East are gradually going into deepening crises on a number of fronts. At least for the moment there does not seem to be the capacity or the will in other non-affected areas to attempt to stem the decline. Issues of religion, weapon proliferation and failing states that are ill-governed have always been challenges that continue to be of concern. The current situation is that no one nation, or even a group of nations, seems to have the ability to address these issues. The perception that the western world, led by the United States, has lost its appetite to maintain a stable world is becoming prevalent. This has produced even more hot spots globally. The world of tomorrow, while it could look very similar to the one we see today, has the potential to very rapidly metamorphose into an entity that cannot be predicted even through acute analysis.

SECTION - IV

MILITARY FORCES: AN ELEMENT OF NATIONAL POWER

THE STRATEGIC INTERFACE

THESIS: The traditional role of military forces—the physical protection of the geographical borders of the nation—has evolved over the past decades to the protection of the sovereignty of the nation, which encompasses the relatively new concepts of national interests and values.

National security, when combined with the nuanced understanding of national interests and values, becomes an all-encompassing term. In the definition of the term in some nations, it goes so far as to include the protection of intangible and esoteric ideas such as the protection of human rights across the world. The broad sweep of the concept has required the employment of military forces in different contexts, diverse conditions and in the pursuit of varied objectives. The military forces—always a fundamental part of the national security calculus—has now become a critical element of national power that cannot be sidelined, irrespective of the context. In the currently prevailing and complex global security environment, national military forces have become the first-choice option amongst the elements of national power to be employed for the protection of national security, considered at its broadest iteration. It has assumed a position at the vanguard of power projection in ensuring that the nation is able to achieve its security imperatives.

INTRODUCTION

Historically military forces have been considered the visible element of a nation's power. Displays of military prowess, spectacular parades, publicly visible conduct of exercises, all are intended to demonstrate the ability of a nation to build, maintain and—in an oblique manner—employ sufficient quantum of military power to secure its interests. The concept of national security was traditionally conceived as the protection of the geographic borders of the nation and therefore was firmly entwined with the ability of the nation's military forces to either deter adversaries through the threat of force or defeat them in case of actual violations of the borders through the actual application of lethal force. In more recent times, the notion of national security has undergone a somewhat diaphanous extension.[1] It now encompasses not only the physical protection of the nation's geographic entity but also involves securing its interests globally. Some nations even go to the extent of including such intangible ideas, like the protection of human rights world-wide, as part of their national security imperatives. The primary development in the evolution of the concept has been the added emphasise placed on a nation's right to protect its economic and trade interests globally through the employment of national power.

This altered perception of national security has transformed the idea of national power being primarily manifest in its military forces to a broader awareness that a nation's economic and diplomatic capabilities could also be leveraged to support national security. This further created a set of national power elements—capabilities resident under the broad categories of military, diplomacy, economy and information—that could be employed in a contextual manner to

---

1 Jablonski, David, 'The State of the National Security State', *Parameters*, Winter 2002-03, US Army War College, Carlisle, PA, 2002, pp. 4-17.

ensure national security. The evolution of the concept of national security also impacted the global geopolitical environment that in turn necessitated the development of a much broader suite of strategies to secure the interests of the nation. This was a simultaneous but parallel development. The strategies employed to ensure national security is now a much wider spectrum than ever before, starting from influencing and shaping activities in the regions of national interest, through to employing deterrence and coercion, and in extreme cases resorting to punishment and then destruction.

The most important factor in delivering this spectrum of strategies is that out of all the elements of national power, only the military forces have the capability to contribute or take the lead in implementing all the strategies directly. Other elements of national power are constrained to function in contributing to the strategies at the lower end of the spectrum and in conflict situations that are of choice rather than necessity. Only military forces have the ability to implement the higher end strategies of punishment and destruction as and when it becomes necessary, In fact, the military force of a sovereign nation is the only element of national power that is authorised to apply lethal force at the behest of the lawful government. This places a responsibility, far greater than that placed on any other element of national power, on the military forces, especially its commanders. The force as a whole will have to shoulder this responsibility through the lawful conduct of the conflict at all times.

Implementing strategies that require the application of lethal force is normally resorted to when the nation faces an existential threat and is involved in a war of necessity, whereas wars or conflicts of choice do not automatically require the use of force. In either case, the use of lethal force needs firm resolution and national determination. The dichotomy is that while the use of force to secure the nation is dependent on such determination, rigid resolve cannot be considered a virtue either politically or militarily. In fact, national security is best served by an adaptable and accommodating political approach to emerging challenges and a flexible military posture that can provide an open and if necessary malleable solution.[2] The application of force is

---

[2] Snow, Donald M., *Thinking About National Security: Strategy, Policy and Issues*, Routledge, New York, 2016. (Part I: Context).

further complicated by the military need to ensure that the adversary is defeated physically and that there is visible perception of having done so. Thus the physical defeat has to overlap into the cognitive domain for the outcome to be long lasting.

There is a subtle difference between military power and the military forces per se. However, they also share a cyclical relationship in that military forces of a nation are the repository of national military power. Military forces therefore have a much broader organisational perspective and carry out functions that enable the application of military power. This could take the shape of activities that generate and sustain military power as well as pursuits that do not have any direct bearing on it, but are peripheral duties that contribute to national security in obscure ways. The complexity of the global security environment demands great flexibility from all elements of national power, especially the military forces that have become the first-choice options for most governments when faced with unforeseen and defused security challenges. This requires the military forces to develop and inculcate robust yet adaptable concepts, multi-function capable systems and training regimes that cater for the extremely broad swath of possible contingencies. Flexibility within the military forces, resulting from these attributes, has become critical because of the increasing proclivity of democratic governments to employ military forces in what were traditionally non-military functions. This has expanded the spectrum of conflict far beyond the historical remit of military forces, placing a broad responsibility on conventional forces.

The international geopolitical environment is not a straight forward mix of nations anymore. It is now influenced by an eclectic mix of rogue states, non-state actors and irregular forces, all of whom have agendas that are not conducive to stability and peaceful coexistence. In these circumstances most nations look to creating credible strategic deterrents to ensure that their national interests are not compromised. Military forces are the obvious choice to create strategic deterrence and to act as visible back up to other less intrusive initiatives to further national interests. In the long term national interests are best served by building institutions that provide the necessary back drop to security initiatives. However, the task of building national institutions and ensuring their continued viability in times of financial stringency and decline in the resource availability is difficult, if not impossible. This is particularly the case with military forces. The national security ethos has to be visionary and the strategic leadership capable of making difficult decisions if long term security is to be assured. The first step towards achieving this is to carefully maintain a balanced national security strategy that lays down priorities at the highest level. This might require giving primacy to one or the other element of national power dependent on the long term view of national security of the nation. Irrespective of the lead agency, the military forces will have to provide the real strength behind national initiatives.

There is a very clear and tangible relationship between the development of strategy and transforming it into operational tasks that together will achieve the desired end-state in conflict. However, this strategy to task methodology is a complicated process since the adversary will also be attempting to implement a strategy of their own in a similar manner. Therefore, one's own strategy must be developed taking into account the possible adversary strategy and putting in place countering tasks as far as possible. To a large extent the success of strategy to task methodology is dependent on the strategic decision-making capability of the military force which is inherently a fragile art. In the contemporary environment national security is defined in an extremely broad manner. This wide-ranging concept of national security makes it necessary for a nation to carry out expeditionary operations, far away from its own geographic borders, to stabilise volatile regions that might otherwise impinge on its own security.[3] This creates its own set of fundamental requirements for the military forces to fulfil.

The military forces also face a number of challenges, some of them constantly evolving, that impact on their efficacy, efficiency and effectiveness. Further, extended periods of peace tend to have a detrimental impact on military capabilities because the importance of military forces to ensuring the security of the nation, irrespective of the nation being at peace or in conflict mode, is diluted by other

---

3   Gompert, David C., 'Preparing Military Forces for Integrated Operations in the Face of Uncertainty', Issue Papers, *Rand Corporation*, San Francisco, 2003, pp. 6-14. https://www.rand.org/pubs/issue_papers/IP250.html accessed on 13 May 2016.

preoccupations that are considered to be of direct consequence to national prosperity. In recent times the international community has unanimously approved the concept of the 'responsibility to protect' in the United Nations. However, the concept is controversial as intervention based on it invariably runs contrary to the traditional idea of national sovereignty. On the other hand, there is an increasing tendency in the developed world to take recourse to intervention in troubled regions. The legal challenges that come with such interventions as well as the legal implications of applying military force at the operational level have the potential to become long-lasting, if not, insurmountable issues.

Space and cyberspace have also clearly become domains of great interest and influence in military operations. There are a number of difficulties that have to be overcome before a military force can claim operational capabilities in space, the primary one being the cost-factor. On the other hand, disruptive operations in cyberspace are not resource-intensive while countering such attacks is extremely difficult. More than being a military threat, cyber-attacks are perhaps best dealt with as threats to national security that require a whole-of-government response.

Employing the military forces of the nation has manifold implications. One of the most important factors that must always be considered by the government is the support that military operations need from the domestic population. A number of disparate factors contribute to creating a sense of war fatigue within the nation. War fatigue, once set in, can become debilitating to the prosecution of the conflict in any meaningful manner, especially when the operation in question is expeditionary in nature and not a war of necessity. Military power, resident within the constituted military forces of the nation has to be very carefully applied in the pursuit of national security.

Chapter 13

THE POWER OF MILITARY FORCES

Military power is the ability of a nation to apply or threaten to apply lethal force in the pursuance of its actual or perceived developmental, security and/or political needs. In the application of military power, the objectives to be achieved, or military objectives, could be fixed at the strategic, operational or tactical level of conflict as dictated by the laid down higher level political objectives. There is a subtle but distinct difference between military power and military forces. Military power is the ability to apply lethal force whereas military forces are the instruments that facilitate the application of such power at the behest of the national government. Further, military power, while critically reliant on military forces for its application, also requires a number of non-military capabilities to be present within the nation for its generation.[1] Clearly, these factors; such as resource availability, national infrastructure, indigenous industrial capacity etc.; are of indirect influence, but nevertheless crucial to the concept of a nation's military power.

Military power therefore, has to be viewed as a broader continuum within which the military forces form the critical nucleus for other factors to coalesce in a credible manner. It is military power that provides the government with options when dealing with security challenges and, in a non-combat situation, the military force provides the wherewithal to back negotiations with covert and overt shows of force. Holistic military power provides the nation with the ability to

---

1   For a detailed discussion of this concept read, Cohen, Eliot A., *The Big Stick: The Limits of Soft Power and the Necessity of Military Power*, Hachette Book Group, New York, 2017.

enforce its will when necessary, at times even without the recourse to the actual application of force through the application of the strategies of dissuasion and deterrence.

Within the strategies that are employed in ensuring the security of the nation, deterrence and coercion rely heavily on military power, whereas the actual application of force in pursuing the strategies of denial and punishment will depend more on the ability of the military forces to apply lethal power to achieve the desired objectives. Deterrence makes recourse to the actual use of force unnecessary by the adversary's acceptance of the preponderance of military power resident in the nation that is employing the strategy of deterrence. By not actually employing military forces, it also helps to preserve the invaluable mystique of military power.[2] Effective deterrence is also based on the purely human function of perception regarding the credibility of the claims regarding military power. The basic fact is that the strategy of deterrence is a direct function of perceived military power and only indirectly influenced by the military forces of a nation. Within the spectrum of strategies with influence and shape on one end and destruction on the other, deterrence, coercion, and punishment make the continuum. The contribution of military power is the highest at the lower ends of the spectrum in dissuasion and deterrence and gradually reduces as the more overt strategies come into prominence where the military forces become the focus of actions being initiated.

The process of selecting a strategy to counter an emerging security challenge is crucially dependent on the prevailing context and circumstances. The implementation of the selected strategy thereafter will depend on two primary factors. First, if the situation has the potential to escalate, necessitating a change of strategy more towards the application of force, the approach has to be strategically holistic with the flexibility to progress to combat operations if required. This would mean that military forces would be kept in short notice readiness. Second, if third nation intervention is anticipated, the diplomatic elements of the nation will need to be involved much more than otherwise to ensure that the regional and international environment can be shaped to one's own advantage. In both cases, the military forces will be the underpinning strength on which the selected strategy

---

2   Harris, Owen, 'Costs of a Needless War,' *The Australian*, Sydney, 18 July 2005.

in implemented. There is a cyclical connection between military power and military forces.

Military Forces

The employment of military forces is awesome in its scope and a capable force will be irresistible when applied with panache. It has enormous capacity to destroy, but by its very ethos is not structured to either control or impose and maintain order in chaotic conditions. The fundamental ethos of a military force is to apply force—at whatever level of lethality—in order to achieve the desired objectives with minimal loss of personnel and materiel to one's own forces while maximising the loss of the adversary. This is incompatible with the needs that have to be met in order to impose order, a policing or stabilising function. While military forces are regularly used in this less 'demanding' role, by virtue of their training, force structure and even equipment, they are sub-optimal in conducting this role.

There is normally only limited understanding within the decision-making bodies of a nation regarding this distinction and therefore it is common, especially in the contemporary security environment, for military forces to be used as a first option alternative to contend with any unforeseen or rapidly evolving circumstances that the nation has to face. Only high calibre civilian and military leadership, capable of functioning together and complementing each other even under stress, will be able to stem this tendency which is detrimental to both the military forces and the well-being of the civilian government.[3] The proclivity to employ military forces as a tool of 'ready resort' has resulted in two unintended consequences.

First, and perhaps more important, the military forces have per force had to expand the spectrum of conflict that they engage in to encompass a range from the provision of humanitarian assistance on the one end to fighting a war of national survival on the other. To cover such a broad spectrum effectively is not a minor task and involves the inculcation of a number of disparate qualities in the personnel and the acquisition of vastly different equipment and weapon systems. Both these requirements by themselves spin off a myriad other necessities

---

3 Art, Robert J., & Waltz, Kenneth Neal, (eds), *The Use of Force: Military Power and International Politics*, Rowman & Littlefield Publisher, Lanham, MD, 1999.

for the operational employment of these sophisticated equipment and their efficient maintenance. There are two ways to achieve effectiveness throughout the spectrum; one, build a force with separate elements to carry out the separate functions or, two, acquire multi-function capable platforms and train the personnel flexibly to operate throughout the spectrum as required. A military force with functionally specialised elements is obviously the optimum solution, but resource constraints that face almost all nations foreclose any attempt to exercise this option. Unfortunately the second option, while feasible, has its own drawbacks, which is the second unintended consequence.

The structuring and development of a force with multi-function systems involves the degradation of specialised characteristics making the systems function at a certain, and mostly acceptable level, of performance. However, when pitted against a function-dedicated system, it is bound to come out second best, not an option in military operations. Further, the training required to make the personnel functionally adequate in different areas will be both time and resource intensive. Military equipment and concepts of operations are inherently technologically sophisticated and some niche capabilities can only be optimised with a great deal of training and experience. Therefore, having a group of generalists does not solve the challenge of having to be competent across the wide spectrum of conflict.

The military force has two primary roles:[4] to be the primary national instrument that deters aggression and if deterrence fails to secure decisive victory when the nation is forced to defend its sovereignty and strategic interests through the application of force in conflict or war. While, these are fundamental to the security of the nation, the contemporary security environment has made both of them complex concepts that require great fidelity from the military forces to achieve.[5] The process to be incorporated to achieve the necessary fidelity is not effortless and also has an element of the unknown in it.

---

4   SSR Backgrounder, 'The Armed Forces: Roles and responsibilities in good security governance', *Geneva Centre for the Democratic Control of Armed Forces*, Geneva, p. 3, https://www.files.ethz.ch/isn/195684/DCAF_BG_10_The%20Armed%20Forces.11.15-1.pdf accessed on 14 May 2016.

5   Edmunds, Timothy, 'What Are Armed Forces For? The Changing Nature of Military Roles in Europe', *International Affairs*, Vol 82, No 6, November 2006, RUSI, London, pp. 1059-1075.

It is this uncertainty that complicates the national security equation. The prevailing context is such that there is a greater requirement for the military forces of a nation to be able to operate within a complex environment while steadfastly maintaining a path to the achievement of national objectives. This requires more than normal flexibility in countering national security challenges.

Another factor that makes it imperative for the military forces to remain flexible is the changing nature of the threats that they face even when employed in the lower end of the spectrum of conflict like in peace keeping or enforcement activities. The use of asymmetry has become a norm, especially when the adversary is a non-state entity, irregular forces or insurgents. In addition the effectiveness of these asymmetric threats has been enhanced with the adaptation of technology at the very base level. The availability and adept employment of modern technology by irregular forces have gradually shortened the gap between unconventional and conventional modes of conflict, further increasing the complexity for military forces in countering their challenge.

Stemming from the increased spread of responsibilities that military forces have been straddled with, there has been considerable change, evolutionary, rapid and at times reactive, in the competencies that a military force must possess to be successful in its endeavours. On the other hand some absolute basic competencies necessary for the efficient functioning of military forces have not altered significantly and continue to be the core around which other, more dynamic, competencies are developed. The core competencies are national will, strategy to task methodology, strategic communications and flexibility of the force in being.

Core Competencies

National Will

Military forces are the instruments through which a nation projects its power to achieve political ends. The process by which military force is translated into intended political effects is developed as a combined civil-military enterprise.[6] In stable democracies this is not difficult to achieve. However, the employment of military forces, especially to implement the strategies of punishment or destruction, requires the support of the general population. Such support becomes even more important if the conflict that the nation is engaged in becomes long drawn-out and starts to affect the wealth and status of the nation in a negative manner.[7] Whether such a war is one of discretion or necessity also plays a very influential role in determining popular support.

One of the most important core competencies of a military force is its 'staying power'. Staying power essentially means the inherent capacity of the force to continue operations at the desired level for the duration required to achieve laid down objectives. A number of sub-factors contribute to determining whether or not a particular military force has the necessary staying power to successfully conclude the embarked upon war, campaign, operation or battle in a circumstantial manner. These factors vary with the level at which the assessment is being carried out. For example at the tactical level, the greatest influence on staying power to win a battle may well be the availability of sufficient ammunition and firepower support. At the other end of the spectrum, one of the most important considerations at the military strategic level would be the bipartisan support of the government for the military actions being initiated. This is dependent on the perception of the public regarding the necessity of the conflict, the progress being made and the casualties being incurred.[8] Public support is the foundation for building national will to continue the conflict, even to its bitter end if necessary.

The core competencies of military forces are built on the national will to succeed in any conflict in which the nation gets involved. Here the reasons for going to war and the processes that democracies have

---

6   Stone, John, *Military Strategy: The Politics and Technique of War*, Continuum International Publishing Group, London, 2011, p. 4.

7   Mueller, John E., 'Trends in Popular Support for the Wars in Korea and Vietnam', *The American Political Science Review*, Vol 65, No 2, June 1971, pp. 360-371.

8   Carden, James, 'A New Poll Shows the Public is Overwhelmingly opposed to Endless US Military Interventions', *The Nation*, 9 January 2018, https://www.thenation.com/article/new-poll-shows-public-overwhelmingly-opposed-to-endless-us-military-interventions/ accessed on 21 July 2018.

put in place to debate the necessity for entering into a conflict situation is outside the context of this discussion. In a direct manner, it is the national will that will provide the necessary resources to develop an effective military force and it is the national will that will sustain it when employed to protect national interests. Economic necessities to be fulfilled for the overall development of the nation will always be a competing force against the expenditures to be incurred to acquire, maintain and operate a sophisticated military force. Without manifest national will the military force of a democracy has the potential to gradually be reduced in capabilities and more importantly status within the national security apparatus.

Strategy to Task Methodology

Strategy is about doing things optimally, applying means to ends, and the best strategy is pragmatic in the extreme. Essentially strategy is the interface between political objectives and military operational capabilities, a medium that connects both and gives both of them tangible reality in the context of national security. Strategy is primarily concerned with the nature of war, and if it successfully aligns with the developments in the actual conduct of war, it will also automatically serve the ends of policy.[9]

In other words, military strategy translates political objectives into subordinate goals that can be achieved through the application of military forces and lays out the tasks for them to perform. This is a straightforward appreciation of military strategy, but identifying the subordinate military goals is a complex and involved process. The scale of the complexity is dependent on one's own ability to predict and anticipate the response of the adversary with sufficient assurance. The selection of military objectives must, therefore, be done in anticipation of the adversary's possible action. The process of developing a viable military strategy is characterised by interdependent decision-making between the two antagonists.[10]

---

9 Strachen, Hew, 'War and Strategy', in Olsen, John Andreas, (ed) *On New Wars*, Oslo Files On Defence and Security – 4/2007, Norwegian Institute of Defence Studies, Oslo, 2007, pp. 14-15.

10 Schelling, Thomas C., *The Strategy of Conflict*, Harvard University Press, Cambridge, Mass, 1960, p. 86.

There is another paradigm that has been discussed over the years—the necessity to disarm the adversary as early as possible so that they are unable to put into practice their strategies to achieve their military goals and, through it, the political objectives. This could be interpreted to mean that irrespective of the political objectives, the military strategic objective should always be rapid disarmament of the adversary.[11] However, the costs of achieving victory has to be commensurate with the advantage that it brings and from a political perspective the complete disarmament of the adversary may not be viewed as an attractive proposition because of the cost involved in both treasure and blood.

Another factor that complicates the strategy to task methodology is the difficulty in calculating the force necessary to be applied to achieve victory, which has to be tailored to specific circumstances. This is fraught with uncertainties regarding the effectiveness of the force being applied vis-à-vis the adversary's ability to withstand it and react, which could have disastrous consequences for one's own forces. Strategic decision-making therefore, requires skill in discriminating and selecting the most important and central objects that the adversary possesses, the destruction of which would be decisive in their defeat.[12] However, strategic decision-making is a difficult art primarily because most of it is based on assumptions and predictions that tend to alter without warning and at times even without the decision-maker being aware of the changes that have already taken place. The assurance of a decision being more right than wrong can be increased by having as good an understanding of the adversary as possible.

The strategy to task methodology is a vital link in creating a military force that can always maintain the link between political objectives and the subordinate military goals. While this is clearly a function of the strategic military leadership, there is a role that has to be played at the grand strategic level of national security. The political objectives to be achieved, from which the military goals emanate, have to be drawn within the bounds of reasonable calculation and possibility of achievement in a cost-effective manner. Any disconnect between the

---

11 Stone, John, pp. 5-6.

12 Clausewitz, Carl von, *On War*, trans. Colonel J. J. Graham, Barnes & Noble, New York, 2004, p. 649.

two would invariably lead to a situation wherein the danger of the military forces failing to achieve their objectives is very high.

Strategic Communications

In the development of military forces clear communication of intent from the national leadership down to the military is of paramount importance. It is based on this higher level policy directive that the force structure and capability development is undertaken. Further this directive also guides the developments of military strategy based on threat assessment and force posture as developed over a period of time in conjunction with the broad doctrine of the force. Fundamental to developing an appropriate military force structure and capability is the identification and articulation of a nation's values and ideals, stated within the realm of reality. Although the government plays a major role in achieving clarity in this process, the identification of national values involves a number of disparate organisations, governmental, private and at times even international bodies. The role of the government is to provide the context in terms of reality i.e. the ability of the nation to defend the values that have been identified. In other words, the government is the one that applies pragmatism to what can otherwise become flights of fantasy. Matching the means to achieve the ends through the formulation of adequate ways is an age-old and successfully demonstrated formula. The difficulty lies in realistically matching the means and desired ends in the contemporary volatile international security environment wherein the ends can and do, shift uncomfortably at the most inopportune moments.

The military forces, functioning at the next level of national security, will have to develop the strategy that will address the realities of the environment but yet protect and support the identified values of the nation. This is an onerous task. Strategy is only the beginning of the efficient application of force, which requires materiel, personnel, concepts and an effective command structure to succeed.[13] The importance of technology is underwritten in this basic fact—the greater the military-technical superiority of a force, the more likely it is to achieve its strategic objectives. However, this truism can be distorted

---

13 Wright, Quincy, *A Study of War*, 2nd Ed, University of Chicago Press, Chicago, Ill, 1965, pp. 290-293.

if it is not understood clearly and has the potential to become counter-productive if applied across the board because of political expedience. For example, technical superiority can be translated, wrongly, to the reduction of the number of troops required to achieve a military objective to a number that does not have the required critical mass to succeed. The corollary is that the same quest for technical superiority can lead to the development of weapon systems with such enormous capacity for destruction that their use is almost completely precluded.

Strategic communications—not in the purely information exchange mode, but in a holistic approach to understanding the security needs and imperatives of the nation—is an absolute necessity for the military force to develop its core competencies within the realm of reality and relevance to the nation. The primary responsibility for this rests with the national government, but the military force has an equal responsibility to monitor the relationship between proclaimed values and ground reality.

Flexibility of the Force-in-being

A fundamental characteristic of war is that it is unpredictable at all levels, from the strategic to the tactical. This has been true throughout the long history of warfare and has necessitated making the military forces to always prepare for the unexpected. Historically this was achieved by maintaining a well prepared standing army that could be employed as and when the need arose to defend the country. The need to cater for uncertainties was primarily at the operational and tactical level when actual combat operations were being conducted. Operational uncertainties were fairly limited since the two forces engaged in visual combat adhering to a basic set of rules regarding the conduct of the war. Uncertainties were manifest most at the tactical level where battles were conducted between elements of the two forces. In effect the uncertainties were not insurmountable and were mostly of a personal nature to the combatants. When holistically viewed, this is not an unsurmountable challenge.

The circumstances under which military forces now engage in conflict as well as the character and conduct of conflict itself have undergone enormous changes. First, the military forces are now considered first-choice option to be deployed to provide humanitarian relief for natural or man-made disasters, to stabilise failing or failed states, to establish and maintain peace between warring states or factions, to counter irregular forces waging asymmetric wars, insurgencies or guerrilla wars, to safeguard national interests and to defend the nation in times of external aggression. This is a very broad spectrum and involves the embodiment of a number of very disparate skills in the personnel and capabilities within the force. Since the force-in-being is a comparatively small one, numerically, the entire force needs to be flexible to accommodate these wide ranging requirements. The answer, if there is one, to this challenge is to build a force that is inherently agile and adaptable, achieved through developing flexible and diverse capabilities within the force.[14]

Agility is the ability to rapidly create a range of effects across a broad spectrum of operations and across a range of circumstances and varied environments. An agile force will be able to maximise effects while minimising, to the extent possible, force requirement. This is an absolute necessity for modern Western military forces that have, in the past few decades, shifted their reliance from numerical superiority to ensuring a capability and conceptual edge over potential adversaries through leveraging the benefits of sophisticated, and expensive, technologies. Their concept of operations has altered focus from massing forces to massing of effects through concentrating them at a selected point of impact. Such agility is not easy to acquire, maintain or proficiently employ. It requires sophisticated and high fidelity processes, command and control and a professionally well-developed force to achieve the desired quantum of agility that can contain all emerging challenges.

Adaptability is the ability to react to new and unforeseen challenges in a time critical manner, to be able to identify and seize

---

[14] For a full treatise on the criticality of flexibility as a war-winning capability for a military force read, Finkel, Meir, *On Flexibility: Recovery from Technological and Doctrinal Surprises in the Battlefield*, Tlamin, Moshe, (translator), Stanford Security Studies, University Press, Stanford, 2011. (Especially Part Two, Flexibility-Versed Recovery: A Theoretical View, pp. 53-120.)

A Book Review of the book referred above by Raphael D. Marcus is also available in *Parameters*, 44 (1) Spring 2014, US Army War College, Carlisle, PA, 2014, pp. 146-148. (https://ssi.armywarcollege.edu/pubs/parameters/issues/Spring_2014/Book%20Reviews/Finkel_OnFlexibility.pdf)

new opportunities and to be able to stay relevant in an ever changing environment. In this context, time criticality is a relative concept in that an adaptive military force will be able to react within an appropriate timeframe to neutralise or contain an emerging challenge and need not necessarily mean an inordinately fast response. A military force that has an inherent core of adaptability will be able to adapt to emerging circumstances without having to change its basic configuration. Once again this is neither easy nor within the capability spread of all but the most advanced forces.

These are the two overarching factors without which a military force will find it extremely difficult to be flexible in any realistic manner. However, underlying these two factors are a number of other subsidiary factors that feed into the process of ensuring adequate flexibility, such as training, availability of technologically advanced systems, policies that permit the implementation of multi-faceted programs and many more. Flexibility remains a core competency for a military force to be considered a relevant, valuable and viable element of national power.

Dynamic Competencies

Drawing from the four major core competencies that are enduring in the build-up of a military force, there are competencies that have to be dynamic by virtue of the fact that they are critical to the force being able to respond appropriately to emerging challenges. While a number of competencies can be listed within this category the primary ones, within which the minor competencies can be encompassed are: ability to adapt to high rate of change in the environment, ability to carry out expeditionary operations, ability to acquire and employ high-end capabilities and the ability to integrate.

Adapting to Environmental Changes

The environment within which a military force functions has two sides to it. One is the external environment made up of a combination of the physical—terrain, geography, climate, weather operating conditions—and the adversary in terms of their capabilities, concepts of operations, objectives both political and military, and their warfighting ethos.[15] The other is the internal environment in terms of

---

15 SSR Backgrounder, *op cit*, pp. 5-6.

the force's own capabilities, doctrine, concepts and constraints under which they operate that could be political, legal or resource related. While the external environment can only be influenced indirectly and that too in a limited manner, the internal development of the force can be carefully tailored to meet the strategic requirements of the nation.

The tailoring of the military force and its efficacy will depend on two factors. One, the ability of the force to adapt to a high rate of change in the operating environment and two, its ability to counter emerging threats in a proactive manner and simultaneously be able to continue a modernisation program. Of the two, adapting to the high rate of change is more important in the short term because it has immediate and very direct consequences to the conduct of a battle and to the well-being of the forces in combat. The capacity to simultaneously counter threats and modernise has long term implications and can also be done gradually, giving it less immediacy. However, both the factors have both long and short term elements to them, making them complex in analysing and understanding.

The external environment needs constant monitoring and assessment to orient the force in the appropriate manner.[16] This requires the force, and by extension the nation, to be able to maintain an advantage in terms of developments in science and technology over potential adversaries. Further, maintaining such advantages is directly associated with the ability of the nation to carryout and maintain adequate research and development activities oriented towards improving military capabilities in a holistic manner. In turn, this is a function of the economic and educational status of the nation. Essentially, in this cycle of development, the well-being of the military forces finally rests on the economic and educational ability of the nation to sustain sophisticated technologies. While the development of modern technologies is an involved and normally lengthy process, its impact on the performance of the military force is of a more immediate nature. A force that is more technologically

---

16 Podhorec, Milan, 'The Reality of Operational Environment in Military Operations', *Journal of Defence Resource Management*, Vol 3, Issue 2, (5) 2015, University of Defence, Brno, Czech Republic, 2012, pp. 41-50, http://journal.dresmara.ro/issues/volume3_issue2/02_podhorec_vol3_issue2.pdf accessed on 19 August 2016.

adept will be more flexible and therefore more capable of prevailing in circumstances that are dynamic. This connection between long term initiatives and their direct impact on short term consequences is not always clearly visible.

The ability to counter threats is an immediate requirement for all military forces. However, the complexity is that this ability is dependent on developing a built-in capability to recognise extraordinary long term changes to the conduct and characteristics of war. The capacity to visualise long term trends is essential to ensure that the modernisation process is correctly aligned. This is a gradual process, but one that ideally should be a perpetual and continual one for two reasons; first, it is necessary to keep pace with the developments and improvements in capabilities that potential adversaries are undertaking and second, a military force that tends to be static will very easily enter a downward spiral in its capabilities and be unable to respond to rapidly emerging challenges. Since the total capacity resident within a force will be divided in simultaneous operations and modernisation is taking place, it will be necessary to distinguish between peer competitors and potential adversaries. Peer competitors can be monitored while one's own modernisation is continuing, but developments within a potential adversary's military forces may necessitate actions that may lead to the curtailment or even complete stop of the modernisation efforts.

Even though adapting to environmental changes is influenced by both short and long term factors, it is a dynamic competency for two reasons. First, it is contextual to an extent wherein the force may be forced to hold long term aspects in abeyance to deal with emergent situations. Second, only continuous adaptation to on-going developments, both in the external environment as well as internal adjustments, based on well-crafted flexibility will maintain the force in a state of readiness capable of dealing with all challenges rapidly. Adapting effectively to environmental challenges is a foundational dynamic competency.

Expeditionary Operations

Contemporary challenges to national security need not necessarily arise at the borders of the nation or even somewhere close to it. Further, the size of most military forces is being reduced for a number of reasons:

financial stringency, political expediency, trade-off with technological improvements, to list a few. These two factors in combination with the proclivity of governments to turn to the military forces whenever the slightest threat to security emanates, irrespective of the cause and effect, leads to the inevitable conclusion that modern military forces must possess sufficient expeditionary capabilities.[17] The ability to mount effective expeditionary operations of the required calibre is a dynamic competency of military forces in a number of ways. There are a number of elements that combine to make up a cohesive expeditionary capability.

First, the military force must be able to operate in an expeditionary mode with minimal footprint. This is relative in that the footprint will be dependent on the size of the force and also on the duration of the commitment. However, the footprint within the borders of the nation into which the expedition is being conducted must be the bare minimum. A large and intrusive footprint has the potential to alienate the local population that could be an impediment to smooth operations as well as to achieving the laid down objectives. Second, a majority of expeditionary operations in the contemporary environment will eventuate in the conduct of irregular wars which could mean that the force must have sufficient niche capabilities like special operations to be successful.

Third, expeditionary operations cannot be conducted without sufficient training and strategic depth within the force. This requires the development of an effective theory, doctrine, and concept of operations to conduct expeditionary irregular conflicts. This is an exacting task and all military forces may not be able to develop such expertise on their own. This situation is further exacerbated because of the fact that most small forces will not have the full spectrum of capabilities resident within the force to contemplate conducting a stand-alone expeditionary operation. However, expeditionary forces must have overarching capabilities that are stand-alone for a definitive period of time for them to be able to function effectively, leading to

---

17 Fry, Robert, Lt Gen Sir, 'Expeditionary Operations in the Modern Era', *The RUSI Journal*, Volume 150, 2005-Issue 6, RUSI, London, 2005, Published online 30 October 2009, pp. 60-63. https://www.tandfonline.com/doi/abs/10.1080/0307 1840509441986?journalCode=rusi20 accessed on 19 August 2016.

the formation of coalitions that bring together military forces with different capabilities to become a force with all necessary capabilities embedded in it. Therefore, expeditionary capabilities become intimately connected to the fourth element, which is the ability of the force to conduct coalition operations. Coalition operations require a force to focus on three fundamental areas—interoperability, all-weather operations and rapid deployment.

Interoperability. Interoperability by itself could become a stumbling block in the formation of an effective coalition. Modern military forces are network enabled and interoperability can only be achieved through having the same or similar network-enabled capabilities. The advantages of having seamless interoperability are many; the agility of the coalition improves dramatically, the forces are able to control the tempo of operations through achieving decision-superiority and from an individual nation's perspective, it becomes possible to economise on the size of the force required to achieve a clearly laid down objective. However, network-enabled interoperability also brings in some vulnerabilities to the entire coalition. First, in case any of the coalition partners or allies has not reached the same level of sophistication as the rest in terms of networks, the coalition will not be able to function at the high level of interface that is required. The simple fact is that coalitions have to operate at the level of the lowest common denominator, which might put the entire force at risk. Second, network-enables interoperability is a complex concept and requires highly developed skills to operationalize, especially between forces from different nations. Third, networks are vulnerable to cyber-attacks and there is as yet no fool-proof defences against them. Network-enabled interoperability, the corner stone around which coalition success is constructed could be targeted as a centre of gravity that, if neutralised, can fatally affect coalition operations. Network-enables operations also have few challenges to overcome—the equipment required are expensive to acquire, maintain and be trained on, and could be prohibitively so for resource strained nations; a long lead time is required to become fully network-enabled and compatible with potential coalition partners; and there will always be a certain amount resistance from the personnel being introduced to this new ways of operating with excessive reliance on networks.

All-weather Operations. The ability to operate unrestrained by weather is a prized capability that is also an asymmetric advantage to conventional forces in conflict with irregular forces. Coalition operations would normally be undertaken against adversaries who need to be defeated to ensure stability and security of a region. The ability of the coalition force to carryout precision strike under all conditions—all-weather, day and night—is crucial to success and to limiting the duration of any conflict. This premises that a coalition force will always have all the capabilities of a balanced force embedded in them and will not be put together with only niche capabilities since that would defeat the whole purpose of creating such a force.

Rapid Deployment. The security environment has changed radically in the past few decades making it necessary for military forces to be able to react rapidly to emerging threats that could be geographically at a great distance from their home base. Rapid deployment capabilities can be built by an individual military force provided it has sufficient resource support. However, translating the same capability to a coalition force is not an easy task. The rapid deployment capability of a coalition force will depend on the readiness status of individual members as well on the collective ability of the members to respond in a timely manner. Once again the coalition force would be able to do so only at the pace of the slowest member. Rapid deployment capability is a crucial element in the overall posture of a coalition force and could well be one that avoids escalation of limited conflicts by early intervention.

Employing High-end Capabilities

In all conflict situations there is a clearly discernible relationship between the tempo of operations, intensity of the conflict and the technology being employed. Weapon systems at the high-end of technology can control the tempo as well as the intensity of operations even when pitched against an adversary with similar capabilities. The control is much easier to achieve when the adversary is an irregular force operating at a lower level of technological sophistication. However, even after such control is achieved, an intelligent adversary will be able to context it by the use of asymmetry that could negate the advantages of technological superiority. The employment of high-end capabilities has to be carefully tailored to meet contextual requirements while ensuring that reliance on them does not become a vulnerability that can be exploited by an adroit adversary.

Within the military force, the air force is perhaps most reliant on high-end capabilities to function optimally. That is not to say that the land and maritime forces are not technology-dependent, they are, but to a relatively lesser degree. Contemporary air power is primarily characterised by its ability to deliver lethal attacks with precision, discrimination and proportionality. This capability is seen as a critical requirement in operations in a highly asymmetric environment and is almost completely reliant on technology. Similarly, uninhabited aerial vehicles make a significant contribution to irregular warfare through their ability to provide persistent surveillance and reconnaissance as well as carryout targeted and time-sensitive strikes. Technology also enhances the manoeuvrability of military forces, which is an important feature of modern warfare. Manoeuvrability is crucial in irregular warfare because it permits a numerically smaller force to cover a large geographic area as well as to retain the element of surprise to a certain degree when in actual combat.

A military force operating at the high-end of technology will find it far easier to scale down the technology to suit a situational requirement rather than having to ramp up technologically from a lower level. This is fundamental to a military force being effective across the entire spectrum of conflict, which is the primary function of all balanced forces. On the other hand, high-end capabilities, while being desirable, are expensive to acquire, difficult to maintain and gain expertise in operating. A military force that has difficulty in incorporating high-end capabilities would, therefore, be one that is not of the required calibre. High-end capabilities are necessary not as a panacea to winning all conflicts but they are essential to ensure that the force is able to function at a level that provides an assured probability of success.[18] This is becoming increasingly important because of the open availability of highly sophisticated weapon systems to even irregular adversaries—a development that has made the clear technology gap

---

18 Biddle, Stephen, Chapter 4: 'The Modern System, Preponderance, and Changing Technology', in *Military Power: Explaining Victory and Defeat in Modern Battle*, Princeton University Press, Princeton, 2004, pp. 52-77.

between conventional military and irregular forces narrow down to an extent where it is negligible in contemporary conflict environment.

The Ability to Integrate

A balanced military force will have all three combat capabilities—land, maritime and air—in adequate quantum resident within it. It is not sufficient for these three disparate capabilities to be available in the force, but the force must have the ability to integrate them into a joint force capable of projecting force as a single entity. In recent times, military forces are endeavouring to operate as seamless systems to achieve the desired effects. Integration of capabilities resident in the three environmental forces is a dynamic ability that is essential for a military force to prevail in conflict. This is because contemporary threats that are to be defeated are best addressed by a combination of capabilities, tailored for the situation rather than by individual capabilities operating independently.

In contemporary conflict the integration process is more pronounced between the army and air force with the naval forces normally being in a stand-off mode. The concept of air-sea battle and amphibious operations are also being developed, but they function at the operational and tactical levels of war. An integrated military force will, of necessity, comprise of both land and air forces as essential components. Land forces are not platform-centric but are primarily focused on prevailing in the mixed-intensity operations that are becoming common place in the prevalent security scenario. Air power is a crucial element in this ability. Further, air power is a multi-function capability that is central to winning the ground battle, especially in the evolving hybrid or irregular wars.

The intent of most modern military forces is to evolve into a seamless system for two reasons. One, seamlessness simplifies the synchronisation of operations that is essential to achieve increased combat effectiveness. In turn, optimising combat effectiveness is necessary to counter the increased sophistication of capabilities and concepts of operations of irregular adversaries, which can effectively challenge the notion of military superiority based on conventional forces. In the current environment high-end weapon systems are available to even non-state and terrorist entities that do not have the same legal or sovereign sanctity as a national military force. Two, only an integrated military force can provide the military answer to the challenges and security needs of a changing and continually evolving world. The essence of military capabilities—flexibility, concentration, manoeuvrability and superior firepower—is only achievable through adequate integration of the three arms of the military forces.

THE CHALLENGES TO MILITARY FORCES

Ever since the emergence of sovereign nations as accepted entities with rights and responsibilities recognised internationally, their military forces have been considered the protector of national sovereignty and therefore granted a special status. At a very fundamental level of national security this is still the case—it is the military force that will be at the forefront of a war of national survival. However, the advent of nations also saw an increasing sense of nationalism being developed in all the states. Nationalism is essentially the identification of a group of people with a nation. There are two perspectives on the origins of nationalism; one that considers nationalism as a reflection of the basic human tendency to be recognised as part of a group based on affinity of birth, and a second perspective that nationalism is more recent in origin and requires the structure of a modern society to exist.[19]

The relationship between nationalism and the role of the military within the state has not always been smooth. This is particularly so in the post-colonial nations where the military is often seen as having been on the side of the colonial powers during the nationalistic struggle for freedom. Even so, the military forces have been considered a critical component of national defence, as opposed to security, and therefore supported by the nation. Further, in times of conflict or war, there is no doubt that nationalism will always buttress the military and its endeavours to protect the nation. It is in times of comparative peace that the divergence between the two becomes visible. Nationalism tends to become inward looking in times of peace, perhaps in the quest for greater well-being of the nation and is manifest externally normally in terms of trade and commerce, pushing the military forces into a subsidiary role. The recent expansion of the concept of national

---

19 Motyl, A. J., *Encyclopaedia of Nationalism, Vol 1: Fundamental Themes*, Academic Press, San Diego California, USA, 2001, p. 251.

security has further diluted the status of military forces and even led to the demand in certain nations for their budgets to be reallocated to aid and diplomatic agencies that are perceived to be more important to furthering the interests of the nation.

There is another factor that influences the broader national understanding of the role of defence forces in the arena of national security. In recent times democratic nations have consciously made attempts at not being seen to improve their military capabilities for fear of being labelled militaristic. Militarism is the belief or desire of a government and people that a country should maintain a strong military capability and be prepared to use it aggressively to defend or promote national interests. In extreme cases, militarism could lead to regarding military efficiency as the supreme ideal of the state and to subordinate all other interests to those of the military.[20] However, in the contemporary international political environment it is considered, with good historical reasons, to be an avoidable trait in a nation. This soft approach to the development of capable military forces and the accompanying reluctance to accept the realities of war has made military forces something of a desirable, but inconvenient part of the government. This dichotomy—of the tacit acceptance of the necessity to maintain a capable military force but the reluctance to accept it—is more visible in democratic nations. The primary reasons for the development, and in certain cases perpetuation, of this situation are economic and electoral. When nations face economic hardships and stringency the requirement to fund social programs will always take priority over spending on defence, especially when the electoral cycle is short-term.

In addition to the pressures that divergent nationalism and reluctant militarism brings on contemporary military forces, they face a number of other challenges in carrying out the fundamental task of protecting the nation and furthering the national interest. These challenges can be clubbed under the very broad categories of morale, civil-military relationship, legal aspects and the issues in the employment of military forces.

---

20 *Free Online Dictionary*, http://dictionary.reference.com/browse/militarism, accessed on 9 May 2012.

Morale

"Man is a feeble unit in the middle of a threatening infinitude."

-Thomas Carlyle

The noun morale means the mental and emotional condition—as of enthusiasm, confidence or loyalty—of an individual or group with regard to the function or task at hand.[21] The term refers to the level of individual faith in the collective benefit gained by performing a task, particularly in times of stress or danger. While morale could be interpreted to be of influence in any organisation, civil or military, its importance to the functioning of a military force cannot be overemphasised. Morale is the most important intangible element of the human dimension in a military force.[22] It is as important, if not more so, as the effectiveness of the weapon systems and training that mark a military force as competent.

There are far too many factors, tangible and illusory, that affect the morale of a fighting force. This is particularly applicable at the lower levels of command and operations with the basic fighting unit being susceptible to a large number of factors. Seemingly insignificant factors, even created by external agencies, could have a disproportionately high impact on the morale of a group.[23] However, in an overarching manner, three major but independent factors that directly affect the morale of a force can be identified.

First is the warrior-ethos of nation. Every nation has its own ethos towards going to war, the actual conduct of operations and the defining of the desired end-state. The ethos is a fusion of history, culture, experience, economy, status of military forces and many other contextual issues. The higher the warrior-ethos built into a nation, the

---

21 Hughes, Barrie, (General Ed), *The Penguin Working Words*, Penguin Books Australia, Ringwood, Victoria, 1993, p. 350.

22 Headquarters, Department of the Army, Washington DC, USA, *FM 22-100 Army Leadership*, November 1998, p. 3-3.

23 Wierzbicki, Sławomir, 'Soldier's Morale as a Chance for Winning the Military Conflict', *World Scientific News*, Issue 72, 2017, pp. 358-363, http://www.worldscientificnews.com/wp-content/uploads/2017/01/WSN-72-2017-358-363.pdf accessed on 10 June 2018.

more its proclivity to employ its military forces as well as endure the hardships that automatically come with conducting a conflict. While a democracy will be more reluctant to enter into a conflict scenario, the ethos of the nation will have a fundamental impact on the decision-making process. Indirectly this 'support' from the nation affects the morale of the military forces while conducting the actual operations. More than the decision to go to war, the warrior-ethos is important in ensuring adequate morale is maintained when faced with adversities. In contemporary terms this has added importance because of the advent of suicide bombing as a weapon of war.

Suicide bombing attacks can perhaps be termed as the cheapest weapon of war with the ability to have the most impact on the morale of the adversary. The impact of suicide bombings, against which most counter measures are ineffective, can be devastating to a military force representing a nation that is averse to accepting casualties. Casualty tolerance is a fundamental requirement for a nation to be able to pursue a long-drawn campaign. A nation with minimal warrior-ethos will have very limited appetite to absorb casualties and continue to conflict till the desired end-state is achieved. In such situations, public opinion can turn against support for the war very rapidly and equally rapidly sap the morale of the fighting forces.

The second factor is the need for the military forces to believe in the society on behalf of which it is fighting the war. This has a tenuous connection to the first factor of national warrior-ethos. The morale of a military force in the deepest sense is affected directly by the mutual trust between them and the society at large. This trust is built over a long period with the society having explicit belief in the moral and ethical correctness of all actions of the military force and in return the military having faith in the population that they are protecting to provide them with the resources and emotional support needed to perform their tasks. There is an implicit covenant between the military force and the government that assures the military personnel that in return for their risking their lives, the government will look after their interests at all times. If this relationship is even slightly frayed, or perceived to be tense, the impact on the morale of the force can be significant. As a continuation, even a slight deterioration in morale will have a quantifiable effect on the fighting efficacy of the force. A voluntary military force is a microcosm of the broader society and cannot function in isolation. The changes in the balance between the military and the society at large therefore, will be immediately felt across all levels of the military. The impact on morale will be immediate and fathomable.

The third factor is focused on the effect of long term deployments and high readiness posture of the force that indirectly affect the morale. This factor is particularly important to numerically small military forces that do not have the overall capacity to sustain open-ended deployments, even if the tempo and intensity of operations are low. Long term deployments and the necessity to rotate personnel into and out of theatre on a regular basis will impinge on the overall readiness of the force for two reasons. First, beyond a certain timeframe, these rotations will be possible only with the reduction in normal training activities wherein the instructors are withdrawn for operational duties. This will be the beginning of a downward spiral that will gradually make the force unable to retain the necessary level of training to ensure adequate proficiency in personnel at all times. Second, repeated deployments that will become necessary in long duration operations will negate the opportunity for individuals to carry out adequate refresher training, contributing to a reduction in overall readiness of the force. The combination of these two can become an insurmountable challenge to a small military force.

A subsidiary issue that will be generated with the onset of inadequacy of training is the possibility of the loss of the ability to operate at full-spectrum capabilities to the desired level. In terms of the efficacy of military application, full-spectrum capabilities are critical to exercise the necessary flexibility that optimises the creation of the desired effects. This regression in capability will add impetus to the degradation of the force capability and increase the rate of decline. Effectively long term deployments are not conducive to the maintenance of high morale in a small military force. Long term deployments also have an adverse effect on the individual through the increase in stress levels. If not properly contained at its onset itself, stress can lead to long term side effects in the individual. Collectively this situation will tend to lower the morale of the force, initially in small units and then spreading to larger formations.

Morale in the deepest sense must be a tangible thread that connects individuals at the lowest tactical level of the military force, to the highest levels of command, through intertwined levels of command, responsibility and authority. Morale is the glue that binds a military force together and makes individuals willingly put their lives at risk for the good and safety of the larger society that they serve. It is built on a large number of intangible factors like esprit-de-corps, loyalty, pride, nationalism, patriotism, courage etc.

Civil-Military Relationship

> "Armies enter combat not merely because two or more of them happen to be hanging around an empty battlefield and decide to fill in some time but because an issue between two or more political entities cannot be settled in other ways and then military means are resorted to."
>
> General Rupert Smith[24]

The military forces of most practicing democracies are controlled by the civilian political leadership, with the military high command willingly accepting the primacy of the elected government in all matters of national security. While the actual mechanisms of such control may vary in different nations, the fundamental arrangement of the elected government exercising supreme authority over the military is the basis of all civil-military relationships. Therefore, the mechanisms used by elected civilian leadership to oversee and control military forces are, fundamental considerations in fostering this relationship.[25] However, over the years this relationship has become contested at times, especially in nations where the military forces have been continuously employed in non-core functions like providing disaster relief and delivering humanitarian aid. Further, in an era where conventional conflict that directly threatens the nation's sovereignty is unlikely, the

---

24 Smith, Rupert, *The Utility of Force: The Art of War in the Modern World*, Alfred Knopf, New York, 2007, p. 13.

25 Feaver, Peter, 'Civil-Military Relations', *Annual Review of Political Science*, Vol. 2, No 1, Paolo Alta, CA, 1999, pp. 211-229.

status of military forces as a critical arm of national security tends to be gradually eroded.

Liberal democratic nations have always been defended by conservative military establishments. Military forces, by virtue of their very profession, are inclined to foster and value the warrior-ethos within its ranks. The success of Western military forces in ensuring that their nations are not threatened in any manner has given rise to a sense of invulnerability to the society at large. This in turn has been instrumental in creating a fairly vociferous segment of society that demands the undoing of the military forces. This contradiction between the ethos of the warrior class within the military and the unwillingness of the beneficiaries of their steadfastness to support them is becoming increasingly visible in a number of democratic nations. This dichotomy can, if not carefully ameliorated by visible and coherent actions, create a civil-military divide that will place the nation at risk from a security perspective.

Although several conflicts have been fought after World War II, the democratic nations of the world have not been required to defend themselves against an existentialist threat since 1945. There is also a less than optimum understanding of military matters and the relationship of the military forces to the very broadly defined concept of national security within the community. Imperceptibly the gap between the civil society and the military forces has increased to an extent wherein a bridge seems to be impossible to build. A combination of these factors has led, over the past six decades, the gradual dilution of the criticality of the military forces within the national security equation in the perception of the broader society. This is emphasised by the gradual decline in the number of parliamentarians who have served in the military forces, in all democracies other than the ones in which compulsory military service is the norm. This decline is also indicative of the disinclination of the larger section of society to embark on a military career since it is not perceived as belonging to the first rung. This is a self-defeating cycle from the military perspective since it fails to attract the 'best and the brightest' of the nation, that in turn will gradually reduce the overall calibre of the military forces thereby diminishing its chances of attracting the persons of the right ability.

The implication of only few parliamentarians having served in the military is that the debate and subsequent decision-making regarding all aspects of the military forces, from conditions of service to acquisition of capabilities, is normally done at a superficial level. Only when national security is directly threatened is there any focused interest displayed in ensuring that the military forces are adequately prepared to meet emerging exigencies. At the fundamental level, the issue is that the society that the military defends has less than optimum interest in the well-being of the military forces, electing to not see or acknowledge their contribution to the nation. When long spells of comparative tranquillity within the nation brings about stability and a sense of invulnerability, which is further deepened with the minority anti-military establishment, the military forces tend to be compared and equated to other areas of governance like welfare and health care. It is no surprise that military forces around the world have faced increasing scrutiny and resource pressures over the past few decades.

The factors mentioned above tend to have a collective influence on civil-military relationship. There is no doubt that good relationship, built on mutual trust and confidence not merely cordiality, is the foundation for building a strong and viable military force that directly contributes to national security. Along with public apathy and the indifference of the civilian leadership towards the military forces, there are a number of other challenges to creating a harmonious civil-military relationship. First, there is insufficient understanding of the functioning of the military machine in the civil leadership. On the other hand, the military considers the elected representatives as short-term masters and do not feel the need to comprehensively be inclusive of the civil leadership in strategic decision-making. In combination, this situation intrusively degrades mutual trust. Second, since the military, by virtue of their non-political stance in democracies, is not seen as a group that will vociferously protest against wrong-doing the civilian leadership tends to discard them as a vote-winning group. The military considers this attitude disdainful and does not make any effort is making their points of view known. The result is a widening divide in the appreciation of the military processes on the one hand and the political system on the other.

An extended period of peace, in its broadest definition where the nation is not in peril, the increasing financial pressures, domestic demographic changes and the altered expectations of the general population regarding the government's and military's role have combined to create an increasing disconnect between the social and political elite and the military leadership. This is true of most democratic nations. However, only a very short-sighted national leadership, both civil and military, will let such a situation continue without being addressed and corrected. The consequences of not doing so are dire and will lead to national security becoming a bargaining point both domestically and within the international arena.[26]

In the contemporary global environment, there are two other factors that have great influence on civil-military relationships. Although not emanating from direct civil-military interaction, they have the potential to create long-term detrimental influence in the smooth functioning of the civil-military interface in democracies. First, there is a noticeable trend in the developed world to embrace universal values at times even when such values are contrary to the national values. While in the long term, this might have the effect of creating a value system that transcends geographical, cultural and ethnic borders, in the short to medium term and in particular reference to the military forces, this could become the thin edge of a divide with the prospective to become a wide chasm. In the case of military forces, the national motivation to subscribe to universally accepted values could manifest as providing care in a bipartisan manner to both international and one's own victims of warfare. When a military force is engaged in combat operations equating the adversary or even neutral personnel

---

26 For detailed discussions and worthy conclusions on civil-military relationship in democratic nations, read the following definitive and authoritative studies:

Huntington, Samuel P., *The Soldier and the State: The Theory and Politics of Civil-Military Relations*, Harvard University Press, Massachusetts, 1957.

Janowitz, Morris, *The Professional Soldier: A Social and Political Portrait*, Originally published 1960, Free Press; reissue edition 2017.

Desch, Michael C., *Civilian Control of the Military: The Changing Security Environment*, The Johns Hopkins University Press, Baltimore, 1999.

Feaver, Peter D., *Armed Servants: Agency, Oversight and Civil-Military Relations*, Harvard University Press, Massachusetts, 2003.

with one's own fighting personnel could act as a morale shattering experience. This has the potential for the military forces to lose faith in the political values of the nation, leading almost immediately to loss of trust in the civilian leadership.

Second, the most nations do not have an appreciation of visible combat operations involving the nation's military forces, although a large number of Western democracies have deployed their forces in expeditionary combat operations for more than a decade. Further, the visible and more often reported contributions of military forces are the actions initiated to deliver humanitarian assistance, disaster relief and peace keeping operations. These are 'good news' stories that even the military forces themselves want to be placed on the nation's conscience in order to garner popular support for them. However, a conscious move towards projecting the military force as harbingers of succour is a double-edged sword. Being actively and visibly involved in humanitarian assistance operations, both domestically and internationally, could reinforce the perception that the primary role of the military forces is nation-building in its broadest explanation. The obvious follow-on to this is that it will not take a long period of time thereafter for the military forces to be seen, and more importantly, treated as civil servants in uniforms, rather than as the primary defenders of the nation's sovereignty. This will almost unequivocally change the civil-military relationship. The down-gradation of status in the national perception can take place in a very short timeframe, whereas recovering the status as a primary element of national power and the cornerstone of national security will be a long and arduous upward trek. Such an upgradation may not be within the grasp of a number of military forces, especially the ones that function as small or middle power forces, automatically and perhaps permanently confining military forces to a secondary status within the national security calculus, at best.

There is no substitute for good civil-military relationship in a democracy to ensure that national security is never compromised. However, in the contemporary environment, achieving a state of harmony requires concerted effort from both the civilian and military leadership. When analysed in an unbiased manner the root cause of most collapses of civil-military relationship can be traced to the civilian leadership placing greater emphasis on domestic political considerations and the electoral cycle than on maintaining the national security imperatives above petty politics in a bipartisan manner. This is also no to say that the military leadership is flawless, since there have been instances, especially in the newly emerged, post-colonial democracies, of the military forces being actively involved in domestic politics and even playing a 'king-maker' role. Being constitutionally subservient to the elected leadership, it is incumbent on the military forces to be the more flexible element in this, often turbulent, relationship. This is a constant challenge to a democratic nation's military force.

Legal Aspects[27]

The legal issues that affect the employment of military forces are encoded in the operations law. The manifestation of a nation's will through the projection of military power, in accordance with the law, is an integral part of the broader military mission. It is internationally accepted that a sovereign nation must carefully consider the legal, moral and political repercussions of the employment of its military forces before committing them to operations. It is incumbent on a responsible nation to adhere to domestic and international law at all times in the conduct of military operations. There are a number of international treaties, dating to different periods, which govern the conduct of armed conflict: the Hague Conventions from 1907; the Geneva Conventions and the Hague Cultural Property Convention from 1949 and 1954; and the Protocols additional to the Geneva Conventions and the Convention on certain conventional weapons from 1997 and 1980.[28] These reflect what could be termed the accepted norms of the time regarding the application of lethal force and the broader employment

---

27 The legal aspect of civil-military relations in democracies was the subject of a Conference organised by the Geneva Centre for the Democratic Control of the Armed Forces (DCAF) in Geneva on 3-5 May 2001. The proceedings of the Conference was published, details given below.

Vankovska, Biljana, (ed), *Legal Framing of the Democratic Control of Armed Forces and the Security Sector: Norms and Reality/ies*, Geneva Centre for the Democratic Control of Armed Forces, Geneva, 2001. http://www.bezbednost.org/upload/document/legal_framing_of_the_democrati.pdf accessed between November 2015 and September 2016.

28 Mulinen, Fredric De, *Handbook on the Law of War for Armed Forces*, International Committee of the Red Cross, Geneva, 1987, p. xv.

of the military forces. However, in the contemporary security scenario the military forces face certain challenges in operating within this rigid set of rules. While it is not being suggested here that sovereign nations' should disregard international law, the proposition is that there needs to be a realistic review of the laws that bind military forces in a disadvantageous manner. The fundamental issue is regarding the moral position vis-à-vis right and wrong of the participants in a conflict and the detrimental effect of restrictive laws practiced in a one-sided manner during actual combat operations.

There are three fundamental challenges stemming from legal issues that military forces face when involved in combat operations. First, is the implication of the implementation of the concept of justice based on reason, which by itself is the bulwark of democracies. In conventional conflict, where the adversaries evenly subscribe to the prevailing laws of armed conflict, justice based on reason normally will not have any detrimental effect. However, the implications become easily visible in the contemporary environment when the conflict is almost always between the military forces of a sovereign nation and non-state irregular forces. In such conflicts only the military forces operate within the ambit of international law while the irregular adversary consciously does not adhere to any preconceived norms of conflict. However, justice based on reason is applied without fail and scrupulously to members of the military force, even for actions undertaken under extreme provocation. Such actions have both advantages and disadvantages. The advantage is that in dispensing justice with an even hand, the nations and its military forces involved automatically demonstrate that they hold the moral high ground and are lauded for their forbearance. This is vitally important for democratic nations to establish the 'correctness' of their actions.

From a purely military effectiveness perspective such actions are bound to have a detrimental effect on the force. The effect will initially be felt only at the tactical level in the fighting units, but will gradually percolate upwards to the entire force, and given sufficient time to the nation as a whole. This is so because starting from individual combatants to tactical level leadership and then to commanders at all levels, the prospect of committing an offence that will not be condoned, even if the decision was taken under life threatening situations will eventually have a negative impact on the decision-making process of the force. It has to be reiterated that the suggestion here is not the complete disregard for laws of armed conflict but that its applications has to be much more flexible and attuned to the context of its implementation. This is a challenge that military forces will be struggling with for the near future.

The second challenge is the appreciation of domestic laws and customs that may or may not have absolute legal sanctity but are still important to be observed from the perspective of being seen to be carrying out the right actions. This is particularly important when military forces are involved in expeditionary operations. Irregular, non-state forces that wage insurgencies are particularly adept at portraying the regular military forces as perpetrators of unjust actions from the viewpoint of local values, customs and beliefs. In most contemporary conflicts the operations take place amongst culturally different populations and geographically diverse areas, as compared to the predominantly Western military forces. Starting from the value placed on the life and status of individuals, to societal and cultural values and the associated dos and don'ts, to understanding the complex ethos of an alien nation in a contextual manner are almost impossible tasks. Most military forces are not tuned or trained to be particularly sensitive to cultural nuances, more so when the deployment and combat operations are initiated at short notice. While the actions in this context only borders on the legal, it can have an all-consuming domino effect on the final outcome of the conflict, with the potential to completely mar excellent military performance for good.

The third challenge overlaps with the effectiveness of the employment of military forces and is related to the selection of the adversary centres of gravity that must targeted to create the necessary effect to achieve the desired objectives. Modern military forces have the built-in capability to identify the appropriate centre of gravity that if attacked and neutralised will create the necessary effects. However, the legality of attacking the identified targets changes with circumstances, the probability of collateral damage and the prevailing public opinion. This dynamic situation where even if the target can be legally attacked, ethical and cultural considerations may negate such an attack adds to the complexity of target selection and prosecution at the execution level of operations. The complexity is further exacerbated by the very limited time available to operational commanders to make decisions regarding target selection and even lesser time available for the operator to decide whether to deliver the weapon or not.

Legal aspects of employing military forces will always be complex and have a controlling influence on the conduct of operations. The challenge is not so much to ensure the legality of military actions, but to ensure that it is possible for the force to create the necessary effects through its ability to operate within the legal boundaries. The distinction is nuanced and has to be carefully considered at the planning stage of all operations.

Employment of Military Forces

The efficient employment of military forces is an arduous task, perhaps the most complex of human undertaking. The effectiveness of military forces is measured in terms of their ability to create the necessary effects optimally in order to achieve the desired end-state. In this context the end-state would be a purely military calculation that in turn will be a subset that contributes to achieving the national political end-state. If there are differences between the military aims and political objectives, they can rapidly escalate to becoming challenges that will invariably lead to divisions if not managed through a process of consultation and discussion at the highest levels of civil and military leadership.[29] The overarching strategic objectives should always be arrived at through balancing political and military imperatives. A competent military force will be able to identify the military end-state at the planning stage and also have the flexibility to adapt it contextually in case of changes to the desired political end-state as the campaign progresses. Further, the primary military objective would be to defeat the fielded forces of the enemy at the earliest in an efficient manner. This efficiency founded on achieving an optimum combination between weapon system effectiveness and operational concepts.

In contemporary conflict, achieving the desired military end-state is predicated on five major factors: the selection of centres of gravity, the targeting process, the sophistication of available weapon systems,

---

29 Stone, John, *Military Strategy: The Politics and Techniques of War*, p. 141.

the balance between target identification and neutralisation capabilities, and the impact of long duration wars.

Centres of Gravity. The selection of the centres of gravity that, if neutralised, would create the maximum effect on the adversary is the most important part of campaign planning. The process selecting the centres of gravity is influenced by a number of considerations. First, the aims of the campaign, both long term and short term, must be clearly identified. While the long term objectives will normally be political in nature, the short term objectives may be more military in nature, in terms of neutralising the adversary's ability to influence the course of events. Second, the process must consider the context within which the campaign is being conducted. This means that the geo-political, cultural and religious environment in the area of operations as well as those of the primary adversary must be carefully analysed before centres of gravities are determined. Further, the repercussions of attacking a particular target, in terms of its moral and ethical fall outs and one's own international standing must be taken into account. Essentially, the selection of centres of gravity must be context specific to the campaign at hand. Third, while targets within the commercial and industrial complexes and the political system can be identified during the military planning process, their prosecution will need to be endorsed at the highest level of government because of the political nature of the targets and a high probability of creating unintended consequences. Even certain military targets that could be conceived as dual-use facilities that if attacked could create collateral damage to civilian infrastructure will need to be cleared above a purely operational military level. The selection of the centres of gravity is an involved process.

Targeting Process. Effective targeting is a complex activity, involving a number of steps that must all align with each other to ensure success. After a centre of gravity has been selected as a target, surveillance and reconnaissance must be conducted to identify the exact location and intelligence gathered to ensure the veracity of the selection. Thereafter the actual strike operation can be undertaken, which in itself has a number of tactical level challenges to be overcome to ensure accuracy, proportionality and discrimination. The targeting process is conducted at the operational level of a campaign but its failure can create cascading effects that could even jeopardise the entire campaign. It is, therefore, necessary for military forces to put in place robust targeting processes and to review them in a contextual manner in each campaign being undertaken. In contemporary conflict that places a premium on being able to carry out time-sensitive targeting, the process is under constant pressure to be compressed. This further emphasises the need for robust and well-practiced targeting processes to be clearly embedded in the operational ethos of the force.

Weapon Systems. At the baseline, the effectiveness of the employment of military forces is measured in terms of their achieving the desired end-state. However, the way in which this is achieved has become increasingly important, to an extent where the way or manner in which a campaign is conducted is at times more important than achieving the ultimate end-state. While this is a paradoxical situation, because of the influence of a number of disparate factors it is seen that it may be more advantageous to achieve subordinate objectives through using visibly correct means rather than strive to achieve the end-state. In this context, guided weapons and precision-guided munitions provide the necessary fidelity to neutralise targets with minimal probability of collateral damage that could lead to unintended consequences. The recent proliferation of such sophisticated weapon systems on the one hand has made offensive action much more effective and on the other, provided a greater ability to resist conventional offensive campaigns.[30] While the accuracy of guided weapon systems has been proven over the past few decades, there is an external factor that impinges on their effectiveness in the broader sense. Their effectiveness is primarily a function of neutralising targets that have strategic impact on the outcome of the campaign, which in turn is a function of the correctness of the selection of targets. Therefore, while sophisticated state-of-the art weapon systems are a necessity, the cycle of selection, and identification of the target, strike and damage assessment is equally important in ensuring effectiveness in the employment of military forces.

Balance of Capabilities. All military forces, by virtue of their basic responsibility to protect the nation, have two primary operational capabilities vested in them. These are the ability to identify targets

---

30 ibid, pp. 134-135.

and the ability to neutralise them when required through the weapon systems made available to them. Obviously the proficiency of these capabilities resident in a military force is intrinsically connected to the availability of systems operating at the high-end of the technology spectrum, especially when operating under restrictive rules of engagement. There is a need to balance the two capabilities in order to ensure that the force development does not become skewed in either direction. An abundance of one capability without sufficiency in the other will not be able to create the necessary effects when the force is employed. Essentially, it is not good enough to be able to select and locate a target if the capability to prosecute it is not resident in the force and as a corollary, having highly sophisticated strike capabilities without the ability to locate selected targets is also equally insufficient to achieve the desired end-state. In recent years, since most of the operations have been conducted in coalitions and because of the financial difficulties being faced by a majority of the developed nations, there has been a visible trend to develop either one of the two. Any imbalance between the two directly diminishes the offensive capability of a force. Such imbalances are particularly noticeable in air forces and become fundamental challenges to their effectiveness in the offensive role. The ability of a joint military force to carry out parallel offensive operations, primarily based on the offensive capabilities resident in the air power component, will also be adversely affected when the capabilities are not balanced.

Long Duration Operations. Traditionally military forces have been designed to fight for short durations, mostly calculated in weeks and months rather than in years. Although the two World Wars and the subsequent Korean and Vietnam Wars did extend to a number of years, they were not wars that the military forces had planned to fight as such. The conflict in Afghanistan, at the time of writing being assiduously scaled down and terminated, was also not expected to last for the more than 12 to 13 years that it did.[31] An important factor to be considered when committing military forces into conflicts that are likely to be extended in nature is the long term fatigue that the force is likely to suffer. When a force has been involved in long duration wars,

---

31 Pernin, Christopher G., Nichiporuk Brian, and others, *Unfolding the Future of the Long War: Motivations, Prospects, and Implications for the U.S. Army*, Rand Corporation, Santa Monica, CA, 2008, Chapters 2, 3, and 4.

the demands of maintaining the desired tempo and intensity necessary to win will always take its toll in terms of reducing the efficiency of the force as a whole. This will become apparent initially in parts of the force that is not directly involved in the conflict, because the focus would be on maintaining the operational tempo. However, the deterioration of capabilities, once set in one area of the force, will rapidly spread through the whole force. Long duration conflicts have the flow-on effect of making a nation averse to the employment of military forces into the near term future after its completion, particularly if the outcome has not been favourable.

The effective employment of military forces has never been an easy task. In the current geo-political environment, the overriding need to be efficient makes this task extremely complex. In addition, contemporary situations demand extreme precision, proportionality and discrimination in the application of force when military forces are employed. A large number of critical and less important factors impinge on the efficacy of employing military forces to achieve the desired national objective. It is difficult under these circumstances to delineate the military end-state necessary to achieve the political objective for which the conflict or war has been initiated. Democratic nations are, therefore, reluctant to employ military forces freely with an overarching remit to defeat the adversary's forces. Invariably, the strategies of deterrence and coercion are the preferred options rather than escalating the conflict to the status of war in the pursuit of a strategy of punishment. The necessity to apply force in a graded manner, with the escalation mechanism controlled by the political leadership, while an unsavoury situation for the military leadership, is a reality that has to be clearly understood. Both the graded application and functioning under externally imposed extreme restrictions are individually difficult situations that make military effectiveness difficult to achieve. In combination, these two factors make the employment of military forces irrevocably convoluted. Extreme dexterity in strategic planning of the campaign and focused direction of application at the operational level is necessary in the military leadership for the campaign to successfully achieve the desired end-states, both military and political.

Concepts and Ideas

> "Every attempt to make war easy and safe will result in humiliation and disaster."
>
> General William Tecumseh Sherman[32]

The one basic concept that guides all other developments in the broader security environment is that the application of lethal kinetic force through the employment of military forces must always be subordinate to efforts that attempt to promote better governance and programs for economic development in the volatile state or region that is being pacified and stabilised.[33] This is so for two reasons. First, in the current context destabilisation of the socio-political ethos and a move towards a conflict situation will invariably start as insurgencies and acts of terrorism. Second, insurgents and terrorists thrive in failed or weak states and make full use of social breakdown and the chaos that it brings. The primary aim of stable nations must always be to avoid these situations.

From a military perspective, the development of concepts or ideas must perform three functions. First, a truly useful concept must be able to solve a significant problem that restricts the optimum functioning of the military forces. It must also be able to recognise or create an opportunity to perform a military function in a better manner through the introduction of innovative ideas. Second, new concepts must always drive change in a positive manner. The introduction of a new concept must make the military more effective and efficient. Third, ideas must be able to move the military organisation towards

---

32 General Sherman (1820-1891) was a Union general during the American Civil War, playing a crucial role in the defeat of the Confederate States and becoming one of the most famous military leaders in US history.

33 Bowdish, Randall G., *Military Strategy: Theory and Concepts*, Dissertation presented to the Graduate College at the University of Nebraska, Lincoln, Nebraska, June 2013, pp. 140-149. Scholarship. 26. http://digitalcommons.unl.edu/poliscitheses/26 accessed several times between November 2015 and October 2016.

better alignment with the broader national security environment. A sound idea must be able to function seamlessly with the nation's efforts to achieve strategic objectives and smooth over any aberrations in the process. In combination, these three functions are necessary to balance and integrate the functioning of the military and civilian elements of national power in a contextual manner to ensure that the national security apparatus is not biased in its application.

Military forces across the world are going through a difficult period of resource restrictions and reducing budgetary allocations. In some cases this has directly translated to non-availability of even basic requirements to function effectively in sustained operations. This situation can only be ameliorated by a concerted effort by both the military and the government to prioritise the tasks that military forces have to perform. Flowing on from such a higher level prioritisation, the military should be able to identify and emerging opportunities to enhance performance levels within the restricted situation. This can be achieved by developing and instituting concepts that will maintain the traditional edge of the military forces against irregular adversaries in operations. In this context, in combat operations, leveraging technology to ensure technology over-match is a foundational requirement. This is of particular importance, especially since lethal and sophisticated technologies have become available to non-state actors, irregular forces and military forces of rogue states.

The contemporary era is populated by adversaries who use disruptive means to overcome the superiority of conventional military forces. Further, military forces generally operate under strict supervision of the civilian leadership in most circumstances. The combination of these two factors decreases the options available to the military forces when they operate against irregular forces. Unconventional thinking that produces discrete but viable concepts that in turn will provide asymmetric advantages to the conventional military forces has to be nurtured and cultivated on a long term basis to ensure the success of military operations. This requirement could lead to accepting the need to invest in asymmetric capabilities within a conventional force.

All wars are tragic and their conduct as well as results is uncertain. It touches the political, economic, cultural, psychological and human aspects and ethos of a nation to varying degrees. However, the credibility of nation in the international arena is very clearly attached to its ability to visibly win, once it has gone to war. It is therefore necessary for military forces to be able to prevail in all contingencies, which requires a coherent and robust set of concepts and ideas that retain the flexibility to adapt to fast-changing circumstances.[34] This capacity—to generate, validate and implement flexible concepts—is of paramount importance for military forces to stay relevant within the broader national security calculus.

There are two factors that a 'thinking' military force must always consider in the generation of concepts and ideas. First, too many concepts will invariably make all of them lack sufficient depth and substance. A modern military force needs a minimum time to digest and adjust to a new concept before it can be applied in combat conditions. Moving from one concept to another in short order is not conducive to the proper understanding of any one concept. Second, in detailing a concept care must be taken to articulate it in concise and precise words. The inability to express ideas clearly and the use of improper terminology interfere negatively with effective and professional appreciation as well as implementation of emerging concepts.

Concepts and ideas are the intellectual underpinnings of a modern military force. The contemporary security environment is in a constant state of evolution and therefore a military force that does not keep abreast of developments will find that its effectiveness reduces rapidly in a short timeframe. The concepts and ideas that are generated must therefore be dynamic enough to keep pace with the changes in the environment and emerging threats. For numerically small military forces this could become an added burden making it difficult to develop or even adapt new concepts into the force, especially if they are involved in sustained operations. The necessary balance to be maintained between achieving the desired operational tempo and continually developing and refining new concepts and ideas has to be carefully managed to ensure that the military force remains an effective element of national power.

---

34 ibid, pp. 184-187.

Summing Up...

Military forces are national instruments that apply lethal force to achieve national objectives at the government's behest. Even though military forces may be considered to be 'stand-alone' capabilities, in reality they cannot function at the optimum level on their own. They require a number of support infrastructure, both virtual and materiel, to be successful. More than ever before, the application of military power has become a whole-of-nation enterprise. Even so, military forces remain the prime movers in implementing national security strategies.

Military forces of all nations are raised and trained to apply lethal force when necessary to achieve the desired objectives as directed by the government. In recent times military forces, especially the ones from democratic nations, have been increasingly employed in less 'strenuous' conditions such as peace-keeping and peace-enforcement. Further, democratic governments have come to rely on their military forces to deliver a range of different outcomes that may not be directly military or conflict related. There is the possibility that such outcomes may not always be compatible with the training that has been imparted and the purpose for which the military forces had been raised in the first instance. However, the inherent flexibility of the military forces permit them to achieve tangible results even in such situations that are new to them. The drawback that comes with such employment is that it could detract from the efficient conduct of their primary mission, especially in numerically smaller forces.

The inherent power of military forces is a direct function of the combination of a number of factors that also influence each other. They could be divided into two categories—core and dynamic competencies. Core competencies are the ones that ensure the efficiency and staying power of the military forces in terms of their employment and are closely linked to the national will to support the employment of military forces. They also encompass the ability of the military force to directly connect strategy to the task at hand in order to achieve the overall strategic objectives, which should always be political in nature. The military force and the government must be able to demonstrate a clear commonality of the objectives to be achieved to the domestic public. This requires strategic communications, which provide a correct appreciation of national intent in terms of the employment of military forces and its relationship to national security imperatives. Flexibility of the force-in-being that in turn creates the necessary agility and adaptability for the force to cater for the rapid changes in the conduct and character of war is critical in this context.

The core competencies, which are enduring, give rise to dynamic competencies that are vital for the efficient functioning of the military force-in-being. The dynamic competencies ensure that the military force is able to retain the full flexibility necessary to cater for the constantly changing operational environment and the incrementally changing capabilities. Dynamic competencies optimise the military forces' capabilities in a contextual manner. In the contemporary security environment the ability to incorporate high-end capabilities and integrate with other domain-centric forces are highly prized dynamic competencies.

Historically, military forces have been the protectors of national sovereignty. However, they face a number of challenges in achieving this fundamental objective. This status is a cornerstone of the rationale for the creation and continued maintenance of efficient military forces by nation-states. In democratic nations, the military forces at times tend to believe that they are not always being given the stature that they deserve as the protectors of the nation. This normally stems from the extreme adulation that they are subjected to during times of war and conflicts, especially if the war is one of national survival, and which gradually gets diluted in times of peace. This sense of entitlement comes into conflict with the realities of a democracy that has to maintain an appreciable balance in the allocation of national resources between military requirements and other priorities of the nation such as welfare, medical facilities, and infrastructure development.

Civil-military relations in a democracy is always a delicate subject and needs maturity in handling from both the political leadership and the higher leadership of the military forces. Both need to be statesmen in order to maintain a balanced relationship, which is absolutely critical for the security of the nation. Civilian control of the military means control by the elected representatives through the parliament, and indirectly, the constitution. However, this control can become entrenched in the hands of civilian bureaucracy to the detriment of the nation. A reasonably good civil-military relationship, devoid of the pitfalls of bureaucratic control, is critical to the well-being of the nation. Civil-military relationship in a democracy is a two-way street where political leadership and military command structure must meet half-way, in mutual respect and trust. Any other manner of conducting the relationship is bound to create unnecessary tensions and avoidable confusion.

The strict adherence to the Laws of Armed Conflict (LOAC) is another challenge that faces military forces in the conduct of high intensity combat and/or irregular warfare. While it is clearly understood that LOAC are inviolable in the conduct of a military mission, the adversary in an irregular war is highly unlikely to be mindful of such niceties. Further, sovereign military forces normally have more restrictive rules of engagement imposed on them by the home government to cater for domestic laws and customs. Therefore, very often the military forces engage in combat situations with a distinct 'handicap' in terms of the freedom to employ their full capabilities. In contemporary irregular warfare these restrictions might become a point of contention between the operational level command of military forces and the political leadership. There is only one answer to this potential challenge—that is to ensure that the application of force by the military forces consciously remain within the bounds of international law.

Military forces, by the very nature of their fundamental responsibilities, need to maintain all-round capabilities. Balancing the necessary high-end with low-end capabilities, in times of fiscal stringency and resource scarcity, will be a constant challenge for all military forces. The development of the appropriate concepts of operations and ensuring the capabilities to implement them will become extremely difficult and challenging tasks. Added to this, long-drawn deployments and conflicts bring their own unique challenges to the military forces. Democratic nations specially are likely to suffer from what has been termed war-fatigue, much the same way as soldiers suffer from combat-fatigue. National will to support military forces engaged in long-drawn wars is bound to wane very quickly, especially when there are high casualties and a war that is seen as not of real consequence to the nation.

Military forces today face the unenviable task of having to ensure a rapid conclusion to all operations, but after achieving the desired objectives and arriving at the required end-state. In any irregular war this is not an easy task. Irregular forces define victory as not being militarily defeated, an amorphous state of affairs. There are far too many variables at play in the current security environment and the power of the military force is also influenced by and dependent on myriad factors. These factors must be brought together in the right proportion in a well-crafted manner to ensure that the application of military force stays focused on achieving national objectives.

Chapter 14

FUTURE CONFLICT TRENDS IMPACT ON MILITARY FORCES

A nation must have the ability to deal with future threats, irrespective of their origin and how they manifest on security imperatives. To a great extent this ability is underwritten by the nation's existing capabilities to secure itself in a volatile environment. In the past few decades this ability has become an optimum combination of military and other elements of national power, employed in a combined manner and adjusted contextually to create the necessary effects most efficiently. The change in visible threats from the military forces of an adversarial nation to diffused and at times non-military threats have been a major factor in necessitating this shift from an overwhelming reliance on military capabilities to a whole-of-nation approach to ensuring national security.

The trend in terms of military operations in the past few decades has been for conventional forces to be employed in small wars more often than being used to conduct large campaigns. In a very broad manner, small wars encompass all military operations conducted against irregular forces, insurgents, terrorists and other non-state actors as well as peace enforcement operations in unstable and volatile areas. Even when relatively large campaigns have been conducted, minor conflicts are likely to continue to be waged in its aftermath, particularly when the operation has been expeditionary and interventionist in nature. Conducting these small wars require a separate set of capabilities as opposed to those needed to fight conventional wars against another military force. The military forces therefore need to have built-in capacity to maintain security while providing humanitarian aid and carrying out nation-building under fire. Essentially these activities are not military roles, but in the absence of any other group with sufficient cohesiveness to carry out these disparate functions, most democracies rely on the military forces to undertake them. However, converting a conventional military force into one that is adept at conducting small wars can prove to be costly both in terms of resource requirements and the long term detrimental effect on the force's conventional warfighting capabilities. In fact the cost of such transition will impact on both human and political aspects of the nation.

The Warrior Ethos. Contemporary combat operations tend to be conducted with stand-off weapon systems and even uninhabited vehicles that can conduct lethal attacks while being controlled from far away. In effect, a large percentage of combat operations have assumed a detached nature. In the case of small or irregular wars, combat operations are likely to become even more detached than it already is.[1] Military forces function in extraordinarily complex situations that can have debilitating effects on the human psyche. Therefore, it is necessary to inculcate a 'warrior ethos' within the force to ensure that it functions efficiently under combat conditions. This ethos becomes a binding force within combat units. By making combat operations detached, the cohesiveness of fighting forces tend to be diluted and over a period of time this could make a military force a very loosely controlled organisation, which is not conducive to good performance as and when closer and more involved combat operations are to be conducted.

The Idea of Joint Military Forces

Military operations are conducted in the three environmental domains of land, maritime and air, as well as in space and cyberspace. However, there is ample evidence to demonstrate that irrespective of the domain in which combat operations are taking place, no single domain Service will be able to achieve the desired end-state by itself. All operations of conventional military forces are, of necessity, joint in nature.[2] This

---

1 Author's discussion with (Late) Lt Gen Michael Short USAF (Ret), ADC Weston Creek, Canberra, 30 Jul 2007.

2 For a comprehensive analysis of the development of joint operations read, Beaumont, Roger, *Joint Military Operations: A Short History*, Praeger, Westport, Connecticut, 1993.

central idea of jointness is based on optimum inputs from each Service dependent on the context of the campaign and always aligned to create the necessary effects to achieve the desired military end-state. In the contemporary security environment, it is more likely for conventional military forces to start the operations with the employment of air power to gather information and also to carryout targeted strikes to eliminate adversary defences as far as possible. However, the effectiveness of such actions will depend on the continued availability of air assets and their combined effectiveness.

The efficacy of joint operations is directly dependent on each Service optimising its own specialisation and being able to operate with the others in as seamless a manner as possible. This would also mean that they do not impinge on the core competencies of the others. A truly joint military force will be able to leverage the ability of each arm in such a way as to ameliorate the disadvantages of the other and thereby be able to project power under all circumstances. In irregular wars, the political necessity of maintaining a limited footprint in alien territory and the probability of land forces being susceptible to higher casualty rates can be overcome by the use of air power to insert, maintain and extract forces on an as required basis.

Doctrine

A competent military force operates according to its stated doctrine. However, in a number of cases the doctrine tends to be biased towards one of the other Service, dependent on a number of factors. This situation is not beneficial for the conduct of joint operations. The impact of biased doctrine is particularly severe on small forces without sufficient mass to absorb minor failures in doctrine and concepts and yet perform at the required level of competency. The development of a truly joint doctrine, from which joint operational concepts to conduct joint operations can be derived, is a complex process and at times not within the grasp of some smaller military forces. However, it is of critical importance for small forces to be doctrinally sound and aligned because they normally will not have fall-back options and therefore are forced to operate at levels where the potential for failure is higher than in the case of medium or large forces.

Success in future operations, irrespective of where in the spectrum of conflict the force is operating from, will be determined by the joint doctrinal perspective that is embraced by all Services.[3] Strategic doctrine must have a direct relationship to the grand strategy of the nation and likewise, operational doctrine should be a flow-on that provides more detailed guidance for the employment of the military forces. At the operational level independent Services must be able to distinguish their unique requirements and carefully align them to the joint campaign requirements. Achieving the desired end-state, it has to be reiterated, will not be possible in any other manner.

Space

The reliance on space to carry out almost all military tasks is already a reality. The space-based assets currently enable and enhance the effectiveness of the military forces across the entire spectrum of conflict. However, currently most space-operating nations continue to use space as a benign environment and at least pay lip service to maintaining it as a non-weaponised domain. There is already a concept to base direct energy weapons in space being debated and it is more than likely that other weapon systems will also be based in space over the coming years. Under these circumstances, there are two primary factors that would influence future trends in warfare. One, space superiority, similar in nature to air superiority, would become a necessity and space-faring nations will need to defend their space assets. This has enormous repercussions for the way in which conflict will unfold in the air, on the land and in the maritime domain.

Two, nations reliant on allies for space-based capabilities, which are the majority of nations, will find it necessary to either be more aligned with their allies or to try and become more neutral in terms of their relationships with the major powers. In either case, the potential for global readjustments in terms of diplomacy and security are high and almost certainly lead to a less stable environment. Space will become a contested domain in the future; the question is only how rapidly this change will take place. Future conflict will automatically become even

---

3   Priebe, Miranda, Rohn, Laurinda L., and others, *Promoting Joint Warfighting Proficiency: The Role of Doctrine in Preparing Airmen for Joint Operations*, Rand Corporation, Santa Monica, CA, 2018. https://www.rand.org/pubs/research_reports/RR2472.html accessed on 5 October 2018.

more complex that it currently is, and increase the influence of stronger nations with indigenous space assets and the ability to operate in space. The capability gap between the military forces of 'space-nations' and others dependent on alliances will become vividly apparent.

Cyberspace

> "We are now, in relation to the problem of cyber-warfare, at the same stage of intellectual development as we were in the 1950s in relation to possible nuclear war."
>
> International Institute of Strategic Studies,
>
> Annual Report 2010

Irregular forces as well as nation-states who chose to operate asymmetrically against stronger conventional military forces and sovereign nations, to bridge the capability/technology gap, find clandestine cyber operations effective tools.[4] The traditional concept of protection has revolved around physical security. In the current environment national infrastructure like water and power as well as essential services like hospitals, transportation and communications are reliant on computer networks for their efficient functioning. Even the military is reliant on cyberspace for their functioning. Cyber-attacks, as a prelude to confrontation, first emerged in 2007, when Estonian computers were frozen prior to the conflict with Russia. However, the primary difference between cyber-attacks and the more visible physical attacks on a nation's infrastructure or military is that it is almost always impossible to determine the exact source of the attack. This makes it difficult to react and curtail the attacks.

The difficulty in coping with a cyber-attack after it has been committed has led to a doctrine of pre-emption that advocates going into foreign computers to destroy malicious software before it can do any harm. However, this would amount to an act of war and invite

---

4 Sawhney, Ashok, Commodore (Retd), 'Cyber War in the 21 Century: The Emerging Security Challenge', *RSIS Commentaries 20/2010*, S. Rajaratnam School of International Studies, NTU, Singapore, 18 February 2010, p.1.

retaliation through counterattacks. There has to be both national and international level solutions that must be put in place to avoid a cyber-war. While individual nations can, and do, put in place cyber security measures, international cooperation is essential for them to succeed since cyberspace does not adhere to any preconceived notion of boundaries. The biggest hurdle to creating a safe cyber environment is the fact that a cyber-war can be initiated as much by responsible nations as by individuals who could be terrorists or just irresponsible citizens. Military forces have to be cognisant of the threat to their effective operations through lapses in cyber-security and also build-in redundancies for efficient operations in the case of cyber-attacks. This is a double edged sword, since no fool-proof security system can be devised and scarce resources will have to be expended in creating sufficiently reliable back-up solutions.

Urban Conflict

Conventional military forces have a preponderance of lethal power as compared to an irregular force. Asymmetry is the obvious tactics that the weaker force will adopt to neutralise this disadvantage as far as possible so that conflict could be joined on a level ground. In open conflict it is difficult to introduce asymmetry of any significance and therefore, the irregular force opts to conduct combat operations in the urban areas where they can employ hit and run tactics more easily.[5] This is further facilitated by their operating within the local population thereby making it difficult for the military forces to distinguish combatants from civilians. Urban areas also normally negate the firepower of conventional military forces because of the higher probability of collateral damage that is politically unacceptable in contemporary conflict. In the current global environment, a majority of the insurgent or irregular forces resort to suicide bombing as a terror tactic. The issue is that there are very few counter tactics that will succeed against dedicated suicide bombers who are determined to lose their lives. In urban conflict this can become a morale lowering factor.

---

5   Sassen, Saskia, 'Welcome to a new kind of war: the rise of endless urban conflict', *The Guardian*, International Edition, 30 January 2018, https://www.theguardian.com/cities/2018/jan/30/new-war-rise-endless-urban-conflict-saskia-sassen accessed on 3 February 2018.

Urban conflict tends to break up the cohesiveness of military forces by imposing the necessity to operate in numerically small elements that become difficult to control and coordinate effectively. It also tends to reduce the surveillance and reconnaissance horizon of conventional forces, thereby reducing the situational awareness on which the success of all operations depend. From a surface operations point of view, urban operations consume a much larger number of personnel than would have been the case if the same objectives were to be achieved in a geographically more open theatre. Effectively, the costs in terms of lives and resources will depend on the adversary's capabilities with very limited connection one's own ability to operate effectively.[6]

As a result, urban conflict is always more resource intensive than other types of conflict. In most cases it also has the potential to inflict larger amount of casualties on the military force while minimising the danger to the irregular adversary. Added to these two factors is the fundamental reliance of conventional military forces on superior firepower, situational awareness and cohesiveness of command and control for their success, which is at least partially denied in such conflicts. In an overarching manner urban conflict become extremely complex for military forces. Urban conflicts against irregular adversaries do not normally produce any tangible victory for the military forces nor does it produce clearly definable defeat for the adversary. When viewed from the perspective of bridging the connection between military end-states and political objectives, such an outcome is tantamount to failure for the military force and the nation concerned.

The Strategy of Coercion[7]

The prevailing international security environment is such that the probability of state-on-state conflict of any large denomination taking place is very low. It is also far more restrictive regarding the lethal employment of military forces than it was even a few decades ago. In

---

6 Hills, Alice, *Future War in Cities: Rethinking a Liberal Dilemma*, Frank Cass Publishers, London, 2004. (Particular reference to Part II that deals with Policing, Enforcement and Warfighting)

7 For an in-depth analysis of the strategy of coercion read, Kainikara, Sanu, *The Bolt From the Blue: Air Power in the Cycle of Strategies*, Air Power Development Centre, Canberra, 2013, pp. 67-88.

addition, the international community has in the past few years put in place legal documents that permit unilateral intervention in a nation's internal affairs with the explicit permission of the United Nations. These factors point to the increased employment of military forces in expeditionary operations that would involve irregular warfare and peace enforcement activities. Almost in direct contradiction to the accepted need to intervene is the reluctance of the international community to commit surface forces to undertake such operations. The reluctance stems from the aversion of the host nation to have foreign military forces within their borders, and the high probability of insurgent actions being initiated if this is done. From the intervening nation's perspective, boots-on-the-ground for an indefinite period of time is likely to be costly both in lives and finances, which could dampen domestic support for such actions and also create circumstances that are not ideal for success. Under these circumstances, military forces will be required to implement strategies that are at the lower end of the spectrum, such as denial and coercion, based on the inherent capabilities of air power, with ground forces being employed only as a last resort.

The power projection capabilities of conventional military forces, enhanced through technology-enabled precision strike and mobility are critical to enforcing the strategies of denial and coercion. This is achieved through the threat of force and the punitive use of force with the ability to escalate the actual employment of force if necessary. In order to ensure that the adversary understands the need to alter their behaviour pattern in response to coercive activities, it may be necessary to resort to lethal application of force at an opportune moment. Military force planning must consider this aspect both in terms of developing capabilities and maintaining an updated and prioritised target system list.

Air Forces

The air power capabilities of most nations are resident within their air forces. However, since air power is a resource-intensive capability to acquire, maintain and operate effectively, a number of nations have air forces that only have few of the elements within the entire capability spectrum of military air power. Nation's that have aspirations to be responsible international citizens and also want to be seen as capable of projecting power, need to maintain a balanced air force with all capabilities resident in them. In the contemporary conflict scenario, the capabilities of a balanced air force will be highly prized to enforce denial and to coerce a reluctant adversary. The major advantages inherent in the employment of air power—minimal footprint; almost no mission creep; low probability of own casualties; and precision, proportionality and discrimination in strike—make it ideally suited to be employed as the first choice in most emerging conflict situations. Military forces must have the maturity to understand the evolving trends in conflict, the political and resource restraints under which military forces are allowed to operate, and the fall-outs that can be expected, both internationally and domestically, from nation committing to expeditionary operations of choice to be able to accept the primacy of one Service above the others in a contextual manner.

Essentially, the military commitment will always have to be of a joint nature, even in instances where the ground forces are not deployed as such. Air forces do, and will continue to, play a decisive role in current and future conflicts. This is so since the chances of ground invasion of one state by another is a very remote possibility under the prevailing global security environment. Paradoxically air forces are increasingly being viewed, especially in democracies with financial troubles, as the Service that can be best reduced and restructured to cater for the reduced resource availability. While this trend has become noticeable, the reduction in air power capabilities will lead to a precarious situation wherein intervention will become an impossible operation to perform.

At the higher end of the spectrum of conflict where wars of necessity will have to be fought and won, a balanced air force is a critical requirement. Accepting that this situation may not arise in the near future for most nations, the risk of failure if such a war has to be fought without an adequate air force is far too high to be ignored. Along with the fact that building an air force of calibre is a long-drawn process that needs time and resources in abundance, the decisions regarding scaling down air forces must be very carefully weighed before being implemented. A nation's long term threat perception, alliance situations, resource availability and a number of other factors must be of fundamental influence in such decisions. Military forces, and within them air forces, are critical elements of national power and must be maintained at an acceptable level of competence at all times. The perceivable trend of future conflict does not permit any other option.

Targeting

Targeting is a critical part of the application of military force. While the process of identifying and then neutralising a target is normally an operational level task, the broad direction of what to target has to come from strategic guidance originating at the highest level of decision making. There are two fundamental areas of the adversary that can be targeted—the will to fight and the means to fight. There is a school of thought that military forces should only be targeting the means, the ability, of the adversary to fight and should not be involved in targeting the will. This assertion is patently incorrect. Military forces can and do influence the cognitive domain when employed with sufficient clarity of purpose. However, the methodology adopted and the application of force would vary dependent on the selected area to target.

From a military perspective, targeting the will to fight does not provide any assurance of success since there are far too many intangible factors involved in creating and maintaining the will of a nation to go to war or continue the fight. Three broad targets can be considered of sufficient importance for the will of a nation that if sufficiently degraded would have a debilitating effect on the overall will. They are leadership, military forces and civilian population. The impact of attacks on each of them will be different in different nations and will be a product of the kind of government in place, nation ethos regarding war, cohesiveness of the nation as an entity and a number of other subsidiary factors. Attacks on leadership could have greater impact on autocratic governments than on democracies. Similarly military forces can be debilitated by focused targeting of command and control hubs that would make the force lose cohesion and unity of command and purpose. The most difficult target to be effective against is the civilian population, since it is almost impossible to correctly judge their relationship with the government. Of the two areas to target, will to fight is the more difficult to neutralise, especially when only the military forces are involved in the conflict.

The means to fight is more straightforward to target and in fact the primary role of military forces is to destroy the adversary's means to fight. The adversary's military forces, conventional or irregular, are the visible means of conducting a conflict. It is supported by a number of other capacities like industry, transportation, warehousing and communication facilities. The adversary's means can be neutralised for the short term by defeating the fielded forces and in the long term by destroying their capabilities to generate military power.[8] In contemporary conflict this is far more difficult because of the spread of irregular conflicts and asymmetric means being employed. The proclivity of the current crop of irregular and non-state forces to devalue human life through the adoption of suicide missions increases the risks to conventional military forces involved in contemporary conflict. In the future, targeting the means to fight could become even more costly in terms of loss of human lives and could become unacceptable. This might require harsher actions on the part of the military force. The ethics and morality of escalating the conflict to the next higher level will have to be carefully factored in the planning of all future conflicts. The trend in this instance is not supportive of conventional forces.

Summing Up...

The future is difficult, if not impossible, to predict. However, by extending the line that joins the past and the present it is possible to understand the evolving trend in the conduct of conflict. A number of new elements will come into play and will increasingly influence the actions of all participants while the effect of the time honoured elements will wax and wane with circumstances and the context of their application. The most important development in to the future will be the very low probability of state-on-state conflict and the clash between two conventional military forces. This will be reinforced by the spread of irregular wars and the proliferation of non-state actors conducting irregular operations in the pursuit of intangible goals and ideals.

---

8 Guiora, Amos N., 'Determining a Legitimate Target: The Dilemma of the Decision-Maker', *Texas International Law Journal*, Volume 47, Issue 2, Spring 2012, Austin, Texas, pp. 315-336. http://www.tilj.org/content/journal/47/num2/Guiora315.pdf accessed on 18 May 2016.

The enhanced capabilities of conventional military forces are evidenced by the greatly increased spread of the spectrum of conflict in which they participate. However, their effectiveness has been brought into question by the asymmetric capabilities and methodologies being adopted by the current, and future, crop of irregular forces. Inherent flexibility of military forces, based on clearly articulated doctrine has so far permitted their holding fast without overt failures. That may not sufficient in the evolving context of conflicts wherein one single step changing concept can fully decapitate an entire force. The visible trends in conflict are ominous. The redeeming factor seems to be that conventional forces are also aware of this lacuna and it must be presumed that both technological and conceptual developments are already in place to contain the fall out.

CONCLUSION

Sovereign nation will continue to rely on their military forces to provide the wherewithal to defend the borders of the country as well as to protect its geographically far-flung interests. Although national security is now being considered a whole-of-nation issue, the military forces will have to be at the forefront not only because of historical precedents but also because of the greatly enhanced spectrum of conflict that military forces have to operate across, making it imperative for them to have enhanced capabilities than ever before. Further, military forces now need both basic and almost unchanging competencies as well as ones that are dynamic and evolutionary to function effectively. They also need sufficient depth and in-built developmental capabilities to ensure that the force-in-being has sufficient flexibility to deal with emerging challenges.

Flexibility, arrived at through being adaptable and agile is built on the force having adequate high-end capabilities that are continually upgraded. The lead-time required to acquire and proficiently employ high-end capabilities is long. In addition, it is simpler for a force operating at the high-end to ramp down its capabilities to function at a lower end of the technology spectrum rather than having to ramp up capabilities even from an intermediary position. Needless to say, in most expeditionary operations, high-end capabilities may not be required to achieve mission success, but the requirement to operate at a lower end in the scale will be better facilitated by the force possessing adequate high-end capabilities.

Military forces function differently to other organisations and departments of the government. By the nature of its responsibilities it employs unique methodologies in fulfilling its functions. There is often a lack of clear understanding and appreciation of the importance of these methodologies and other processes for the optimum functioning of military forces. A fundamental factor for the development of this situation is that the more sophisticated military forces of the developed world have not been required to fight a war of necessity for more than 60 years. These nations have taken granted that their military forces will perform to the desired level. This has also led to a less than harmonious civil-military relationship that is at times acrimonious and divisive. The need in all democratic nations is to have a supportive civil-military relationship that in turn will create the necessary infrastructure and policies necessary to support all national security initiatives.

Military forces have always faced challenges that emanate not from adversaries in the field of battle but from internal developments and influences that are perhaps more difficult to counter effectively. These internal challenges stem from within the nation as a result of evolving cultures, national ethos, increased awareness of human rights, the quest for more individual freedoms as well as gender and religious equality and the demand for stability for a nation and its people to prosper. In addition, there is increasing pacifism—meaning an aversion to the employment of military forces—especially in the more developed nations of the world. This questioning of the need to apply lethal force through the employment of military forces is generally a moralistic stance of societies that have evolved considerable and are resident in stable democracies. Capable military forces are resource intensive and in times of financial stringency would seem to be wasteful expenditure. This attitude towards the military forces is further emphasised by the perceived lack of direct threat the nation in most cases. A combination of these three factors makes military forces and the expenditure they incur a source of embarrassment for pacifist nations. In the absence of severe existential threats it is difficult to influence groups with such extreme views.

All democratic nations need to develop concepts and ideas that clearly articulate the connection between national objectives, its threat perception and the necessary military capabilities to underpin the minimum necessary security for the nation to prosper. Future risks to national security must be assessed and balanced at the highest levels of government so that the role of military forces can be easily understood. This might require shifting strategic priorities not only in terms of national developmental ambitions, but also setting security priorities to be achieved through the employment of national power elements, including the military.

National security is ensured through the implementation of a number of strategies that spread from influencing and shaping the environment in a benign manner to applying lethal force to destroy selected targets. The strategies of deterrence, coercion and punishment form the continuum between these two extremes. All elements of national power are involved in the lower level strategies but as the spectrum moves towards punishment and destruction, the predominant role is that of the military forces. The essential difference is that in the beginning, only implicit and thereafter explicit threat of the use of force and other more 'soft' power inducements are employed. However, even for such approaches to work, a nation must have demonstrated military power at its disposal. When it comes to the higher strategies, it is almost purely military power and forces that apply it to the necessary scale. Among all the elements of national power it is only the military forces that can be used to employ strategies across the entire continuum. This is a unique capability, and not well understood or appreciated in civil society.

The interpretation of what entails national security has become almost all encompassing and this is reflected in the evolving concept of national security and its many definitions. The thread of continuity in this process is that the military forces have always been considered a crucial part of the elements of national power that ensure the security of the nation. However, in recent times there is a discernible attempt in the democracies of the world to limit the role of the military forces and to make them peripheral in the broader national security equation. It is only when the nation's geographic integrity is threatened that the military forces are considered to be in the forefront of national security. This is a short-sighted view of national security and the role of the military forces and implemented at the peril of the nation becoming increasingly vulnerable to even minor threats. Military forces are an indelible element of national power and the dilution of any of their capabilities will have immediate and far-reaching consequences for the overall security of the nation.

SECTION - V

THE SWORD ARM

MILITARY FORCES IN THE 21ST CENTURY

THESIS: In a global environment that creates evolving threats to national security, threat mitigation is best achieved through enforcing a whole-of-government approach to the security enterprise, with the military forces in the vanguard.

Military forces have always been at the forefront of ensuring national security and their employment is guided by the national security strategies derived from the Grand Strategy of the nation. The efficacy of the military forces is a direct function of the availability and adequacy of resources and the effectiveness of its employment is a function of the national ethos and the strategic culture of the nation. Irrespective of the merit and capability of the force, the military will continue to be an instrument of policy for democratic nations. Military forces have to be strengthened in 21st century democracies considering the increasing uncertainty and volatility of the global security environment. Strengthening the military forces, especially in times of relative peace will be troublesome for a democratic government since resource allocation will always be affected by conflicting demands. Even so, the military forces must become entrenched as the vanguard in ensuring national security within a strategy that revolves around a whole-of-government approach.

INTRODUCTION

The end of the Cold War in the last decade of the 20th century was a decisive turning point in the development of military forces in the Western world. It also had a salutary impact on the foreign policies of the democratic nations of Europe and the United States. The Cold War had, over a period of time, established an accepted order to the international system.[1] At the same time it had also provided the rationale for the continued expansion of the national security establishment, of which the military was a recognisably large part. The collapse of the Soviet Union brought about a state of flux in the global security environment that has lasted the past few decades.

The world has seen the emergence of large and well-organised terrorist groups taking recourse to extreme violence. Even though this cannot be considered a new development, the rapidity of the proliferation of these groups has surprised even the most pessimistic assessment of the early 2000s. While terrorist groups have been most active enmasse in the Middle-East and South Asian regions, the evolution of security threats has normally been contextual and the manner of their progression has been dependent on a number of factors, mostly unique to the region and nation. However, at the absolute base level some amount of strategic commonality could also be observed.

Mitigating direct and indirect threats to the nation requires delineating the roles and functions of all elements of national power. The role of the government is to bring together the appropriate capabilities necessary to contain the threat in the required proportion. Such a whole-of-government approach to security is a strategic

---

1 Hadar, Leon T., *Quagmire: America in the Middle East*, Cato Institute, Washington D.C., 1992, p. 6.

necessity. Threat mitigation by itself is a very broad spectrum where the strategies start at the lower end from influencing a potential adversary and goes at the other end to preventive and/or pre-emptive strikes. The application lethal force is the realm of military forces and therefore they have to be an integral part of the threat mitigating process.

Irrespective of the manner in which national security is defined, a nation cannot be assured of its sovereignty in the absence of an efficient military force.[2] Military forces are the anchoring foundations in any evaluation of national security. Unfortunately, this fundamental status given to military forces also brings it into direct competition with other, necessary, nation-building priorities in all but the most resource-rich nations, especially those that adhere to democratic norms. The tension between the two requirements come to the fore and is exacerbated during times of relative peace, when the direct connection between military forces and national security is obscured by the smoke cover of stability.

The traditional precedence of building a large enough, and capable enough, military force when the nation is physically under threat is not a viable process to be adopted in the 21st century. The lead-time required to build, equip and field a competent military force, fit-for-purpose, is now longer than ever before in history. The long lead-time inherent in the process makes the old system of building when necessary redundant. The situation points to the fact that military forces of the 21st century will be required to fight as they are when necessary. In turn, this means that nations have to maintain a 'standing force' of sufficient calibre to fulfil national security imperatives. Further, in order to maintain the military force at peak effectiveness it would have to be continually modernised, which equates to additional and repetitive costs. The allocation of resources at the national level will always be a vexed issue in democratic nations, irrespective of available wealth.

Military forces cannot function in a vacuum of their own and need to be connected directly to the national security strategy to

---

2 Villanueva, Adrian, 'Don't underestimate need for strong military', Forum, *The Straits Times*, Singapore, 30 January 2016.

derive their objectives and develop the military strategy.³ The military strategies range from influencing and shaping, deterrence all the way to destruction with coercion and punishment in between. In the contemporary world, foreign military interventions in unstable and volatile regions of the world are becoming common-place. Majority of these interventions are undertaken by the military forces of the established democratic nations, mainly from the relatively more developed world. Further, the need for such interventions has been reinforced by the UN doctrine of 'responsibility to protect'; a doctrine that has been used and misused in the recent past. Military forces involved in interventions, have used the entire spread of strategies that have been listed above, not always successfully. The reasons for the intervention, the modus operandi and the objectives that have been laid out at the start of the intervention need to be analysed in order to rationalise the employment of military forces.

In functioning democracies, the military forces are always under the control of the civilian government apparatus. Civilian Government has to be clearly understood as the constitution and the parliament and not individuals holding the positions. This concept is not clearly comprehended by some of the elected representatives and could become warped. It is the responsibility of the strategic military leadership to ensure that the sublime meaning of civilian control is understood in the same way by both sides of the equation. Normally the military forces are permitted to function without any restrictions, other than the internationally recognised laws of armed conflict, only when the nation is engaged in a war of national survival. In all other cases a number of self-imposed restrictions on the application of military power is invariably enforced by the government of the day to ensure a higher than normal morality and ethics. At times, these extra restrictions, called rules of engagement, could be detrimental to the efficacy of the military forces and their attempts to apply lethal force in order to create the necessary effects.

Even functioning within the rules of engagement, over the past few decades, military forces have started to play an increased role in all

---

3 Lykke Jr, Arthur F., 'Towards an Understanding of Military Strategy', Chapter 13 in Cerami Joseph R., & Holcomb Jr, James F. (eds), *Guide to Strategy*, US Army War College, Carlisle, PA, February 2001, pp. 179-186.

aspects of national security. At the same time, the concept of national security itself has undergone a sea-change, with broadened definitions that encompass virtual objects also as worthy of being protected. For example, in some definitions of national security, the 'values' of a nation are also included as having to be protected to ensure national security. The breadth of threats against which the nation has to be protected has widened enormously and is now a vast plethora of items and ideas. Three factors—the enormity of the threats, the rapidity with which they encompass the nation, and the ever-changing face of these threats—make the military forces come to the vanguard when the nation is faced with security challenges. They are the only 'ready force' capable of meeting and defeating the challenges to national security. However, the downside is that in numerically constrained forces, the load could become too heavy manage without failing in other responsibilities. This situation could rapidly spiral out of control if not immediately recognised and controlled. The solution to avoiding heavy burden on the force could be to adopt multi-specialisation within the personnel of a force. At the same time, this solution would require higher calibre personnel to be inducted, which in itself might prove to be a difficult task. Military forces, especially smaller ones, face a long-term issue.

War today is complex and convoluted. Further, the security environment is extremely dynamic. Faced with a combination of these two factors, the military forces of a nation will have to maintain a force structure that is flexible enough to rapidly alter the force posture in accordance with the evolving security challenges that face the nation. In addition, it can be observed that a single-nation operation, or a conventional state-on-state war where only two nations are involved, have become an impossibility. Coalition operations are the norm of the times, and for the foreseeable future, and therefore, military forces will have to retain the agility needed to function effectively alongside other nation's forces. Military forces need to be multifaceted in order to carryout coalition operations alongside other forces with whom they have previously not worked.

In no uncertain manner, the military force of a nation has assumed a position as an indispensable instrument of national policy. This is not a contestable statement and remains true for all nations that strive to maintain their sovereignty. Leading from this assertion it then becomes necessary to strengthen the capabilities resident in military forces so that its capacity to ensure national security is always more than what is demanded of it. A strong military force can only be created with adequate resourcing, a stable civil-military relationship built on mutual respect, steady national support for all military operations, and the nation employing the military forces only within acceptable moral and ethical circumstances.

Military forces in the 21st century face multifarious challenges—in terms of its status within the nation, its operational efficiency against complex and evolving security threats, and the influences of domestic political developments, especially in democratic nations. They have the onerous task of overcoming these challenges and at the same time ensuring that the nation is defended against all threats, which span a large spectrum.

Chapter 15

THE EVOLUTION AND MITIGATION OF THREAT

The end of the Cold War was presumed to be the beginning of an era of peace and prosperity, with the disparate nations of the world coexisting without any tangible threat being felt by even the smallest of states. Laudable as this utopian dream was, it never came to pass. Indeed the reverse was true. The nationalistic, ethnic and religious feelings that underpin the ethos of nations and peoples that were suppressed during the Cold War because of the distinctly bipolar characteristic of the global strategic environment during that time were rapidly brought to the fore. Almost simultaneously there was the creation or aspiration of minor ethnicities to create sovereign states for themselves, again a manifestation of the three fundamental traits that distinguish a people—religion, ethnicity and ideology. The result was an eruption of skirmishes, conflicts and wars—large and small—that constantly destabilised nations and regions. With the international system being intimately interconnected, it was seen that even minor regional upheavals tended to leave remarkably visible ripples globally. In effect, the threats to nations increased and became multifarious rather than diminishing and fading away.

From the mid-1990s the global security environment has been in a state of flux.[1] The unipolar world that was envisioned at the collapse of the Soviet Union failed to create the level of stability necessary

---

1 Ries, Tomas, *The Global Security Environment 2030 and Military Missions*, Swedish National Defence College, Stockholm, October 2010, (Chapter 3: Deep Trends) pp. 18-23 & 28-31

to craft global peace. Even while this fact was becoming apparent, the speed with which instability crept into the security equation was not anticipated by most nations. The global implications of ill-advised initiatives by the only super power in the early years of this century further contributed to the complexity of the security environment.[2] The global financial crisis broadened the instability by leaving the developed world in economic chaos that is bound to take up a great deal of time and resources to overcome. This situation exaggerates two implications. One, the policing of global hot spots that was a default responsibility of the developed 'Western' nations is no longer an attractive proposition for these financially strained nations. In turn this could encourage smaller nations and non-state entities to become more adventurous in pursuing their national interests even if such actions could lead to destabilisation. Two, it provides an opportunity for emerging powers to emphasise their independent stance even in matters of global importance. This could lead to lack of consensus in international bodies regarding intervention to stabilise deteriorating security situations resulting in inaction by the global community even in circumstances that could lead to extreme instability if not contained.

Through the history of nations, threats to a nation's security and interests have always been an integral part of the calculations of national sovereignty. In analysing and understanding the concept of threat, there are two fundamental factors to be borne in mind. First, the differences over time are only in terms of the intensity and implications of the threat, rather than in terms of whether a threat exists or not. A nation is always under threat in varying degrees. Second, the difference is the ability of a nation to mitigate actual and emerging threats at a particular time, which could vary with a number of interlinked and independent factors such as the prevailing economic capacity of the nation at that time and domestic political stability. There is another overarching element in considering the mitigation of threat—the role of the military forces of a nation. It is seen that the severity of a threat and its direct impact on a nation is indirectly proportional to the visible and demonstrated military capabilities of a nation. Even though a number of other elements of national power have started

---

2 Khalilzad, Zalmay, &Shalapak, David, 'Overview of the Future Security Environment', Chapter 2 in Khalilzad, Zalmay, & Lesser, Ian O., *Sources of Conflict in the 21st Century*, Rand Corporation, Santa Monica, CA, 1998, pp. 12-16.

to be influential in ensuring national security, the primary element still remains the military force. The expanding spectrum of conflict and employment of military forces by sovereign nations is testimony to their primacy in the arena of national security. The evolution of threats and their mitigation therefore is greatly influenced by the status—strength, capability and capacity—of a nation's military forces.

The Evolution of Threat

The evolution of threats to a nation's security is contextual, although there is an underlying strategic commonality in it. It is contextual because threat perceptions are directly influenced by the understanding and definition of national security, which differs from one nation to another. On the other hand, there is strategic commonality because at the absolute basic level, national security involves the physical security of the nation and its people from external aggression and threats to this primary requirement can be common to all nations. Since there is a dichotomy between the fundamental threat to nations and the more nuanced threats that may not be applicable to all nations, their evolutionary process will also be different. However, in a very broad manner, the evolution of threats can be analysed within a common construct.[3]

There is no nation that does not perceive some form of threat to its well-being at all times. This is a statement that can be considered as an overarching fact in any analysis of national security. The threats may be minimal and easily overcome or could gather momentum to become increasingly difficult to contain. In a broad manner, the possible impact of these threats will dependent on the nation's ability to perceive the emergence of the threat at an early stage and the capacity to ameliorate it effectively through the employment of national power elements before it evolves into greater proportion. In an indirect manner the state of preparedness of the elements of national power will determine this capacity. Threats do not develop without notice. Even the ones that seem to mature at a rapid rate provide sufficient warnings and indications that can be noticed if there

---

3 Davis Jr, Major John R., 'Defeating Future Hybrid Threats', *Military Review*, September-October 2013, Army University Press, Fort Leavenworth, KS, pp. 21-19.

is a robust national threat monitoring mechanism. The evolution of threat is a process that can be understood by analysing the differences and the connections between vulnerability, risk and threat. Further, there is also a distinct continuity between dependency, vulnerability and risk.

All nations have vulnerabilities. Every nation will attempt to find the vulnerabilities of their neighbours, even when they are not even potential adversaries, if only to be aware of them because vulnerabilities are the indicators of the potential of a nation to be a stable and responsible state within the international order. The strength of a nation lies in the manner in which it addresses the existing vulnerabilities and neutralises them with minimal disturbance to the normal functioning of the state. The capacity to do this effectively determines the ability of the nation to forge a pre-planned path to achieve its desired national objectives. Vulnerabilities if not perceived when they become apparent and/or not addressed in an appropriate timeframe and manner can gradually evolve into palpable risks. On the other hand, vulnerabilities can also be such that they are apparent only for a limited period of time after which they automatically disappear. It is also possible for a few vulnerabilities that are simple and at the lowest end of the spectrum to be of very limited consequence because even if they were to be exploited by an adversary, they would not have the potential to create any tangible disruption to the nation. In effect, most simple vulnerabilities will become self-relieved over a period of time.

Long term vulnerabilities, normally complex in nature, will invariably pose challenges to national security. The inherent complexity of these vulnerabilities and their long term nature makes it imperative to alleviate them at the earliest opportunity, failing which they can become entrenched as challenges to national security.[4] In comparison, challenges are more difficult to address. This is the first step in vulnerabilities exposing the nation to security challenges. Challenges

---

4 Fleming, Major Brian B., 'Military Problems in the Operational Environment', in his monograph *The Hybrid Threat Concept: Contemporary War, Military Planning and the Advent of Unrestricted Operational Art*, School of Advanced Military Studies, Fort Leavenworth, KS, 2011, pp. 23-26.

that are identified and dealt with adequately then erase the vulnerability from which it developed and the nation returns to a tangible security equilibrium. However, challenges that are not immediately recognised and addressed are prone to fester within the national security equation and broaden their impact and influence on the security status of the nation. The complexity of the circumstances and vulnerability that initially posed the challenge will be a contributing factor to the influence that it will have on national security. From this stage the challenge could very rapidly become an unmitigated risk, growing into a threat with ease. The rate at which the transformation of vulnerabilities into threats take place could vary, dependent on a number of factors such as the complexity of the vulnerability, the national ability to identify and take remedial action to recognised vulnerabilities and the basic concept on national security itself. However, the pace of transformation is generally slow in the beginning and tends to increase after the vulnerability has started to challenge national security and the subsequent risk matures as an issue. The amelioration of vulnerabilities, and even challenges, is far easier than addressing the same issue after it has grown out of proportion into a risk and further become a threat.

Vulnerabilities are distinctly different from threats, when viewed through the prism of national security, although there is also a discernible connection between the two. In fact, threats do not normally emanate directly as threats at the outset itself, but evolve from vulnerabilities. Vulnerabilities are easily assuaged whereas threats take concerted effort by one or a combination of the elements of national power to neutralise. Therefore, national security is best ensured by lessening vulnerabilities at an early stage than after they have matured into threats. Although this is a logical solution, it is a rather simplistic one for two reasons. First, vulnerabilities are not easy to identify and requires a constant watch through the institution of an elaborate infrastructure to monitor the process of identifying and neutralising vulnerabilities. Vulnerabilities spring from national dependencies which are perhaps easier to identify in a broad manner. Second, even if a particular vulnerability has been identified, it may not be possible to initiate the actions to nullify it. This could be because of a number of reasons such as domestic political compulsions, the close relationship between the vulnerability and economic development of the nation, and inadequacy of the national infrastructure necessary to do so. The continuum is very clear—national dependencies almost always become vulnerabilities, which when not allayed develop into risks and very rapidly evolve into threats to the nation.

There is another facet of the evolution of threats that need to be highlighted. In the contemporary security scenario, threats need not always originate directly from national vulnerabilities. They could be fallouts from global causes and global reactions to emerging trends in the broad security environment. In an obtuse manner, this is a repercussion of global cooperation in terms of economy and development. The global financial crisis that has had sweeping impact across all nations of the world is a prime example of global causes creating threats to individual nations that need not have manifested as an initial and individual vulnerability. The fundamental fact is that each threat to national security has to be considered individually to understand its source, monitor its pace of evolution and analyse the remedial measures that can be instituted. This has to be done with the clear understanding that there are certain fundamental factors that will remain common for the process, irrespective of the individuality of the threat and its manifestation.

While threats are omnipresent, it is also true that a nation cannot continue to function effectively for an indefinite period of time when under threat. It cannot presume that a threat will not develop into something that physically or virtually starts to interfere with the wellbeing of the nation or that the probability of such an eventuality is so miniscule that it can be safely ignored. Therefore, all nations try to put in place strategies to address the threats at an opportune moment, normally when they still remain vulnerabilities or risks. Nations with adequate stability and resource availability will go one step further and attempt to minimise dependencies so that vulnerabilities do not emerge without adequate notice and they do not become apparent to external observers. The fundamental issue with vulnerabilities is that even if they do not develop into becoming threats, but are clearly visible to other nations they easily become centres of gravity that can be targeted with great effect to the detriment of national security.

Mitigating Threats

Threat mitigation is one of the primary roles of a government and should have the highest priority at all times, whether in times of peace or when circumstances are more volatile. A number of factors influence a government's ability to alleviate threats to national security through the development of adequate strategies to do so. Therefore, essentially, mitigating threat will have to be analysed within two areas—factors that impact the government's ability to develop strategies and the veracity of the strategies themselves and the efficiency of their implementation.[5]

The Role of the Government

The international social and politico-economic environments have overlapped each other for a considerable period of time. Today the security environment is an amalgam of social, political, economic and religious paradigms that do not make a homogeneous mix and therefore is prone to upheavals and instability. Since the security environment is volatile the need for mutual consultation, consensus building and a willingness to accommodate contrary views and opinions in inter-state relationships is of crucial importance to stability, both regionally and internationally. Mitigating threat is a unique process for all nations, no two processes being the same and in most cases not even being similar. Even common factors will exert different influences and therefore have distinctive implications on the process being adapted by individual states. There are three common factors that illustrate this point; the perception of the role of the United Nations, shifting international relations, and the interpretation of international law.

United Nations.[6] The instantaneous global connectivity provided by leapfrogging technological innovations makes even minor regional instability rapidly assume global proportions unless contained within a very short time span of its initial outbreak. This is one of the major

---

5 Winter, Donald C., 'Adapting to the Threat Dynamics of the 21st Century', *Backgrounder No 2603*, 15 September 2011, Washington D.C. 2011, http://thf_media.s3.amazonaws.com/2011/pdf/bg2603.pdf accessed on 11 May 2017.

6 Waxman, Mathew C., 'Regulating Resort to Force: Form and Substance of the UN Charter Regime', *The European Journal of International Law*, Vol 24, No 1, Oxford University Press, Oxford, 2013, pp. 151-189.

reasons for the increased importance being placed on the role of the United Nations (UN) by Western powers. The contrast here is that the less developed or developing nations, especially in the Asian region, do not place the same amount of reliance or give importance to the UN. The interpretation of the role of the UN in the global security environment therefore varies drastically between those of the West and the rest of the world. From a purely threat mitigation point of view, especially in nations with small economies and large number of dependencies, the UN does not fulfil the requirements to be considered an international agency that can ensure national security. Governments, therefore, tend to seek other ways to mitigate threats to their security than rely on the UN. Unless a comprehensive reorientation of its perceived role can be undertaken and satisfactorily completed, the UN is likely to remain a forum for academic debate for majority of the world and an institution for manipulation for the Western powers to suit their interpretation of the global role of the UN.

International Relations. In addition to the different interpretation of the role of the UN, there is another factor that most governments tend to factor in, when considering threat mitigation—the shifting foundations of international relations. The end of the Cold War, initially thought to bring about an era of peaceful coexistence, instead brought about a more complex security environment wherein even minor nations—in terms of their economy and international political influence—could create ripples in international relations that could not be ignored. In effect, the checks and balances instituted by the two super powers that provided international stability during the Cold War vanished and it did not take long for major and unforeseen shifts to take place in international relations. This has been detrimental to the sense of security in smaller and developing nations. Currently the trend is for most nations to weigh inter-state relations on a case by case basis which is not conducive to long term stability. This situation does not permit the maturation of the threat mitigation processes in the less stable nations.

International Law. There are a number of international protocols that provide the basis for the conduct of diplomatic initiatives as well as the basic guidelines for bilateral and multilateral relations between states.[7] Similarly the Laws of Armed Conflict provide clear guidance for the conduct of armed conflict if it becomes necessary. A majority of independent sovereign states are signatories to these and should automatically adhere to them. However, in practice this is not the case. Although these are international conventions, there is no body with the remit to enforce them with the result that the breech of any of them goes unpunished. While this has been an issue for a number of decades, in more recent times there has been a noticeable tendency for the more powerful nations to interpret and apply these laws in a biased manner that is advantageous to them. The smaller, less powerful nations, but with sufficient internal energy to destabilise the security equation, view this situation with a certain amount of concern since by extrapolation, manipulation of international law could have damaging repercussions to their own security environment. This is particularly so in small nations where the governments may not yet be mature democracies and who do not possess the economic, political and military clout to ensure a stand-alone sovereignty. The process of mitigating threat under these conditions takes on a life of its own and becomes unpredictable from an external point of view.

Government Functions

Irrespective of the type of government in being, the development of the process of mitigating threat and the strategies to be implemented can only emanate from the highest level of the government. The veracity of the threat mitigation strategies and its effective implementation within a broad national security strategy will depend on a number of factors internal to the government. Even though these factors are internal, they are by themselves also affected by external influences that must be taken into account during the process of the development of mitigating strategies. There are six major internal factors that directly impinge on the government's ability to create adequate processes for the development and implementation of robust strategies.

---

[7] There are a number of books on 'International Law' that have been published over the years. A good example is Dixon, Martin, *A Textbook on International Law*, 7th Edition, Oxford University Press, Oxford, 2013. The book comprehensively covers basic topics such as the basis for international law and systems, sources, sovereignty, the use of force etc.

First, is the ability to identify vulnerabilities and differentiate the ones that needs to be analysed and addressed before they develop into risks and thereafter into threats. Particularly important in this activity is the ability to delineate single points of vulnerability because they are more likely to evolve into overarching threats. Second, is the analytical capability resident within the government that directly supports the activities to identify and classify vulnerabilities. Predictive analysis is an extremely important element within this capability without which the analysis will only have very short term validity. Third, is the ability to consider conventional issues in a comprehensive manner at a fast pace and then superimpose collective lateral thinking on to the results to ensure that even non-mainstream threat possibilities are covered. Collective lateral thinking, while complementing the first two, is by itself a difficult ability to develop and foster within a governmental process because governments tend to be risk averse in their analysis and conventional in their collective thinking process. Lateral thinking does not come naturally to the predominantly bureaucratic make up of government agencies and persons with such abilities are normally considered to be unsuitable for the decision-making required of the government. However, lateral thinking is an essential influence on the development of threat mitigation strategies to ensure that emerging threats do not pose unforeseen challenges to national security.

The fourth factor is the ability of the government to protect the values of the nation. This is an onerous task and the ability required equally diffused to develop to the necessary calibre and thereafter to maintain at the required level of competence. However, in the contemporary security scenario a nation must expect an attack on its core values, normally through asymmetric means and other indirect methods. The subtlety of attacks on national values could also prevent them being detected early, making their repudiation more difficult. Fifth, is the necessity for the government to be able to manage the perception of the general population regarding vulnerabilities and threats facing a nation. This is a complex issue by itself and needs careful consideration and handling. Free media is a necessity for the progress of democratic traditions in all nations. However, in times of national security crisis, the media could become a vulnerability on its own, if the dissemination of information is not meticulously managed. The objective should be to ensure that the media becomes and remains a strategic asset as opposed to being a security liability. The management of perception through the entire gamut of the media is a battlespace to be contested and won. The importance of doing this is far greater when the nation is involved in exploiting strategies that involve expeditionary and irregular operations. As an extreme measure the government could consider some form of benign control—ensuring that the truth is always reported without bias—to ensure that the media remains an asset rather than one more challenge to be contained.

Sixth is the competency of the leadership within the government. This is the factor that binds all the others together to produce the necessary impetus and guidance to develop mitigating strategies and, more importantly, to implementing them successfully. The quality of decisions is a paramount stimulus in creating the wherewithal to mitigate threat and to ensuring that the selected strategy is contextually suitable and effective. The other aspect of governmental decision making is that it needs to be relatively quick in this particular instance. As discussed, vulnerabilities that remain unaddressed have the potential to speedily become threats and therefore, decisions must be made at a relatively fast pace. This could be anathema to cautious governments and lead to situations wherein the national security equilibrium is unbalanced. This will be a direct threat to national security and the effort and time necessary to revert the imbalance will be much more than the time it took to become unbalanced. If not directly addressed and remedial action initiated, the unbalanced state could become untenable. The challenge is to ensure the quality of the decision while maintaining the necessary speed of decision-making, a dual requirement that sometimes could be seen to be at odds with each other.

The role of the government in mitigating threats is vital and all-important. However, it is also influenced by a number of challenges that is both extraneous to it as well internal to its functioning.[8] Developing threat mitigating strategies is a complex endeavour and needs dedicated attention to be paid to the prevailing security circumstances of the nation, its resource availability, domestic political condition, and the

---

8 Jennings, Will, Bevan, Shaun, and others, 'Effects of the Core Functions of Government on the Diversity of Executive Agendas, *Comparative Political Studies*, Vol 44, Issue 8, Sage Publications, California, May 2011, pp. 1001-1030. http://journals.sagepub.com/doi/abs/10.1177/0010414011405165 accessed on 12 Jun 2017.

status of the military forces as well as the other elements of national power. Irrespective of the size of the nation and its alliances, it will be a foolhardy government that does not pay sufficient attention to this aspect of governance. In fact, an often used threat mitigation strategy is to evoke alliance and treaty obligations of friendly nations to assist in overcoming threatening situations. Once again, the acceptance of such a strategy underpinning national security will depend on domestic circumstances and the broader view of the population of the nation.

Threat Mitigation Strategies

At the core of all national security calculations there will always be a realistic assessment of the threats that a nation is likely to face, immediately, as well as in the short, medium, and long term. These will also be assessed in terms of their intensity and the likely duration that they will affect the nation, both directly and indirectly. A nation with tangible strength and power will invariably develop strategies to use them in order to protect itself. Ideally these strategies should be aimed at mitigating the threat rather than confronting them in an effort to defeat them. Obviously, defeating a threat would require the use of military force and has the potential to escalate the actions into a more general conflict. The commonality between mitigating and defeating a threat is that in both cases the military forces of the nation will be a major contributor in employing the selected strategy. Threat mitigation is best achieved by altering the perceptions of the potential adversary, primarily an activity in the cognitive domain. On the other hand, defeating a threat will invariably require the employment of the military forces to physically defeat the adversary, which may or may not be followed by actions to influence the cognitive domain. Actions in the physical domain normally neutralises the immediate and short term threats only, but are necessary to achieve the immediate suppression of emerging threats.

Threat mitigation is normally achieved by the military forces through defence, deterrence and offensive preventive attacks.

Defence

At a fundamental level defence is always an easier and cost-effective option than offensive action. A well formulated defensive strategy is difficult to overcome without prohibitive expenditure of resources, both materiel and personnel. In case the defensive arrangements are put in place in a calculated manner they can also compensate for weaknesses that might otherwise be visible for exploitation by an adept adversary. Defensive actions can be initiated to mitigate both physical and virtual threats to the nation, internally and outside the borders of the state.[9] This is an important factor that could be deciding factor for nations that are inherently non-aggressive in their overarching security considerations.

A defensive stance does not automatically mean that a nation will not possess any offensive capabilities at all. The essence of defence lies in the ability to take concerted offensive action as and when necessary to demonstrate and firmly establish the defensive capabilities. Defence is also a matter of perception, in that the strategies that could be employed in maintaining a defensive posture almost always will have a component of external perception of the nation's capabilities as an influence. Defence is primarily built on the strategies of influence, deterrence and coercion, all of which relies on the perceived capabilities of the elements of national power, in particular those of the military forces. Influence is the most benign strategy and does not normally include the use of military forces other than in times of disaster relief or in stabilisation operations as a preventive measure to ensure that instability caused by natural or man-made calamities does not deteriorate into making the nation a failing or failed state. Normally, such activities will be regional rather than global. Deterrence on the other hand involves the demonstration of military capabilities through a number of methods such as exercises, forward posturing and if necessary show of force without the actual application of lethal force. The surveillance and intelligence gathering capabilities of military forces will be of great significance in ensuring that potential adversaries are deterred from initiating any action that is inimical to the national interest. Coercion, as a strategy of defence borders on the nation transitioning to an offensive stance and could include the use of lethal means as punitive measures to coerce a recalcitrant adversary

---

9 Green, James A., &Grimal, Francis, 'The Threat of Force as an Action in Self-Defense Under International Law', *Journal of Transnational Law*, Volume 44, Vanderbilt University, Nashville, TN, 2012, pp. 289-295. https://www.vanderbilt.edu/wp-content/uploads/sites/78/green-cr.pdf accessed on 17 June 2017.

or to deny manoeuvre capabilities to an enemy force before the actual outbreak of hostilities. Although the three strategies contribute to a defensive posture, it is deterrence that is the centre piece in threat mitigation without recourse to the actual use of force.

Deterrence

Deterrence is perhaps the best option in terms of threat mitigation for it provides for the security of the nation without having to enter into conflict and incurring all the penalties that armed conflict involves.[10] Deterrence is the ability of a nation to display sufficient power so that other nations, adversarial or otherwise, are disinclined to carry out any actions, overtly or covertly, that could prompt the employment of such power. This could be translated to the threat of the use of force as well as the demonstrated capability, and more importantly, the national will to use it in case required. From a deterrence point of view, there is an inherent relationship between the measures initiated to support a deterrent posture and the actions as well as the reactions of the potential adversary. The concept of deterrence is based almost totally on the perception of the adversary regarding the ability of the deterring entity to go through with the implicit threat of the use of force. This perception could be based on the history of the nation or entity in question in the use of force in support of the concept of deterrence, the exhibited success of such actions and the ability of the nation to repeat the necessary actions if necessary. However, if it becomes necessary to repeat the application of force to enforce deterrence, the posture being adopted would have to be re-examined since the necessity to repeat the actions indicate a less than optimum situation to further pursue deterrence. In case the use of force does not create the necessary effect, repeated employment of force itself becomes a direct threat to the viability of deterrence.

Although deterrence as a concept is a powerful tool, especially considering that it has the potential to avoid unnecessary bloodshed and damage and destruction of infrastructure, there is a fundamental factor that must be weighed, analysed and understood before it is adopted as a primary concept on which national security is based.

---

10 Kainikara, Sanu, 'The Strategy of Deterrence and Air Power', *Working Paper 27*, Air Power Development Centre, Canberra, 2008.

Essentially, in the absence of any credible and visible threat to the security of a nation, there is no method by which the concept can be clearly validated. This is because deterrence is primarily based on the perception of the adversary whose absence makes it impossible to evaluate the effectiveness of the deterrent posture that has been developed by a nation. Under these circumstances it would not be appropriate to build the national security structure with deterrence as one of the cornerstones.

Pre-emptive and Preventive Strikes

From the threat of using force to carrying out punitive action to bolster the credibility of such threats is a very distinctive change in the spectrum of threat mitigating activities. The punitive actions could be in the form of either pre-emptive or preventive strikes that reinforce the perception of intent and demonstrated will in the cognitive domain of the adversary. There is a subtle difference between pre-emptive and preventive strikes—pre-emptive strikes are carried out to neutralise the immediate threat being posed when there is reasonable belief that the adversary is in the final phases of gathering resources and that an attack that is inimical to one's own security interests is imminent, whereas preventive attacks are planned and executed to nullify the capability of an adversary to initiate and sustain any action that is contrary to one's own national interests. Essentially, pre-emptive strikes are meant to create effects that are more short-term and preventive ones have more long-term goals. However, dependent on the built-up capability of the adversary, theses strikes may only have limited effects and may not shift the balance of power in the final analysis.[11]

There are three fundamental disadvantages that must also considered before resorting to carryout strikes of this nature. First, the effectiveness of such strikes is dependent to a great degree on the diplomatic initiatives that underpin such actions. Failure to ensure sufficient support for pre-emptive and/or preventive action could lead to a dilution of the effects that are sought to be created as well as lead to diplomatic isolation in extreme cases. Second, strikes

---

11 For a detailed history of pre-emptive strikes and the principles underpinning them explained through case studies that span modern warfare from the Napoleonic wars to the recent invasion of Iraq read, Flynn, Matthew J., *First Strike: Preemptive War in Modern History*, Routledge, New York, 2008.

carried out before the break-out of hostilities could be outside the security concepts of allies and other friendly nations who may not contribute to the concept of first-strike. Since punitive actions have a high potential to escalate into conflict, being the initiator could create a situation wherein even traditional allies become reluctant to offer materiel and diplomatic support. Therefore pre-emptive and preventive strikes must be undertaken after clear support has been garnered, especially from strategically important allies. Third, if the regional and international perception is such that the punitive actions are perceived as being undertaken without sufficient cause, it could create a backlash through the slightly weaker nations cooperating with each other to diplomatically isolate the initiating state. In the long-term such an action will always be detrimental to the security of the nation. In other words pre-emption could become a provocative act rather than a threat mitigating strategy.

Both pre-emptive as well as preventive actions, if conducted with panache, provide the advantage of having surprise one one's side as well as retaining the initiative for further action. By retaining the initiative, they provide the opportunity to control the tempo and intensity of the subsequent actions, whether diplomatic overtures or escalation of military action. Further, these actions must be taken with the clear understanding that they could lead to escalation, although such escalation need not yield commensurate results or even further the security status of the nation. In fact, the opposite may be the case in certain circumstances, especially if the strikes are seen widely as unjustifiable; ensuring security through the expansion of punitive strikes is normally a double-edged sword. Therefore, pre-emptive and preventive strikes must never be undertaken without careful consideration of the pros and cons, the prevalent context, own and adversary capabilities, and the support and understanding of allies as well as possibly neutral nations.

Summing Up...

Threat mitigation is best achieved through the demonstrated ability to protect the nation's sovereignty and far flung interests, with the use of force if necessary. Ensuring this is an involved and sophisticated process in the prevailing international security environment wherein the explicit use of force, through the employment of military capabilities, is not considered a viable strategy. In these circumstances, more subtle and non-intrusive concepts such as deterrence take centre-stage. However, these concepts are highly refined and are based on influencing the cognitive domain of the adversary, which is difficult to achieve and even more problematic to measure with any clear assurance. The use of force, even in a punitive manner, is emblematic of the more evolved processes not having created the necessary effects to yield the desired end-state, and in the final analysis unlikely to do so. Further, the diffusion of threats make the entire process of their mitigation even more complex, with the necessity to develop extremely nuanced concepts that do not have to take recourse to the fundamental use of force.

Chapter 16

THE DYNAMICS OF RESOURCES

The strength and status of the military forces of a nation is indelibly connected to the resilience and development of its economy in combination with the will of the nation to expend it in support of military power. Military power is viewed in different ways in different countries and is influenced by a number of factors, some of which are intangible and therefore difficult to fathom or measure. However, the type of government in a nation normally has a direct influence on the resource allocation for the acquisition and maintenance of military power. It can generally be noticed that autocratic or dictatorial governments allocate more than sufficient resources towards the build-up of military power whereas democracies are more reluctant to do so. The dynamics of resource allocation is also prejudiced by other factors such as threat perception, alliances and the fundamental ethos of the people that constitute the state. All autocratic regimes have unique characteristics but are normally dependent on military power to retain control of the state. Therefore, the resource allocation for military forces would almost always be without restraint. This chapter discusses the dynamics of resources in the context of a democracy.

Economic solvency of a nation that leads to financial adequacy for the military forces can be considered a weapon by itself.[1] However, the cost of national defence, primarily based on having a viable

---

1   Gajewski, Gregory R., *Democracy, Resource Abundance and Growth: The Debate*, The Louis Berger Group Inc., New Jersey, October 2012. https://www.louisberger.com/sites/default/files/Democracy_Resource_Abundance_and_Growth_The_Debate.pdf accessed on 19 June 2017.

military force capable of projecting adequate military power to ensure the security of the nation, is always scrutinised in a democracy even in times of financial stability. This is fundamentally because of a combination of factors. First, in times of comparative peace the role and necessity of having even a moderately large standing military force gradually recedes. This is because the collective memory of the utility of such a force and its direct contribution to national security that has ensured the very same peace tends to be befuddled and diluted. It is not uncommon in such situations to have other elements of national power gradually assume the lead role in a retrospective manner for having created the existing peace. Second, in times of prosperity brought about through the relatively secure peace, it becomes fashionable for the political leadership to criticise the expenditure within the military forces as being wasteful and therefore, needing more scrutiny and the introduction of external oversight. This invariably leads to the reduction of resource allocation to military forces. In democracies this situation is further exacerbated by the fact that the military forces are expected to be apolitical and subservient to the civilian leadership, which is an effective way to muffle any dissent from the military leadership. When a nation does not have a direct threat to its sovereignty, as defined according to convenience by the political leadership, this situation can become completely unbalanced with the military forces being gutted completely from within. This amounts to political intolerance of the cost of maintaining a credible military force with the ability to project power of the required calibre. In stable democracies, there are four fundamental factors that create political intolerance towards adequate resource allocation for military forces—domestic compulsions, intervention fatigue, the need for transparency, and accountability.

Domestic Compulsions. Domestic compulsions, essentially impinging on the civilian leadership of the country, are direct products of the electoral cycle and internal politics. Dependent on the threat perception, particularly within the opinion-moulding elements of the society, the domestic opinion could be swayed in favour or away from supporting resource expenditure on military forces. Generally it is seen that in times of comparative economic stability the military forces are provided the necessary resources for development and acquisition. However, it is in times of economic crisis that resource constraints are imposed on the military forces and financial support is begrudged to them. This approach not only creates difficulties in ensuring an even development of military power but also entrenches a perception within the broader population that the military forces are a body that needs to be supported only in times of economic prosperity. In democracies, domestic politics tends to overshadow all other inputs in relation to military power, especially when the nation has not been directly threatened for a relatively long period of time.

Intervention Fatigue. In recent times the democratic world has intervened militarily on a number of occasions in different parts of the world for a variety of reasons. However, there is a very thin delineation between foreign intervention within the concept of right to protect and violating the sovereignty of a nation. The United Nations recognises only four mass atrocity situations when intervention is sanctioned—genocide, war crimes, crimes against humanity and ethnic cleansing.[2] Interventions in accordance with this concept have been carried out, by and large, by military forces contributed by nations that support the United Nations and its initiatives. Further, interventions can be of a short duration or protracted and be of very high tempo and intensity or of a more prosaic nature. Irrespective of its characteristics, every nation has a fatigue threshold with regard to intervention.[3] This threshold is also not a constant and varies with the intent, domestic perception and human and material cost of the intervention. Irrespective of the resilience of the nation towards loss of life, once this threshold has been reached, the nation will suffer from intervention fatigue that will almost immediately translate to the withdrawal of its forces from interventionist activities. In an indirect manner this will translate to the cutting down of resources to the military forces, since it will be perceived that resource requirements would have also reduced with the withdrawal from intervention. In actuality the reverse may be the case, with the military requiring greater investment of resources to make good the capabilities and capacity that have been expended.

Transparency and Accountability. True democracy is built on transparency of government activities to the general public. This

---

2 Latif, Asad, 'The World of the Secular Pope', *The Straits Times*, Singapore, 4 January 2013, p. A25.

3 O'Toole, Molly, 'UN Ambassador Warns Against Intervention Fatigue', *Defense One*, Atlantic Media, Boston, 19 November 2014, https://www.defenseone.com/threats/2014/11/un-ambassador-warns-against-intervention-fatigue/99485/ accessed on 19 June 2017.

translates to all areas of resource allocation, although some parts of national security remains shrouded in a certain amount of secrecy because of the sensitive nature of the activities being undertaken. In an effort to assuage the public demand for more transparency in the resource distribution within the nation, a number of democratic governments tend to curtail resource allocation to the development of military forces so that they can be seen as being more transparent in governance. This situation is also demanded because the military forces tend to obfuscate their expenditure in bureaucratic explanations that get to be seen as attempts at not being accountable for resource expenditure. The combination of the military reluctance to be open to civilian scrutiny and the government's proclivity to play to the gallery, especially when in the election mode, makes it difficult to ensure that adequate resources are made available for the development of military power. While the reluctance is understandable in most cases, this is an area wherein the civilian and military leadership has to work together to ensure that fallacies are cleared and the military forces are appropriately resourced. A corollary of transparency is the question of accountability that is a fundamental principle of democratic governments. The elected representatives have an onus of responsibility to be accountable to the constituents to ensure that public funds are allocated and utilised in accordance with the prevalent norms of the society. This requirement is closely related to transparency and the need for good governance. In times of relative peace, when the requirement to have strong and robust military power appears to be a superfluous requirement, the need for accountability is often placed as the reason for stringency in resource allocation for military forces.

The Geopolitics of Military Spending

The end of the Cold War in the early 1990s converted the world from a bipolar entity to a unipolar one and therefore, was a turning point in global politics. However, it is less obvious that it was also a turning point for the geopolitics of the global system by creating a fundamental geographic shift in international politico-economic focus.[4] It can now be clearly seen that the end of the Cold War marked

---

4 Jane's Editorial Staff, 'Global defence spending to hit post-Cold War high in 2018', IHSMarkit, I, 18 December 2017, https://ihsmarkit.com/research-analysis/global-defence-spending-to-hit-post-cold-war-high-in-2018.html accessed on 20 January 2018.

the end of the European era, in which Europe had been the centre of the global system for a number of centuries. In the past few decades Asia, particularly the Indo-Pacific region, has become the nucleus for international economic, political and security activities. The tangible repercussions of such a geographic shift is that it will have military implications that manifest, *in extremis*, as an arms race and at the very least as a steady build-up of arms that could lead to rivalry for influence and control.

Inevitably this transfer of focus will also mean a shift in military spending from the traditional European economies to those of the developing world. As fiscal austerity takes hold of the Western democracies in the wake of the global financial crisis (GFC) and the more apparent security flash-points shift to the Asia-Pacific region, where the economy has not been as heavily affected as the rest of the world, military spending is also bound to gradually shift. It has been reported that the difference in the cumulative defence spending between Europe and Asia has reduced considerably and that Asia may, for the first time, overtake Europe in military spending in 2012-13.[5] There is no doubt that from both economic and security perspectives, Asia-Pacific is the future, in fact the value of trans-Pacific trade has far outstripped trans-Atlantic for decades now.

This shift in global focus to the Asia-Pacific will also bring about changes to the manner in which military forces will be developed. Wars until now, perhaps with the exception of some campaigns in World War II, have been fought for the control of territory—this has been true from the Peloponnesian wars to the most recent Libyan intervention. Therefore, it was perceived that the fundamental arm of the military force was the land component. However, recent developments in global politics and international relations have made intervention on the ground or capture of enemy territory unacceptable in terms of broad public opinion since they represent the concept of invasion and occupation. As a consequence, in the past few decades, huge land forces have been gradually replaced by technologically advanced navies and air forces that have the ability to coerce an adversary without having to physically establish a presence in enemy territory. This development has been assisted by the closing of the technology gap between the

---

5   *Stratfor 41/12*, 'The Geopolitics of Shifting Defence Expenditure', Austin, Texas, 12 March 2012.

industrialised nations and the developing ones to insignificance, which has facilitated the entrenchment of the concept of reliance on navies and air forces rather than on large armies to ensure national security.[6] The Asia-Pacific is fundamentally a maritime region containing the busiest maritime choke point in the world—the Straits of Malacca—with almost all the nations dependent on energy and raw material imports to sustain the growth of their economies. That the sustainment of these economies is critical to global economic stability is perhaps a moot point in the current international equation. It is therefore, not surprising that the nations of the Asia-Pacific are rapidly building up their maritime power projection capabilities through the development of their own navies and air forces. The region is not merely an area of competition between the United States and China—Japan, despite its pacifist constitution fields one of the most capable military forces of the world and South Korea is not far behind. Of greater interest from a geo-security evaluation is the fact the nations that are native to the South China Sea, namely Philippines, Vietnam, Malaysia, Indonesia, and Singapore have put in place initiatives to strengthen their military power by investing in maritime forces reliant on sophisticated, state-of-the-art high-technology navies and air forces. In the Asia-Pacific security equation, while the nations of the region acknowledge US primacy, they are also preparing to create a power balance based on a relationship of equality between themselves and more importantly between the regional powers. European military power, hamstrung by extreme financial cutbacks, is gradually becoming irrelevant in the global arena, a situation that would have been inconceivable even two decades ago. A combination of factors—the appreciable shift in the geopolitical dynamics; a financial crisis termed global, which is actually European; and unsustainable models of welfare-oriented state governance—have made Europe irrelevant in the larger scheme of global economy and stability. For the foreseeable future military spending will be centred on the developing economies of the Asia-Pacific.

Cost Factor

In order to maintain the necessary level of competence on a continuous basis, all military forces need to be able to absorb two types of

---

6   ibid.

expenditure—operational costs and modernisation costs.[7] Operational costs are the ones incurred for the day-to-day functioning of the military forces that would primarily consist of training and maintenance costs; costs incurred to meet replacement requirements to make good losses due to normal wear and tear of equipment; costs involved in recruiting and retaining the right calibre of personnel that would involve ensuring adequacy of pay and other allowances at par with the civilian sector; and the expenditure necessary to maintain adequate peacetime infrastructure to sustain training and other necessary activities of the force. Operational costs are recurring and the amount will be a direct function of the size of the military force, its level of sophistication, and the nation's expectations of it, underpinned by national economy and national security perceptions. When the military force is actually deployed to undertake operations, the costs involved are normally met through extra allocations since peacetime projections of expenditure will not meet the expanded requirements of conducting a deployed conflict. Nations that do not cater for the cost of conflict separately will find that the military forces are incapable of meeting the additional costs from within their allocated resources and therefore, will suffer from lack of resources in a short period of conflict. Operational costs also carry a certain amount of flexibility in that they can be varied according to the projected long-term threat perceptions of the nation. However, the reduction of operational costs based on flawed threat predictions could very rapidly become catastrophic for the security of the nation. This is a fact that may not be given the necessary importance in the broader debate regarding the priorities within the national budget allocation—at times deliberately so, to cater for narrow political purposes. The consequences can be disastrous for national security. In the current financially constrained conditions that most democracies find themselves, manipulating operational costs for short term political gain is being seen as an attractive option. It is perhaps under these conditions that democratic nations across the world are pruning the operational costs of military forces.

---

7 For detailed analysis of the cost factor in acquiring, maintaining and operating high-technology modern day military equipment and systems read, Bolton, Joseph G., Leonard, Robert S., and others, *Sources of Weapon System Cost Growth: Analysis of 35 Major Defense Acquisition Programs*, RAND Corporation, Santa Monica, CA, 2008. https://www.rand.org/content/dam/rand/pubs/monographs/2008/RAND_MG670.pdf accessed on 18 June 2017.

Contemporary military forces need to be upgraded and modernised on a regular basis to retain their effectiveness because of continuous enhancements in system capabilities brought about through technology-enabled innovations. Modernisation costs are influenced by two independent factors—the extremely high cost of acquiring new systems and the rising costs of maintaining ageing systems in at least the minimum required effectiveness. The combination of these two factors place defence in what can be termed a 'death spiral'. The highly increased cost of new systems, albeit with much greater capability and broader capacity that the one it is replacing, translates to a nation with finite financial ability not being able to replace the entire ageing systems and having to contend with only a certain percentage of the holistic capability being modernised. In the past few decades modernisation costs have skyrocketed with fewer platforms or systems costing more to acquire and maintain than the ones that they are replacing while not providing a complete capability replacement. This is a dichotomy that defies amelioration and one that is causing insurmountable resource management conundrums. The situation is further complicated by the inability of the military forces to predict the operating costs of the new systems with sufficient accuracy, thereby bringing in uncertainty into calculation of the overall operational cost calculation for the force in its entirety. This situation of flux detracts from the credibility of the military forces' ability to be seen as fiscally responsible while still delivering the necessary power projection and security needs of the nation. In democratic nations, where financial scrutiny is of a very high order, the inability of the military forces to clearly articulate their requirements tends to mire them in fissiparous debate with the civilian leadership. When financial constraints of a nation make it imperative for the government of the day to examine resource distribution minutely, this kind of vagueness regarding expenses will always bring about scepticism of the military forces ability to be fiscally responsible. In combination with the general belief that military forces have for years been allowed to run riot with their budgets not having been strictly controlled, there is bound to be an impending clamp down on military expenditure. Coming as it does in a time when the cost of military capabilities is rising steeply, this situation does not bode well for the broader health of military forces.

Budgetary Calculations

The GFC has impacted all nations and therefore is a global phenomenon.[8] However, the impact of the GFC has not been felt similarly in all nations with the variation being very large. The so-called industrialised European nations that have so far followed a welfare-oriented governance model have been the hardest hit and the more conservative and cautious states of the Asia-Pacific have weathered the crisis much better than all others. Particularly the major economic powers of Asia—China, India and South Korea—have managed to steer clear of financial pitfalls and have cautiously increased their defence budgets to meet perceived and actual changes to their security environment. Therefore, the GFC although considered global and does have global implications, does not have the similar influence or repercussions across all nations. However, in an overarching manner, security strategies must be developed cognisant of two fundamental dynamics that stem from budgetary calculations that take into account the influence of the GFC on one's own as well as other nations' military forces.

First is the necessity to maintain the correct or optimum balance between operational requirements and the available budget. This has to be achieved at the highest level of military financial planning and must take into account not only the budget but also the changing capability and capacity requirements of the military forces vis-à-vis national security perceptions and the government's expectations of them. There is no doubt that most military forces will attempt to reduce their size while trying to retain capability at the same level and in some cases might even be able to trade size for increased capability. However, improving capability while reducing actual size will depend on the availability of finances since the enhanced capability will always come at a higher expenditure. This requires a finely balanced trade-off between capability and size since maintaining the minimum level of capability while effecting sufficient reduction in size that would create meaningful financial savings. In the contemporary security environment, a fundamental operational requirement would be the ability of the military force to maintain strategic agility. Strategic agility

---

8 Shah, Anup, 'Global Financial Crisis', *Global Issues*, 24 March 2013, http://www.globalissues.org/article/768/global-financial-crisis accessed on 19 June 2017.

assumes increased importance because the current trend, one that will continue for the near future, is for conflicts to erupt with very little notice, making it necessary for military forces to be able to deploy rapidly. Challenges to security can develop abruptly—technology-enabled global shocks can create unpredictable instabilities that can only be contained by a force with adequate strategic agility. While size does not automatically create strategic agility, reduction in size beyond a critical minimum for whatever reason will have a detrimental effect on a force's ability to respond to emerging crisis.

Second is the necessity to establish the minimum required military size, capability and capacity to meet the government's desired needs and then match it to the approved budget in order to let the government know if there is a gap between the two. From a national security perspective this is an imperative step to ensure that there is no shortfall in military capabilities and if there is a disparity it is either addressed directly. In certain cases ameliorating the situation may not be possible because of resource and financial constraints, in which case the lack of assurance of complete security of the nation must be made known to the general population. While making the lack of security public may not be the preferred option of a government for obvious reasons, such action is necessary for the military to be able to perform its ultimate duty of safeguarding the nation when required. In the very broadest term, historically, elected representatives have been seen to be less than open with the public when it comes to accepting the shortfall in the security of the nation that have come about because of their studied neglect of the military forces. In order to have the desired level of military capability the national interests—opportunities to be exploited or threats to be mitigated—must be first established, both for the short-term and long-term. The rest of the budgetary calculations can only be done after analysing and establishing this baseline. Budgetary balance between capability and operational requirement has to be understood in holistic terms of the national requirement to be involved in conflict or other kinds of military operations and not in terms of environmentally divided capabilities like land, maritime and air.

In this continuous and constant battle to maintain an optimum balance between the budget and military capabilities, there are two underlying factors that must always be implicit. One is the need for the government and the public—as well as the military force—to be aware that resource and financial expenditure on the military force will at best manage the risks and challenges to national security, but never completely eliminate them. Second is for the military force to appreciate and differentiate the mandatory capabilities that are required to perform their role optimally from those that are desirable or optional to create added assurance to necessary capabilities. The correct choice in this process will not only improve the chances of success, but is critical to ensuring success in all military endeavours—conflict or otherwise. In each of the factors discussed above budgetary calculations play an extremely influential role in deciding the choices that are to be made while ensuring the necessary military readiness to guarantee national security in its broadest definition.

Other elements

There are two other elements that influence the dynamics of resources in all nations, to a greater or lesser extent dependent on a number of extraneous factors—the ability of the defence industry to leverage technological innovation and the role of the indigenous defence industry. Technological innovation has always been critical, and perhaps central, to military modernisation.[9] The modernisation of military forces is a holistic process that involves changes to doctrine, organisation, as well as strategy and tactics wherein technological innovation is almost always the commencing point. Technological innovation is a resource intensive process and therefore the slowing down of economies has directly impacted the ability of defence industries to pursue cutting edge technologies to improve military capability. Innovation has become evolutionary and incremental—providing new and better ways to employ existing technology—rather than being revolutionary, which creates the necessary backdrop for dramatic and far-reaching capability overhaul.[10] In the absence of adequate fiscal support for innovative changes to technology, the defence industry has been forced to slow down capability improvement programs that would also have been

---

9 Bitzinger, Richard A., 'Can the Defence Industry Still Innovate?', *RSIS Commenatries No 080/2012*, S. Rajaratinam School of International Studies, Nanyang Technological University, Singapore, 8 May 2012.

10 ibid.

long-term resource saving measure. The fall-out of the GFC has been a situation where short-term measures have assumed a greater priority than the long-term development of capabilities to the detriment of military forces.

Over the past five decades, the defence industry has gradually been consolidated and today companies that have capability to design and manufacture of high-value and state-of-the-art systems are concentrated in a few nations. Although euphemistically they are termed multi-national companies, because of their establishing purely manufacturing plants in nations with cheaper labour or outsourcing the production of minor items of the system, they are bound by the laws and restrictions of the home nation for the export of the weapon systems. In other words, the availability of high-end weapon systems to a military force is controlled by the major four or five industrialised nations of the world. In this context, the role of the indigenous industry takes on a different hue. Especially in emerging economies, attempts are being made to create indigenous defence design and manufacturing and to enhance their performance after that. While self-sufficiency is a far away dream, a number of economically stable and advanced nations have established indigenous industry. This is indeed laudable but comes with a penalty of its own. The technology base required to develop and produce highly sophisticated military hardware is not easy to create and foster and therefore, more often than not indigenous industry is not able to deliver the necessary capability on time or within the allocated budget. Obviously this increases the cost of acquisition of a capability and more importantly impacts the overall readiness and force projection capability of the force. Indigenous development is not beyond the technology development of emerging nations and therefore not an impossible task, provided sufficiency of financial outlay is assured, if necessary even beyond the projected requirement.

Summing Up…

There are two elements at work simultaneously with regard to the dynamics of resources for military forces. One, the changes in political attitude towards the military forces along with the greatly enhanced envelope of activities that they are required to undertake; and two, the global financial downturn that has affected all nations and their military forces in some way or the other. The focus of geo-politics and security is gradually shifting to the Asia-Pacific while the GFC has not affected the nations of the region as much as it has Europe. In combination, Asia-Pacific is witnessing a military build-up like never before, although the rate of technology innovation has somewhat reduced because of a number of reasons. In the final analysis, it is safe to assume that the dynamics of resources will eventually slow military capability development as well as curtail extensive build-up of military power projection capabilities in most nations. The conflicting demands on finite budgets and changed perceptions of national security and interests will coalesce to diminish the status of military forces from the exalted place that they held in the aftermath of World War II.

Chapter 17

MILITARY FORCES AND SECURITY STRATEGIES

National security strategies are the foundation blocks for the development of military forces and these cannot be replaced with any other input as the primary source for the advancement of concepts of operations and the actual conduct of conflict. Since national strategies are evolved to achieve strategic objectives of the nation, it becomes necessary to have national consistency of a very high calibre in determining national objectives. The long-term goals of a nation must not be fickle, but placed at a high enough position strategically for them to be almost 'set in stone'. While this is a difficult task all strategic decision-makers must endeavour to achieve this objective. The veracity of the military force will depend on the consistency of national strategic objectives. Another aspect national security strategies is that they should form a continuum involving both military and non-military approaches to security. The end-state being sought is always assured security of the nation and this can only be assured with the employment of all elements of national power, which goes far beyond military capabilities. Further, the legitimacy of any action initiated to ensure national security is also dependent on the selected strategy being implemented within the accepted international laws and norms. In this context the perception of 'correctness' of the actions of a nation plays an important part in getting acceptance of the need to apply force if necessary and the actual conduct of the conflict.

The contemporary security environment is characterised by change and ambiguity.[1] Further, the environment has become much more interconnected compared to the situation even a couple of decades ago and therefore, no nation can afford to analyse the security scenario in isolation. Irrespective of the size, capability and status of a nation, it will have to take into account the influence of even the smallest state when considering its options to secure itself against all challenges to its sovereignty. In these conditions, while pragmatism is an important ingredient to the development of a coherent and viable strategy; pragmatism by itself cannot be considered a strategy.[2]

War and Conflict

Armed conflict wherein force is used to achieve the objectives of the nation is not always inevitable. However, the current international strategic environment is such that most nations will face some form of armed conflict directly or indirectly at some time or the other. The application of force is normally considered the mandate of the military forces and in contemporary times comes with the caveat of a 'no harm to civilians and property' policy. There is a dichotomy in this situation. The essence of employing military forces in conflict is the legal application of lethal force within a national security strategy. When such strategies support attrition and destruction as an integral part of the application of force, the military is normally unable to meet the 'no harm' stipulation of the government. When the need to avoid collateral damage becomes an overriding priority for the government, the effectiveness of a military force starts to diminish.

Collateral damage has become an emotive issue in most countries. It is influenced by both international and domestic political aspects, as well as by operational demands and imperatives. Finding the correct balance is critical to managing the external perception of the conflict.

---

1   Abigail, Major General Peter, 'Preparing the Australian Army for 21st- century Conflict: Problems and Perspectives', in Evans, Michael, Parkin, Russell, Ryan, Alan (eds), *Future Armies Future Challenges: Land Warfare in the Information Age*, Allen & Unwin, NSW, 2004, pp.238-241.

2   Conin, Dr Patrick, 'The US and China in a Changing Asian Security Environment—A US Perspective', Keynote Presentation in ASPI-Boeing China Seminar on *'US-China Relations and Australian Policy Options'*, held in Canberra on 12 August 2009.

However, the balance required would shift dependent on the kind of conflict or war that is being undertaken. The acceptance of collateral damage would be different between wars of choice and necessity. Superimposed on this would always be domestic perceptions not only regarding collateral damage but also the broader issue of the use of force. While collateral damage was not considered an issue during World War II, but as the term implied, it was 'something unavoidable that happened when legitimate targets were being attacked'. The advent of precision-guided munitions and an increased sense of morality changed this perception and imposed the necessity to avoid collateral damage on military forces.[3]

Another development that has taken place in the realm of war and conflict is that there is now a clear understanding that conflict must be shifted from the purely physical to an amorphous combination of influencing the physical and cognitive domain. There is no doubt that wars have always been won in the cognitive domain, however the actions that brought about victory was almost always conducted in the physical domain. The actions in the physical domain brings about destruction and annihilation whereas the cognitive domain deals with thought, perception behaviour pattern and belief system. In this kind of a combined approach to the conduct of war, there is a greater understanding of the combat environment that in turn provides the ability to perceive a larger number of options that could be considered possible courses of action. This would have the advantage of imposing greater complexity to the adversary's actions. However, even this sophisticated methodology to the conduct of a war will not eliminate the probability of collateral damage, but will definitely minimise the chances of unwanted destruction. More importantly, this combined approach is perhaps a better option from a moralistic point of view.

Military Power within the National Power Balance[4]

Unlike even a decade ago, the current international system surrounds military forces in ambiguity. This is not to suggest that it has lost its

---

3   John Stone, *Military Strategy: The Politics and Technique of War*, p. 134.

4   For a comprehensively researched analysis that provides a holistic understanding of this topic read, Tellis, Ashley J., Bially, Janice, and others, *Measuring National Power in the Post-Industrial Age*, RAND Corporation, Santa Monica, CA, 2000 (Particularly Chapter 2 Power and National Power: Some Conceptual Considerations)

importance, but to point out that it is now not the only strategically decisive component within the elements of national power. In the contemporary security scenario the strategic balance can be conclusively influenced by any of the power elements in a contextual manner. However, it is also to be noted that military power becomes less usable with the increase in its destructive power, even if precision and proportionality is also enhanced side by side. The dichotomy is that conventional military forces continue to remain fundamental instruments of national policy. Its frequency of employment in this strategic mode is in direct contrast to the perceived need to use lesser force in its employment.

Another aspect of military power that needs to be considered is the influence of few strategic drivers in the development of military capabilities. The primary strategic drivers are the global security environment and its effect on the regional security architecture; the international and domestic political geometry and interaction between the two; and the balance between the availability and requirement of resources. The global security environment will be determined by factors over which a nation will have only limited influence at best and no influence at all in a worst case scenario. However, the global environment will always have a salutary influence on the regional security architecture. The development of military forces is invariably influenced by the prevailing and future security environment in the region in which the nation is located. There is a cyclical relationship between the security scenario and international political developments—each influencing the other in a marked and visible manner. However, domestic political developments will have a greater impact on military build-up as well as on the role of the military in the national security system. The international political scenario may not have a direct influence on the development of military forces other than through its impact on the nation's domestic political processes.

Perhaps the most important strategic driver in military development is the resources equation. In times of relative peace, resource allocation to the military forces is considered to be 'wasteful' and therefore arbitrarily reduced. This is very clearly seen in democracies, wherein governments of all persuasions tend to look at the military budget as the first option to exercise budgetary prudence.

While allocation of extra resources in times of security challenges could create a credible military force in the mid-20th century, the lead time required to field a potent force has now increased to an extent where a just-in-time allocation of resources will not yield a force of the necessary calibre. The dichotomy that faces a government is to ascertain the minimum required force to ensure national security and then to allocate the required resources to achieve the needed level of capability. The efficacy of a military force is directly dependent on the economic resources that it can access, which in turn is a function of the robustness of the economic activities of the state.[5]

National Strategic Reach. A nation's position within the comity of nations is, to a large extent, dependent on its national strategic reach. Strategic reach—the ability to influence events beyond the immediate area surrounding the geographic boundaries of the nation—has to be assiduously built based on a number of elements of national power and some other factors. The core elements of national power; economy, diplomatic strength, military capabilities and information accessibility; as well as the ability to integrate technology and the ability to create an environment for efficient development of the nation and its surroundings are essential to create strategic reach. A nation must at all times attempt to increase its strategic reach in order to ensure that its sovereignty and security remain sacrosanct and inviolable at all times. While the core elements of national power and their relation to strategic reach is almost self-explanatory, the other two need elaboration. The capacity to integrate technology is a fundamental requirement for the military to remain effective, for the economy to grow at the required rate and for information accessibility. The creation of an efficient environment is necessary to have a well-developed research infrastructure, a stable social fabric and the necessary support infrastructure to ensure seamless and directed development. These are primary requirements for the overall development of the nation.

Foreign Military Intervention

Foreign Military Intervention (FMI) is not a new concept. It is a phenomenon that is endemic in the current international political system, manifest more prominently since the end of the Cold War and

---

5 Gray, Colin S., *Modern Strategy*, Oxford University Press, Oxford, 1999, pp. 31-32.

the demise of the Soviet Union as a counterweight to the hegemony of the United States. Further, the United Nations has passed a resolution within the coercive Chapter VII of its Charter proclaiming the responsibility to protect (R2P) even through military intervention, if necessary.[6] So far (at the time of writing) the only instance wherein the R2P clause was invoked was in the NATO led intervention in Libya that led to the fall of the Gaddafi regime. There is also a prevalent opinion that in this instance the UN authorisation had been stretched beyond the scope of R2P.[7] FMI under any caveat is not readily acceptable to the recipient nation. Another factor in FMI, for whatever reason and whether or not it is authorised within a legal framework, is that there is no connection between the type of government and its propensity to intervene in another nation. Three factors influence a nation's decision to intervene—the capability to do so effectively; the domestic political situation and support for the intervention in the intervening nation as well as the target nation; and the prevailing international politico-economic situation.[8]

Even when the factors that influence foreign intervention are conducive to a successful intervention, most nations are averse to initiating a military intervention. Historically it is seen that in most cases the decision to intervene is arrived at in a gradual and reluctant manner.[9] There are a number of reasons for this display of reluctance. First, the decision to commit military forces to a conflict is momentous,

---

6   United Nations, *Charter of the United Nations and Statute of the International Court of Justice*, available at http://www.in.org/en/documents/charter/index.html, accessed on 11 August 2013.

7   Thakur, Ramesh, 'Responsibility to Protect: Libya as a Case Study', in Brent, Keith (ed), *Air Power and Coercive Diplomacy*, the Proceedings of the 2012 RAAF Air Power Conference, Air Power Development Centre, Canberra, 2012, pp. 43-44.

8   Levite, Ariel E., Jentleson, Bruce W., & Berman, Larry, (eds), *Foreign Military Intervention: The Dynamics of Protracted Conflict*, Columbia University Press, New York, 1992, pp. 14-16.

9   The exception to this generality could be the NATO intervention in Libya in the pursuance of the principle of R2P under a UN mandate. The alacrity with which the French and British governments deployed military forces belied the assertion that this was not a pre-planned operations that was only awaiting the rubber stamp of the United Nations.

which directly and indirectly influences a large number of other basic functions of the nation. Therefore, generally the decision is taken only when a critical threshold has been crossed and the broader interests of the nation is directly impacted. Second, the translation of the political goals to military objectives is a complex process in the case of military interventions. This in turn makes it difficult to adapt the overarching military strategy to the slightly lesser grade of application that is normal in the initial phases of a military intervention. Third, even if the intervention commences at a relatively low level of conflict, dependent on the dynamics of the environment it could escalate rapidly into full-scale war. The intervening nation may not be prepared for such an exigency both politically and militarily. Fourth, military success in an intervention need not always and automatically culminate in a political solution or settlement. In fact military intervention does not even assure creating a favourable political situation for the intervening nation, if the premises and planning of the intervention had been incorrect.[10]

The most important and difficult part of military intervention is the phase of withdrawal. The decision to withdraw military forces is as critical as the decision to intervene. It is possible for the intervening nation to decide on a unilateral withdrawal, which is a viable if last option since it does not constitute loss of territory. However, such a withdrawal, without achieving the aims of the intervention, will almost always have other repercussions in terms of loss of status for the intervening nation and a detrimental impact on the military forces. A classic example is the protracted US intervention in Vietnam and the withdrawal that had to be affected in disorder. A withdrawal of forces does not automatically mean that foreign intervention has ceased. It could well be that a sizeable foreign military force is permitted to remain in the host country to ensure stability and also to influence further developments. The intervention in this respect could be through the influence that can be brought to bear by activating other elements of national power.[11]

---

10 Levite, Ariel E., Jentleson, Bruce W., & Berman, Larry, (eds), *Foreign Military Intervention: The Dynamics of Protracted Conflict*, p. 18.

11 ibid, pp. 19-20.

There are certain basic ideas that must be clearly analysed by the intervening nation, failing which the intervention is unlikely to succeed in achieving the desired military and political objectives. The first idea that must be considered and analysed in detail is to think through the consequences, for all nations concerned, of the employment of military forces, the military outcomes to be achieved, the connection of the military objectives to the ultimate political goals and the stability to be maintained after military action has stopped and/or the war won. This would essentially need a reconstruction plan to be made an integral part of the military plan. This reconstruction plan may be activated and conducted by an agency other than the military, although in a number of cases the reconstruction phase would also need the military forces to be in the lead. This phase will only succeed if the post-conflict civil-military relationship is based on mutual trust and understanding of the different but intertwined roles that both have to play in order to stabilise the situation. The second idea is that the use of military forces limits the options that can be activated and limits the boundaries of a government-to-government interaction. Therefore, military forces must only be employed as the absolute last resort option, when all other efforts have been tried and have conclusively failed. The third idea to be kept at the forefront is to repeatedly check and assure that the use of force is being done in a manner that it enhances the national interest at all times. It is in this context that strategic weapons have a greater value than having to 'invade' the host country with a large force. FMI has always been, and continues to be, a double-edged sword that invariably produces less than optimum results for the intervening as well as the recipient nation. However, in the current international socio-political, security, and economic environment there will be circumstances wherein an alternative may not present itself and FMI will have to be resorted to, however reluctantly.[12]

---

12 For in-depth analysis and consideration of various factors that influence Foreign Military Interventions read:

1. Levite, Ariel E., Jentleson, Bruce W., & Berman, Larry, (eds), *Foreign Military Intervention: The Dynamics of Protracted Conflict,* Columbia University Press, Columbia, NY, 1992.

2. Aydin, Aysegul, *Foreign Power and Intervention in Armed Conflicts*, Stanford University Press, Stanford, CA, 2012.

National Security Strategy

All nations, small and large, weak and powerful, need to have an articulated national security strategy that provides a clear indication, to friends and foes alike, of the national security posture. The national security posture has primacy in determining the overarching security strategy of a nation. The national security strategy must always be viewed within a historical perspective with the aim of connecting the political process to the development and deployment of military capabilities. Therefore, it is imperative that the development process of the national security strategy must have continuous political guidance at the highest levels throughout. This will also facilitate the interaction between political guidance and campaign planning when the decision to employ military forces have been taken.

The international security environment is now more interconnected than ever before leading to the requirement to ensure that a viable national security strategy will be able to cater for and contain the global spectrum of threat. It should also be cognisant of the fact that state-on-state conflicts are less likely to occur and that securing the physical borders of the nation is only one part of what the strategy is meant to achieve. Increasingly, the need is to be able to protect the networks that are the sinews that hold a nation together and that they can be targeted with minimum effort in case their protection levels are not sufficiently high and robust. Effectively there is a visible shift in the imperatives of national security. There are some other factors that must be considered in order to ensure that a national security strategy that is developed meets all the requirements of the nation. One, it must be able to encompass deductive thinking in order to understand the balance of power and the impact of power shift in developing the security strategy. Two, the national security strategy must retain the flexibility to introduce and implement a capability-based planning cycle dependent on the information available regarding the military capabilities of potential adversaries and of other nations within the sphere of influence of the nation. Three, while it is clear that linking the strategy to lower order tasks will be difficult, this process must be clearly identified and embedded in the developmental cycle. Four, the relationship and dynamics between the different elements of national power and the distribution of power between the departments that control them within the government must be studied and determined before a security strategy development is embarked upon. The underlying requirement for the national security strategy to be robust is that the changes that need to be incorporated to cater for the future and those that are required to cater for the emerging present will have to be balanced. National security strategy should not be placed at such a position that it becomes a completely visionary concept, devoid of any real-life connection.

A good national security strategy should be able to leverage off the spectrum of strategies form the most benign influence and shape to the other end when destruction becomes necessary to achieve national security objectives. This spectrum spreads across through deterrence, coercion, and punishment. From a military perspective, implementing the strategy of punishment and destruction is seen as their exclusive preserve, whereas other elements of national power contribute in different scales, dependent on context, to the implementation of the other strategies. However, the contribution of the military forces towards the implementation of the strategies of deterrence and coercion are finely nuanced and needs to be carefully tailored. The combination of deterrence and coercion can be considered to have a continuum that commences at persuasion, and goes through dissuasion, deterrence and compulsion at the highest end.

The lower levels of the spectrum can also be clubbed under the guise of diplomacy wherein persuasion and dissuasion can be used to create a more benign environment to pursue national interests without having to take recourse to the threat or actual use of force. Such diplomacy can be enhanced by the presence of military forces who could put on a show of force to reinforce the hard power of the nation. At the higher end of the spectrum of strategies, the nation may have to resort to punishment and destruction of the adversary in order to ensure national security.

The prevailing security environment of the 21st century is such that nations tend to resort to irregular wars rather than involve themselves in conventional wars. At the same time the tendency of nation-states to employ force has visibly increased in the past few decades. There is a sense of impatience that can be observed in the dealings between nations with the result, the strategy of punishment is used more often than ever before. Along with the spread of irregular war as the preferred modus operandi of smaller powers, foreign military interventions have also proliferated. More small-scale wars are being fought across the world as compared to the situation during the Cold War.[13]

In an overarching manner, it could be surmised that national security strategies, if they have been applied, had failed, when a nation has to fight a war of national survival. However, after the end of World War II, there has not been any distinctive wars of national survival that have been fought, at least from the perspective of stable democratic nations.

National security strategies cover a broad spectrum and at any given time one or the other of these strategies will be in use at all times in a nation. Imperatives of national security will force the change of the selection of strategies and it will move across the spectrum. In addition, the intensity of the application of these strategies will also vary with the context of their application. Choosing the correct strategy, especially when it involves the application of lethal force has to be carefully done and is an art. The application of the chosen strategy must be carefully crafted, since the outcome will have a direct bearing on the status of nation vis-à-vis other contemporary states.

Summing Up...

The global security environment is today more flexible and in flux than ever before, characterised by change and ambiguity. With nations becoming increasingly interconnected through commerce and trade, this inherent ambiguity of the environment tends to get enhanced. Another aspect that has become more visible is that the expanding interaction between nations also create an atmosphere conducive to conflict. Such conflicts involving diplomacy and competitiveness are inevitable although the use of force is not. In fact nations should be able to resolve bilateral and even multilateral issues through negotiation. However, when the use of force becomes unavoidable, the military forces come under enormous pressure to avoid collateral damage—to both infrastructure and more importantly to civilians in the war zone.

---

13 Johnson, Loch K., *The Threat on the Horizon: An Inside Account of America's Search for Security After the Cold War*, Oxford University Press, New York, 2011.

In recent times collateral damage has become an emotive issue in the perception of both domestic and international communities, making the political leadership extremely wary of even the slightest collateral damage.

The development of military capabilities is primarily driven by the resource equation of the nation. While resource availability is critical in this context, there is also the nuanced effect of domestic political pressures that tend to superimpose itself on resource allocation. This is an unavoidable factor that all democratic nations face and one that normally restricts the military capabilities rather than improve it, unless there is a clear, direct, immediate and visible threat to national security. Military commanders and planners have to be cognisant of this actual reluctance of the political leadership to invest in the military forces. In other words, capabilities will almost always be less than what would have been the optimum when a military force is operationally deployed. In the current global scenario, this is just a fact that needs to be accepted.

The question of foreign military intervention is complex and needs to be clearly enunciated within the national security strategy. Such interventions have the capacity to go drastically wrong and could have disastrous consequences for the intervening nation and its government, even in the short term. In all such interventions it has to be ensured that national interest is kept as the paramount factor in determining whether or not to intervene as well as the level of intervention that is envisaged. Even so, there may be instances when an intervention is undertaken purely for altruistic reasons, although such occasions may be few and far I between and the actual intervention would in all likelihood be the act of a coalition rather than that of an individual nation. A coalition intervention would mean that a larger interest is at stake and also that there would normally be international approval for the actions being initiated. In all cases, whether national interests are directly affected or not, military intervention remains a double-edged sword, with the intervening nation also likely to face detrimental consequences, both in terms of resource expenditure and possible military casualties.

Chapter 18

MILITARY FORCES IN THE 21st CENTURY

Introduction

There has been a subtle change from the traditional employment of military forces in the past few decades. They are no longer the primary arbiters of national security in a sweeping manner under all circumstances, although they continue to be the foundation on which the concept of security and sovereignty is built. However, nations continue to raise and sustain military forces even if their capabilities are limited, in order to emphasise the independence and sovereignty of the nation. At the same time, the employment of military forces have increasingly become multi-faceted, not merely as defenders of the border.

In the relatively new concept of a whole-of-government approach to national security, military forces have become one of many elements that a nation employs to ensure its stability and security. The military forces are normally employed in their traditional role only after careful consideration. Even in the rare occasion when military forces are employed to apply lethal force, success of their actions depends on defining clearly achievable end-states that are aligned with national security imperatives.

Over the modern era i.e. the post-World War II period, it has been observed that few fundamental principles should be adhered to before employing military forces, especially since the prevalent security scenario has become extremely dynamic. Further, military power now works in tandem with the diplomatic prowess of the nation and often overlaps in creating the desired effects to achieve national security.[1] Contravening these basic principles in the employment of military forces risks failure in achieving satisfactory results.

The concept of national security has been evolving ever since the term was formally accepted when it was enshrined in the National Security Act of 1947 in the USA.[2] Since the military forces continue to form the foundation of activities aimed at ensuring national security, their role of military forces also continue to change to fit the circumstances and context. The result has been an expansion of the activities that have become the responsibility of the military forces. This expansion has been largely towards the non-warfighting side of activities in the broad spectrum of military functions. These functions, such as the delivery of humanitarian aid and provision of disaster relief, have gradually been under the umbrella of 'military operations', with their own changing tempo and intensity. The span of military operations are now very broad. As a consequence numerically smaller forces will have difficulty in optimally meeting all the demands that have started to be placed on military forces.

The military forces are the only element of national power that is oriented towards delivering an organised and rapid response to emerging crisis situations.[3] Therefore, governments turn to military forces when a challenge to national security arises, as the choice element for a first response action. At other times, the military forces are also the proverbial 'stick' that accompanies the 'carrot' that is the developmental aid and other assistance that is provided by the more developed world to lesser developed nations. In the liberal mindset, these should be given with absolutely no caveats attached, which is an

---

1 Kainikara, Sanu, 'Principles of War and Air Power', *APDC Working Paper 31*, op cit.

2 *Milestones: 1945 – 1952*, National Security Act of 1947, Office of the Historian (USA), https://history.state.gov/milestones/1945-1952/national-security-act accessed on 17 July 2018.

3 Mills, John R., 'All Elements of National Power: Re-Organizing the Interagency Structure and Process for Victory in the Long War', *Strategic Insights(E-Journal)*, Volume V, Issue 6, July 2006, Centre for Contemporary Conflict, Naval Postgraduate School, Monterey, California., 2006. http://www.nps.edu/Academics/centers/ccc/publications/OnlineJournal/2006/Jul/millsJul06.html accessed on 17 July 2018.

utopian dream. In the real world, aid is always accompanied by some demands of the receiving nation as a quid pro quo and the military is a fall-back option to entrench the deterrence.

The roles and responsibilities that are placed on the military forces only increase in numbers and seriousness as the world moves on to a more dynamic and volatile security environment. This situation is becoming clear in an overarching assessment of the capacity of other elements of national power to ensure security. At the strategic level of national security it is seen that most of the other elements of national power are struggling to define their roles in the broader national security equation. For these elements national security is not the main focus, but is considered the by-product of their core actions that seem to be focused on some other factors, at times with no connection to national security. There is a fundamental necessity in democratic nations to do a comprehensive overhaul of the contribution of the elements of national power and their connection to national security.

In the second half of the 20th century, a large number of independent states emerged as a result of the rapid de-colonisation that took place at the end of World War II.[4] In many of these newly independent nations, struggling with establishing democratic norms, the military force was the only stable element within the government. Their role in ensuring the stability of the nation became a critical element to retaining the sanctity of fragile states. In these circumstances it became easy for the military leadership to take over the government, especially when the civilian leadership proved that they were not up to the task of guiding the nation through the initial uncertainty that comes with 'independence'. Unfortunately a number of military forces and their leadership succumbed to the temptation, almost always with disastrous and long-lasting results. The military forces, especially of the newly de-colonised nations, must keep the needs of the nation paramount and resist the temptation to assume power. Democracy can only survive when the military force ensures its paramountcy.

Contemporary military forces have also been forced into a situation of having to wage Information Warfare that now adds to the total

---

4   *Decolonization*, https://www.ssag.sk/studovna/files/Decolonization.pdf accessed on 17 July 2018

effect that can be created in times of conflict. This has been the result of contemporary conflicts evolving into amorphous and asymmetric employment of lethal force. Contemporary conflict has been termed, Irregular War or Hybrid War and information warfare contributes to creating the desired effects to achieve the necessary end-state and objectives. Because of the complex nature of contemporary conflict, communications assume added importance in the employment of military forces in the modern context. All these requirements make the military forces itself a complex organisation that could become a monolithic entity, if not carefully crafted. This the main reason why force structure and force posture have assumed critical positions in any modern military force.

The Cold War ended around 1989–1991. However, even after three decades, the military forces of the democratic world continue to be influenced by the Cold War context in their appreciation of the challenges they would face and the response actions required of them. In the meantime the security environment has changed rapidly and drastically. Even if the military forces have realised that their own conceptual development is not keeping pace with the changes taking place in the global security arena, there has not been sufficient impetus or focus to ensure that measures necessary to bring the military forces 'up to speed' have been instituted. The rate of evolution of the military forces have been far too slow in relation to the security environment. This drawback will result in the military forces having to catch up after the crisis has erupted. Obviously this is not the optimum situation.

Even though the conduct of combat operations continue to remain the primary role of military forces, there are a plethora of other missions also thrust on them. In the context of an irregular war, another major role given to the military forces is to influence the local people that has been termed as 'winning the hearts and minds' in common jargon. However, winning over the favour of the local population in an irregular war scenario requires a large number of military personnel on the ground, which would be far in excess of the numbers that nations normally permit to be employed in the contemporary context. Irregular wars, the normal contemporary conflict, is war among the people, fought for winning the support of the people. Achieving this objective would require a different set of capabilities in the military forces and is likely to stretch the capacity of these forces.

21st century military forces face the challenge of having to conduct humanitarian aid and disaster relief operations on one end of the spectrum of operations, while being ready to rapidly transition to the conduct of high-end conventional warfare on the other end. Transitioning from the low-end of the technology spectrum to the highest end is a formidable task, made more difficult by the need to do so rapidly. The employment of military forces also has a variable tempo and intensity, making the entire exercise complex and complicated. In addition, the current trend is for military forces to be engaged in coalition operations, which brings with it its own compound and involved challenges. The military forces have to develop and imbibe a different group of skill sets to be successful in coalition operations.

From being defenders of a nation-state's sovereign borders a century back, a national military force has evolved into a totally different entity, built around its core role of ensuring national security and all that involves. An efficient military force will encompass the capacity and capability to respond to a constantly changing security environment that alters the very concept of national security in a contextual manner.[5]

Fundamentals of Employing Military Forces

All independent nations maintain military forces of some sort, even if the competence of some of these forces is questionable. This fact testifies to the acceptance of the fundamental requirement to have at least a minimum level of military capabilities within the national elements of power. In a number of cases, the military forces may not even have the capability to ensure the security of the nation but are still maintained as an institution for the purpose of emphasising the independent status of the nation. The employment of military forces in support of national security has undergone significant changes in the past few centuries. Unlike in the 19th and first half of the 20th

---

5 O'Rourke, Ronald, 'A Shift in the International Security Environment: Potential Implications for Defense—Issues for Congress', *Congressional Research Service Report*, Washington, 26 April 2018. https://fas.org/sgp/crs/natsec/R43838.pdf accessed on 17 July 2018.

centuries, they are no longer employed as the only tool to protect national interests. This is so since the perception of national security itself has undergone dramatic changes and is no longer confined to the physical protection of the national boundaries. National security is now very broadly defined as the protection of national interests and values that may not even be physically connected to the geographic boundaries of the state. It is accepted now that national security is a combination of an undefined 'sense' of security within the population and the objective reality of freedom from aggression.[6] In these conditions, the concept a whole-of-government approach to national security would deliver optimum results. Such an approach would mean that all elements of national power—grouped for ease of understanding under the generic heads of diplomacy, information, military and economy—would have to be brought to bear at the appropriate level and intensity to ensure national security.

In these circumstances, the employment of military forces would have to be done within some clearly defined parameters and principles. However, in democracies certain factors will always impinge on their effective employment. First, the strategic aspects of war and peace are diffused in nature and not clearly understood by everyone involved in the employment of military forces. This is particularly so of the civilian political decision-makers who at best would only have a superficial knowledge of military affairs. There will be a great deal of difficulty in making the political masters understand the nuances of the application of military force in the pursuit of national security. There is a secondary issue that rises from this less than optimum situation. The military leadership would have to stand-up to the political decision-makers when the expectations of what the military is tasked to achieve are unreasonable. However, they should also be able to maintain a balance in achieving the political objectives within the capacity of the military. This is an onerous and complex balancing act to perform. Failure to achieve the right balance could see the military being either stretched beyond its capacity or becoming an under-achieving entity that would have its own tangible repercussions.

---

6 Omand, Sir David, 'Securing the State: National Security in Contemporary Times', *RSIS Working Paper No 251*, S. Rajaratnam School of International Studies, Singapore, 6 November 2012, p. 6.

The second factor that will have to be carefully considered is the methodology to apply military force to achieve limited objectives. By virtue of its very nature, military forces are oriented towards destroying the assets of the adversary and 'neutralising' the opposing forces. This was perhaps an acceptable feature even as late as World War II. However, sensibilities and the level of acceptable damage have changed and in the current circumstances, more often than not the military forces are not permitted to bring to bear the full extent of their warfighting capabilities. The requirement to achieve limited objectives creates a dichotomy within the concepts of its application that is normally aimed at obtaining victory in conflict. Here again, the military leadership will have to shoulder the burden of de-conflicting the disparate requirements and to achieving the strategic goal of the nation. These are limiting factors that must be recognised and overcome to pave the way for the employment of military forces to be successful.

More important than mitigating the limiting factors completely is the necessity to adhere to certain basic principles in the There are four principles that must be considered before resorting to the application of military forces. First, is a fall out from the fact that the prevailing security environment is dynamic and will continue to be so at least into the mid-term future. These circumstances will create friction or struggle between policy and strategy, which will be difficult to ameliorate. No conflict or war can ever be a set-piece affair and the military forces that prevail would always be the one that is able to adapt to the ever-changing priorities of the battlefield faster than the adversary. Such adaptations will invariably lead to an intense interplay between policy and strategy. On the other hand, the day a military force stops to adjust to the evolving conflict scenario is the day that it will start to lose battles, campaigns and subsequently wars. In the present context, it is more likely that a conventional military force would be involved in irregular wars (IW), wherein success is iterative and not decisive. The unique feature that develops from this situation in which no decisive victory is possible is that strategy will have to evolve along with the conduct of the conflict.[7]

---

7   Mullen, Admiral Mike, 'Chairman's Corner: Three Principles for the Use of Military Force', *Release to American Forces Press Service*, http://www.au.af.mi./ aunews/archive/2010/0506/Article 0506/Mullen0506.htm accessed on 18 March 2010.

Second, in the contemporary world, military power can never be considered the last resort of the nation and it should not be used as such. It could perhaps be the first element of national power to be employed directly, but it should never be the only one to be used in the long term. The flexibility and rapid response capability of military forces invariably make them the first-choice option in times of emergencies ranging from providing humanitarian aid in response to natural or man-made calamities to the other extreme of a dire national security challenge. However, in every case, the immediate reaction through the military has to be followed up by other elements of national power at the appropriate time. Military power and diplomacy are no longer discrete elements but must complement each other at all times.[8] In fact diplomacy thrives within the shadow cast by military power projection capabilities and it can be seen that when military capabilities of a nation are in decline, the diplomatic persuasiveness and coercive power also tend to become limited. The military shadow is a safe place for the other elements of national power to operate under. In the case of IW it would seem prudent to employ military forces only after all other elements of national power has been committed, other than for the initial phase when physical stabilisation of the environment might be necessary.

Third, the actual application of force, especially in the case of IW, should be done carefully in a precise and principled manner. Carefully applied force would mean not only that it is accurate, but also that it is both proportionate to the need and discriminate in neutralising targets. Such an approach tends to improve the chances of limiting collateral damage,[9] which is one of the fundamental dictums of the application of force in IW. In IW, the strategic battlefield is the minds of the people and winning in that space requires a fundamental understanding of the thought-process of the adversary and the target population, as well as limiting unnecessary damage to life and property—avoiding collateral damage.

The fourth principle is the prerequisite to have the depth of force necessary to be able to maintain the required tempo of operations for the desired timeframe. This is of particular importance since campaigns

---

8   ibid.

9   ibid.

and operations can, and usually do, last longer than envisaged in the planning stage. Depth of force requires nuanced balancing of strategy, capability and resources. This an arduous task that can only be achieved by professional masters of military science. The understanding of resources—financial, materiel and human—comes from experience, training and knowledge that is gathered over a long time. Further there will always be debates and disagreements regarding decisions based on accepted policies and the execution of strategy. The need is to keep the gaps between policy decisions and strategy execution from becoming dichotomies that cannot be resolved.

The Evolving Role of the Military Forces

The role of the military forces was well defined and stayed the same for a few centuries till the mid-20th century. After World War II, the concept of national security started to evolve at a much faster pace than was initially envisaged in the 1950s. This automatically meant that the military forces, until then almost the sole element in ensuring the sovereignty of the nation, also had to evolve to fill the new areas that they were required to operate in and to accept certain amount partnership from other elements of national power. This development also meant that in some cases, the military forces would function in a supporting role or in rare occasions may not even have direct involvement in the actions being initiated in the pursuance of national security. In essence, the role of the military forces have now become far more inclusive than to merely fight and win wars. However, even without having to fight wars, the tempo of operations of the military force in the 21st century will remain high as they are saddled with an increasing number of disparate roles.

Today, the military forces of a nation is tasked with a broad spread of tasks to perform ranging from the benign to the application of catastrophic force—from humanitarian assistance and disaster relief (HADR) to fighting a war of national survival. This has come to pass because along with the changing perceptions of national security the democratic governments have also recognised the need to have a proactive and reactive element of national power that can be finely tuned to be in full alignment with national security priorities. With its built-in flexibility and adaptability, as well as ready availability, the military forces became the choice option to create such a standing force. Over the past few decades military forces have therefore been gradually transformed and have become rare and valuable assets that are now regularly used to signal concern, intent and willingness of a nation to act, both internationally and domestically.[10] Military forces are now the first element of national power that is used to demonstrate humanitarian concerns as well as political determination to safeguard national interests.

With a whole-of-government approach to national security becoming prevalent, all elements of national power become involved in operations to a greater or lesser extent in a contextual manner. In this scenario, military forces become a critical element in ensuring a safe and secure environment for the other agencies to operate in an uninhibited manner. In the case of providing humanitarian assistance or operating in an expeditionary manner, building relationships through interaction between the military forces of like-minded nations also assumes an important role in enhancing mutual understanding that underpins stability. Three major factors have dramatically increased the importance of military forces to democratic governments around the world, making them a crucial, if not critical, element in any national security calculus.[11]

First, the present day military forces have a large spread of capabilities that can be brought to bear in myriad circumstances. This ability automatically catapults the military forces of a nation to a position of pre-eminence when there is a need to act to preserve national security. Global airlift capabilities, enhanced agility in contenting with multiple and disparate challenges simultaneously, rapid reaction capabilities that can be brought to bear in both military and non-military situations, and in extremis, the ability to apply force with lethality, precision, proportionality and discrimination makes military forces a formidable element of national power that can only be ignored at the peril of diminishing national security.

Second, while the risk of conventional conflict between states has reduced considerably, foreign relations now play an increased role in

---

10 Yates, Athol, 'What Defence Really Does', *Canberra Times*, Canberra, ACT, 2 July 2012.

11 ibid.

securing a nation. At the same time providing foreign aid, diplomatic initiatives and trade policies that favour a particular nation have all declined in their usefulness as tools to effect influence in order to secure the nation because of their reduced impact on the recipient country. Therefore, an increasing number of nations have come to rely more on their military forces to stiffen their ability to implement foreign policy initiatives. This employment is more in the soft power region through implied and actual coercion and delves into the hard power part of military forces in extreme cases. In these rare cases, foreign policy initiatives could be considered to have failed. Military forces, employed in a nuanced manner is an effective sign of a nation's foreign policy intent.

Third, in most democracies, there is a trend for the public to take more interest in the military forces that they effectively own, even if in an indirect manner. This greater sense of ownership is the result of years of keeping the military forces under a cloak of semi-secrecy from the public and the subsequent disconnect felt by the military and civilians alike regarding the real purpose of expending the resources that keep a military force battle ready. In the 21st century, active democracies have become extremely transparent and it is not possible to obfuscate the employment of military forces or conceal military operations and their aftermath in terms of own and enemy casualties, financial and other resource implications and most importantly, a comparison between the result that was intended and achieved. While on the one hand these circumstances could be viewed as being restrictive to the freedom of action of a government, they could also be a factor in making it easier for the government to employ military forces within a broader set of circumstances. This would lead to the government having a larger number of options to choose from in the event of a national security challenge.

The primary function of military forces will obviously continue to be ensuring the security of the nation although the discharge of that responsibility could involve them carrying out a number of roles that were not so far within their remit. This is a consequence of the evolving definitions and perceptions of national security. The priority has subtly shifted from the physical defence of the nation's borders towards a broader and long term security option achieved through the protection of national interests wherever they may happen to be, in a global manner. Accordingly the military forces should have the ability to deploy to far flung areas at short notice and also offer affordable flexibility to respond to emerging threats. By any measure these requirements are onerous and military forces will find it hard to meet them effectively. The answer to this vexed issue could be the adoption of an effects-based approach in the application of military forces. This would focus the effort required to achieve the desired end-state thereby reducing the need to employ the full spectrum of military capabilities to an as required basis. In an obtuse manner this could be termed an asymmetric approach by a conventional force to gain the advantage over the adversary.

Without doubt this approach and the broader responsibility leading to a larger spectrum of possible roles for the military forces would have a direct impact on its force structure. The increasing spread of roles that a military force would be expected to perform would mean that creating and maintaining a fully balanced force would become extremely resource-intensive. This will be beyond the capacity of most nations to achieve, especially in the current cash strapped environment. The alternative therefore will be to create a focussed force with sufficient built-in flexibility to be able to switch roles when necessary. Since it is unlikely that a military force would be required to engage in the full spread of its possible roles simultaneously, this approach would seem to be a viable option.

Military Forces in Fragile States

The decolonisation that enveloped the world in the wake of World War II also created a large number of 'independent' nations, which in short order became untenable in terms of economic viability and societal stability. The common factor across all these fragile nations was that the colonial powers had left behind a relatively coherent military force. With the nation decidedly declining into chaos, it was tempting for the newly appointed commander of the military forces to assume control of the government machinery. Most such takeovers were well meant and done in the spirit of looking out for the nation than to further personal ambitions. However, the old adage that power corrupts and absolute power corrupts absolutely, almost always comes into play. It is a noticeable trend that once the military takes over a nation, they are reluctant to hand the nation over, or to institute democratic processes to bring back civilian rule. The coups in Fiji and Pakistan in the past few decades are examples that can be studied to demonstrate this challenge.

The role of the military in fragile and failing states is critical to their stability.[12] Most of these nations are not established democracies and suffer from economic, social and political instability. While they flirt with democracy in the initial period immediately following the decolonisation, these states lack the depth of education necessary for a people to understand the basics of democracy and even the elected representatives do not follow a strict code of conduct. This situation inevitably leads to decline in government control, opposition to the ruling party and eventually to armed insurgencies—a climate tailor made for the intervention of the military. The military in most of these cases consider themselves the guardians of national sovereignty and feel the moral compulsion to intervene to put things 'right'. There have been a few instances of the military willingly handing back power to an elected government after the military has conducted elections and then returning to the barracks. However, these are perhaps the aberrations rather than the rule.

One of the reasons for the military to hold on to power after they have taken over, even for altruistic reasons, is the control of the military-industrial complex or external aid that comes through the military forces. Considering that the fragile states being analysed are all on the brink of economic collapse, the commercial and economic stakes, both personal and national, become too high for the military leadership to willingly hand over control. It takes a mindset not commonly found in human beings, to be able to act in complete harmony with the needs of the nation while subsuming personal ambition and wellbeing.

Contemporary Conflict: War in the Information Age

Conflict at the tactical level has remained the same for centuries—it is about neutralising the adversary's ability to inflict damage to oneself by taking appropriate measures, including killing adversary forces when required. The methods adopted to achieve this end-state has changed

---

12 Carlin, Mara E., *Building Militaries in Fragile States: Challenges for the United States*, University of Pennsylvania Press, Philadelphia, 2017.

with a number of factors, the most important being the technology-facilitated improvement in the efficacy of applying force. While the fundamentals at the tactical level have remained the same, colossal changes have taken place in the manner in which a conflict is fought at the strategic level, the medium in which the most effective actions are undertaken and perhaps most importantly, the political end-state that is required to be achieved.

Contemporary conflict is principally about ensuring the support of a population, a fight to win the hearts and minds of the people on a massive scale. More than fifty per cent of the conflict is conducted within the medium of communications or in the information sphere. In fact conflict can now be assumed to be fought as much in the broader virtual area of communications as in the physical sphere. The fundamentals of conflict is straight forward. Conflicts arise when two parties (individuals, groups, nations) do not agree with each other or when their fundamental beliefs are not compatible. Essentially this means that conflict takes place at both the physical as well as the cognitive domain. In other words, conflict manifests as divergent and at times contradictory behaviour patterns that in turn leads to physical actions that are detrimental to peaceful coexistence. The dichotomy in behaviour patterns and, at the highest level of the cognitive domain, in the belief system creates a situation wherein the conflict has to be fought and won both in the battlefield and through the medium of the 'communications revolution' that is sweeping the world.[13] The use of internet proxies to attack the adversary is becoming more prevalent in all conflicts. In turn this situation demands a cultural shift in the military forces in the understanding and approach to conflict in order to be effective, they have to understand and be able to function in the sphere of Information Warfare (IW).

Information. Information is the end product of the collection and collation of data and the first step towards knowledge generation. Uninterrupted information flow is the critical ingredient to creating the level of knowledge necessary to ensure a robust decision-making process that is in turn necessary to move the military forces towards

---

13 Lonsdale, David J., *The Nature of War in the Information Age: Clausewitzian Future*, Frank Cass, London, 2004. (Chapter 4: How Strategic is Strategic Information War?)

a position of superiority. Information is fundamental to creating Situational Awareness (SA) in the decision-making body, which then can create a rapid response and also transfer the necessary information to the appropriate agencies. From a military perspective, real-time communications assume great importance to ensure the veracity of decisions. Further, the success of information operations in a joint campaign depends on the military hierarchy creating a single focal point for the creation of information superiority and SA. This point should also be able to function as a filter to avoid the politicisation of information that is used to direct military operations in the field.

Information Warfare

IW is low risk and comparatively less resource intensive while being able to achieve the same or similar results as conventional wars. If a nation and its military forces have the capability to wage IW on an 'industrial' scale, the chances of success increases manifold. There are distinct advantages to adopting IW as one element of a multi-elemental military capability. Primarily, effective IW will be able to influence the morale of the adversary at a far lower cost in both military and political costs as well as with minimal resource expenditure. If conducted within a strict protocol, IW can be converted to deliver the proverbial 'death by a thousand cuts' by gradually bleeding the adversary of the capacity of their elements of defence to function properly.

It is not difficult to imagine that a modern conventional conflict will have an equal part being played out in the IW arena as the physical application of force. Only a military force that is capable of functioning in a congruent manner in the economic and information spheres while also being able to conduct warfare with the kinetic application of force as well as proxy wars will succeed under these circumstances.[14] This is a broad sweep of capabilities, which are resource-intensive and therefore, most nations would find it difficult to embody all of them in their military forces. This circumstance is being addressed by the formation of alliances between like-minded nations that compensate

---

14 Richards, General Sir David, *Future Conflict and Its Prevention: People and the Information Age,* address to the International Institute of Strategic Studies, London, 18 January 2010.

for the inability of individual nations to resource military capabilities adequately.

Information warfare as such is not a new concept—it has been practiced from ancient times whenever wars have been fought. Further, information has been the basis for decision-making during war and peace from time immemorial. The change that has taken place in more modern times is the access to information and the generality of such information that is disseminated in an uncontrolled manner. In recent times access to information has changed from a situation of producer push to customer pull, which makes concise military responses to information leak difficult.[15] Such fundamental shifts in inputs to warfighting is not a common occurrence and happens only once in a few generations. Changes that have taken place in IW are to be considered in this realm.

The quantum leap in information technology and its ubiquitous spread into the military forces that in turn has directly affected the conduct of war compels all competent military forces to question old assumptions. It is pertinent to note here that modern military forces, especially in the more stable democracies of the world, had been lulled into complacency at the end of the Cold War. Information gathering became a purely technological enterprise at the cost of losing the vast network of human intelligence gathering machinery. The information revolution that brought about a borderless entity to defend almost immediately highlighted the gaps in intelligence gathering which is the foundation for information availability. The military forces are now faced with a situation where the physical sovereign borders of the nation have become the easiest to defend while the vast borderless expanse of information is becoming increasingly difficult to protect and complex even to police effectively. There are no clear-cut borders to defend anymore.

Another aspect of information technology is the speed and reach on modern media and the direct influence that they bring to bear on all aspects of national security, particularly when the military forces are employed. Media now plays an extremely important role and can be considered to be part of IW. The irregular forces that fight insurgencies

---

15 ibid.

for a variety of reasons tend to manipulate the media through the control of information denial as well as information dissemination processes. In the past few decades it has been seen that regular military forces are not 'media-savvy' or as adept at information manipulation as the irregular forces that they confront. This could be the result of excessive secrecy traditionally associated with military operations and the reluctance of governments to permit information access to the media for fear of compromising on-going operations. From an IW perspective, this could be self-defeating and military forces have been forced to reform their rules regarding the engagement of media during conflict situations.

Contemporary Conflict: The Military Response

From the perspective of conventional national military forces, contemporary conflict is multi-faceted and therefore, a multi-agency and normally a multi-national enterprise. In addition, the adversaries have become increasingly agile, are primarily irregular in nature, and are experts in the employment of unconventional and constantly evolving tactics. In essence they have mastered the art of creating asymmetry to avoid the overwhelming combat power of conventional military forces. The situation is volatile since the development of tactics and counter-tactics is a continuous process and the success or failure of a battle, operation or campaign could hinge on the ability of the force to adapt rapidly to emerging situations. The amorphous form of the irregular force with diffused and decentralised command and control processes, where they do indeed exist, makes them far more adept at adjusting to emergent situations. From experience the military forces have understood the central lesson of having a command and control structure that is capable of rapidly catering to changes that take place in the battlespace. This entails not merely the adaption of a previously existing and proven command structure, but the creation of innovative structures that can be put in place and undone with equal ease. An agile command and control structure is a foundational requirement for military forces to succeed in achieving their objectives.

The military forces have the onerous responsibility of having to cater for the ever-changing strategic and economic environment. This is not an easy task and adding to the complexity is the greater emphasis that is being placed on conflict prevention in recent times, rather than engagement in physical combat to achieve victory. This is because the international community has recognised the need to prevent conflict if failing states, especially in the economic sense, are to be assisted out of their current situation and avoid their becoming failed states with all the security challenges that it brings. In these circumstances the military is required to participate in the capability building required to transform a failing state into a stable situation. The military contribution in this case would be creating a viable security apparatus as well as developing other non-security elements of national strength.

The Military Dilemma

Military forces of the democratic world still suffer from a throw-back to the Cold War era, when the primary requirement was to oppose an adversary who was almost a replica of themselves. The global security scenario has altered considerably in the intervening nearly three decades between the end of the Cold War and the current environment. This preoccupation with pure conventional capabilities have made the military forces more prepared to enter into combat operations more suited to a previous era rather than being able to cater for emerging trends in warfighting.[16] In other words, the relevance of some of the military forces to the prevailing context in which they operate can be questioned. In this context the budgetary pressures that all military forces of the world are being subject to have to be considered as a crucial factor in their inability to adapt and alter their basic structure.

While the ability to conduct combat operations is a primary and critical requirement for all military forces, this capability is no longer sufficient in itself for the force to be considered a balanced one. Modern employment of military forces require them to be able to influence the people while they are operating amongst the populace. This requires mass in numbers, something that flies in the face of determined rolling back of the numerical capacity of military forces in most democracies. Further, influencing people requires the military to be able to be able to show their presence on the ground and other areas of the littoral as well as deep within the adversary territory. This requires the numbers

---

16 Smoler, Fredric, 'Fighting the Last War—and The Next', *American Heritage*, Vol 52, Issue 8, November/December 2001, https://www.americanheritage.com/content/fighting-last-war%E2%80%94and-next accessed on 19 June 2017.

necessary to put 'boots-on-the-ground', sufficiency in littoral landing crafts, adequate number of transport aircraft and helicopters to project power rapidly in faraway places when necessary. The ratio of military personnel who could interact with the target population has to be high if the influence is to be at least semi-permanent. It is also necessary to ensure that the military personnel entrusted with the interaction be of high quality so that the possibility of misinterpretation of interactions is minimised. This situation translates to the calibre of personnel itself being converted to capability.

While the battle to influence the target population could be considered a low-end mission when the area of operations is not heavily contested military forces will also have to continually maintain high-end capabilities of the appropriate calibre in order to deter potential adversaries. At the same time, at the tactical level, the need to fight and win hard battled with the adversary will not recede or even become secondary in priority. The determining factor in developing capabilities would be the threat perception and the perceived employment of the military forces in a contextual manner. The tempo of operations and the scale of the possible employment will be the key discriminator in determining the quantum of capabilities necessary as well as the development of the force structure. The two almost contrary requirements—of having to influence a target population predominantly through the application of 'soft power' although in the guise of military forces; and maintaining a level of high-end and lethal capabilities within the same force—while also being assailed by budgetary constraints creates a dilemma for all military forces. There is no simple solution to ameliorating these twin challenges, but careful planning through capability and force structure development processes can lessen the impact.

Contemporary conflict is a war for the people, fought on the human terrain, and require a minimum critical mass in terms of personnel in order to have a chance at succeeding. This would entail encompassing the capacity to reach and influence ungoverned areas through sufficiency in airlift and brown water littoral capabilities. On the other hand a war of technology permits, in certain circumstances, the replacement of personnel with technology, ideas, concepts and processes. However, this is not an optimum solution and could fail if the technology being brought to bear can be bested by asymmetry. Therefore, a calculated balance between technology and mass must be maintained in the structure of the force being employed. Such a balance is necessary since purely high-end warfighting capabilities alone will not be sufficient to win an irregular war.

Force Structure

Force structure is the basis upon which the fighting abilities of the military force is built. There will always be debate regarding the correct balance to be maintained between high- and low-end capabilities, between technology reliance and people-delivered capabilities, and between the tactical requirements of the force in relation to the balance to be maintained with strategic capabilities.[17] The decision will have to be made taking into account a number of factors, the most important being the perceived characteristics of the next conflict. As discussed earlier, the optimum situation will be to maintain the structure for creating a balanced force-in-being. However, this may be beyond the financial and other resource capabilities of a majority of nations and therefore a careful judgement has to be made between creating the structure for a balanced force and one that could be termed a 'focussed' force. A focussed force would be one that has the in-built ability to be optimised for a chosen conflict scenario rapidly while still having a minimum overall balance.

It is certain that in the immediate to mid-term future, military forces would be required to combat irregular forces, probably in an expeditionary mode. The prevalent and emerging international security environment suggests this to be true. While the combat capabilities required to overcome these threats would be conventional in nature, they have to be extremely sophisticated and capable of adapting at short notice. The need to maintain a minimum level of balance while also being able to focus points towards the development of multi-role capabilities as opposed to narrowly focussed ones. This would also entail the loss of niche capabilities, but would maximise flexibility

---

17 Cancian, Mark, 'Military Force Structure: Trade-Offs, Trade-Offs, Trade-Offs', *Breaking Defense*, 27 February 2018, https://breakingdefense.com/2018/02/military-force-structure-trade-offs-trade-offs-trade-offs/ accessed on 3 March 2018.

and minimise operational sustainment costs. In the current resource constrained circumstances there is no other option.

Attributes of a 21st Century Military Force

Military forces of a sovereign nation represent the values that are important to the people and are supposed to be the sentinels of 'freedom' for them. The characteristics of such a military force have altered through history, even while the fundamental requirement has remained unchanged. Over the years the attributes necessary for the military force to be an effective element of national power have changed. A 21st century military force must embed certain characteristics in itself to ensure that it remains relevant to the nation and its security imperatives. The essential attributes are briefly explained below.

Expanding Spectrum of Roles. In the past few decades the role of the military forces have expanded beyond all conceivable limits. They now span a spectrum that start at the lowest end of delivering humanitarian assistance to ward off natural and/or human created disasters, through armed conflict to total war. Beyond that the responsibility goes on to encompass post-conflict stabilisation and even reconstruction. It is critical for the military forces to have this expanded capability spectrum to ensure the nation's ability to influence and shape regional and global security trends.

Assessment. At the strategic level, the military forces should be able to carry-out accurate assessment of the threat scenario, both existing as well as emerging. This capacity must be augmented by the ability to project future threats with considerable accuracy. Only based on these capabilities would the force be able to arrive at considered risk management strategies. The ability to analyse and inform at the highest levels of national security considerations is vital to the effectiveness of a 21st century military force.

Inter-operability. In any of the possible security scenarios in the 21st century, national security cannot be assured by the military forces alone. All challenges to the sovereignty of a nation will have to be faced with the employment of all elements of national power. Such an approach is the most efficacious way to ensure the safety of the nation. In order to optimise such an approach, the military forces should be able to operate seamlessly with all government agencies and even with some non-government agencies under certain conditions.

Balanced Force. Military forces will need to be balanced with the right mix of capabilities that provide it with both flexibility and adaptability—two increasingly valuable characteristics. These cannot be developed overnight and therefore involves careful forward planning. A balanced force will also need to be interoperable with allies, neighbours and possible coalition partners. The likelihood of a nation going to war or conflict on its own is increasingly becoming remote. Therefore, interoperability with other military forces will have to be incorporated as an essential element through tailored doctrine, commonality of equipment and war-fighting systems, and joint training.

Countering Threats. The concept of protection of the state will have to be achieved in a different manner in the 21st century. The traditional threat of a military intervention, conflict or war has almost vanished, especially in the case of established democracies. The emerging threats are amorphous and non-traditional. They have not been part of the threat perception of military forces in the 20 century. The more serious emerging threats that have global significance can be listed.[18]

- Climate changes that become threat multipliers in already fragile regions

- Increasing competition over resources leading to rivalry between nations. This is compounded by the need to have assured ability to secure vital resources form troubled regions. Military forces would have to 'run interference' in certain cases.

- Uncontained population growth, especially in the less developed parts of the world, that exacerbates poverty-related challenges to security.

- Mass urbanisation and the associated growth of crime that feeds into an international network of security challenges.

---

18 Lee, Marc, 'Avoiding Future Shock as Global Instability Grows,' *Jane's Defence Weekly*, 5 September 2007, p. 27.

- Large-scale migration, at times in waves, from the poor to rich nations that have the potential to destabilise the receiving nations.

- The collapse of governments and the accompanying break-up of societies in fragile and failing states across the world.

Rogue States. More than ever in the past, there are a number of rogue states that want to destabilise their region for a number reasons. Dealing with them is not a purely military matter, it takes a whole-of-government approach. However, military forces will have to take the lead in a number of activities to contain these states and in extremis, resort to the lawful application of force. One attribute of a 21st century military force is its ability to apply the entire cycle of strategies, starting from influencing and shaping the region to carrying out destructive activities, at the appropriate level to contain a rogue state.

Disruptive Technologies. The fast paced changes taking place in developing technologies always bring out some that are disruptive to normal activities. Irregular forces are increasingly looking towards these technologies to defeat conventional military forces. The future forces will have to have the inherent capacity to leverage of these same disruptive technologies to further improve their advantage over irregular forces. There is an increasing need for military forces to function within the disruptive envelope to neutralise the asymmetry of irregular forces. A military force that is reliant only on conventional capabilities will find its combat edge eroding fast in a modern battlefield. The changing demands of national security demands that modern military forces be able to leverage the most disruptive technologies to their own benefit.[19] Success in doing so will be dependent on the ability of the force innovate, adopt and adapt.

Information Age Requirements. The 21st century is the century of information. The Information Age is already a reality and any military force that has not realised this truth and adapted accordingly will become a redundant force within the next few years. Information age demands that military forces be able to analyse and interpret huge volumes of data in order to enable quick and correct decision-making

---

19 Cox,Laura, 'Technology & the Military', *Disruption*, 5 June 2017, https://disruptionhub.com/technology-the-military/ accessed on 20 June 2017.

at all levels of command. Decision-making and robust command and control systems are the foundations for military victory. This fact is being reinforced in the Information Age where the relative speed of decision-making itself becoming a war-winning element in military conflicts.

Military Operations

The role and responsibilities of military forces in securing national interests have continually widened in the past fifty years fundamentally because of the failure of the other elements of national power to assume carriage of their parts of the broad spectrum of activities necessary to secure the nation. In turn this has led an ever widening spectrum of military operations that starts on the benign end at the delivery of humanitarian aid and disaster relief and moves on the other end to the conduct of wars of national survival. The spread in between encompasses all possible situations that a disciplined set of personnel can contribute towards ameliorating. While this has brought greater recognition of the military contribution to the broad concept of national security it has also brought about a situation wherein almost all employment of military forces is now fraught with the real possibility of mission creep. Most of the military forces are capable of absorbing a certain amount of mission creep. However, when operating in an expeditionary mode, mission creep could become unsustainable for a number of reasons, primarily the lack of pre-planning and the non-availability of adequate resources—both personnel and materiel—required to undertake the additional tasks. The outcome is that the combination of the increased spread of the operational spectrum and unavoidable mission creep increases the susceptibility of the military forces to fail.

Armed Humanitarian Intervention

The provision of humanitarian aid and disaster relief is a role that military forces have undertaken for more than half a century. It is now taken for granted that in difficult circumstances the military would be at the vanguard in delivering the necessary assistance to people affected by natural calamities as well as facing man-made disasters. However, the next step in the spectrum is armed intervention—peace keeping and peace enforcement, which could occur in any order. It is also not necessary for such interventions to be a preparatory phase for the delivery of humanitarian aid. Essentially the intervention is almost always aimed at preventing or putting an end to an incipient civil war that is certain to make the country involved a failed state.[20] Such interventions have also been termed 'Foreign Military Intervention' which is perhaps a better descriptor of the actions undertaken in such operations. Although the tempo and intensity of such operations may not always be high, there will be times of spikes in both and therefore, the success of such interventions will be directly dependent on the military forces' ability to adapt to the emerging situation in a contextual manner.

There are a number of pitfalls that must be understood by the intervening nation, especially where the actual employment of force becomes a necessity. Fundamentally, if the intervention has been undertaken in a unilateral manner without sufficient legal backing from the UN, it is certain to draw condemnation from some quarter of the international community. The end of the Cold War was supposed to usher in the era of a unipolar world wherein all nations worked in tandem for world peace. There has not been a greater fallacy. The world today is multipolar and the feeling of international insecurity is all pervasive. Therefore, any intervening country must be able to weather the storm of international criticism. Second, since the intervention is almost always an attempt at putting a lid on a civil war, the military force must ensure that the civilian casualties that will invariably happen as collateral damage must be far less at the final count than would have been the case if the civil war was allowed to run its course. Of course, the ideal would be to avoid civilian casualties all together, but that is almost an impossibility when military forces are employed within the population as will be the case in peace keeping/enforcement operations.

The third issue is that an intervention invariably spawns insurgencies of varied strengths. These will either gradually wither away or become another security challenge to be dealt with. Because such a development is certain to take place, the end result of a military

---

20 Frowe, Helen, 'Judging armed humanitarian intervention', Chapter 6 in Schied, Don E., (ed), *The Ethics of Armed Humanitarian Intervention*, Cambridge University Press, Cambridge, UK, 2014, pp. 95-112.

intervention is always mixed. There have been very few instances of an intervention having been universally declared as a complete success, even when there has been bipartisan support and approval for the intervention per se. From a strategic viewpoint military intervention, while absolutely necessary at times when humanitarian considerations and the concept or 'responsibility to protect' has been evoked, is at best likely to have only an even chance at success. It is more likely to bring in contentious results and accusations of bias on the part of the intervening nation.[21] It is highly unlikely that the intervening nation will emerge from an intervention smelling of roses.

Coalition Operations

In a changing world order, even the most powerful of nations need the legitimacy that a coalition provides to undertake operations that would otherwise have been unilateral. The concept of a 'coalition of the willing' emanated from this need, wherein the lead nation can carry out the campaign as it needs to within the broader umbrella of a coalition. International opinion is something that cannot be shunned anymore. However, creating a coalition is a relatively easy task when compared to making it function as required. The tensions in the actual conduct of operations become much higher when the coalition partners are not traditional allies and when the contribution of the lead-nation is disproportionately high and that of many partners only token. There will invariably be resentment and mistrust, especially if the rules of the coalition are such each partner is following its own rules of engagement and no nation can overrule the selection of targets at the planning level and at the tactical level of operations. In these circumstances holding the coalition together becomes a difficult task. If a coalition breaks up before achieving the desired end-state, it risks losing its legitimacy and is certain to be questioned regarding the legality of its actions.

Coalitions also need to manage risks and threats to keep them at a level that is acceptable to all partner nations. This is like looking for the lowest common denominator and has the potential to 'defang' the coalition if not carefully managed. The level of acceptability of risk, while different in different military forces, will have to be carefully

---

21 Bellamy, Alex J., 'The responsibility to protect and the problem of regime change', Chapter 10 in Schied, Don E., (ed), *op cit.*pp. 166-185.

managed in order to make the coalition effective.²² Further, the acceptable level of risk will also be influenced by circumstances and the context in which the force is being employed. It is also not necessary that traditional allies will automatically have similar threat acceptance levels. A combination of these factors has also had a considerable influence in the development of the concept of the coalition of the willing.

The US has been the lead nation in a large number of coalitions that have been built over the past century. If one single factor stands out regarding the overriding requirement for the success of a coalition it is that at the highest level of the coalition operations, the vision must be that of the needs of a strategic war to be won rather than clamouring for victory in tactical battles. Unfortunately in a majority of the cases, tactical victories have been considered, and touted as, the achievement of strategic objectives. In some extreme cases it can also be seen that there were no strategic war objectives laid down and the desired end-state has been constantly moved along as the campaign progressed. There is no better ingredient to ensure failure of a coalition.

Summing Up...

Military operations have become common place in the past few decades to an extent that there has been no time when at least a peace enforcement mission has not been on-going in some part of the world. That this was not the anticipated state at the end of the Cold War is extraneous to this discussion. Only military forces have the speed, reach, reliability and redundancy to meet emerging national security challenges that now span a very wide spectrum. However, the constant use of military forces makes it difficult for them to train for the future, a lacuna observed specially in numerically small forces. The operating tempo becomes such that training requirements are difficult to meet in their entirety, which in turn leads to a gradual and imperceptible, but continuous degradation of the overall capabilities of the force. This is an unacceptable situation and must be recognised and remedied directly. Military forces have to always be ready to fight the next war,

---

22 Bowman, Steve, 'Historical and Cultural Influences on Coalition Operations', Chapter 1 in Marshall, Thomas, and others (eds), *Problems and Solutions in Future Coalition Operations,* Strategic Studies Institute, US Army War College, Carlisle, PA, 1997, pp. 12-16.

not the last with the complete understanding that the next will never be like the last. The trinity of change that will make this possible is—people, concepts and technology.

The employment of military forces will only meet the national security objectives if there is a transparent relationship between the demonstrated foreign policy fundamentals of the nation and the revealed military capabilities. When this connection is lost, or worse cannot be established, the employment of military forces will invariably be unfocussed, meandering and almost always open-ended. There can be no better recipe for military disaster. Such a situation will be exacerbated when the civilian leadership—that should logically be the controlling element—draws lessons from recent operations that are different and at variance with those the military themselves have distilled. This dichotomy will bring up differences in almost all aspects of capability and force structure development and in extremis can lead to a complete mistrust between the two establishments. Once again, the nation will be on the brink of a security disaster waiting to happen.

Chapter 19

THE MILITARY FORCE AS AN INSTRUMENT OF POLICY

The military forces of a nation can carry out many tasks but their uniqueness is based on the fact that only the lawfully constituted armed forces of a nation is permitted to apply lethal force in the protection of the sovereignty of the nation. They are the only legitimate instrument of the polity permitted to do so. This situation is exemplified by the fact the soldier, while acting on behalf of the nation is said to be employing force rather than being violent. This nuanced distinction in language is necessary to make the principle clear.

In order to establish the status of military forces in 21st century democracies, it is necessary to analyse the utility of force in current times. Their application is seen most of the time to be for constructive purposes, but the damage and destruction that they bring to bear seem to far exceed the benefits that such actions bring to bear. It becomes necessary to focus attention on the employment of military forces through the prism of few factors that have come to signify the important aspects of such actions.

Codifying War

The motivation for a nation to go to war is usually political and from an international perspective it is considered legal if war has been 'declared'. Organised violence, which is considered legal, is always the defining character of war. Since the term violence has unsavoury connotations, the term 'application of force' is normally used in depicting the actions of military forces in prosecuting a war to couch the violence involved and its repercussions. Democratic nations with a clear understanding of the violence that its military force can unleash normally attempt to curtail its use and are reluctant to employ the forces to their fullest extent.

There is an indelible relationship between the conduct of war or the application of force by military forces and the accepted contemporary world order. Contemporary world order is a concept that combines politics, legality of a nation's actions, moral and ethical considerations, socio-economic and cultural ethos of individual nations and their strategic military capabilities.[1] Each of these factors influence the development of the others in different ways and to different extents at different times. Therefore, the world order is never static, it is always in a process of evolution. There is a tendency within liberal democracies to consider the world order and its fluid state to be based on cultural evolution. This is a mistake. This focus on cultural aspects of a nation and its impact on world order overlooks the military facet that shapes world order. Primarily the capacity resident in military forces to deter and coerce, at time through punitive actions, is one that continuously influences the evolution of world order.

War is destructive—in all possible meanings of the word and conducted through the application of the entire cycle of strategies. Democratic nations, considering that they are the flagbearers for the more humane face of the world, attempt to make this harsh truth palatable by adopting two methods. First, they try to legitimise war through the application of altruistic concepts to justify the violence that military forces unleash in the name of fighting a war and the need to win; and second an attempt is made to mitigate the death and destruction through the application of legalistic moral principles of precision, discrimination and proportionality to minimise collateral damage. Further, the democratic nations enforce strict and restrictive Rules of Engagement (ROE) on their military forces as a physical means of making the destruction acceptable and almost unavoidable. This attempt is shored up by developing concepts of operations,

---

1 Gray, Colin S., *Hard Power and Soft Power: The Utility of Military Force as an Instrument of Policy in the 21st Century*, Strategic Studies Institute, US Army War College, Carlisle, PA, April 2011, p. 23.

techniques of application and tactics that seem tailored to reduce the devastation that accompanies war.

In attempting to legitimise the violence that accompanies war, the democratic nations essentially adhere to the 'just war' theory. They accept that the violence perpetuated by a nation, especially when it has been done to defend national sovereignty, can be condones if a moral ethical dimension can be superimposed on their actions. However, at the fundamental level wars are not about the ethics, morality or legality. To a minor extent the legitimacy of the actions in the eyes of the beholder may have a salutary influence on its conduct. Purely from a military perspective, national military forces always fight to win. The 'warrior-ethos' assiduously cultivated across the rank and file of the military force is not about losing or even achieving a stalemate in a war; it is about winning, even if it means the application of unmitigated violence on the adversary.

The Laws of Armed Conflict (LOAC), international law based on common humanity is a commitment to the moral principles that should guide the conduct of war. In real-life situations the LOAC is almost always constrained in its implementation, since complete adherence to it would invariably limit the effectiveness of the application of military force. The laws that have been formulated are broad enough to be left open to interpretation and can normally be exploited to justify the actions of the military forces. The moral aspect of the legal principles lends itself to debate and contest, in terms of whose morality is being enshrined? This brings out the basic question, is there a universally accepted definition of morality?[2]

Democracies attempt to 'civilise' the application of force through the implementation of a number of restrictive initiatives to lessen the impact. However, if a war is fought to win, which is as it should be, death and destruction is an inevitable consequence. The balance to this opposing requirements is to regulate the quantity of destruction and keep it to the bare minimum required to achieve 'victory' as defined by the State. Achieving this balance itself is a double-edged sword: if the application of force is measured in carefully administered doses, its effectiveness reduces, even worse the use of force itself may become

---

2 Kennedy, David, *Of War and Law*, Princeton University Press, Princeton, NJ, 2006, Chapter 3. (For a detailed examination of morality and legal principles)

unpalatable on moral, ethical and political considerations; on the other hand, unrestricted use of military force could lead to the same conclusions, but through a different path. The ability of a military force to deter and coerce is almost completely dependent on its demonstrated capability to apply force in order to punish and destroy. By regulating the capacity of military forces to apply force, democracies are pushing towards making the national forces redundant. This is a slippery path that could gather a momentum of its own, to the detriment of national security.

Democratic nations clearly understand that despite unprecedented technological advances in the methodology, the application of force invariably manifests as violence that creates death and destruction. Military forces are crafted to do just that. Therefore, in open societies they cannot be protected from the moral, ethical and political debate that must essentially follow each war. They will not and cannot also remain above controversy in liberal democracies. While the effectiveness of military forces has improved in the past few decades by an unimaginable quantum, the expectations regarding their ability to achieve the desired end-state with minimal destruction has also been raised, perhaps even more than the technological improvements can deliver. It is inevitable that the nation will sit in moral and political judgement of their actions in a strategic situational and contextual manner.

The nature of war does not change—it has been consistent throughout history. Only its character changes with circumstances and myriad other influences. Clausewitz clearly warned against the pitfalls of confusing the character of war for something that it is not. He also cautioned against attempting to transform war into something that is alien to its nature.[3] In recent times theorists have started to argue that war's nature is somewhat variable and also that Clausewitz had been ambiguous in explaining the nature of war.[4] There is no doubt in the

---

3 Howard, Michael &Paret, Peter, (eds& trans), Carl von Clausewitz, *On War*, Princeton University Press, Princeton, NJ, 1976, p. 88.

4 For a detailed examination of this concept of the variation in the nature of war and an interpretation of Clausewitz on the same theme see, Echevarria II, Antulio J., *Clausewitz and Contemporary War*, Oxford University Press, New York, 2007.

mind of this theorist that political objectives remain the ultimate goal to be achieved by the application of force by military forces.

Since the nature of war remains a constant, it cannot and should not be treated as an extension international law and accepted ethics. Warfare is a violent manifestation of political will and cannot be curbed or wished away through the application of legal and/or ethical restraints. The only possible aberration when war will assume a life of its own will be if and when warfare starts to govern politics rather than the other way. This is a tenuous situation, and all democracies must be aware of this major pitfall. The moral, legal and ethical restraints that liberal democracies attempt to place over the application of force is effective only when a political community capable of imposing them exists as an entity. In this respect, the logic of war and its connection to politics is more important than the actual conduct of the conflict itself.[5]

The Strategic Culture of a Nation

In the past few decades two trends have become clearly visible in the overall security environment. First is the exaggerated importance being placed on the utility of military forces in maintaining world order, which is a US-led concept. The second is the idea of the strategic culture of a nation that is being explored and debated as never before. There is the beginning of a culture of strategic conceptualisation that is applied in a contextual manner and with adequate situational awareness that directly connects to national security.[6] In a similar manner military forces have demonstrated their utility within the national security calculus as an instrument of policy. However, their application to further national security has to be carefully tailored to suit emerging requirements.[7] The application of force and its overarching utility as an instrument of policy at the grand strategic level is influenced by four factors.

---

5 Howard &Paret, *op cit*, pp. 602-5.

6 Colin S. Gray, *op cit*, p.15.

7 For a detailed analysis of the employment of military forces and the broader application of force in pursuance of political objectives read, Rupert Smith, *The Utility of Force: The Art of War in the Modern World*, Allen Lane, London, 2005.

First, military forces are complex entities and cannot be reduced to simplistic organisations. It requires specially trained professionals to manage and direct efficiently. Second, they are meant to be employed in warfare. Contemporary warfare encompasses a very broad spectrum that is varied and multifarious—from conventional to irregular and hybrid types—which require extremely agile professionalism from the forces if they are to succeed. Third, it requires strategic effectiveness to achieve the desired political end-state, upon which the status of the military force depends in terms of its utility as an instrument of policy. The demonstrated strategic effectiveness of the force will in turn also determine the quantum and timeframe of its application. Fourth, military forces cannot assume that the application of force will be homogenous in all cases. There will always be differences in the cultural and strategic approach of adversaries and the desired political end-state will be different in individual circumstances. The strategic circumstances will be continually evolving and in turn will alter application of force.

From the perspective of the utility of military forces as an instrument of policy, the rapid changes taking place in the global security environment must be viewed as evolutionary. Even though some of the changes are fairly rapid in their manifestation, from a policy perspective they will not be revolutionary in their impact. In military forces, only the tactical and lower level operational aspects need to be attuned to accepting rapid changes that may be necessary to be instituted. At the strategic level the flexibility of military forces should be such that all changes are imposed in a gradual evolutionary manner.

Principles and Necessity

Democratic nations normally function within a set of broad and self-imposed principles that have acceptance because of historic use and perceptions. Most of the time, the she strategic culture of a nations fits into the principles, although there is a cyclical inter-dependency between the two. As a general rule, more permissive the fundamental guiding principles of a nation are, more flexible will be the strategic culture. At the next lower level, the spectrum for the application of military forces will be the largest when the strategic culture is the most flexible.

The national principles of a nation is always impacted and trimmed by its perceived necessity. Further, the choice whether to employ force to achieve national objectives is available to a nation most of the time, except in extreme cases of threat to national survival. Even so, the utility of force as a principle of national security is not an abstraction. However, it is necessary to superimpose Clausewitz's 'friction' on to the violence that is an inevitable accompaniment to the employment of military forces.[8]

Paradoxically, moral restraint influences national policy much more than it is given actual credit for in regular discourses. It is one of the fundamental factors that limits the ferocity of war and enhances the political aspects. Functioning within the broader set of national principles, considered morality restrains a nation from moving towards absolute war and the use of catastrophic force to achieve its objectives. Since war has the potential to achieve mutual destruction, the moral aspect of political principles holds this possibility in check. On the other hand, the utility of military forces is determined by political objectives and their achievability vis-à-vis national capacity and only peripherally influenced by the character and capability of the force per se. Therefore, it is highly unlikely that a war will be fought completely free of any moral or political compulsions.

The right to go to war is a discretionary phenomenon, even when it is done within the ambit of international law. However, under duress in actual war conditions, the restrictions—moral, ethical, legal—are allowed to slip, as long as the military forces are seen to be functioning within the legal boundaries laid by international law. In these conditions, national policies that are devised within the 'conventions of war' will tend to be tempered with self-interest more than moral or ethical considerations. The fact is that necessity always trumps altruistic principles. National rules of engagement (ROE) are always determined in terms of what is most advantageous for the nation in order to dominate the conflict environment.[9]

---

8 Howard & Paret, *op cit*, pp. 117-123.

9 Schelling, Thomas C., *Arms and Influence*, Yale University Press, New Haven, CT, 1966. See for a detailed analysis of the conventions of war, international law, national interests and the application of military forces, especially Chapter 1.

There is an indelible connection between national principles and policies. In an utopian construct policies should reflect principles fully. However, there is a dichotomy in attempting to achieve this rather esoteric outcome. Policies are pragmatic appreciations of contemporary and near-term future and are almost always prescriptive, whereas principles are designed to permit ambiguity and broad interpretations. The effective employment of military forces is done by optimising the balance between principles, policies and strategy to achieve political objectives. Within the national security equation this makes the military forces the ultimate instrument of policy, because it is a clear expression and manifestation of state violence.[10] In this environment, the imposition of ethics and morality are essentially contextual.

Under normal circumstances, military forces will be employed within principles considerations and laid down national policies. The debate is regarding the understanding of what is 'normal' in a generally accepted manner and thereafter how a nations defines its own 'normal'. Even when this conundrum has been effectively solved, it is seen that principles will get left behind on the wayside when the situation evolves beyond the accepted 'normal'; pragmatic policy will take over the strategy for the employment of military forces.

Soft Power, Military Forces and Economic Strength

Soft power is a nebulous and imprecise concept and therefore is defined as what it is not, rather than for itself—anything that is not hard power is soft power. Hard power is defined as 'the ability purposefully to inflict pain or reward in the pursuit of influence.'[11] In the case of a nation, it is convenient to directly identify hard power with military and economic instruments of policy. Soft power is difficult to calibrate or measure and to manipulate as an entity making it difficult to apply precisely.[12] The challenges to applying soft power as an instrument of national policy are far too many for it to be successful. There is

---

10 Gray, Colin S., 'Moral Advantage, Strategic Advantage?' in *The Journal of Strategic Studies*, Vol 33, No 3, June 2010, Taylor and Francis On Line, pp. 333-365.

11 Gray, Colin S., *Hard Power and Soft Power: The Utility of Military Force as an Instrument of Policy in the 21st Century*, p. 28.

12 Nye Jr, Joseph S., *Soft Power: The Means to Success in World Power*, Public Affairs, New York, 2004, p. 5. See for detailed explanation of the concept of 'soft power' and the greater possibilities of its utilisation.

also a palpable tendency amongst its proponents to exaggerate its effectiveness in achieving national objectives. Even so, there is less than optimum understanding of how soft power is to be applied, how it can be controlled effectively and also how it influences potential adversaries.

The soft power of a nation is derived from its own values. Since no nation can claim to be possessed of universal values, the relevance of soft power as an instrument of influence is also reduced. Ignorance of the inherent culture of the adversary makes the employment of soft power more difficult. In the arena of power projection, military forces are considered blunt instruments that are prone to producing unintended consequences. When power projection is attempted by a combination of hard military power and soft power it almost always creates second and third order effects that cannot be predicted or understood in advance.[13]

Although the foundations of national hard power, military and economic power are optimally used when employed as instruments of coercion. However, coercion as a strategy is not fully reliable since the coercee, the nation or entity being coerced, is at liberty to refuse to be coerced, irrespective of the illogicality of the refusal and the cost of such belligerence. Autocratic regimes, where the connection between the general population and the national leadership is tenuous at best, are more prone to illogical behaviour patterns and more difficult to coerce. In these circumstances a judicious combination of hard and soft power is most likely to succeed. The difficulty in fine-tuning and manoeuvring the application of soft power makes the task of employing it as a primary instrument in the implementation of policy almost impossibly difficult. This indicates the necessity to employ hard power, resident in military and economic capabilities of the nation, to achieve base level political objectives. Soft power can subsequently be used to win the peace and achieve the necessary influence to stabilise the situation.

Military Forces – Instrument of National Policy

It is a fact that military forces may not be the 'right' element of national power to be employed under all circumstances. When applied inappropriately, their effectiveness cannot always be assured. Therefore,

---

13 Gray, Colin S.,op cit, p. 41.

as the 21 century is progressing, the relevance of military forces as an element of national power and their utility in ensuring national security has started to get questioned. The resource-intensive nature of military forces adds further to this debate. However, war fought by military forces is a necessary option in international relations. It is not possible to solve all 'conflicts' through political, diplomatic or other non-military means or settled through negotiated compromise.[14] Even so it has to be accepted that war may not deliver a politically satisfactory outcome.

There is a contemporary trend to view the employment of military forces in their lethal form, even if the operations stop short of war, as evidence of policy failure at the political level. This approach is at best a blinkered view of the political process. The importance of military forces as an instrument of national policy is demonstrated and underpinned by historical fact. Even a cursory analysis of the history of the world clearly brings out the fact that wars—fought by military forces—have altered and shaped the history of the world more comprehensively and unalterably than any other element in human experience.[15]

In the past few decades, Western democracies have displayed an increasing proclivity to use military forces as the first option element of national power to enforce their will on other nations, even when such employment borders on the questionable side of international legality. There is of course concerted political attempt to ensure that such applications are within the norms of legal and ethical correctness. The threat is that if the pendulum of political correctness swings so far in this direction, it could destroy the necessary effectiveness of military forces. When military forces are employed, they must prevail, meaning win; a nation must not enter into a war or warlike situation unless it has the will and wherewithal to fight and win. As a corollary, the people of the nation must know fully that wars cannot be fought without pain.

---

14 Thucydides, *The Landmark Thucydides: A Comprehensive Guide to The Peloponnesian War*,Strassler, Robert B., (ed), Free Press, Touchstone Edition, Cambridge University Press, 1998, p. 43.

15 This is the gist of the thesis in Gray, Colin S., *War, Peace, and International relations: An Introduction to Strategic History*, Routledge, Abingdon MA, 2007.

The formulation of appropriate strategy for their employment is critical for the success of military forces. Further, this has to be done at the highest level of decision-making in the security hierarchy of the nation. Only when such directions are given to the military forces will they be able to produce the necessary effects that elevate them to the status of an instrument of national policy. In a liberal democracy, optimised utilisation of military power is achieved when it is controlled by public policy as enacted by elected lawmakers in parliament.

The most contentious issues in the application of lethal force by the military forces of a sovereign nation are the legal and ethical precepts, which must not only be interpreted correctly, but also be seen to have been adhered to in both the domestic and international context. However, both law and ethics are prone to permissive interpretation and can be used in a self-serving manner through glib argument to justify questionable actions. There is also a moral dimension to all conflicts that stem from the broad universal acceptability of ethics in the employment of military forces. This is especially applicable in wars that have an international flavour.[16] This concept continues to reside at the academic level of debate since the accepted morality can never be imposed on any belligerent nor can a defaulter be punished.

Ethics are more complex and its appreciation varies greatly with differences in culture, tradition and philosophical development of a nation and its people. The overarching universality in morality that could be superimposed on military actions cannot be applied to the case of ethics; its limited commonality is lost in differing priorities and values of different peoples. However, human beings as the prime movers in all wars and warlike activities adhere to some basic level of ethical tradition that forms the basis for moral judgement.[17] This belief of the moral 'correctness' of the cause for which a military force is fighting is crucial to achieving victory. If and when this confidence in the morality of its action is shaken, there will be a sharp drop in the effectiveness of the military force in question and the chances of ultimate victory immediately diminishes. Even minimal doubts

---

16 For an authoritative modern analysis of the moral factors that must be considered in wars, read Burleigh, Michael, *Moral Combat: A History of World War II*, Harper Press, London, UK, 2010.

17 Gray, Colin S., *op cit*, p. 51.

regarding the morality of fighting a war can be debilitating to military efficiency.

There is an existing dichotomy in the human requirement of a military force and those of a liberal democracy. The military forces inculcate a warrior-ethos into their cadre whereas liberal democracies are oriented towards being peace-loving. Military forces are directly affected by this dichotomy, since the human factor in them are a microcosm of the larger society. Military forces demand professionalism within its ranks in order to be effective and such professionalism demandscultivating and conserving an elitist warrior spirit, which is the bedrock of militarism. The natural society tends to shun any form of militarism. From a purely human perspective this creates a complexity within the mind that some soldier-leaders find difficult to straddle effectively. This dichotomy will to exist as long as liberal democracies continue to deploy their military forces as instruments of national policy.

It is absolutely necessary for military forces to be oriented to create strategic effects to meet the ends of policy. Only warrior-leaders will be able to deliver this outcome effectively. Military forces are instruments of national policy. They are also complex entities that need exemplary understanding of their strengths and weaknesses from both civilian as well as military leadership if they are to perform the critical functions demanded of them. The absolute fundamental fact is that liberal democracies will find it impossible to secure themselves unless the elements of national power are fully backed by an efficient military force.

Summing Up...

War, also labelled as organised violence, is legal when it has been declared. However, for it to be declared there has to be an identifiable and coherent enemy, normally a State with all the trappings that make it a recognisable entity. This is becoming more difficult to achieve in the modern world, where wars are being fought between non-state entities with no legal status of their own. The other aspect of war is that all nations involved in one recognises and understands that war begets violence and therefore it should be only entered into as a last resort. Even so, the other side of the same coin is that wars are necessary to ensure world order. In an obtuse manner it could be stated that the maintenance of world order is influenced by the employment of military forces.

Humankind has accepted that war is a destructive enterprise while at the same time accepting the necessity of fighting a war to move towards a space where wars would become unnecessary or at least few and far in between. In fact, the history of warfare is also a history of mankind's attempt to humanise its conduct and limit the destruction that it brings about. At the same time the lethality of military forces is improving exponentially. There is a paradoxical dichotomy in this situation. The attempts to humanise the conduct of war are centred on three major initiatives. First, enforcing legal restrictions to the application of force; second, attempting to limit the damage being created through the employment of technologically sophisticated weaponry; and third adhering to the three fundamental principles for the application of lethal force—precision, proportionality and discrimination.

Even though laws have been created and enacted for the actual conduct of war, its legitimacy has been ensured through the theories of 'Just War' that have been propounded. These theories are applied when national security is threatened and a nation has decided to go to war in order to protect its interests. The just war theories also justify the use of force through the employment of national military forces, which invariably leads to death and destruction.

By their very nature, human beings are prone to be violent. The creation of organised military forces could be considered an attempt to curb this inherent tendency on the one hand and on the other it could conceivably be thought to expose the base nature of human beings. The evolution of mankind can also be traced through the attempts at controlling the instinctive barbarity of human beings that is inherent in wars. In order to continually 'civilise' the conduct of war, society has created, and tried to enforce, a large number of restrictions and constraints in the application of lethal force. However, keeping pace with this activity has also been the habitual process of not adhering to the constraints that are placed on the use of force. Historically, adhering to the societal norms has not always been aligned to achieving success in the application of force. There is an inherent dichotomy in this situation wherein the efforts to civilise the conduct of war runs contrary to the needs of the military forces to achieve success. War is an irrational activity but its very nature demands its conduct to be done with the utmost care and planning. This is a paradox that has to be very clearly understood at the strategic level of command in the military forces.

There is a tendency in the modern times to view war as a necessary evil, to be conducted and concluded at the earliest, as fast as possible. This attitude has two deficiencies. One, it makes the employment of military forces an easy decision, while it is actually not. The employment of military forces is the most serious decision a government can take and therefore must not be done in an off-hand manner. Two, the complexity of the conduct of a modern war is such that even planning for a quick end to the conflict is fraught with the very real possibility of failure. The long drawn irregular wars of the past few decades, some still festering wounds, is clear examples of long-drawn and indecisive wars. From these two pitfalls, two facts can be discerned. First, it is certain that wars will continue to be fought and its nature will remain unchanged. However, its character, intensity, tempo and the destruction that it brings about will vary contextually with no two battles, conflicts, or campaigns being the same. Second, in all cases, the 'end' of a war does not ever indicate the end to fighting. Skirmishes and battles will come up one after the other even after the war has been officially or formally declared as over. The battles will keep being fought with monotonous regularity.

Military forces remain the only instrument of national policy that retains a coherent form and focused ability for rapid reaction to emergent challenges. Further, military forces are the foundation on which other elements of national power is able to build their own policy options to support national security alternatives and imperatives. This fundamental truth has not changes throughout history. The difference between medieval and modern times is that, in medieval times the military forces of a kingdom was the first and last arbitrator of national security, whereas in modern times more elements of national power join with military power to create instruments of national policy, especially when national security itself is understood in a more nuanced and sophisticated manner.

Chapter 20

STRENGTHENING MILITARY FORCES IN A DEMOCRACY

Military forces, by their inherent nature, tend to be forward looking in their attempt to anticipate emerging challenges that they would have to face. An appreciation of what the future is likely to bring in terms of technological developments that would enhance their capabilities as well as that of their potential adversaries is also necessary for the build-up of an appropriate force. These activities have to be conducted within a broader national security equation which is essentially a political process and involves all elements of national power. In these circumstances most competent military forces articulate a vision for themselves that range from the grandiose to the mundane. However, a vision by its very definition is something that a body or individual aspires to attain, a perception that is almost unattainable, and once attained it does not stay as a vision anymore. Vision is essentially 'the ability or an instance of great perception, especially of future developments.'[1] While a vision is necessary for the development of a military force, it will only become an aspirational goal if supported by a well-thought-through strategy for the development of capabilities that would pave the way ahead.

In the contemporary world, military forces of almost all nations would at some stage be required to operate away from the geographical limits of the home State. In a majority of cases such deployments would be to function at the lower part of the spectrum

---

1   Dictionary.com at http://dictionary.reference.com/browse/vision?s=t, accessed on 1 October 2014.

of conflict in the peace keeping/enforcement roles and may not require the employment of high-end combat capabilities. Keeping the possibility of expeditionary operations in mind, military forces must consciously develop their doctrine and force structure to cater for operations in distant lands as well as in the primary role closer home in the protection of the sovereignty of the nation. In effect no other element of national power is as influenced as the military forces by the combination of national security objectives, strategic necessities and geographic realities that shape the security stance of a nation. Standing as it does in the vanguard of national security imperatives, military forces need to clearly influence the mindset of the nation and the political decision-making process, especially in democracies.

Civil-Military Relations in Democracies

Civilian control of the military forces of a nation is a fundamental and essential principle of the Westminster System of democratic governance. In this case 'civilian' means the minsters appointed from amongst the elected representatives of the people who form the Parliament and embodies the ultimate and direct control exercised over the military forces of the nation by the Parliament and indirectly by the people of the nation as a whole.[2] There are two advantages to this system—it keeps the military forces institutionally apolitical and professionally devoid of any political involvement; and it provides a clear perception of the mutually agreed reciprocal obligations between the military forces and the government of the people. Civilian control at no time means the bureaucratic control of the military by civil servants, although some of the more senior civilian officials at the centre of power in democracies tend to think otherwise. Constitutionally and legally, control of the military in a democracy is vested in the Parliament and no other body or individual, including the appointed minister.[3]

In the 19th century, Great Britain had experimented with a system in which the Parliament studiously kept away from interfering in the internal matters of the military and did not exercise any control over it. This was perpetuated by the towering personality and personal achievements of the Duke of Wellington who was considered to be the

---

2   James, Neil, 'Stephen Smith and the ADF', *Canberra Times*, 16 March 2012, Canberra, p.17.

3   ibid.

greatest of military commanders that Britain had ever produced. The Parliamentarians, including most Prime Ministers of the time deferred to his view.[4] The result was a system of officering the forces through purchase of commissions that created a class of officers who were definitely not selected on the basis of merit but had a disproportionate in military matters, most of them being knighted gentry. This led to a decline in the professional competency of the force and finally to the debacle that has been named, and celebrated, as the Charge of the Light Brigade in the Crimean War.[5] This was a classic example of a civil-military relationship in which one side differed to the other with disastrous consequences. The balance between the two elements of the decision-making body on national security has to be equitable to avoid decisions that have catastrophic effects being made.

At the core of national security in a democracy resides civil-military relationship. It is influenced by national security imperatives and in turn influences the strategic politico-military process that ensures overarching national security. The balance between civilian and military leadership and control of the military at the strategic level has been at the centre of the concept of national security since antiquity. This balance did not matter too much in the monarchies of the Middle Ages since the authority of the State and command of the military forces were almost always vested in the same individual—the king. However, in democracies the authority of the State is vested in elected representatives, whereas the military forces are commanded by a band of professional soldiers. One has the temporal and moral authority, the other directly controls the more tangible and demonstrable power of modern military forces. A clear balance between the two is essential for the smooth functioning of the State and therefore it is almost always in flux.

All security issues that face a nation have to be addressed jointly by the two institutions, which in ideal conditions should be complimentary to each other and share the responsibilities equally.[6] However, the nature of civil and military decision-making and the

---

4 Woodham-Smith, Ceil, *The Reason Why*, Penguin Books Ltd., Harmondsworth, Great Britain, 1958, pp. 70-74.

5 ibid, pp. 240-247.

6 Gomart, Thomas, *Russian Civil-Military Relations: Putin's Legacy*, Carnegie Endowment for International Peace, Washington D.C., 2008, p.87.

processes involves are very different to each other although they are forced to function in close proximity to each other to ensure national security. The fundamental civil-military relationship will determine the ability of a nation to act decisively and control the factors that influence its national security essentials.[7]

Leadership—Political and Military

In democracies the ruling and opposition parties do not normally have the same policies to deal with matters of state-governance, although ideally they should have the betterment of the nation as the ultimate goal. While the parties struggle continually to gain power through winning elections, political unity on matters of national security is a must for having a strong foundation to building a viable national security policy. Bipartisan support to national security issues will provide a visible cohesion within the political entity and enhance public support for even difficult decisions that may have to be made in this sphere. This status has to be achieved by the political leadership while consciously ensuring that corruption and mismanagement throughout the political process is completely ruled out. While this should ideally be the case in all aspects of government, it must be ensured that the taint of corruption does not touch the leadership and decisions made on military matters.

From a military perspective, the leadership has a much more onerous duty to fulfil. There are three fundamental requirements that must be vested in senior military leaders to avoid major pitfalls in their decision-making. First, they must have a clear understanding of the culture of the adversary that they are, or may have to, fight and defeat. This knowledge will have to be tempered with an even clearer appreciation of one's own culture and the underlying social ethos of the nation. Second, the senior leadership of the military must be able to detect and weed out incompetence at the operational level of command, which would mean instituting an efficient system of evaluation and promotion of middle level officers. Operational failures invariably create strategic consequences. Third, is the requirement to constantly look for ways and means to improve the command structure of the force as a whole to improve its operational

---

7   ibid.

effectiveness.[8] The need is for senior leadership in the military to be statesmen and not merely competent tactical level warriors although all future commanders should have proven themselves as competent 'warfighters' in the first instance.

The military, unlike other arms of the government has a unique requirement to acquire equipment that are fundamental to building its capability to perform its stated roles. Since military capabilities are resource-intensive to both acquire and maintain, a certain amount of fiscal control is always exercised by the civilian leadership on this process. This is a desirable situation, especially in democracies, where the military forces should be fully under the control of the civilian parliament. However, the process of acquisition has become somewhat skewed in most democracies and not all decisions are made above-board. Corruption, not merely in the economic sphere, but also in the temporal area is a constant threat in the military capabilitiesrealm since the finances involved are usually very large. Keeping the decision-making on the capability requirement purely as a military exercise and then having an independent body doing a constant oversight of the acquisition process could limit the chances and temptation towards corruption. However, corruption is a constant threat to the veracity of military capability acquisition.

Civil-military relations are at the core of the performance envelope of a military force in a democracy. A number of factors—some clearly measurable and others intangible—influence the relationship. Fundamentally, the relationship has to be built on mutual trust created through the appreciation of the professionalism of the military leadership and the non-partisan approach of the political leadership towards issues of national security. This tryst plays out in the public arena and can be adversely affected by any sort of bias displayed by either party in their dealings with each other. In this aspect the media, which should be free in a democracy, plays an important role in building perceptions in the public arena regarding the strength of the relationship. While in an ideal situation the relationship should be trouble-free, this may not always be possible. The robustness of the

---

8   Conversation of the author with (Late) Lt Gen Michael C. Short, USAF (Ret), in Australian Defence College, Weston Creek, Canberra, Australia on 30 July 2007. (Referred with permission)

relationship would be tested constantly and only maturity on the part of individuals in leadership positions during the particular situation will smoothen the way forward amicably. This is a must if the larger national security interests are to be furthered.

Major Influences on the Military Forces

There are four factors that have to be considered in analysing the influences on the development of military forces in a democratic nation—the character of the force; alliances and coalitions; self-reliance in military capabilities; and rules of engagement. It can be noticed that other than the character of the force, the other factors are derivatives of the political process of the nation involved.[9] These factors individually and in differing combinations create the direction of development that every individual military force adopts. In effect these factors are the building blocks on which the capabilities and capacities of a force is continually built and revised.

Character of the Force

The optimum nature for a military force in a democracy is for it to be an all-volunteer one without having to resort to conscription at any stage. An all-volunteer force provides greater moral authority to the State when it employs the military force to ensure national security. However, nations with smaller populations would find it difficult to maintain a standing force of the strength that is necessary because of the disparate demands on the demographics of the nation. In these circumstances it would be necessary to resort to some kind of compulsory military service for all citizens in order to maintain a pool of trained personnel that can be called on to add the necessary mass to the military forces in times of crisis. In normal circumstances such a military force would be manned by a core group of professionals, numerically far lesser than the necessary numbers to employ the full capabilities of the force. A democracy should not have to resort to conscription under normal circumstances.

---

9   Freedman, Lawrence, 'Military Power and Political Influence', *International Affairs*, Vol 74, No 4, October 1998, Oxford University Press for RUSI, London, 1998, pp. 763-780.

The corollary to creating an all-volunteer force is that it can only be done if the military forces are given a status within the society that will then attract the right calibre of people into the force. In other words the socio-economic conditions under which the military functions have to be comparable to the rest of society in order to attract competent people into the force.[10] In modern societies it is also necessary to ensure that the conditions of service such as postings, family welfare activities and opportunities for the family to continue their own professional developments must be ensured in order to retain the trained personnel. The traditional mould of the military being a life unto itself will no longer suffice as the model for the military force of the 21st century. The nature of the force has to be adapted to ensure recruitment of the appropriate personnel and perhaps more importantly the retention of these people who will be trained at enormous cost to perform exacting specialist tasks.

There is another factor that tends to alter the character of the force from an operational perspective. If a military force is employed in internal security duties within the nation, it will invariably have a subtle influence on the operational calibre of the force. A volunteer force within a democracy will be a cross section of the larger society and therefore initiating action against their own countrymen will not come as a natural extension of their training. The training, operational ethos and the final outcome desired in constabulary or policing duties are very different from that of a regular military force. Dual usage inevitably makes the military force lose its combat edge, a fact that has been demonstrated in a number of actual cases. Therefore, it imperative that a military force is not employed in internal security duties for long durations.

Alliances and Coalitions

Modern military forces are unlikely to be employed unilaterally as stand-alone entities because of the prevailing global political, security and economic conditions. They would invariably function within a coalition that could consists of purely allies, or could be made up

---

10 Brotz, Howard, & Wilson, Everett, 'Characteristics of Military Society', *American Journal of Sociology*, Vol 51, No 5, March 1946, The University of Chicago Press, Chicago, 1946, https://www.journals.uchicago.edu/doi/abs/10.1086/219845?journalCode=ajs accessed on 20 June 2017.

of different national military forces that have come together for a particular campaign. The latter coalitions would be bound together by unity of purpose and will have no long-term implications. Such coalitions will invariably face difficulties in the command and control structure as well as in enforcing the rules of engagement (ROE), since the constituent nations will have different sets of ROEs. A military coalition of different nations will be ponderous in its operational effectiveness and when faced with a competent adversary could find achieving the desired end-state difficult. The difficulties encountered in creating a cohesive coalition in the 1990s led to the US moving towards constituting what has thereafter been termed as a 'coalition of the willing', which essentially means nations that have similar command and control structure as well as operating under the same set of ROEs. This eases the inherent tensions resident within a coalition and enhances the operational effectiveness of the coalition as a whole.

Alliances are different to coalitions.[11] While coalitions are created to face a particular challenge or necessity, alliances exist at all times, in times of peace as well as conflict, and can either be bilateral or multilateral. Prime examples of long-standing alliances are the NATO and ANZUS treaty. From a military operational perspective, the forces will find it easier to operate with allies since they would have exercised together regularly and there would also be greater inter-operability both in terms of equipment as well as in tactics, procedures and doctrine. However, there are some strategic challenges that will have to be carefully addressed and redressed to ensure that an alliance withstands the tests and tensions that are bound to appear with time.

Alliances are focused on achieving a common goal and therefore may need minor compromise of some national goals to arrive at a consensus that is agreeable to all parties. In most cases, the compromise would be greater on the part of the junior partner(s) of the alliance. Ideally alliances are meant to be the equal sharing of the burden of collective security, although in actual fact this can never be the case. The long history of alliances demonstrate that they are almost always uneven in character and the more powerful partner will have a greater

---

11 'Alliances, Coalitions, and Ententes – Terminology', in *Encyclopedia of the New American Nation*, http://www.americanforeignrelations.com/A-D/Alliances-Coalitions-and-Ententes-Terminology.html accessed on 21 September 2017.

say in its functioning. This situation means that the compromise required to create consensus will also be more on the part of the lesser powers. The question that has always been asked is regarding the correctness of such a situation. How far should a smaller nation go in compromising its fundamental goals in order to be sheltered under the umbrella of an alliance? Since alliances are long-term understandings and cannot be dispensed at short notice, the degree of compromise cannot be done in a contextual manner and has to be thought through in a bipartisan manner by the nation concerned.

The other challenge is for the alliance partners to identify the basic factors that sustain an alliance and the price that each member has to pay for admission. This is vital for the good health and longevity of the alliance. It is in this sphere that the larger partner will be able to compensate for the greater compromise of the smaller nations by taking the responsibility of shouldering a greater share of the resources necessary for the smooth functioning of the alliance. On the other hand, the price of admission for a small nation could well be the moral and political support necessary for the greater power to push forward with an agenda that could be beneficial for the entire alliance, even if the benefits are not equal for each nation. The general consensus that exemplifies and alliance would be able nullify the fallout for this disparity. Sustaining an alliance at the optimum level of cooperation is a complex task and needs sophisticated understanding of not only the international security environment, but also the socio-economic and political situation that is prevalent within each member nation.[12]

Successful alliances will be able to create a long-term sense of balance between the at times disparate requirements of the members by managing to keep the expectations of each to a deliverable level. This will need the creation of a joint vision of collective security that avoids divergence of views and large variations in national security imperatives. The second step to success is the need for all members to articulate their expectations of the alliance as well as of each other so that in times of crisis there are no misunderstandings regarding the responsibilities of each. Third is the requirement for the alliance

---

12 For detailed descriptions of alliances and coalitions read, Weitsman, Patricia A., *Waging War: Alliances, Coalitions, and Institutions of Interstate Violence*, Stanford Security Studies, Stanford University Press, Stanford, CA, 2014.

to coordinate diplomatic actions and ensure political sustainability of actions that are being contemplated. Military alliances will invariably have to resort to operations at some stage r the other in the neutralisation of emerging challenges and cooperative actions in the diplomatic and political arena will be a foundational requirement for military success. Underlying the success of all alliances is the necessity to have clear awareness at the strategic level of leadership—both political and military—regarding the ultimate joint aim of the alliance. Even if there is divergence in though within the members, the general acceptance of the broad aims of the alliance is a must for its robustness.

Self-reliance

Self-reliance in military and economic terms is a virtue that every nation tries to cultivate. However, a self-reliant situation is a difficult position to achieve, even for major powers. In military terms, self-reliance is intricately connected to the concept of self-sufficiency, one cannot exist without the other. In military terms, self-sufficiency is achievable for a very small number of nations who have the financial and resource capabilities to create stand-alone industries that produce the necessary military materiel and equipment. All other nations are dependent, in some way or the other, on these military industrial nations for the development of their military capabilities and therefore cannot be considered as being self-sufficient. Since military capability is built on the twin-pillars of equipment and personnel, availability of equipment becomes an important factor in the development of military forces. Indirectly, such availability is directly proportional to the relationships that a nation has cultivated over the years and the political influence that it can bring to bear on friends and allies.

Self-reliance on the other hand is concerned with the usage of military capabilities in ensuring national security and supporting national initiatives to safeguard its interests. This involves the development of security concepts that could be applied individually by the nation considered. The notion of self-reliance has an element of time built into it. Self-reliance is therefore a contextual concept that could be interpreted in a slightly different manner in different circumstances. The element of time is a critical part of self-reliance since it is the deciding factor in a nation being considered self-reliant or otherwise. The fundamental requirement is for a nation to be able to ensure its security for a designated period of time with its own resident capabilities before allies and friends can come to its assistance. A nation that is self-reliant within the bounds of its requirements cannot, and should not, in anyway be considered as being self-sufficient in meeting its security needs. This caveat is more important in the contemporary global security environment wherein military operations are almost always conducted in coalitions.

There are a number of issues that influence a nation's ability to achieve the necessary level of self-reliance. Fundamental to this is the historical underpinnings, especially of the last few centuries, that defines a nation. A broad analysis brings out the fact that post-colonial nations of the late 20th century are less self-reliant in meeting their security requirements in comparison to even the smallest of European nations. While a number of reasons related to the trauma of colonisation, including its psychological impact, has been listed as the fundamental causes for the situation, it has to be accepted that a majority of these nations have made colonisation in the late 19 and early 20 centuries the reason for their inability to function efficiently as sovereign states. There is a shadow of truth is this accusation in certain cases, but it is definitely not the overarching case. Endemic corruption, resorting to autocratic rule, tribal bias to governance and an all-encompassing dereliction of duty towards the nation has been the bane of post-colonial nations. In security and military terms, the developing world is only now grappling with the concept of self-reliance, with self-sufficiency a far-away dream.

Rules of Engagement[13]

The military forces of a sovereign nation is distinguished from irregular forces by the fact that they adhere to the Laws of Armed Conflict (LOAC) that are internationally recognised. Other lesser differences like wearing the prescribed uniform of the nation and having a recognisable command structure are also differentiations that could be prominent under some circumstances. In contrast, irregular forces do not observe these rules and more importantly, do not have allegiance

---

13 For an exhaustive treatise on the Rules of Engagement read, Hosang, J. F. R. Boddens, *Rules of Engagement: Rules on the Use of Force as Linchpin for the International Law of Military Operations*, University of Amsterdam, Netherlands, 2017.

to a nation, but are normally aligned to an ideology—either political, or religious; and at times a combination of both. The contemporary security environment is such that state-on-state conflicts, where the military forces of one nation battles those of another sovereign state, is a rare occurrence, if at all one takes place. The prevalent trend is for the military forces of a nation to be conducting operations against irregular adversaries. The constitution of these forces, their ideological underpinnings and the support they receive from different areas is superfluous to the discussion in this thesis.

Military forces engaged in physical combat operations with an irregular adversary battles under few disadvantages, especially if the constituted military forces are operating in an expeditionary mode, operating far away from their own country. A major factor is the legitimacy of such deployments within a global viewpoint. All expeditionary operations tend to be looked upon as intrusive by the recipient nation, irrespective of the security conditions prevailing within the country. Therefore, it becomes critically important for the military forces to not only operate within the LOAC but also to be overtly seen to be doing so in order to ensure that the legitimacy of the campaign is not questioned.

The LOAC is a generic set of laws and is interpreted in different ways—some more stringent than others—by different nations.[14] The interpretations depend a lot on the domestic laws of the nation concerned, as well as the historic antecedents vis-à-vis the nation's approach to war and conflict. The proclivity of a nation to commit its military forces to combat will also play an important part in determining the interpretation of LOAC. In this situation individual nations create their own 'Rules of Engagement' (ROE) that is binding on their military forces. Normally these are more restrictive than the LOAC and takes into account a number of factors such as the campaign objectives, the constituents of the coalition, the international legality of the operation and the domestic political support for it. When military forces are

---

14 'Law of War/Introduction to Rules of Engagement', *Student Handout, Basic Officer Course*, US Marine Corps Training Command, Camp Barrett, VA, https://www.trngcmd.marines.mil/Portals/207/Docs/TBS/B130936%20Law%20of%20War%20and%20Rules%20Of%20Engagement.pdf accessed on 2 November 2017.

deployed to show solidarity with an ally, rather than to employ ultimate force to achieve an objective, it will be noticed that the ROE will be far more stringent than when the political leadership of a nation is convinced that certain military objectives have to be achieved. ROE therefore directly influence the character of the military forces in a contextual manner and not on a permanent basis.

Summing Up...

Military forces have emerged as a forward looking element of national power, even though they have been derided for preparing to fight the last war. To a certain extent this derisive comment is correct since the primary role of the military force is to ensure a stable peace. Stability and peace, essential for the material prosperity of a nation, depends to a large extent on the ability of the military forces to maintain the status quo in the socio-political and strategic security environment. In turn this can only be achieved by being able to defeat existing and emerging threats in the near-term. The military forces of a nation must therefore be able to counter threats to its sovereignty in the present while also being able to understand and accept the future.

In democracies, the civilian leadership is given primacy over the military forces. The fundamental principles of democracy are supported and enforced only under these conditions. However, it is incumbent on the civilian leadership to be fully aware that the primacy is not vested on an individual or group of political leadership, but is conferred on the constitutional head of the nation—the collective body of the elected representatives of the people, the Parliament. In a number of so-called democracies, this absolute truth is discarded to the nation's detriment. On the other hand, military forces must also scrupulously maintain an apolitical stance. The political neutrality of the military force can be ensured by its leadership—the officer-cadre—remaining loyal to the constitution of the land and not to individual or collective political leadership.

Military forces function as the central point to ensure national security in most democracies and the most basic requirement for the military to be effective is the stability and reliability of the civil-military relationship. This relationship functions at the centre of the politico-military interaction process and, in normal circumstances, be the focal point that ensures national security. Civil-military relationship is the most important factor to ensure stability in a democracy. A functioning democracy must ensure the necessary balance between the temporal and moral authority of the constitution through the parliament and the more tangible and physical authority of military command.

As is possible with any relationship in which human beings are the primary actors, civil-military relationship can become distorted and biased for a number of reasons. Mostly such distortions emanate from political dissentions wherein the ruling and opposition parties are not aligned regarding the policies that are applied to military forces. A bipartisan political approach to dealing with military forces across the spectrum of its activities—operations, governance, procurement, and the fundamental raise, train and sustain function—is of the highest priority. It is the only way to ensure that the fundamentals of national security remain stable. The onus of responsibility to ensure bipartisan support to the military forces rests with the political leadership, and is not difficult to achieve in an established political and parliamentary process that is the hallmark of a mature democracy. Challenges arise in newer and developing democracies that do not have traditions and established structures to support its progress.

The military leadership would have to adopt a more nuanced approach to nurturing the civil-military relationship when compared to the political leadership. The military leaders would have to be professionally competent in terms of their profession of arms while also being adept at mastering the political structure and processes that are critical to understanding national security imperatives. It is no more sufficient for military leadership to have tactical and operational brilliance—they must also be strategically astute in order to be able to draw the connecting line and maintain the link between military endeavour and national security, defined at its broadest.

Military forces are complex organisations and the more successful ones are always in a state of continuous evolution. The path of this evolution is influenced by few major and myriad minor factors. Further, the evolution towards a particular future point could start at the tactical level and move in a 'bottom-up' approach or could be originated at the strategic level and encompass a more traditional 'top-to-bottom' approach. Each iteration of the evolution could be short-term or long-term and their effects continue even after they have reached their culmination points in one area, influencing other related spheres.

The national character is a major influence on the performance of its military force since the force is a microcosm of the society at larger population of the nation. Therefore, the military force would automatically reflect the prevailing societal norms within the country. At the operational level, the national character will be reflected in the formation and application of rules of engagement that are imposed on the military force. The restrictiveness or openness of the rules under which the military force functions will depend almost entirely on the national character and its appreciation of the enormity of applying force in the pursuit of national security. While the factors that influence the evolution of military forces must be carefully analysed by the strategic leadership of the nation and if necessary conditioned to ensure that the strength and cohesiveness of national military forces are not diluted. This is particularly important in times of relative peace when the military forces and their contribution to national security could be pushed to the background.

In times of a volatile security environment, the military force becomes the element of national power that comes to the fore to assure national sovereignty. At the same time democracies have an unfortunate tendency to ignore military requirements in terms of resource allocation and sustainment of the force. This approach is flawed, especially in modern times when the lead-time required to field a competent force is long and almost always the military will be asked to 'fight' as they are at the time of the requirement arising. The emergence of the threat will be rapid and will not provide the necessary time to build up the force to required standard.

Democracies and their military forces share a symbiotic relationship, one that is mutually beneficial if conducted within the accepted norms of a democratic society. Mutual strengthening of this relationship is a continuous process and is necessary for the well-being of democratic nations.

CONCLUSION

All nations face threats to their well-being on a continual basis, with the evolution of these threats being contextual in almost all cases. The corollary to the evolution of the threat is that most of them have a common thread that aligns them with the broader threats originating in the region and which impact most of the other nations. However, this may not always be the case. Threats do not spring without warning and normally emanate from vulnerabilities of a nation that have been permitted to fester without being corrected. It is also natural for every nation to search for the vulnerabilities of its neighbours so that they could be exploited for one's own advantage. Vulnerabilities are distinctly different from threats and can be neutralised much more easily, if they are identified correctly and addressed appropriately.

Threat mitigation is a priority function of governments, especially in democratic nations. The mitigation process itself will be different in different nations and will also be different for different threat scenarios in one nation itself. In all practising democracies, the mitigation process will be influenced by the nation's relationships with other nations, international bodies and the international law. Within these constraints, threats can be mitigated through the application of a number of strategies. The success, or otherwise, of the process will depend on the capacity of the government to choose the 'right' strategy to be applied in order to ensure that emerging threats are fully contained and neutralised. The security of a nation is almost fully a function of the government's ability to identify the threat at the earliest, choose the right strategy and apply it astutely. This procedure is complex and riddled with potential pitfalls, making it prone to failure at least as often as it succeeds.

Military forces of a nation, by virtue of their inherent qualities of cohesion and flexibility and their capability and competence are placed at the forefront of the threat mitigation process. This position at the vanguard of national security is further emphasised by the fact that they are the only element of national power that is legally permitted to apply lethal force in the pursuit of national security objectives. Theoretically, the application of lethal force should come as a strategy of last resort in the continuum of strategies that ensure national security. However, in recent times it can be observed that lethal force through the employment of military forces is more easily being resorted to by many nations, even when other less exacting options are readily available. This has been an unfortunate development in the late 20th and early 21st centuries.

It is a universal fact that military forces are expenders of resources; a fact that brings to focus the fundamental tension in the resource allocation process in democratic nations, especially during times of relative peace. Historically it is seen that the utility and criticality of military forces to ensuring national security are not focus areas in democracies during protracted periods of relative peace, which will also normally coincide with economic development and political stability. Since there are never adequate resources in any nation to meet the disparate demands of a developing country, during times of relative peace, the military forces almost always get short-shift in resource allocation. Further, in democracies the political leadership always play to the public with an eye on the next election and the necessity to win votes. It follows that invariably the military forces are the ones to suffer from resource constraints.

Carefully crafting the military spending of a nation is a requirement rather than a luxury in the 21st century. In the pre-World War II period, it was possible to resource and build a capable military force when the requirement to field them arose, as long as a competent nucleus had been maintained for the new force to coalesce upon. Such an indulgent comfort is not available anymore. Modern military forces need a long lead-time to be formed, trained and operationally deployed, making it imperative that when conflict knocks on the door, the force will have to fight and win with what it has got at that moment. In other words, a military force fights the way it is, without being 'beefed up'.

In combination with the fact that threats now emerge with little or no warning, the situation is not conducive to an under-resourced military force to be given resources at the last moment to create a force that would prevail over the adversary in short notice. The circumstances have changed to an extent where such a process is impossible to undertake.

Contemporary military forces have a continual need for resource allocation, a situation that is not clearly understood by most political leadership in democracies. The situation is exacerbated by the fact that in most democracies, the political leadership is bereft of military experience and the new breed of 'politicians' are more adept at wheeling and dealing rather than experts at dealing with national security challenges. It is, therefore, not surprising that military forces suffer from benign neglect in most democratic nations.

Even as a military force is looked upon as a wasteful but necessary part of the national security calculus, it is possible for the military to contribute to the nation materially. Today's military forces are users of high-technology weapon systems and a nation can create an industrial base to support it. Defence-related industries have the capacity to contribute to the national economy and thereby offset the resource expenditure on the military. However, the caveat is that the contribution of the defence industry and its technology absorption capability will be a direct function of the resource allocation to this enterprise. The process is an eternal cycle and needs careful nurturing by the political leadership, if it is to prove beneficial to the nation.

In democracies, military forces will have to function within the broad national security enterprise, normally delineated by the national security strategies. However, the political leadership of democratic nations tend to prefer a situation wherein national security strategies and imperatives are left in a vague state and in some cases unarticulated. The security imperatives therefore become invisible to cursory examinations, remaining more implied than clearly defined. From a military point of view, it is necessary to have an articulated national security strategy that provides clear guidance regarding national security priorities. The absence of a clearly defined national security strategy will be disadvantageous for capability and force structure development of military forces.

Military forces should be able to leverage the national security strategy and create flexible solutions to their own operational imperatives and challenges. A combination of national security strategies and available resources will directly impact capability and force structure as well as concepts of operation for the military forces. On this development, indirectly, will depend the national security posture of a nation.

In modern times, the role of the military forces as the primary arbiters of national security has been diluted for a number of reasons. Fundamentally, the approach to national security has changed and most nations now take a whole-of-government approach to securing the nation. This change has been necessitated by the fact that threats to nations are not purely military in nature anymore. In fact, most threats require a collaborative application of all elements of national power. Within this complex matrix and balance of national power elements, the status of military forces is a function of their demonstrated competence. While this competence is difficult to measure, it is an intangible factor that is gauged independent of the capabilities provided by the hardware acquired by the force.

In democracies, the decision to employ military forces is the prerogative of the elected government and parliament and is normally not done without an exhaustive debate and elaborate consideration of all the disparate factors that influence the decision and further actions. Optimally, in all cases the employment should be done within clearly defined parameters, principles and laws. Ideally, the military forces should also be given clear and achievable objectives that are aligned with national security imperatives. By enforcing this cycle, the employment of military forces not only gets the necessary legal sanction but will also be supporting national security.

The role of the military forces is evolving and broadening on a continuous basis. Today, its role is not merely the traditional physical protection of the nation's borders. National security has been defined in much more amorphous and wider manner in recent times and military forces are now required to do much more than ensuring the physical sanctity of national borders. The military forces are in constant flux of adapting to these changes, leveraging their inherent flexibility to its optimised best. The expanding spectrum of responsibilities that have been thrust on the military forces and other external influences have made force structure development complicated. It has become difficult to keep pace with the changed, and ever changing, requirements of the battlefield, making it seem that the military forces are always preparing to fight the previous war. Such is not the case. Force structure development and the implementation of necessary changes to the existing structure is time consuming and may not always keep up with radical changes. At such times, the inherent flexibility of the military forces fill the gap adequately, while the transition is still in process.

21st century military forces need a broad set of capabilities in order to be effective. This requirement is made more complex by the increasing technological sophistication of military systems and the accompanying complexity of operating them efficiently. Today, military operations are no more simple and straight-forward, victory in battle, campaign or war is not defined and wars are named conflicts, because wars are not declared anymore. The advent of asymmetry has created another facet to military responses to emerging threats. From asymmetry and the accompanying irregular war, it has become apparent that modern conflict is fought on the human terrain—for control of the cognitive domain of the adversary. Success in these endeavours is never clearly visible and can be understood only in a long-term perspective.

Under these conditions in which the military forces are compelled to function, it becomes the responsibility of democratic governments to strengthen them to ensure their resilience. This is a function of the civil-military relationship that should not be personality driven and one where both the leadership should meet based on mutual trust as equal partners in the national security equation. Failure to do so will the harbinger of a debacle for the nation, which will jeopardise national security.

Even though the employment of military forces is a complex undertaking, judged by any standards, they continue to remain the primary instrument of state policy. The military force of a nation is the only agency that supports all other elements of national power and acts as a last-resort back-up when all other means have failed—the only entity that is legally permitted to apply lethal force against an adversary.

Irrespective of the changes taking place in the understanding of national security, the primary role of the military forces has remained unchanged over the centuries—ensuring the safety, security and stability of the nation under all circumstances. This fundamental role will remain unchanged into the future.

CONCLUSION

THE 21ST CENTURY MILITARY FORCES

Democracies across the world are struggling with the same issues manifest in different degrees—balancing the budget, fighting the forces of separatism in different forms, contributing to the alleviation of human misery to the extent possible, and meeting the expectations of the domestic population—while ensuring that national sovereignty is not jeopardised, national security imperatives are conserved, and national interest objectives are adequately met. None of these are easily achieved and require a cohesive and comprehensive national security strategy that is not only articulated, but also closely monitored in its implementation. With the complexity of ensuring national security continually increasing, governments invariably tend to view the military forces of the nation as the immediate panacea for all challenges. The result has been the increasingly broad spectrum of activities that is now considered as the normal spread of responsibilities for a traditional military force. In turn, this has led to two further developments—the military force has had to widen its professional expertise far beyond the requirements to be a viable fighting force; and flowing from it, the military forces have been compelled to adapt and alter their force structure as well as capability development processes.

It is perhaps an understatement that military forces have evolved over the past few decades. Ever since the end of World War II, the character of war has been changing, initially at a slow pace that could be studied and absorbed and in step changes in the last few decades, which has not given staid military forces sufficient time to adapt to the changed circumstances. It is a paean to the resilience of military forces that they have acquitted themselves as well as they have in these trying conditions. However, the bottom line has been that the capabilities of conventional military forces, especially ones that have capacity and numerical constraints, have been stretched beyond acceptable limits in most democratic nations. The solution lies in the ability of a nation to accept this somewhat bizarre situation for what it is and initiate an honest review of the military budget, modernisation plans and projected force structure as a first step. This must be followed by actions to implement the recommendations that such a review, conducted at the highest levels of national security decision-making, put forward. Lacking this, the military forces of the future will be marching towards failure.

The Security Dilemma

The contemporary trends of globalisation and fragmentation are important dialectics of the prevailing global security environment. Globalisation has brought about increasing inter-connectivity between and within nations in an overarching manner. This connectivity transcends the 'status' of the nation in terms of economy, socio-political developments or global influence. Such a situation encourages the spread of good governance, even if at a gradual pace, and can improve all-round development and also address human rights issues in marginalised countries. Overall, globalisation can be considered a force for good, a force that encourages positive changes.

On the other hand fragmentation leads to isolation, separatism and fanaticism. In turn any one, or a combination of these developments can create a proliferation of conflict-inducing situations with the potential to spiral out of reasonable control. The end-result in such situations is almost always state failure and rampant regional instability. The downside of globalisation will be felt in such an environment with the regional challenge rapidly mushrooming to become a global issue. The fallout from a global and uncontrolled challenge is invariably increased and unpredictable migration trends with the potential to affect the demography of an entire region. Further the circumstances also favour the development of non-state actors who increase the volatility of the situation. In a broad sense, fragmentation is a negative force that works against peace and stability.

While the two dialectics mentions above are continuously at play in the international politico-social environment, they also spawn two new threats to global security. First is the rise of hegemonic non-state actors who seamlessly assume the roles that were the purview of traditional nation states. The counter to such entities will have to be nation-states, but since these are 'non-state' groups they function across conventional geographical borders, making it difficult for a single nation to neutralise them. The security environment becomes complex with no direct solution that can be applied effectively. The second is the indirect threat to human well-being in an overarching manner, brought about through poverty and social exclusion. The challenge is exacerbated by social, economic and political expectations not being met.

A combination of these two factors creates a complex and ambiguous internal security challenge to nation states. Even if the threat has originated elsewhere, it can travel rapidly into the borders of a nation and tend to get internalised within its borders. There is no ready remedy for such emerging and amorphous threats. An inter-state system of mutual respect, assistance and forbearance could perhaps create a shield of protection for nations within a region.[1] However, the weak link in such a collective defensive shield will always be the nation with the least resilience and the most diversity. Nations that have a tenuous hold on a system that provides for military-economic sovereignty will succumb first. The need of the hour is to create a modernised version of the 1648 Peace of Westphalia that embeds a reformed concept of a politico-economic-social system acceptable to the global community.

The Threat Scenario

The two decades that have gone by in the 21st century provides a somewhat blurred blue print for emerging threats, at least for the mid-term future. The current threats have introduced radical and total changes to the system that existed in the late 20th century. They have ushered in the era of asymmetric insurgent warfare with its mainstream conduct and global implications. In the past decade, non-

---

1 Brown, Seyom, *New Forces, Old Forces, and the Future of World Politics*, Harper Collins Publishers, New York, 1995, p. 46.

state entities have assumed the status of nation states, effortlessly. This development institutionalises terrorist tactics and insurgent strategy, which exploits local/regional poverty, lack of education and social connectivity, and global awareness of the declining situation. Over a very short period of time these non-state groups become a threat to stability and subsequently become a direct challenge to the existence of traditional nation states.

The power to 'make war' is in-built within the non-state entities and they are uniquely tuned to creating and exploiting violent conflict situations. Such irregular conflicts destroy the personal security of individuals, radically change the characteristics of a nation state by inducing a civil war and through rapid proliferation of insurgent conflict to neighbouring countries and regions threaten the status quo of global order.[2]

Future Military Forces

The future military forces will have to be able to adapt and change at short notice rapidly. This will be the primary requirement to achieve modernisation while not compromising on the efficiency of the force. This is a fundamental requirement in contemporary times since the onset of conflict cannot be predicted with any assurance other than that it will happen with insufficient lead-time to create the necessary changes in the standing force to face the emerging threat. Further this threat will always be different to the ones the force has faced and defeated before. Three elements need to be analysed in order to understand the characteristics that need to combine to ensure military success—the security environment; strategies; and the conduct of operations.

Security Environment

The security environment in which the military forces will be forced to operate in the 21 century will be governed by surprise and uncertainty. Accordingly, the environment is bound to be volatile and evolving at all times. The rate of evolution will depend on a number of factors

---

2 Fisher, Kimbra L., 'Challenging the Hegemon: Al Qaeda's Elevation of Asymmetric Insurgent Warfare into the Global Arena', in Robert J. Bunker (ed), *Networks, Terrorism, and Global Insurgency*, Routledge, London, 2005, pp. 115-128.

and will continue to remain unpredictable. The only assurance will be the fact that the security environment that was prevalent even a month ago would have changed in some way on a daily and weekly basis. The uncertainty that emanates from such an environment will create multiple and complex challenges to the efficacy of military operations. The element of surprise, an attribute that even conventional military forces attempt to create whenever possible, will remain an important factor in the calculations of non-state adversaries.

The evolving security environment is conducive to the development of decentralised threats that in turn is an asymmetry that irregular adversaries leverage to neutralise a conventional military force's preponderant advantage. The trend that was set in the last decades of the 20 century—of the military forces of democratic nations of the West operating in expeditionary mode in the developing world—is bound to continue unabated. This means that the military forces will be operating in nations that are not at war with one's own nation. These nations could be in the throes of internal strife, rebellions, religious revolts or sectarian violence. The military forces will be forced to function in an atmosphere where the terrain, operating environment and the local culture would all be alien. A tangible drop in the efficiency of the force and a certain amount of tactical mistakes can be expected under these circumstances.

Strategies

The time-tested strategies that have been used by military forces in previous conflicts are unlikely to succeed in the changed circumstances of contemporary conflict. Military forces of the 21 century will have to conceptualise strategies that are tailored to deter rogue nations and even non-state entities to stop initiating actions that are inimical to the security requirements of the region, as well as in an international context. The spectrum of strategies must also cater for the need to undertake preventive intervention, mostly in an expeditionary mode, to proactively stop regional challenges from becoming crises that could spin out of control.

Future military strategies must be developed at a level that it directly influences a nation's national security strategy. It cannot be merely a recipient of directions from the higher national security imperatives.

Such influence on higher level policies is necessary in order to shape the future development of the military forces and to ensure that the appropriate response mechanisms are resident in the force to counter the ever-changing threat scenario. This is vital to keeping the military forces at the cutting-edge of capability vis-à-vis the possible challenges that it will face at the operational and tactical levels. Developing and implementing such a strategy is the only assured way in which the force can be moved towards implementing a clearly capability-based planning and force structure development. The absence of a clear strategy will detract from the focus required to achieve these vital steps in the creation of a viable military force that is fit for purpose.

Conduct of Operations

At the risk of sounding dogmatic, it has to be stated that the only way in which success in military operations cane be achieved it to pursue an effects-based strategy that is directly linked to effects-based targeting in operations. The effects that have to be created must have a direct connection to the strategic objectives to be achieved and the targeting must permit a visible line to be drawn between the two. All operations must be effects-led. The military forces of the 21st century must be able to conduct mobile, expeditionary and multiple asymmetric operations with the built-in capacity to switch and swing roles rapidly.[3] The inherent volatility of the security environment would require the military forces to react to emerging situations. The capacity to achieve this effectively is dependent on the force being able to maintain an optimum teeth-to-tail ratio. The 20th century military forces had become so reliant on logistic support that rapid reaction capabilities had diminished to a level that it was non-existent at the operational level. The conflicts of the 21 century have demonstrated the need for sustainment self-sufficiency at the operational level. A complete

---

3 The terms 'switch role' and 'swing role' are commonly used within air forces. Switch Role capability denotes the necessity for a system to be 'down-timed' to change the role that it has been conducting so far, meaning that it will not be available for combat use while the change in role is being effected. A Swing Role system on the other hand is one that is capable of moving from the conduct of one role into another without needing any down-time to alter the system. Such a system is of great importance in modern and future military forces since it increases the effectiveness of the force as a whole by a factor of magnitude.

review of the teeth-to-tail ratio in order to optimise it is necessary for the efficacy of the future force.

In the past few decades, the concept of joint, combined and integrated forces have been argued about, debated and even questioned at times. At the operational level success in conflict is a product of jointness at all stages of a campaign, starting at the planning stage itself. This is true irrespective of the domain in which the combat takes place, even if it is predominated by one domain. The need, as the military forces face ever more complex challenges, is for them to move towards the concept of an integrated force while continuing to maintain domain-centric professionalism. This will be difficult to achieve, but must remain the focus of all forward thinking military forces. The next factor that is a cornerstone for the success at the operational level is the availability of actionable intelligence in a timely manner. In order to ensure such availability the military forces have to focus on generating information and knowledge on a continuous basis. Creating actionable intelligence cannot be left to the last minute since it is the product of long term gathering of information and its analysis.

In campaigns conducted far away from home, at the operational level, it is necessary to have reliable and dynamic partnerships with local forces. The need into the future would be to have sufficient interoperability in both equipment and tactics to ensure smooth coalition operations. In certain situations it might entail the building up of partner capability to a higher level to ensure smooth operations. Capacity building of the local forces is an important element in achieving operational success. Such developments will need to focus on both technology acceptance capabilities as well as operational efficiency.

Concluding Thoughts on Future Prospects

The application of military forces in the 21st century needs an all-encompassing and comprehensive review. This need is particularly acute as the century progresses through its first two decades. The first two decades have been littered with the debris of seismic shifts in international relations, exemplified by the pitfalls of the formulation of policies on the run. This ground reality has been further aggravated by two challenges that face the established democracies of the world.

The first is that the contemporary understanding of the Grand Strategy within which a nation functions is flawed and in some cases non-existent. This leads to a decision-making process at the highest levels of national security that will not, and cannot, bring together the political objectives and the effects created by elements of national power to achieve it.

Second is the increasing influence that emerging power bring to bear on global issues and challenges. International political jousting is no more a bipolar activity. The arena is now crowded with participants, both large and small, who all have their own agenda to pursue and are also capable of making short-lived alliances to defeat another bloc. This is visible in the gradual shift of global weightage in international decision-making from the Western nations to those of the Asia-Pacific region. It has become difficult for nation to increase the power of the military forces and thus emerge as a regional or global hegemon since the 21st century has steadily moved on to becoming a multi-polar world.

The Emerging Status of Military Forces

Military forces have clearly moved beyond the role of pure warfighting to undertaking a broad spectrum of operations, some of them decidedly of a benign nature. The reason for this enlarged spectrum as well as the inclusion of non-traditional roles is a complex mix of political, humane, ethical and moral factors. The end of World War II was the dawn of the post-colonial era that brought about the sharpened divide between the so-called developed and developing nations. That the newly independent nations, coming out of extreme exploitation that in some cases lasted centuries, were clubbed together as developing nations should not come as a surprise. The new nations inevitably clashed with each other since in most cases the colonising nations left ambiguous borders that were disputed from their very inception. Peace enforcement and peace-keeping became a necessary role for the military forces of the Western nations, gradually adding these roles to their militaries. There was an underlying belief that the onus of responsibility to ensure peace in their erstwhile colonies automatically rested on the Western nations and the military forces accepted this new role.

The other factor is that in most of the democracies, the military forces were the only government agency that was attuned to reacting in an orderly manner to emerging natural catastrophe, which required immediate response to save lives and return the affected area to normality. Disaster relief operations also got thrust on the military forces. In an incremental fashion, whenever a rapid and concerted effort was required to be implemented, the military forces of the nation were called to assist. In some nations, like India for example, the military has become the centrepiece of fighting insurgencies and maintaining internal law and order. This narrative is not exploring the negative impact of such employment on the warfighting efficiency of the military force in question.[4] The result has been a relatively rapid spread of the spectrum of military operations. The unfortunate part of this development is that the military forces have been left to their own devices to create the appropriate training methodologies to successfully implement the government's less than well-crafted policies.

In the nearly two decades that have passed in the 21st century, military forces have been thrust into the role of arbiters in all kinds of conflicts. In case there have been warfighting involved, such a role is understandable, but in cases where diplomacy and coercion would suffice and perhaps even be better, military forces are routinely given the responsibility to bring the tensions to an end. Such actions no doubt improve the status of military forces in the eye of the public but internally they create a schism because of the professional competence required to excel in these disparate activities. Lacking the resources to create separate cadres for each of these dissimilar tasks, the military forces of the democratic world have been struggling to meet the expectations of the government and the larger nation. Here it must also be stated that for diplomacy and coercion to work, they have to be backed and reinforced by demonstrated military power and the willingness of the nation to employ them. The question here is of the element of national power that should assume the lead in pursuing the selected strategy.

---

4   The impact of being employed in internal security duties on the efficiency and warfighting capabilities of regular military forces is an area of study that has produced a number of articles and monographs. The discussion is not germane to the thrust of the current chapter.

The situation is precarious. The elevated status that the military forces have been given is based on their performance in a variety of tasks. In recent times, most of their tasks have been outside the ambit of the traditional military role. It will only take a single failure to deliver the necessary effects to make the military force look to be in a status and position that they do not deserve. In this case, the judgement form the government and the people will be stringent and hurtful. The military forces of the 'free world' are treading a path that could see them pushed to the sidelines by other more ambitious organisations, within the democratic world. Already, the proverbial daggers are out in many nations. The currently elevated status of military forces cannot be considered an assured fact in the 21st century.

Throughout the later part of the 20th century, the effectiveness of international institutions have diminished. Therefore, the international community of nations have lesser faith in the ability of these institutions to ensure global stability. The result has been increased reliance on national power, a concept being pursued by all middle powers and even by few small powers. Building up the military forces through the acquisition of technologically sophisticated military systems has become the norm across the world. While the terms 'arms race' and 'proliferation' have been used for this phenomena, the trend brings into sharp focus the greater importance being placed on military forces to ensure national security. The downside of such acquisitions is that the receiving nation normally becomes politically subservient to the supplying nation with follow-on rippling effects that alter the geo-strategic situation in the region.

The status of the military forces influence the national security equation and security perceptions. The status given to military forces therefore tend to alter the broader security environment of a region. Any such alteration impinges on global stability in some manner, even if it is minor in nature. The cumulative effect of many such changes cannot be predicted easily, although it is certain that the move will be towards a more unstable situation.

The Importance of Civil-Military Relations[5]

Civil-military relations is the term usually used for the interaction between the elected representatives of a nation and the military forces.[6] In most democracies, the constitution provides the basis for the military forces to be subservient to the governing body, usually the parliament. In matured democracies, this relation is maintained as something sacrosanct, with a tacit understanding of the need to balance the two entities as equal parts of the national security calculus and serves the nation well, both in peace and in war. However, the relation gets skewed when either party assumes that it is the more important part of the dual entity that ensures national security. In a number of cases, the supremacy of the parliament is transferred, by default or on purpose, to the entrenched bureaucracy with disastrous results for the military forces. The civil-military relations in India, the largest democracy in the world, is an example worth an independent study as an epitome of a failing relationship.

Purely from a national security viewpoint, the military forces have to decide on the stance it will take in terms of the advice that it renders to the government. The military forces would have to decide whether the advice should be providing the best course of action to neutralise an emerging challenge or whether the advice should be the best course of action that it believes can be implemented by the government.[7] The answer to this slightly vexed question will indicate the prevailing status of civil-military relations in that country. Further, there is no correct answer to the above question. The government and the nominally subservient military forces are equally responsible to the people to ensure national security in its broadest definition.

---

5 For an in-depth analysis of the importance and historic background of civil-military relationship read, Samuel Huntington, *The Soldier and the State* Harvard University Press, Boston, 1957.

6 The relationship between the government and military forces in a nation being ruled by a dictator or an autocratic regime is not being discussed in this chapter. Any analysis of the status of military forces in such nations is superfluous to the arguments being placed here.

7 Feaver, Peter, 'Is It Worth Giving Obama Advice He Won't Listen To?' *Foreign Policy*, 4 September 2015, *foreignpolicy.com/2015/09/04/is-it-worth-giving-obama-advice-he- wont-listen-to/*, accessed on 16 October 2017.

Therefore, the judgement of both the entities have to be balanced and must complement each other at all times, to achieve optimum security.

In the 21st century, the employment of military forces has increased in the Western nations, the so-called matured democracies. The dichotomy in this development is that such employments are mostly outside of the traditional roles of the military without the government providing additional resources to develop the necessary skill sets for the military to be successful. In some cases, even a casual observer can see that the civil-military relations are strained to a breaking point. The resignation of the French Chief of the Armed Forces, General Pierre de Villiers, in July 2017 is a case in point where the civil-military relations is on the verge of breaking down completely. This trend is incompatible with the emerging security environment that demands a cooperative approach to national security. The strain in the relationship is likely to exacerbate as the century progresses.

The increasing complexity of the security environment makes efficacious policy implementation difficult and at times impossible. Such a situation could lead to frustration on both sides and carries the potential to initiate a breakdown in the relationship. In such a case, there could also arise the distinct possibility of the military forces stepping outside the traditional norms of the relationship. If this situation eventuates, it would be disastrous for the nation as well as for the continuance of democratic traditions. In democracies the traditional role of the military leadership has always been to provide the best professional and unbiased advice. This advisory role is confined to influencing the policy-making process devoid of public advocacy or dissent. It is also not meant to influence the actual policy implementation, so that it maintains a strict and ethical non-partisanship.[8]

It may not be apparent to the lay person in democracies, but there seems to be a growing schism between the civilian and military leadership, especially in situations where decisions are being made regarding the use-of-force. This growing distance may be the result of the relative rigidity of the military in implementing its advisory mechanism

---

8 Headquarters, Department of the Army, ADRP1 – *The Army Profession*, Washington, DC: U.S. Government Printing Office, June 2015, pp. 3-6.

and its decision-making process, both of which are based 'military professionalism'. In turn, this rigidity brings about an expectation of a tangible civilian reaction. However, the extreme flexibility that civilian political leaders crave to maintain goes completely against the grain of the military ethos. Broad flexibility in military forces is a prized characteristic at the operational level and narrows to a very specific dimension at the strategic decision-making space. This difference n approach creates a distance in the civil-military relationship that could lead to mistrust between the two leadership groups.

In addition, detailed military planning is done by a system that is designed to create a plan that ensures 'victory'. This system is not capable of producing multiple options and secondary plans at a rapid rate since the ultimate end-state is always 'victory' as defined in military terms. On the other hand, the civilian leadership demands the creation of plans that may achieve partial victory or even just maintain the status quo. Military plans that are based on fundamental calculations and specific definitions, or at least broadly aligned with, the concept of ends-ways-means tend to be out of synchronisation with the civilian leaderships expectations and decision-making culture.[9] In extreme cases, this cultural divide will result in the civil-military combined decision-making process become dysfunctional.

In all democracies this friction between the civilian leadership and the military hierarchy is visible to a greater or lesser degree and is unlikely to be mitigated completely.[10] In case this friction gets totally resolved, the State will either become fully militarised or the military forces will be 'emasculated' and become a sidelined bit-player in the national security arena. Therefore, this friction must be embraced by both the sides of the equation, which is the only way to ensure a robust national security process. The test of maturity is the inherent ability of the institutions to maintain the right balance without letting

---

9 Janine Davidson, 'Civil-Military Friction and Presidential Decision Making: Explaining the Broken Dialogue,' *Presidential Studies Quarterly*, Vol. 43, No.1, March, 2013, Center for the Study of the Presidency and Congress, Washington D.C., pp. 129-145.

10 Snider, Don M., 'A New Era in Civ-Mil Relations: Rendering Advice to Those Who Do Not Want It', *Strategic Insight*, 2 November 2015, US Army War College, Carlisle, 2015.

the relationship lapse into acrimony. When asked just before his retirement, what military leaders could do to change the situation, the then-Chairman of the Joint Chiefs, General Marty Dempsey, replied, 'Elected officials are hardwired to ask for options first and then reverse engineer to objectives. And the military is hard wired to do exactly the opposite... Now what do we do about that situation? Nothing frankly. But that is the environment we live and work in'.[11]

A functioning democracy will base grand strategic decision-making on the credibility of both the civil and military leadership and the mutual trust that this group holds for each other. Such decisions, of necessity, will have to be argued and negotiated, playing to the strengths of the nation and made taking into account the context under which it is being made. The civil-military relationship must be based on a very clear and mutually inclusive understanding of few fundamental facts. First, that the military will always give the best possible advice and not what it thinks the civilian leadership wants to hear. The second-guessing of the civilian leadership is a dangerous trend and will inevitably lead to the politicisation of the military forces and end in sycophancy. Second, the military professionalism must be built to a level that creates unblemished credibility so that it automatically enthuses trust within the civilian leadership. Third, an acceptance, based on proven track record, that military professionalism has not been tainted or sacrificed at the altar of parochial opportunism. Lastly, an appreciation of the necessity to keep the moral compass of grand strategic decision-making as the guiding force in national security issues.[12]

Unlike in the years following World War II, 21 century demands much more sophistication in conceptual thinking from the military leadership. They need to be able to offer the civilian leadership a variety of options, all of which should be aligned with the desired political objectives if they are to retain their influence on policy making. The need is to develop military leadership with sufficient strategic mindedness

---

11 Collins, Joseph and Hooker, Richard, "From the Chairman: An Interview with Martin E. Dempsey," *Joint Force Quarterly*, Vol. 78, 3rd Quarter, 2015, National Defense University, Washington D.C., pp 2-13, quotation from pp. 7.

12 Freidson, Eliot, *Professionalism: The Third Logic*, University of Chicago Press, Chicago, IL, 2001, pp. 220-221.

that will overcome the traditional operational warfighting ethos of the military. The experience of the nearly two decades of the 21 century that have gone past indicates that improved dialogue between the civil and military leadership tend to produce better policy options and optimised strategies to achieve them.[13] Military leaders have to play an increasingly larger role in this vital area if the employment of military forces are to lead to true victory.

Concluding the Book

This book is an amalgam of five theoretical concepts—at once independent of each other and yet interconnected, influencing each other's development in subtle and nuanced ways. In democracies across the world, whether one that is newly emerged after de-colonisation or one that has been established for a few centuries, the thread that connects a nation to its national security, policy and strategy is the one that retains the concept of its established sovereignty. In recent times, the continuing evolution of the definition of national security, a process itself that is constantly evolving, has made it imperative for the strategic leadership to review the relationship between national policies and the grand strategy of the nation. Needless to state, the pursuance of national security is also becoming a complex and involved exercise in the application of national power.

The emerging 21st century world, at this time of the end of its second decade, is not a pretty sight. The human race seems to be mindlessly hurtling itself on a path that can only lead to its obliteration, even while the signposts that this is indeed the case are being blissfully ignored. The inability of 'world leadership'—if there is such a body—to be visionary and to set a sustainable goal for the future is appallingly obvious. The diminishing influence of the great powers, willingness of some nations to support violent groups that function outside the accepted legal framework, and the inherent immaturity of emerging powers combine to destabilise the global geo-political environment. At the same time, emerging powers are altering the power balance within

---

13 Rapp, William E., 'Civil-Military Relations: The Role of Military Leaders in Strategy Making', *Parameters*, 45(3) Autumn 2015, US Army War College, Carlisle, pp. 25-26.

the international comity of nations—there is now embryonic space for the emergence of a new and multi-polar world.

War and armed conflict have been constant companions of the human impulse to secure what a group of people—a tribe, clan or nation—have considered their possession, irrespective of the material value attached to the so-called possession. The intrinsic value of something, tangible and visible such as land or intangible and merely 'felt' by human nature, is what makes that something worth defending and spilling blood over. While the military forces of a nation stands at the forefront of securing it from attack, the conduct of conflict has altered inexorably in the past few centuries. All through history, war has never been only about combat operations by the military forces of a nation. Physical combat that involves death and destruction has only been one part of a nation's actions to secure what it considers worth protecting—both material and virtual assets. In the past few decades, the characteristics and conduct of armed conflict have altered far more than any comparable period of time in history. The principles of Just War Theory and the accepted Laws of Armed Conflict have been almost completely abandoned and a conventional military force has been left wondering as to how victory in war is defined.

There is no vouchsafing the fact that military forces are meant to uphold the sovereignty of a nation at all times by 'securing' the state. It is in the understanding of what constitutes safety of the nation that both evolutionary and revolutionary changes have taken place in the past six or seven decades. As the appreciation of human values, the rights of individuals and the esoteric concept of human equality have taken hold, the definitions of national security have also evolved, broadened and become almost all-encompassing. In this process of evolution, the thread of continuity in the national security equation has been the military forces that have continued to be a critical element in the national power balance. Unfortunately, in recent times, partisan practitioners of the other elements of national power have made attempts—successfully it seems—to limit the role of the military forces in the national security equation. Moving the military forces to the periphery of the national security construct is not only a detrimental step, but one that will eventually lead to the nation being left wide open to the vagaries of successful adversary attacks. The national security leadership at the strategic level has to clearly understand that the military forces continue to stand at the vanguard of national security, now defined in the broadest possible terms that encompass the protection of national interests and values.

There is no doubting that the threats to national security have become increasingly complex and multi-faceted. The responses to the rapidly changing threat scenario have not been able to keep pace with the changes, to the detriment of national security itself. A whole-of-government approach to national security has been an innovative way to bridge this merging gap between threats and responses. It may not be out of place here to mention that of all the elements of national power, the military forces understand and appreciate this concept more than any other power element. Even so, in times of a volatile security environment, the military force becomes the element of national power that comes to the fore to assure national sovereignty. This capability to assume the lead in extremely difficult circumstances makes the military force a critical element in ensuring the security of a nation. The clear message that military forces send out is that threat mitigation is optimally achieved through adopting a whole-of-government strategy, with the military forces in the lead.

In a short, trite sentence; military forces ensure national security. In the contemporary world, this fundamental truth is often shrouded in vague concepts of 'peaceful co-existence', international political order, and at times a naïve belief in human goodness. Democracies, especially the merging nations seem to have a proclivity to focus on the other, non-lethal elements of national power to further national interests and ensure the security of the nation. Again, this is a utopian understanding of the world, viewed from an ivory tower, completely devoid of the ground realities of international relations and geo-strategy. All soft power elements invariably derive their strength from the hard power of national military forces. This hard power, an inherent capability of the military forces, have also to be demonstrated to others through their employment and exercises. Even such demonstrations will be of no importance if the nation does not clearly exhibit the will to employ their military forces through emphatic and pragmatic civilian leadership, ably supported by the military hierarchy.

A nation that does not understand and cater to this basic concept of national security built on the foundation of a strong and flexible military force will be gambling with its sovereignty.

BIBLIOGRAPHY

Books

Albanese, Jay S.,& Reichel, Philip L., (eds), *Transnational Organized Crime: An Overview of Six Continents*, Sage Publications India, New Delhi, 2014.

Alexander, Bevin, *The Future of Warfare*, WW Norton & Co Inc., New York, 1995.

Art, Robert J., & Waltz, Kenneth Neal, (eds), *The Use of Force: Military Power and International Politics*, Rowman & Littlefield Publisher, Lanham, MD, 1999.

Ashdown, P., *Swords and Ploughshares: Building Peace in the 21st Century*, Orion Books, London, 2008.

Aydin, Aysegul, *Foreign Power and Intervention in Armed Conflicts*, Stanford University Press, Stanford, CA, 2012.

Basevich, Andrew J., *The New American Militarism: How Americans Are Seduced By War*, Oxford University Press, New York, 2005.

Beaumont, Roger, *Joint Military Operations: A Short History*, Praeger, Westport, Connecticut, 1993.

Biddle, Stephen, *Military Power: Explaining Victory and Defeat in Modern Battle*, Princeton University Press, Princeton, 2004.

Bobbitt, Philip, *The Shield of Achilles: War, Peace and the Course of History*, Penguin Books, London, 2002.

Bongiovanni, Francesco M., *The Decline and Fall of Europe*, Palgrave Macmillan, UK, 2012.

Brent, Keith (ed), *Air Power and Coercive Diplomacy*, the Proceedings of the 2012 RAAF Air Power Conference, Air Power Development Centre, Canberra, 2012.

Brown, Harold, *Thinking about national security: Defense and foreign policy in a dangerous world*, Westview Press, Boulder Co, 1983.

Bryson, Bill, *At Home: A Short History of Private Life*, Transworld Publishers, London, 2010.

Buck, Susan J., *The Global Commons: An Introduction*, Earthscan Publications, Abington, UK, 1998.

Burleigh, Michael, *Moral Combat: A History of World War II*, Harper Press, London, UK, 2010.

Calleo, David P., *Rethinking Europe's Future*, A Century Foundation Book, Princeton University Press, Princeton, 2003.

Cerami Joseph R., & Holcomb Jr, James F. (eds), *Guide to Strategy*, US Army War College, Carlisle, PA, 2001.

Carlin, Mara E., *Building Militaries in Fragile States: Challenges for the United States*, University of Pennsylvania Press, Philadelphia, 2017.

Clausewitz, Carl von, *On War*, trans. Colonel J. J. Graham, Barnes & Noble, New York, 2004.

Cohen, Eliot A., *The Big Stick: The Limits of Soft Power and the Necessity of Military Power*, Hachette Book Group, New York, 2017.

Collins, John M., *Military Strategy: Principles, Practices, and Historical Perspectives*, Brassey's Inc, Washington D.C., 2002.

Confucius, *The Analects*, Translated by Dawson, Raymond, Oxford University Press, Oxford, UK, 2008.

Davies, Richard, *Hamas, Popular Support and War in the Middle East: Insurgency in the Holy Land*, Contemporary Terrorism Studies, Routledge, Abington, U.K., 2016.

Desch, Michael C., *Civilian Control of the Military: The Changing Security Environment*, The Johns Hopkins University Press, Baltimore, 1999.

Dixon, Martin, *A Textbook on International Law*, 7th Edition, Oxford University Press, Oxford, 2013.

Doniger, Wendi, & Smith, Brian K. (trans), *The Laws of Manu*, Penguin Books, New York, 1991.

Dorman, A., Smith, M.,& Uttley, M., (eds), *The Changing Face of Military Power: Joint Warfighting in an expeditionary Era*, Cormorant Security Studies Series, Palgrave Macmillan, UK, 2002.

Drozdiak, William, *Fractured Continent: Europe's Crises and the Fate of the West*, W. H. Norton and Company, New York, 2017.

Echevarria II, Antulio J., *Clausewitz and Contemporary War*, Oxford University Press, New York, 2007.

Ernest R. & Dupey, Trevor N., *The Harper Encyclopedia of Military History: From 3,500 B.C to the Present*, Harper-Collins, New York, 1993.

Evans, Gareth, *The Responsibility to Protect: Ending Mass Atrocity Crimes Once and For All*, Brookings Institution Press, Washington D.C., 2008.

Evans, Michael, Parkin, Russell, Ryan, Alan (eds), *Future Armies Future Challenges: Land Warfare in the Information Age*, Allen & Unwin, NSW, 2004.

Farewell, Byron, *Queen Victoria's Little Wars*, Harper and Row, New York, 1972.

Feaver, Peter D., *Armed Servants: Agency, Oversight and Civil-Military Relations*, Harvard University Press, Massachusetts, 2003.

Fernandez-Armesto, F., *Millenium*, Bantam Books, London, 1995.

Finkel, Meir, *On Flexibility: Recovery from Technological and Doctrinal Surprises in the Battlefield*, Tlamin, Moshe, (translator), Stanford Security Studies, University Press, Stanford, 2011.

Flint, Colin, & Taylor, Peter, *Political geography: World Economy, Nation-State and Locality*, Prentice Hall, New Jersey, 2007.

Flynn, Matthew J., *First Strike: Preemptive War in Modern History*, Routledge, New York, 2008.

Fotion, Nicholas, *War & Ethics: A New Just War Theory*, Continuum International Publishing Group, London, 2007.

Gelvin, James L., *The Arab Uprisings: What Everyone Needs to Know*, Oxford University Press, New York, 2012.

Geutsh, Eliot (trans), *The Bhagawad Gita*, Holt, Rinehart and Winston, New York, 1968.

Gray, Colin S., *Modern Strategy*, Oxford University Press, Oxford, 1999.

_____*War, Peace, and International relations: An Introduction to Strategic History*, Routledge, Abingdon MA, 2007.

Green, Leslie C., *The Contemporary Law of Armed Conflict*, 3rd Ed, Manchester University Press, Manchester U.K., May 2008.

Hadar, Leon T., *Quagmire: America in the Middle East*, Cato Institute, Washington D.C., 1992.

Herd, Graeme P. (ed), *Great Powers and Strategic Stability in the 21 Century: Competing Visions of World Order*, Routledge Global Security Studies, Routledge, Abington, UK, 2010.

Hildinger, Erik, *Warriors of the Steppe: A Military History of Central Asia, 500 B.C to 1,700 A.D*, Sarpedon, New York, 1997.

Hills, Alice, *Future War in Cities: Rethinking a Liberal Dilemma*, Frank Cass Publishers, London, 2004.

Holsti, Kalevi J., *The State, War and the State of War*, Cambridge University Press, Cambridge, UK, 1996.

Hosang, J. F. R. Boddens, *Rules of Engagement: Rules on the Use of Force as Linchpin for the International Law of Military Operations*, University of Amsterdam, Netherlands, 2017.

Howard, Michael & Paret, Peter, (eds & trans), Carl von Clausewitz, *On War*, Princeton University Press, Princeton, NJ, 1976.

Hughes, Barrie, (General Ed), *The Penguin Working Words*, Penguin Books Australia, Ringwood, Victoria, 1993.

Huntington, Samuel P., *The Soldier and the State: The Theory and Politics of Civil-Military Relations*, Harvard University Press, Massachusetts, 1957.

Janowitz, Morris, *The Professional Soldier: A Social and Political Portrait*, Originally published 1960, Free Press; reissue edition 2017.

Johnson, Loch K., *The Threat on the Horizon: An Inside Account of America's Search for Security After the Cold War*, Oxford University Press, New York, 2011.

Kagan, Robert, *The Return of History and the End of Dreams*, Atlantic Books, London, 2008.

Kainikara, Sanu, *The Bolt From the Blue: Air Power in the Cycle of Strategies*, Air Power Development Centre, Canberra, 2013.

Keegan, John, *A History of Warfare*, Knopf, New York, 1993.

Kennedy, David, *Of War and Law*, Princeton University Press, Princeton, NJ, 2006.

Khalilzad, Zalmay, & Lesser, Ian O., *Sources of Conflict in the 21st Century*, Rand Corporation, Santa Monica, CA, 1998.

Kilcullen, David J., *Counterinsurgency*, Oxford University Press, New York, 2010.

Kissinger, Henry, *World Order*, Penguin Books UK, 2014.

Lamy, Steven L., Masker, John S., and others, *Introduction to Global Politics*, Oxford University Press, New York, Fourth Edition, 2017, (First published 1997).

Lauzon, Dru, & Vine, Andrew, *'Security and Governance: Foundations for International Stability'*, Colloquium Brief, published by Strategic Studies Institute, US Army War College, Carlisle, PA, 2010.

Lazenby, J., *Hannibal's War*, Warminster: Aris & Phillips, Oxford University Press, Oxford, UK, 1978.

Legge, James, (ed), *The Chinese Classics,* Adamant Media Corporation, Boston, 2000, (First published in 1894).

Levite, Ariel E., Jentleson, Bruce W., & Berman, Larry, (eds), *Foreign Military Intervention: The Dynamics of Protracted Conflict,* Columbia University Press, New York, 1992.

Libicki, Martin C., Shatz, Howard J., & Taylor, Julie E., *Global Demographic Change and Its Implications for Military Power,* RAND Publications, Santa Monica, CA, 2011.

Liddell Hart, B. H., *Strategy,* Second Revised Edition, Meridian Printing, USA, 1991.

Lippman, Walter, *Liberty and the News,* Dover Publications, New York, 2010 (First published 1920).

Lonsdale, David J., *The Nature of War in the Information Age: Clausewitzian Future,* Frank Cass, London, 2004.

McKeon, Richard, (ed) *The Basic Works of Aristotle,* Random House, New York, 1941.

Mo Tzu, *The Basic Writings,* Translated by Watson, Burton, Columbia University Press, New York, 1963.

Modelski, George, *Principles of World Politics,* Free Press, New York, 1972.

Morrissey, John, *The Long War: Centcom, Grand Strategy and Global Security,* University of Georgia Press, Georgia, 2017.

Motyl, A. J., *Encyclopaedia of Nationalism, Vol 1: Fundamental Themes,* Academic Press, San Diego California, USA, 2001.

Mulinen, Fredric De, *Handbook on the Law of War for Armed Forces,* International Committee of the Red Cross, Geneva, 1987.

Munshi, Surendra, & Abraham, Biju Paul (eds), *Good Governance, Democratic Societies and Globalisation,* Sage Publications India, New Delhi, 2004.

Nye Jr, Joseph S., *The Paradox of American Power*, Oxford University Press, New York, 2002.

_____*Soft Power: The Means to Success in World Power*, Public Affairs, New York, 2004.

Paleri, Prabhakaran, *National Security: Imperatives and Challenges*, Tata McGraw-Hill, New Delhi, 2008.

Plato, *The Republic*, trans. by Jowett, B., The Modern Library, New York, 1941.

Pernin, Christopher G., Nichiporuk Brian, and others, *Unfolding the Future of the Long War: Motivations, Prospects, and Implications for the U.S. Army*, Rand Corporation, Santa Monica, CA, 2008.

Priebe, Miranda, Rohn, Laurinda L., and others, *Promoting Joint Warfighting Proficiency: The Role of Doctrine in Preparing Airmen for Joint Operations*, Rand Corporation, Santa Monica, CA, 2018.

Randle, Robert F., *Issues in the History of International Relations: The Role of Issues in the Evolution of the State System*, Praeger, Westport, Conn, 1987.

Rangarajan, L. N., *Kautilya: The Arthashastra*, Penguin Books India, New Delhi, 1992.

Rapoports, Anatol, (ed), *Clausewitz On War*, Penguin Books, Middlesex, England, 1968.

Regan, Richard J., *Just War: Principles and Cases*, The Catholic University of America Press, Washington D.C., 1996.

Ries, Tomas, *The Global Security Environment 2030 and Military Missions*, Swedish National Defence College, Stockholm, 2010.

Richards, Julian, *A Guide to National Security: Threats, Responses, and Strategies*, Oxford University Press, Oxford, UK, 2012.

Rid, Thomas, & Keaney, Thomas, *Understanding Counterinsurgency: Doctrine, operations, and challenges*, Routledge, Abington, 2010.

Romm, Joseph J., *Defining National Security: The Nonmilitary Aspects*, Council of Foreign Relations Press, New York, 1993.

Rupy, Kendra, & Rustad, Siri Aas, *Trends in Armed Conflict 1946-2017*, Peace Research Institute, Oslo, 2018.

Russell, James A., & Wirtz, James J., (eds), *Globalization and WMD Proliferation: Terrorism, transnational networks, and international security*, Routledge, Abingdon, UK, 2008.

Schelling, Thomas C., *The Strategy of Conflict*, Harvard University Press, Cambridge, Mass, 1960.

_____*Arms and Influence*, Yale University Press, New Haven, CT, 1966.

Schied, Don E., (ed), *The Ethics of Armed Humanitarian Intervention*, Cambridge University Press, Cambridge, UK, 2014.

Seybolt, Taylor B., *Humanitarian Military Intervention: The Conditions for Success and Failure*, Sipri, Oxford University Press, Oxford, UK, 2007.

Sirohi, Captain R. K., *Guerrilla Warfare*, Prashant Publishing House, Delhi, 2009.

Smith, Dan, *Trends and Causes of Armed Conflict*, Berghof Research Centre, Berlin, 2004.

Smith, Rupert, *The Utility of Force: The Art of War in the Modern World*, Alfred Knopf, New York, 2007.

Snow, Donald M., *The Case Against Military Intervention: Why We Do It and Why It Fails*, Routledge, New York, 2016.

_____*Thinking About National Security: Strategy, Policy and Issues*, Routledge, New York, 2016.

Solomon, Hussein, (ed), *Challenges to Global Security: Geopolitics and Power in an Age of Transition*, I.B. Tauris & Co, London, 2008.

Spiller, Roger, *An Instinct for War: Scenes from the Battlefields of History*, Harvard University Press, Cambridge, 2005.

Steingerg, S. H., *The Thirty Years War and the Conflict for European Hegemony 1600-1660*, W. W. Norton and Company Inc, New York, 1966.

Stone, John, *Military Strategy: The Politics and Technique of War*, Continuum International Publishing Group, London, 2011.

Strassler Robert B., (ed), *The Landmark Thucydides: A Comprehensive Guide to the Peloponnesian War*, Free Press; Touchstone Edition, New York, September 1998.

Taylor, Alan J. P., *The Struggle for Mastery in Europe 1848-1918*, Oxford Press, Clarendon, 1945.

Tellis, Ashley J., Bially, Janice, and others, *Measuring National Power in the Post-Industrial Age*, RAND Corporation, Santa Monica, CA, 2000.

Thornton, Rod, *Asymmetric Warfare: Threat and Response in the Twenty-First Century*, Polity Press, Cambridge, U.K., 2007.

Thucydides, *The Landmark Thucydides: A Comprehensive Guide to The Peloponnesian War*, Strassler, Robert B., (ed), Free Press, Touchstone Edition, Cambridge University Press, 1998.

Tuchman, Barbara W., *The March of Folly: From Troy to Vietnam*, Ballantine Books, New York, 1984.

Van Creveld, Martin, *Technology and War: From 2000 B.C. to the Present*, The Free Press, New York, 1991.

Waltz, Kenneth N., *Man, the State, and War: A Theoretical Analysis*, Columbia University Press, Columbia, 2001.

_____ *Theory of International Politics*, McGraw-Hill, New York, 1979.

Waters, R. F., & Mcgee, T. G., (eds), *Asia-Pacific: New Geographies of the Pacific Rim*, Crawford House Publishing, Bathurst, NSW, 1997.

Watson, Adam, *The Evolution of International Societies: A Comparative Historical Analysis*, Routledge, London, 1992.

Weir, William, *Guerrilla Warfare: Irregular warfare in the Twentieth Century*, Pentagon Press, New Delhi, 2009.

Weitsman, Patricia A., *Waging War: Alliances, Coalitions, and Institutions of Interstate Violence*, Stanford Security Studies, Stanford University Press, Stanford, CA, 2014.

Woodham-Smith, Ceil, *The Reason Why*, Penguin Books Ltd., Harmondsworth, Great Britain, 1958.

Worth, Robert F., *A Rage for Order: The Middle-East in Turmoil, from Tahir Square to ISIS*, Farrar, Straus and Giroux, New York, 2016.

Wright, Quincy, *A Study of War*, 2nd Ed, University of Chicago Press, Chicago, Ill, 1965.

Monographs, Magazines, Articles, Papers, Reports Etc.,

Ahmed, Ali, 'Political Dimensions of Limited War', *IDSA Comment*, Institute of Defence Studies and Analysis, New Delhi, 29 March 2010.

Baille, Mark, 'Know your enemy: Not just terrorism,' *Defense News*, Virginia, 11 April 2005.

Bitzinger, Richard A., 'Can the Defence Industry Still Innovate?', *RSIS Commenatries No 080/2012*, S. Rajaratnam School of International Studies, Nanyang Technological University, Singapore, 8 May 2012.

Cohen, Ariel & Hamilton, Robert E., 'The Russian Military in the Georgia War: Lessons and Implications', *ERAP Monograph*, Strategic Studies Institute, US Army War College, Carlisle, PA, 2011.

Davis Jr, Major John R., 'Defeating Future Hybrid Threats', *Military Review*, September-October 2013, Army University Press, Fort Leavenworth, KS, 2013.

Edmunds, Timothy, 'What are the Armed Forces For? The Changing Nature of Military Roles in Europe', in *International Affairs*, Vol. 82, Issue 6, 2006, Royal Institute of International Affairs, London, 2006.

Emmers, Ralf, 'The Role of Five Power Defence Arrangements in the Southeast Asian Security Architecture,' *RSIS Working Paper No. 195*, S. Rajaratnam School of International Studies, Nanyang Technological University, Singapore, 20 April 2010.

Feaver, Peter, 'Civil-Military Relations', *Annual Review of Political Science*, Vol. 2, No 1, Paolo Alta, CA, 1999.

Fleming, Major Brian B., *The Hybrid Threat Concept: Contemporary War, Military Planning and the Advent of Unrestricted Operational Art*, School of Advanced Military Studies, Fort Leavenworth, KS, 2011

Freedman, George, 'Geopolitics, Nationalism and Dual Citizenship,' in *Stratfor* 116/10, 21 July 2010.

Freedman, Lawrence, 'Military Power and Political Influence', *International Affairs*, Vol 74, No 4, October 1998, Oxford University Press for RUSI, London, 1998.

Fry, Robert, Lt Gen Sir, 'Expeditionary Operations in the Modern Era', *The RUSI Journal*, Volume 150, 2005-Issue 6, RUSI, London, 2005.

Gaub, Dr Florence, 'Predicting the Arab Spring: What we got wrong', *Jane's Defence Weekly*, 8 February 2012.

Gomart, Thomas, *Russian Civil-Military Relations: Putin's Legacy*, Carnegie Endowment for International Peace, Washington D.C., 2008.

Gompert, David C., 'Preparing Military Forces for Integrated Operations in the Face of Uncertainty', *Rand Issue Paper*, Rand Corporation, San Francisco, 2005.

_____ 'Constraints of military power: Lessons of the past decade', *The Adelphi Papers 17-133*, International Institute for Strategic Studies, London, 2008.

Gray, Colin S., *Hard Power and Soft Power: The Utility of Military Force as an Instrument of Policy in the 21st Century*, Strategic Studies Institute, US Army War College, Carlisle, PA, April 2011.

_____ 'Moral Advantage, Strategic Advantage?' in *The Journal of Strategic Studies*, Vol 33, No 3, June 2010

Gupta, Sanjay, 'The Doctrine of Pre-Emptive Strike: Application and Implications', *International Political Science Review*, Vol 29, No 2, March 2008, Sage Publications, California, 2008.

Harris, Owen, 'Costs of a Needless War,' *The Australian*, Sydney, 18 July 2005.

Interview with Keith Alexander, General US Army, in *Jane's International Defence Review*, November 2010.

Jablonski, David, 'The State of the National Security State', *Parameters*, Winter 2002-03, US Army War College, Carlisle, PA, 2002.

Kainikara, Sanu, 'Principles of War and Air Power', *Working Paper No 31*, Air Power Development Centre, Canberra, June 2011.

_____'The Strategy of Deterrence and Air Power', *Working Paper 27*, Air Power Development Centre, Canberra, 2008.

Kalha, R.S., 'Is the Arab spring over?', *IDSA Comment*, Institute for Defence Studies and Analyses, New Delhi, 26 June 2012.

Laksmana, Evan A., *RSIS Commentaries 169/2010*, S. Rajaratnam School of International Studies, Nanyang Technological University, Singapore, 14 December 2010.

Latif, Asad, 'The World of the Secular Pope', *The Straits Times*, Singapore, 4 January 2013.

Lauzon, Dru & Vine, Andrew (eds), 'Security and Governance: Foundations for International Stability', *Colloquium Brief*, Strategic Studies Institute, U.S. Army War College, Carlisle, PA, June 2010.

Lee, Marc, 'Avoiding Future Shock as Global Instability Grows,' *Jane's Defence Weekly*, 5 September 2007.

Lele, Ajey, 'Space Code of Conduct: Inadequate Mechanism', *IDSA Comment*, Institute of Defence Studies and Analyses, New Delhi, 18 June 2012.

Long, Tom, 'Small States, Great Power? Gaining Influence Through Intrinsic, Derivative and Collective Power', *International Studies Review*, 19(2), Oxford University Press, Oxford, June 2017.

Marshall, Thomas, and others (eds), *Problems and Solutions in Future Coalition Operations*, Strategic Studies Institute, US Army War College, Carlisle, PA, 1997.

McInnis, Kathleen J., 'Lessons in coalition warfare: Past, present and implications for the future', *International Political Review*, December 2013, Vol 1, Issue 2, Palgrave Macmillan, UK, 2013.

Mueller, John E., 'Trends in Popular Support for the Wars in Korea and Vietnam', *The American Political Science Review*, June 1971, Vol 65, No 2, Sage Publications, California, 1971.

National Research Council, *Understanding the Changing Planet: Strategic Directions for the Geographical Sciences*, The National Academies Press, Washington D.C., 2010.

Nurkin, Tate, 'Getting Creative to Fight Future Battles', *Jane's Defence Weekly*, 23 November 2011.

Olsen, John Andeas, (ed), *On New Wars*, Oslo Files: On defence and Security – 04/2007, Norwegian Institute for Defence Studies, Oslo, 2007.

Omand, Sir David, 'Securing the State: National Security in Contemporary Times', *RSIS Working Paper No 251*, S. Rajaratnam School of International Studies, Singapore, 6 November 2012

Owen, William F., 'The War of New Word: Why Military History Trumps Buzzwords', *Armed Forces Journal*, Virginia, November 2009.

Podhorec, Milan, 'The Reality of Operational Environment in Military Operations', *Journal of Defence Resource Management*, Vol 3, Issue 2, (5) 2015, University of Defence, Brno, Czech Republic, 2012.

Popescu, Leonard and Nicu, *A Power Audit of EU-Russia Relations*, report by the European Council on Foreign Relations, Brussels, November 2007.

Rose, Gregory, 'Irregular warfare blows hole in Geneva rules', *The Australian*, 26 August 2011.

Sawhney, Ashok, Commodore (Retd), 'Cyber War in the 21 Century: The Emerging Security Challenge', *RSIS Commentaries 20/2010*, S. Rajaratnam School of International Studies, NTU, Singapore, 18 February 2010.

Skinner, Tony, 'US Power 'likely to wane', warns NIC Report', *Jane's Defence Weekly*, London, 26 November 2008.

Stratfor 41/12, 'The Geopolitics of Shifting Defence Expenditure', Austin, Texas, 12 March 2012.

Thayer, Carlyle A., 'The Five Power Defence Agreements: The Quiet Achiever,' *Security Challenges*, Volume 3, No. 1, Kokoda Foundation, Canberra, February 2007.

Verity, Julie (ed), *The New Strategic Landscape: Innovative Perspectives on Strategy*, Palgrave Macmillan, New York, 2012.

Villanueva, Adrian, 'Don't underestimate need for strong military', Forum, *The Straits Times*, Singapore, 30 January 2016.

Waxman, Mathew C., 'Regulating Resort to Force: Form and Substance of the UN Charter Regime', *The European Journal of International Law*, Vol 24, No 1, Oxford University Press, Oxford, 2013.

Wolfers, Arnold, 'National Security as an Ambiguous Symbol,' in *Political Science Quarterly*, Vol 67, No 4, December 1952, The Academy of Political Science, New York, 1952.

Yates, Athol, 'What Defence Really Does', *Canberra Times*, Canberra, ACT, 2 July 2012.

Resources accessed on-line

Baily, Martin Neil & Elliott, Douglas J., *'The U.S Financial and Economic Crisis: Where Does it stand and Where Do We Go From Here?'* The Brookings Institution, http://www.brookings.edu/papers/2009/0615_economic_crisis_bailey_elliott-aspx?p=1

Bloom, David, & Canning, David, 'Global Demography: Fact, Force and Future', *PGDA Working Papers No 1406*, 2006, http://ideas.repec.org/p/gdm/wpaper/1406.html

Bolton, Joseph G., Leonard, Robert S., and others, *Sources of Weapon System Cost Growth: Analysis of 35 Major Defense Acquisition Programs*, RAND Corporation, Santa Monica, CA, 2008. https://www.

rand.org/content/dam/rand/pubs/monographs/2008/RAND_MG670.pdf

Brotz, Howard, & Wilson, Everett, 'Characteristics of Military Society', *American Journal of Sociology*, Vol 51, No 5, March 1946, The University of Chicago Press, Chicago, 1946, https://www.journals.uchicago.edu/doi/abs/10.1086/219845?journalCode=ajs

Bowdish, Randall G., *Military Strategy: Theory and Concepts*, Dissertation presented to the Graduate College at the University of Nebraska, Lincoln, Nebraska, June 2013. http://digitalcommons.unl.edu/poliscitheses/26

Carden, James, 'A New Poll Shows the Public is Overwhelmingly opposed to Endless US Military Interventions', *The Nation*, 9 January 2018, https://www.thenation.com/article/new-poll-shows-public-overwhelmingly-opposed-to-endless-us-military-interventions/

Feld, M. D., 'Information and Authority: The Structure of Military Organization, *American Sociological Review*, Vol 24, No 1, February 1959, https://www.jstor.org/stable/2089578?seq=1#page_scan_tab_contents

Freedman, Lawrence, 'On War and Choice', *The National Interest*, The Centre for National Interest, Washington D.C., 20 April 2010, https://nationalinterest.org/article/on-war-and-choice-3440

Gajewski, Gregory R., *Democracy, Resource Abundance and Growth: The Debate*, The Louis Berger Group Inc., New Jersey, 2012. https://www.louisberger.com/sites/default/files/Democracy_Resource_Abundance_and_Growth_The_Debate.pdf

Green, James A., & Grimal, Francis, 'The Threat of Force as an Action in Self-Defense Under International Law', *Journal of Transnational Law*, Volume 44, Vanderbilt University, Nashville, TN, 2012, pp. 289-295. https://www.vanderbilt.edu/wp-content/uploads/sites/78/green-cr.pdf

Guiora, Amos N., 'Determining a Legitimate Target: The Dilemma of the Decision-Maker', *Texas International Law Journal*, Volume 47,

Issue 2, Spring 2012, Austin, Texas. http://www.tilj.org/content/journal/47/num2/Guiora315.pdf

Hughes, Dr Geraint, *Predicting Future Trends in Warfare*, Defence-in-Depth, Defence Studies Department, King's College, London, 2018, https://defenceindepth.co/2018/02/21/predicting-future-trends-in-warfare/

Jane's Editorial Staff, 'Global defence spending to hit post-Cold War high in 2018', IHS Markit, I, 18 December 2017, https://ihsmarkit.com/research-analysis/global-defence-spending-to-hit-post-cold-war-high-in-2018.html

Jennings, Will, Bevan, Shaun, and others, 'Effects of the Core Functions of Government on the Diversity of Executive Agendas, *Comparative Political Studies*, Vol 44, Issue 8, Sage Publications, California, May 2011. http://journals.sagepub.com/doi/abs/10.1177/0010414011405165

Milestones: 1945 – 1952, National Security Act of 1947, Office of the Historian (USA), https://history.state.gov/milestones/1945-1952/national-security-act

O'Rourke, Ronald, 'A Shift in the International Security Environment: Potential Implications for Defense—Issues for Congress', *Congressional Research Service Report*, Washington, 26 April 2018. https://fas.org/sgp/crs/natsec/R43838.pdf

Orwell, George, *Notes on Nationalism*, First Published by Polemic, London, Great Britain, May 1945, http://orwell.ru/library/essays/nationalism/english/e_nat

O'Toole, Molly, 'UN Ambassador Warns Against Intervention Fatigue', *Defense One*, Atlantic Media, Boston, 19 November 2014, https://www.defenseone.com/threats/2014/11/un-ambassador-warns-against-intervention-fatigue/99485/

Quiggin, John, 'China's Imminent Collapse', *The National Interest*, http://nationalinterest.org/commentary/chinas-imminent-collapse-5880

Sachs, Stephen E., *The Changing Definition of Security*, http://www.stevesachs.com/papers/paper_security.html

Sassen, Saskia, 'Welcome to a new kind of war: the rise of endless urban conflict', *The Guardian*, International Edition, 30 January 2018, https://www.theguardian.com/cities/2018/jan/30/new-war-rise-endless-urban-conflict-saskia-sassen

Shackman, Gene, Xun Wang & Ya-Lin Liu, *Brief Review of World Population Trends*, http://gsociology.icaap.org/reprot/demsum.html

Shah, Anup, 'Global Financial Crisis', *Global Issues*, 24 March 2013, http://www.globalissues.org/article/768/global-financial-crisis

Shaw, Martin, 'The Legitimacy of War Today', *E-International Relations*, 26 July 2008, https://www.e-ir.info/2008/07/26/the-legitimacy-of-war-today/

Smoler, Fredric, 'Fighting the Last War—and The Next', *American Heritage*, Vol 52, Issue 8, November/December 2001, https://www.americanheritage.com/content/fighting-last-war%E2%80%94and-next

Strategic Insights (E-Journal), Volume V, Issue 6, July 2006, Centre for Contemporary Conflict, Naval Postgraduate School, Monterey, California., 2006. http://www.nps.edu/Academics/centers/ccc/publications/OnlineJournal/2006/Jul/millsJul06.html

Vankovska, Biljana, (ed), *Legal Framing of the Democratic Control of Armed Forces and the Security Sector: Norms and Reality/ies*, Geneva Centre for the Democratic Control of Armed Forces, Geneva, 2001. http://www.bezbednost.org/upload/document/legal_framing_of_the_democrati.pdf

Ward, Thomas J., 'The Political Economy of NGOs and Human Security', *International Journal on World Peace*, Vol 24, No 1, March 2007, https://www.jstor.org/stable/20752764

White, Jeffrey B., *Some Thoughts on Irregular Warfare: A Different Kind of Threat*, Centre for the Study of Intelligence, Washington D.C., April 2007, https://www.cia.gov/library/center-for-the-study-of-intelligence/csi-publications/csi-studies/studies/96unclass/iregular.htm

Wierzbicki, Sławomir, 'Soldier's Morale as a Chance for Winning the Military Conflict', *World Scientific News*, Issue 72, On-Line Journal, Poland, 2017. http://www.worldscientificnews.com/wp-content/uploads/2017/01/WSN-72-2017-358-363.pdf

Winter, Donald C., 'Adapting to the Threat Dynamics of the 21st Century', *Backgrounder No 2603*, 15 September 2011, Washington D.C. 2011. http://thf_media.s3.amazonaws.com/2011/pdf/bg2603.pdf

Encyclopedia of the New American Nation, http://www.americanforeignrelations.com/A-D/Alliances-Coalitions-and-Ententes-Terminology.html

Development, Doctrine and Concept Centre, Ministry of Defence, UK, Strategic Trends Program, *Global Strategic Trends – Out to 2045*, Fifth Edition, London, 2014.

https://assets.publishing.service.gov.uk/government/uploads/system/uploads/attachment_data/file/348164/20140821_DCDC_GST_5_Web_Secured.pdf

United Nations, *Charter of the United Nations and Statute of the International Court of Justice*, available at http://www.in.org/en/documents/charter/index.html

INDEX

A

Activities in Space   132

Afghanistan   99, 101, 122, 294

Air Power   vi, 239, 309, 340, 364, 372, 454, 457, 464

Algeria   123

Alliances and Coalitions   419

APEC   101

Arab Spring   95, 106, 123, 145, 152, 228, 230, 231, 243, 463

ASEAN   101

Asia-Pacific   100

Asymmetric warfare   213, 215, 217, 218

Attributes of a 21st Century Military Force   391

    Balanced Force   392

    Countering Threats   392

    Disruptive Technologies   393

    Expanding Spectrum of Roles   391

    Information Age Requirements   393

    Inter-operability   391

B

Balban. *See also* Ghiyas Ud-Din Balban

Battle of the Somme   171

Battlespace   208, 240, 241, 245, 337, 387

Borderless ideology   152

BRICS (Brazil Russia, India, China and South Africa)   164

Brown, Harold   45, 454

C

Caliphate   96

Chagatai Turks. *See also* Mughals

Challenges of Immigration   144

Civil-Military Relationship   67, 283

Clausewitz   3, 198, 266, 402, 405, 454, 455, 456, 459

Coalition Operations   396

Codifying War   399

Cold War   4, 13, 22, 23, 43, 83, 87, 91, 92, 96, 97, 98, 141, 155, 158,

164, 166, 228, 321, 327, 334, 348, 363, 369, 374, 386, 388, 395, 397, 457, 468

Contemporary Conflict   387

    The Military Response   387

    War in the Information Age   383

Conventional Military Forces   206

Cyber-attacks   203, 307

Cyberspace   134, 307

D

Defeating Irregular Forces   217

E

Employing High-end Capabilities   275

Ethnic clashes   120

European Union   88, 93, 116, 133, 229

Exclusive Economic Zone (EEZ)   131

Expeditionary Capabilities   218

Expeditionary Operations   272, 273, 463

F

Forced migration   120

Future Conflict Trends   303

Future wars   238, 245

G

Gaza   122

Genghis Khan   64, 73

Geo-political stability   83, 86, 139, 140, 141, 154, 156, 159

Global Financial Crisis (GFC)   16, 114

Grand Strategy   vii, 64, 69, 73, 74, 216, 319, 442, 458

Great power status   158

    Economic Capacity   159

    Power Projection Capability   161

      hard and soft power   162

Guerrilla Warfare   209, 210, 460, 461

H

Hannibal   171

Humanitarian assistance and disaster relief (HADR)   379

I

Impact of Urbanisation   126

Industrial Revolution   119

Information Warfare   220, 373, 384, 385

International Code of Conduct for Outer Space   133

International Law   334

International Relations   334

Interoperability   5, 6, 50, 234, 236, 274, 392, 441

Iraq   33, 96, 99, 122, 243, 341

Irregular Forces   212, 217

  Asymmetric warfare   213

  Characteristics and Conduct of Operations   212

  Defeating Irregular Forces   217

  Expeditionary Capabilities   218

  Information Warfare   220

  Local Support   215

  Long War Strategies   215

  Modus Operandi   214

  Unconventional War   216

Irregular Warfare   viii, 209, 217, 469

Islamic doctrine   154

Islamic social movement   153

Islamic state   154

Islamic State (IS)   96

J

Jauna. *See also* Muhammad Tughluq

Just War Theory   13, 177

  jus ad bellum   177

  jus in bello   177

K

Kautilya   3, 62, 70, 459

Khalif Rasul Allah. *See* Caliph

L

Laws of Armed Conflict (LOAC)   17, 150, 197, 401

Libya   186, 188, 364

Liddell Hart, B. H.   65, 71, 458

Limited Wars   184, 185

Lippman, Walter   43, 458

Long War Strategies   215

M

Machiavelli   3, 70

Middle East   88, 94, 95, 96, 101, 106, 116, 123, 127, 152, 195, 230, 231, 250, 321, 454, 456

Military coup   2

Military dictators   2

Military Forces   iii, viii, ix, 7, 69, 206, 207, 235, 256, 259, 261, 278, 291, 303, 304, 359, 371, 375, 379, 382, 406, 407, 413, 418, 438, 442, 463

  Fundamentals of Employing   375

  Instrument of National Policy   407

  Major Influences on   418

  The Evolving Role of   379

Military Intervention   186, 187, 363, 364, 365, 366, 395, 458, 460

Military power   257, 259, 345, 378

Military Spending   348

Moghul Empire   91

Moon Treaty of 1979   133

Muammar Gadhafi   188

Muhammad Tughluq. *See also* Jauna

Muiz u-Din Fateh Mubarak Shah. *See also* Mubarak Shah

N

Nano-technology   233

National Defence College   44

National Military Forces   235

National Military Strategy   69

National Research Council   139

National security   xi, 21, 41, 43, 45, 46, 53, 55, 58, 59, 61, 62, 66, 69, 72, 74, 251, 317, 359, 368, 369, 376, 432

  Changing Definition of   42

  Governance   51

  Impact of the Economy   56

  Limiting the Military Influence   54

  Natural Resources   52

  Primary Features of   46

  Security, Defence and Contemporary Issues   49

  Through Military and Economic Prisms   53

National security objectives   1, 3, 11, 15, 74, 240, 368, 398, 414, 430

National Security Strategy   69, 367

Nation-State   35

Non-government organisations (NGO)   112

Non-state entities   14, 83, 129, 130, 136, 137, 178, 189, 194, 195, 197, 198, 199, 204, 208, 212, 214, 218, 247, 328, 410, 437, 438, 439

Northern Ireland   123

O

Ottoman Empire   156

Outer Space Treaty   133

P

Pakistan   118, 122, 383

Peace of Westphalia   31, 33

Peloponnesian War   62

Peloponnesian wars   349

Post-Colonial Nations   42

Power Projection Capability   161

Prevention of Arms race in Outer Space   133

Princely States   29

Q

Qutb Minar. *See also* Qutub Minar

Qutb ud-Din Mubarak Shah. *See also* Mubarak Khan

R

Rapid Deployment 275

Responsibility to protect (R2P) 208, 364

Rise of Ethnicity and Nationalism 90

Roman Empire 158

Rules of Engagement (ROE) 400

S

Security and Foreign Policy 70

Soft Power 259, 400, 406, 454, 459, 463

Strategic Communications 267

Strategy of Coercion 309

Sub-Saharan Africa 127

Sun Tzu vi, 3

Sword Arm i, iii, v, viii, xi, xii, xiv, 1, 7, 319

Syrian Civil War 96

T

Theatre Military Strategy 69

The Evolution of Threat 329

The Idea of Joint Military Forces 304

Theory of Strategy 71

The principles of war 239, 245

The Responsibility to Protect 33

Threat mitigation 322, 333, 338, 342, 429

Defence 338

Deterrence 340

Pre-emptive and Preventive Strikes 341

Strategies 338

Tiananmen Square 77

U

Unconventional War 216

United Nations Environment Program 127

Urban Conflict 308

US CYBERCOM 203

V

Vagaries of War 179

W

Wahabi doctrine 153

War in the Information Age 383

War on Terror 99

Weapons of mass destruction (WMD) 98, 231, 232, 233, 243, 460

Whole-of-Government Approach to Security 6

World Trade Centre 98

World War I 156

World War II 9, 22, 32, 42, 43, 44, 58, 94, 105, 114, 141, 145, 155, 237, 284, 349, 357, 361, 369, 371, 373, 377, 379, 382, 409, 430, 435, 442, 448, 454

Y

Yemen 122

Youth Population Growth 122